The
Birth of the
Elizabethan Age

A History of Early Modern England
General Editor: John Morrill

This new series will provide a detailed history of early modern England. Its distinctiveness lies in the fact that it aims to capture the spirit of the time from the point of view of the people living through it. Each volume will be broad in scope covering the political, religious, social and cultural dimensions of the period.

Published

The Birth of the Elizabethan Age
England in the 1560s
Norman Jones

In preparation

The Birth of the Jacobean Age
England 1601–1612
Pauline Croft

England in the 1590s
David Dean

The Rule of Charles I
England in the 1630s
Kenneth Fincham

England in the 1650s
Ann Hughes

England in the 1690s
Craig Rose

England in the 1700s
W. A. Speck

The
Birth of the
Elizabethan Age

England in the 1560s

Norman Jones

BLACKWELL
Oxford UK & Cambridge USA

First published 1993

Blackwell Publishers
108 Cowley Road
Oxford OX4 1JF
UK

238 Main Street
Cambridge, Massachusetts 02142
USA

British Library Cataloguing in Publication Data
A CIP catalogue record for this book is available from the British Library.

Library of Congress Cataloging-in-Publication Data
Jones, Norman L. (Norman Leslie), 1951–
    The birth of the Elizabethan Age: England in the 1560s / Norman Jones.
    p.   cm.   — (A history of early modern England)
    Includes bibliographical references (p.) and index.
    ISBN 0–631–16796–X (alk. paper)
    1. Great Britain—History—Elizabeth. 1558–1603.   2. England—
    Civilization—16th century.
I. Title.   II. Series.
DA355.J65   1993
942.05–dc20
                                                                93–1116
                                                                CIP

Copy-edited and typeset in 10 on 11½ Baskerville
by Grahame & Grahame Editorial, Brighton
Printed in Great Britain by T. J. Press Ltd, Padstow, Cornwall
This book is printed on acid-free paper

Contents

List of Illustrations

Abbreviations

Add.	Additional Manuscripts, British Library.
APC	J. R. Dasent (ed.), *Acts of the Privy Council*, 32 vols (London, 1890–1907).
BCP	John Booty (ed.), *The Book of Common Prayer 1559. The Elizabethan Prayer Book* (Washington DC, 1976).
Bodl.	Bodleian Library, Oxford.
BL	British Library, London.
Bullein	William Bullein, *A Dialogue . . . Against the Fever Pestilence* (1573) [STC 4037].
CPR	*Calendar of Patent Rolls Preserved in the PRO, Philip and Mary, Elizabeth, 1553–1572*, 9 vols (London, 1937–66).
CSPD	Robert Lemon and M. A. E. Green (eds), *Calendar of State Papers, Domestic, 1547–1580*, I (London, 1856).
CSPD, Add.	M. A. E. Green (ed.), *Calendar of State Papers, Domestic Series, Addenda, 1566–1579* (London, 1871).
CSPF	Joseph Stephenson et al. (eds), *Calendar of State Papers, Foreign, Elizabeth*, 23 vols (London, 1863–1950).
CSP Rome	J. M. Rigg (ed.), *A Calendar of State Papers, Relating to English Affairs, Preserved Principally at Rome . . .* (London, 1916).
CSP Sp.	M. A. S. Hume (ed.), *Calendar of State Papers, Spanish, Elizabeth*, 4 vols (London, 1892–9).
CSP Ven.	Rowden Brown (ed.), *Calendar of State Papers, Venetian*, 9 vols (London, 1864–98).
CUL	Cambridge University Library.
ER	*The English Reports*, 158 vols (Edinburgh, 1901–30).
Grindal	William Nicholson (ed.), *The Remains of Edmund Grindal* (Cambridge, 1853).
Hartley	T. E. Hartley (ed.) *Proceedings in the Parliaments of Elizabeth I* (Leicester, 1981), vol. I.
HEH	Henry E. Huntington Library, San Marino, CA.

H&L	P. L. Hughes and J. F. Larkin (eds), *Tudor Royal Proclamations*, 3 vols (New Haven, 1969).
HLRO	House of Lords Record Office.
HMC	Historical Manuscripts Commission.
Lansd.	Lansdowne Mss.
LRO	Corporation of London Record Office.
MacCaffrey	Wallace MacCaffrey, *The Shaping of the Elizabethan Regime* (Princeton, 1968).
Machyn	J. G. Nichols (ed.), *The Diary of Henry Machyn* (London, 1848).
Parker	J. Bruce and T. T. Perowne (eds), *The Correspondence of Matthew Parker* (Cambridge, 1853).
PRO	Public Record Office, London.
Smith	Mary Dewar (ed.), *De Republica Anglorum by Sir Thomas Smith* (Cambridge, 1982).
STC	W. A. Jackson and K. Pantzer (eds), *Short-Title Catalogue of Books Printed 1475–1640*, 2nd edn (London, 1976, 1986, 1990).
Stowe	James Gardiner (ed.), *Three Fifteenth-century Chronicles, with Historical Memoranda by John Stowe. Camden Society*, n.s. 28 (1880).
Strype, *Annals*	John Strype, *The Annals of the Reformation*, 7 vols (Oxford, 1824).
Tawney & Power	R. H. Tawney and Eileen Power (eds), *Tudor Economic Documents*, 3 vols (London, 1964).
Whythorne	James M. Osborn (ed.), *The Autobiography of Thomas Whythorne* (Oxford, 1961).
ZL	Hastings Robinson (ed.), *The Zurich Letters*, 2 vols (Cambridge, 1842, 1845).

Preface

In writing this book I have been supported, helped and encouraged by friends, colleagues and institutions. Time and money, those most essential ingredients, have come from Utah State University. Provost Karen Morse, Deans Robert Hoover and Joyce Kinkead, and Director Ann Leffler have always been responsive to my needs, and Ed Glatfelter, Chair of the History Department, has consistently helped me make the best use of whatever resources were available. Carolyn Fullmer, the Executive Secretary in History, has brought her impressive skills to bear on all sorts of computer, travel and organizational problems, saving me years of time.

The Henry E. Huntington Library generously provided me with an Albert Jones Fellowship, making it possible for me to spend a term using its collections and interacting with the scholarly community of Southern California. I owe a deep debt to the Master and Fellows of Clare College, Cambridge, for giving me rooms and dining rights for a term while I worked in the Cambridge University Library. Manchester College, Oxford, gave me a home while I worked in the Bodleian Library. Important parts of this book were researched in the Institute of Historical Research at the University of London, that wonderful home-from-home for those of us in British history.

My debts to colleagues are legion. Christopher Coleman, JoAnn Moran and Retha Warnicke deserve special thanks because they helped me find my way in areas that I did not know well, pointing out manuscripts that might be of use to me.

Conrad Russell, Marjorie McIntosh and Jean Brink have provided forums in which I could work out the shape of this book, and provided valuable discussion along the way. Leonard Rosenband, Bob Cole and Ed Glatfelter have all been sounding boards for my ideas, and the members of The Edge and MOU have provided intellectual stimulation, useful counter irritation and sheer entertainment. My students, especially Eric Olsen, Caroline Patrick-Jones and DeAnn Lester, have all taught me while being taught.

Ann Leffler, Anne Butler and Mildred Johnson read and commented on parts of the manuscript, protecting me from innocent errors. Mark Damen and Fran Titchener have patiently checked my Latin translations and traced obscure classical references with enthusiasm.

Sir Geoffrey Elton has, as usual, been my Mæcenas and good friend, welcoming me back to Cambridge and Clare. Wallace MacCaffrey deserves special thanks for his friendship and support, and for his knowledge of Elizabethan high politics which he has shared with me, both in print and in person, for years. David Dean has played the role of co-conspirator. I learned a great deal from him about the Elizabethan world, had his help in hammering out the shape of the book and, not least, lived in his flat during research stints in London.

This book is dedicated to three women who, each in their own way, have played an important role in my scholarly and personal life. First to my 'gossips' (using the term in its Elizabethan sense) Joyce Kinkead and Ann Leffler. Joyce's delightful conversations have taught me to see my writing and my life in a new light. Ann's friendship, intelligence and integrity have sustained me through hard times and have been an integral part of the good ones. And equally to Lynn Meeks, who is the good times. Her belief in me has given me a new life.

Norman Jones

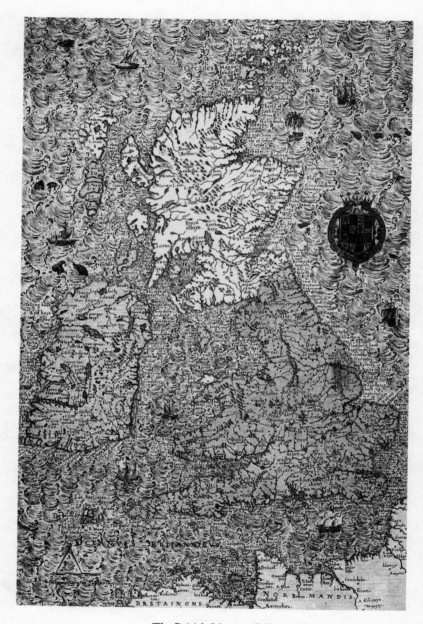

The British Isles in 1567

1

Prologue

This book is Virginia Murphy's fault. A commissioning editor for
Blackwell Publishers, she softened my mind with a particularly good
curry before asking if I wanted to write a history of England in the
1560s from a contemporary point of view. I pondered a moment and
decided 'Why not?' I knew the 1560s well – or thought I did – since I
had been doing research around and about them for years. It was only
later that it began to dawn on me that this could not be a normal sort
of history.

To write about how contemporaries experienced a decade is to break
with historiographical traditions and literary conventions. Historians
generally ask a question which, by narrowing the subject, allows the
researcher to follow the vein of the query through the stratas of
evidence. Once the tunnel has been excavated the historian leads the
readers back up it, eventually emerging into the light of understanding.
Lives, however, are not lived in historical tunnels. We are fond of talking of history as a seamless web, but we are forced by necessity to take
our shears and cut it into tiny fragments to make it understandable. The
tradition of question-asking and tunnel-digging in which I was raised,
I quickly discovered, would not serve for writing a history that depicts
the experience of living in the 1560s.

After some thrashing about I finally realized that it required me to
combine a set of historiographical systems. In fact, that became the
main attraction of the project. Its narrow focus allowed me the scope
to combine the political, religious and legal history in which I normally
work with the social history that has taught us to see the underlying
currents of life cycles, disease, food supply and gender that provide the
contexts in which political, religious and legal choices are made. This
has been done with some success in micro-histories by Natalie Davis,
Steven Ozment, Eugene Brucker and Carlo Ginsburg, to name a few,
but could it be done for a larger society?

I was not sure if it could, and I knew that I would drown in seas of manuscripts and books if I did not develop a set of working assumptions. The first assumption I made, in the tradition of Sir Geoffrey Elton my doctoral mentor, was to read the primary sources first. Of course I knew the basic secondaries already, but I had to read the primaries, even the ones I knew, with a different eye than ever before. I had to read them 'whole', rather than using them for a single purpose, listening for what the authors found important rather than ransacking them for clues to what I considered important. To that end I immersed myself in both manuscript and printed contemporary sources, noting the mysteries that kept turning up, such as why the calf with a child's face born in 1562 was important enough to be widely reported.

From this reading the shape given by contemporaries to their experiences began to emerge. Under the microscope I started to see mountains where previous historians, flying over the territory on their way to more important events, saw only molehills. The sheer angst of the 1560s struck me: the fear of hunger and disease taught them by experience, the troubled economy and the unstable political situation, and all the other worries that were the prelude to the golden Elizabethan Renaissance. The ways in which the people of the 1560s chose to deal with these problems shaped their future, but it was a future unknown to them. Because they did not know it I concluded that I ought to minimize it in the book. People living through events do not know their outcomes.

The label 'a history of' invokes a recounting of events, and I did not wish to abandon the events of the 1560s. They were the formative experiences of life in the decade: the high politics that sent English troops into battle in Scotland and in France, and the rebellions of 1569; the *Sturm und Drang* of the vestiarian controversy and Catholic resistance; the tension over Elizabeth's marriage and the succession. All these are well known from previous histories, but they had to be in mine, too. However, rather than separating the political and religious events from one another I wanted to keep them in the complex setting in which I found them. To divide Elizabeth's marriage proposals from general ideas about a woman's place, or religion from the uses of religion in times of need and celebration, would drain the events of their import for contemporaries.

Listening to people from the 1560s did not guarantee that I understood them; but neither did they understand themselves in their context. So once I had identified the contours of the world as they saw it I needed the help of other scholars to make sense of what I was seeing. One scholar in particular has been invaluable to me: Wallace MacCaffrey, without whose *Shaping of the Elizabethan Regime* I might have been forced to write a political history of the decade. Because it exists I did not need to rewrite it. I have also leaned heavily on the work of historians of demography, disease, childhood, women, and all the other specialties that have helped me make sense of the stories told by people in the 1560s.

The debts I owe to some scholars are indicated in the footnotes, but I have tried to use as much original material as possible, attempting to match historians' generalizations with contemporary proof. I wanted to let Elizabethan people speak for themselves.

I have tried to steer clear of historiographical debate in the text. Although there are some points on which I wished to argue with other historians, such as Mortimer Levine's treatment of the Hertford–Grey marriage, I concluded that if the reader was to listen to the concerns of people of the 1560s he or she should not be distracted by the historians squabbling in the next room. My colleagues can expect a spate of articles as I take up these issues.

Once when I was describing this book to a group in Cambridge, Adam Fox asked if the people I talk about were 'representative'. It is a question that, given our historiographic traditions, is a fair one. I can only answer that every person who lived in the 1560s had unique experiences as well as sharing experiences with their fellows, so I consider every life to be equal to every other. Even Queen Elizabeth ate breakfast and caught cold like the peasants, and even peasants worried about Elizabeth's marriage prospects. That neatly sophistical device allowed me to do what the sources forced on me, to use the few existing narratives to their fullest extent. The reader will come to know Thomas Whythorne well before the book ends because his autobiography is a unique source for the period. There was no one else like him, but he *did* experience and reflect on the decade. My poverty of these sorts of first-person accounts had to become a virtue. Whenever I found people who could be heard in their own voices I gave them cameo roles.

In the end I hope I have created a compound of social, political and intellectual history that crosses the history of events with the history of life cycles to produce a hybrid: a history that portrays the way those living through the 1560s experienced and understood them.

2

In the Beginning: 1559

The first Elizabethans did not know they were Elizabethans. When Queen Mary died just before dawn on 17 November 1558 her passing did not mean to contemporaries the beginning of the reign of Gloriana, the Virgin Queen Elizabeth whose rule would be synonymous with English greatness. It meant more political and religious confusion to overlay the difficulties and joys of life.

Late on the morning of the seventeenth Elizabeth was proclaimed Queen of England, France and Ireland and Defender of the Faith. In the afternoon the churches of London rang their bells welcoming their new ruler while their churchwardens prepared for a night of celebrations. As night fell bonfires were lit in the streets, tables were laid with food and drink, and the populace 'made merry for the new queen'.[1]

Around those fires the conversation of those not too far gone in drink would have been sober. The arrival of a new queen, the fourth ruler in twelve years, heralded hope of change, but it also brought fear. For English people the late 1550s were not a happy time, and the uncertainty of a change of government added a layer to their distress, a distress that would deepen over the next few years. The 1560s would not be an easy decade because they marked the beginning of tremendous change in English society as well as more hunger, disease, war and rebellion.

The people toasting the new queen were faced with difficult problems of existence as well as with a new regime. Food shortages, disease, crime, unemployment and a poor business climate robbed people of their security and bred fear: fear of God, fear of strangers, fear of usurers, fear of those who were different, fear that things beyond the control of the individual were lurking on the edge of life, ready to destroy it.

The new regime brought added worries as well as hopes. Elizabeth, it was assumed, would once again change religion. Protestants would no longer burn, but Catholics might be executed, and more social division and revenge were expected. England, allied with Spain, was in the midst of a disastrous war with France and Scotland. With Mary's death would her husband, Philip II of Spain, abandon England and make a separate peace? Would the Scots invade the North? A spinster Queen was frightening in itself. After all, a woman would be ruled by her husband – witness Mary's willingness to go to war on Philip's behalf – so the future of English policy was in the hands of an unidentified royal spouse. But the Queen must marry as soon as possible lest the realm be left without an heir if she died, leaving it to be inherited by one of many claimants and their quarrelling supporters.

One piece of advice prepared for the new government by Armigal Waad, a veteran civil servant and diplomat, summarized what he designated 'the distresses of the commonwealth'. This skeletal analysis had seven heads: the poverty of the Queen; the penury of the noble men, and their poverty; the wealth of the meaner sort; the dearth of things; the divisions within the realm (class and religion); the wars; and the want of justice.[2] Waad expatiated on these in order, but Lord Paget, a leading member of Mary's Privy Council, pithily summed up the uncertainty of the times, writing 'God save us from the sword, for we have been plagued of late with famine and pestilence'.[3]

The arrival of a new monarch did not ameliorate most of the troubles of the time – they were beyond policy – and it made the remaining ones worse. To thoughtful English people the future was very uncertain. Their economy was poor, suffering from the effects of a disastrous war with France that had cost them their last continental possession, Calais. With Calais went the trade that had passed through it, to the great distress of the merchant community and the Crown's coffers. The war, and royal policy, had fed the scourge of inflation as money was called in, melted down, adulterated and reissued. As its value deflated prices inflated. Part of the 'great inflation' that plagued the century, it meant that most incomes lagged behind the escalating prices.

A devaluation of the coinage at the beginning of the 1550s had caused a boom in the export of cloth, England's major industry. This was followed by a collapse of the market in mid-decade, causing widespread underemployment. As English people understood them, the economic ills of the country grew out of the greed, social climbing and lack of discipline that disordered the ordained structure of the commonwealth and drew down God's wrath in the form of plague and famine. Convinced that social hierarchy and economic hierarchies were fixed, many saw social climbing as a sin, economic aggrandizement as sinful and antisocial, and economic and social change as threatening.

To modern eyes the distresses caused by disordered hierarchy look like economic depression and class division, but that is not the way contemporaries would have classified them. Rather than depersonalizing the causes they personalized them, identifying mis-behaviour, sloth and sinful natures driven by greed as the roots of social distress. These personality traits occurred at all levels of society, each manifesting itself in a way appropriate to its place, proving the universality of original sin.

At the very bottom were the 'sturdy and false vagabonds' – who were frequently nothing more than unemployed or seasonal labourers migrating in search of work – 'living only upon the spoil of simple people'; they were especially dangerous because they had no masters to be responsible for them.[4] Masterless and wandering, they were beyond the control of a society that governed on a very local scale. Fearing them out of proportion to the crimes they committed, stable people believed they should be punished harshly and forced to work.

In 1559 a draconian proposal was made for preventing servants and labourers from moving out of the hundred in which they dwelt, fixing their wages, and forcing them to carry sealed testimonials about their previous employer issued by the churchwardens. The proposal justified itself by invoking the concept of divine hierarchy, claiming it would reduce servants to obedience,

> which by degrees shall reduce to obedience to the prince, and to God also, which is now by looseness of times, come to such contempt, that there is now none other remedy left, but by awe of law to acquaint men with virtue again, whereby the reformation of religion, which without a reverent discipline and appearance, and severe laws withall, cannot continue, may be brought in credit, with the amendment of manners . . .[5]

Apprentices, adolescent boys, were a frequent source of concern because they, too, were hard to control. But they presented another problem. Greedy parents apprenticed their sons in trades that allowed them to distort the social scale, rising above the places into which they were born, exalting them over their betters by virtue of wealth. This opportunism was believed to create a shortage of farm labour. Learning a skilled trade or becoming a merchant was, according to the same 1559 proposal to Parliament, a major source of economic distortion:

> through the idleness of those professions so many embrace them that they are only a cloak for vagabonds and thieves, and there is such a decay of husbandry that masters cannot get skilful servants to till the ground without unreasonable wages.[6]

The love of money was the root of these evils and the ruling classes saw it as their duty to curb the natural affection for money that, they believed, led their employees to wander in search of higher wages. If employers did not have the power to control their servants the national decline would continue.

The 1560s would see a series of proclamations and statutes aimed at stopping the mobility that would increasingly become a feature of Elizabethan life. The magistrates, like King Canute flogging the tide, were defending what many English people believed to be the proper distribution of order, responsibility and wealth. Just as they tried to prevent the lower orders from rising, they sought to keep the upper from lowly occupations.

Only gentlemen had the right to be leisured, and they should not work in a trade. Elizabeth's first Parliament passed a law forbidding any person worth more than £40 a year to become a tanner.[7] There was much talk of protecting the gentry from those who would drag them down the social scale. Husbandmen, yeomen, artisans and merchants overcharged their customers, it was believed, using the income to buy land, apeing the gentry while taking away their livings. As one observer put it, this 'is the ground of dearth of victuals, of raising of rents and hath made them rank and disobedient'. Moreover, allowing merchants to invest in land and houses rather than trade decayed the princes' customs and encouraged 'the maintenance of usury, and spoil of young gentlemen'.[8]

Usurers, taking their living from unfortunates who were forced to pay interest contrary to God's law, ruined everyone. Their greed pulled down their betters and gave them, mere moneylenders, the lands and incomes of gentlemen. John Yonge, writing in his 1559 New Year's gift to Elizabeth, noted that the interest rates available to merchants of good credit were at least 20 per cent, and complained that usury was destroying the Queen's most valuable subjects. Take the case of a gentleman 'that either for your Majesty's service in war, or for other cause of necessity is driven to borrow'. For him the interest rate would be 30, 40 or even 50 per cent, 'which kind of colored usury eats up both gentlemen and commoners'.[9]

Blinded by greed, people such as usurers forgot their proper station in society, threatening the foundations of the commonwealth. Robert Crowley published a dialogue that bluntly pounded home this truth. In it a prophet of God tells a farmer who wants to maximize his income by lending at interest:

> You are called to live
>   after twenty pound by year,
> And after that rate
>   ye should measure your cheer.
> . . . . . .
> Ye are not born to your self
>   neither may you take

That thing for your own
    where of God did you make
But steward and bailiff.[10]

The loud complaints against those who were threatening to advance
beyond their station tell us that many were doing so, and that it made
their 'betters' nervous. The worry that these perverters of order were
degrading those born to rule gave the wealthy upstarts a share of the
opprobrium that was being heaped on those blamed for causing inflation. Since their economic models were monetarist and static, English
folk believed inflation was caused by greed and devalued currency. Middlemen, foreign merchants and luxurious tastes for expensive foreign
goods made all this visible.

Regrators, engrossers and forestallers were a popular set of villains.
By buying up goods and withholding them from the markets they
manufactured shortages where there were none, reaping the reward
of artificially inflated prices. If only, people said, these distortions of
the market were stopped, inflation would end and they could afford
to live.

Take the price of shoes. Early in 1559 it was complained that in the
previous six months it had risen from 12s 6d to 20s.[11] This jump was
caused, according to a statute regulating the price of leather passed in
1559, because a previous Parliament had repealed the law forbidding
the engrossing of tanned leather. Its repeal had, it said, 'brought shoes,
boots, males, saddles and all other kind of wares made of tanned
leather, to great and unreasonable prices'.[12]

For some reason the framers of this act did not connect the rise
in price of leather directly to market forces. This is demonstrated by
another 1559 statute against exporting tanned leather. Its authors saw
the export trade in terms of personal greed, rather than in terms of
demand driving up the price. The price of tanned leather had hit
historic highs because 'divers and sundry covetous and greedy persons
now late having more regard to their own singular lucres and gains,
than unto the maintenance and preservation of the commonwealth'
were exporting it.[13]

The greed of the middlemen was matched by the corruption of the
artisans, whose shoddy merchandise was over-valued and poorly made,
robbing the people and hurting foreign trade. Frequently Parliament
stepped in, attempting to force up the quality of goods produced.
If only they made better goods, it was believed, the markets would
improve. If only the lust for money of 'certain evil disposed and
deceitful persons' could be curbed the people could be assured of
getting what they paid for.[14]

Although greedy merchants and manufacturers were well-known

causes of the economic troubles, the willingness to blame human sinfulness for economic woes meant that the consumers came in for their share of criticism. People who took this line decried the lust for foreign goods that deprived English workers of their livelihoods and caused the export of precious money.

The concern over imports was vague recognition that England had a very unbalanced foreign trade. Depending for exports primarily on cloth and wool – with tin, lead, hides, grain and fish making up the balance – England imported an enormous range of goods. The London Port Books for 1559 list imports of alum, soap ashes, tennis balls, canvas, carpets, Holland cheeses, eels, feathers, figs, flax, gingerbread, glasses, gloves, hats, hops, iron, linen, lemons, oil, pins, pitch, ropes, soap, sugar, thread, bed ticks, wormseed, yarn, spices and dried fruits of all sorts, and nearly £67,000 worth of wine into the capital. Industrial raw materials, especially dye stuffs such as woad, and finished products dominate the list.[15]

The fact that England did not produce many essential goods, such as gunpowder, copper and steel, was not lost on contemporaries, but since no English people competed in the markets for those necessities they came in for less criticism that did imported luxuries. Non-essentials such as wine, and fancy goods such as gilt spurs and Spanish leather, were decried as wasteful causes of unemployment and national impoverishment.

Worse, those who consumed the imported goods were often seen as the victims of unctuous foreign merchants who, it was believed, bribed their way through the courts, carrying off the kingdom's wealth. The Baltic merchants in London's Steelyard, whose exemption from customs duties had long given them an advantage over native merchants, were objects of mistrust, even though their privileges had been revoked in 1552. Italian traders controlled the Mediterranean traffic and were despised for both their business acumen and their soft manners:

> the Italians above all other to be taken heed of, for they in all times pass to go to and fro everywhere and for themselves serve all princes at once, and with their perfumed gloves and wanton presents, and gold enough to boot if need be, work what they list and lick the fat even from our beards.[16]

When they were not blaming human frailty for the economic depression, thoughtful English people considered the effects of the debased coinage. Thomas Gresham, the leading merchant in the realm, summarized their belief when he coined Gresham's Law: 'Bad money drives out good.' With the trust in English coin undermined along with its bullion content, prices were, it was assumed, bound to rise. At the same time, English money lost value on the foreign exchanges, driving up the cost of imports. This was widely understood and when Elizabeth formed her new government it was deluged with advice about the necessity of reforming the coinage. Armigal Waad pronounced that it had to be done quickly since 'the longer the sore festereth the harder it will be to provide remedy', and John Yonge called for a return to bullion content of twenty years before.[17] It seems that Elizabeth, building on work done by Mary's Privy Council, began planning a recoinage from the first day of her reign.[18]

However, though many thought that a recoinage would revive the economy, many others feared it. Inflation was an advantage to debtors and those whose rents were fixed. Moreover, many justly feared a sudden revaluation would catch them with debts denominated in old pounds but payable in the more valuable new ones.[19]

The economic picture at Elizabeth's accession was gloomy, but at least there was a hope that government policy could brighten it. Sharp laws against greed and corruption and reforms of the coinage could be enacted. Perhaps if they were God would smile on England and send good harvests.

The food supply for England was dependent on weather and the weather was fickle, making it uncertain whether, from year to year, there would be feast or famine. Unusually wet summers caused failed grain harvests, as in 1556 and 1557, creating widespread hunger and misery. That of 1558 was good; 1559 was even better; and 1560 would be bad.[20] The undependable food supply caused anxiety and wide fluctuations in the price of food with accompanying attempts by governments to assure supply and control prices.

Parliament's frequent attempts to keep land under cultivation and out of the hands of graziers, and to stop the export of food, indicate how seriously contemporaries took the recurring famines and the social dislocations they caused. As with other parts of the economy, there was a tendency to blame the shortages on the greed of individuals as much as on meteorological or metaphysical causes. Thus in 1555 Parliament forbade the export of wheat, rye, barley, butter, cheese, herring, beer and wood without a license because 'sundry covetous and unsatiable persons seeking their only lucres and gains' had caused 'wonderful dearth and extreme prices'.[21]

These kinds of laws reflect the terrible toll food shortages took in a society that was primarily agricultural. A bad harvest emphasized the social divisions between the poor and the rest of society, pushing them into desperation and threatening riot and revolt. Hungry, the agricultural labourers had reduced income and reduced consumption. Their masters, lacking produce to sell, curtailed their spending, depressing other sectors of the economy. Food of all sorts began to disappear from barns, ponds and fields as theft supplemented the diets of the starving.

In short, the weather put the harvests, and the entire economy, on an unpredictable roller-coaster ride.

Historians have debated the connections between famine and the rates of disease, but in the late 1550s these two horsemen of the apocalypse ravaged the country. In 1557 a disease known as the 'new ague' – a type of influenza – appeared. In combination with plague and the mysterious sweating sickness it made 1558 the worst year for disease-related mortality in the century. The historian John Strype, writing in the seventeenth century, encapsulated the situation when he wrote that 'hot burning fevers, and other strange diseases, began in the great dearth of 1556 and increased more and more the two following years'.[22]

In the terrestrial realm the proximate cause of disease was the unbalancing of the elements and the humours. Evil conjunctions of planets, hot and damp weather, noisome garbage, and other things were seen as the environmental sources of disease. Individuals threatened by corrupted air could increase or decrease their chances of illness by changing their diet and their residence. Bonfires were lit in the streets to purify the air; blue crosses were affixed to the doors of the infected, warning the healthy away; those who could moved to the country; and many changed their diets and were bled. Evil diet was especially dangerous since, as one doctor explained, 'through evil diet repletion, which brings purtrifaction, and finally mortification'.[23]

The authorities, following the prevalent theories of disease, took actions to cleanse the streets and isolate the sick, but their best efforts availed little. In the face of the threat people turned to God, but God's role was never clear, since disease might be, for some, a chastisement for their sins, a kindly prod to conversion; for others a Job-like test of their faith. In either case renewed devotion was the best cure – although it was well to remember that God has purposes that no mortal can probe, killing many who seem models of the faith. Ultimately a resigned acceptance of God's will was the best the sufferer could achieve. Nations, too, were punished or tested by God's whip of disease.

Avoiding God's anger and finding solace in the face of fear was made more difficult by the frequent changes of official religion that had begun in the 1530s, leaving it uncertain what God expected of the faithful. What Catholics valued, Protestants devalued. Each could blame the other for the disobedience that brought God's microbial wrath upon the nation, and both were aware that extremists on both sides would happily kill their opponents. Catholics had proven their willingness to kill heretics in Mary's reign when, according to a contemporary, 'gospelling preachers [had] a sweating sickness in Smithfield, and their Bible burnt'.[24] The burning of Protestants in Smithfield conducted by the Catholic bishops and Mary's government had sent many into exile on the continent or forced them to hide their dissent. Resentful and angry, they were ready to do the same to Catholics if given the chance. Many feared a civil war over religion.

Advice given to the government in the first month of Elizabeth's reign makes it clear just how much religious tension there was. Assuming Elizabeth would lead the nation back to Protestantism, these advisers urged extreme caution. 'This case is to be warily handled,' wrote one, 'for it requires great cunning and circumspection, both to reform religion and to make unity between the subjects.' 'I pray God,' he continued, 'to grant us concord both on the arguments upon the cause and state of religion, and among ourselves for the account of Catholics and Protestants.'[25] Another adviser urged that the leading Catholic bishops be imprisoned and that all the arms, weapons and horses they had be seized.[26]

Their fears were justified in the sense that some bishops were stirring their flocks to defend Catholicism. In a famous sermon at Queen Mary's funeral Bishop White warned the audience that the wolves of heresy were coming out of Germany, 'and hath sent their books before, full of pestilent doctrine, blasphemy and heresy'. Likening himself to a faithful dog who barks to warn his master of danger, White bayed against these Protestant wolves who would spread heresy and rebellion.[27] Reminding the audience that there was no salvation outside of the Catholic Church, he pointedly said Mary had been greater than Elizabeth.[28]

The tensions between the ardent Catholics and the various sorts of ardent Protestants left many people confused about religion, and nervous about discussing it. Many became 'jacks of both sides' – neuters who cloaked and dissembled their lack of religious principle so that they could coexist with all. Not altogether gone from Catholicism, and not utterly divorced from the 'gospellers,' they tried to walk in the middle, the safe way, in order to keep peace, substance, honour and dignity.[29] For English people late in 1558 this was a sensible position if they wished to avoid disrupted lives and, perhaps, execution. Nonetheless, this confusion and dissembling led to 'nulla fidianism', or absence of faith. One nulla fidian in a dialogue whispers, after dismissing his servants, 'there are many of our sect. Mark our doings.' But, 'beware of blabbes. There are many Protestants.'[30]

These same people, who cared more for peace than doctrinal purity, preferred what the future bishop John Jewel described as 'a golden, or as it rather seems to me, a leaden mediocrity'.[31] Elizabeth's government did too, as its early actions would make clear.

Six weeks after Mary died a royal proclamation stopped preaching of all kinds. Even though it also granted Protestants the right to use an English litany, it was clearly designed to prevent more outbreaks of religious violence.[32] Already there had been a number of disturbing incidents, as when a Protestant mob broke into the Italian church of St Augustine in London. Once inside, their preachers, according to an Italian witness, attacked Queen Mary and Cardinal Pole, 'vituperating the people for the errors they had committed in believing their former teachers'.[33] Iconoclasm, assaults on Catholic clergy and other anti-Catholic activities continued in the first months of the reign. The Queen's government, though sympathetic, was right to fear violence if religious expression was not carefully controlled.

Even when Parliament had returned England to Protestant worship, these tensions would not abate. Fear of Catholic revolt went hand-in-hand with the carping of the more radical Protestants. As Thomas Earl, the vicar of St Mildred's, Bread Street, noted in his commonplace book, the end of the Latin mass in June 1559 was 'to all mens comfort except a few of Calvin's church' and 'peevish obstinate' papists.

Lord Keeper Bacon recognized this in his speech at the end of the Parliament in 1559. Addressing the problem of religious division and reactions to the new settlement of religion he wisely observed:

> And here great observation and watch should be had of the withdrawers and hinderers thereof: and especially of those, that subtly, by indirect means, seek to procure the contrary. Amongst those I mean to comprehend, as well those that be too swift as those that be too slow; those I say, that go before the laws, or beyond the laws, as those that will not follow; for good government cannot be where obedience faileth, and both these alike break the rule of obedience; and these to be those, who in likelihood should be beginners, and maintainers, and upholders of all factions and sects, the very mothers and nurses to all seditions and tumults, which necessarily bring forth destruction and depopulation.[34]

To many at the beginning of the reign it must have felt as if the Crown was riding the runaway horse of religion, trying desperately to keep its head down. The speculation and nervousness about religion must have been palpable around the accession bonfires.

For all English people, but especially those toasting the new Queen in Berwick, Carlisle, York and the villages of the north, the religious question was mingled with fear of invasion from Scotland. England and Spain were at war with Scotland and France and it was expected that a combined army of Scots and French would pour across the border in early spring, seeking victory and, as a bonus, to enforce Mary of Scotland's claim to be the legitimate Catholic heir to the throne of England.

The concern was heightened by the instability of the Crown itself.

The 1550s had already seen the death of two monarchs. Elizabeth, the third ruler of the decade, was a childless spinster of twenty-five. Ominously, her unmarried state left the kingdom hanging in uncertainty. Whoever she married would take a major role in the nation, and the religion, nationality and even temperament of the king might change the fate of the country. Moreover, until her marriage was settled England's place in the international order was questionable. If she married a Habsburg – Philip II, or the Archduke Charles of Austria, perhaps – the old Anglo-Spanish alliance would remain intact, keeping England on the diplomatic course it had been sailing since the beginning of the century. This was especially important because of the continuing war against the Franco-Scottish alliance, an alliance cemented by the marriage between Mary, Queen of Scotland, and Francis, the dauphin of France, in April of 1558. If Francis and Mary produced a child it would have a claim on the English throne by blood, and because the Catholic church considered Elizabeth illegitimate and unable to inherit the throne. Under the circumstances a continued Habsburg alliance would be doubly valuable.

If, on the other hand, Elizabeth chose to marry a Lutheran prince such as the King of Sweden, England's diplomacy might move away from the Spanish. Marriage to an Englishman was also possible, but whoever she married, he would presumably become the dominant partner in ruling the nation.

Marriage was important diplomatically – Elizabeth's hand was, as the diplomat Thomas Challoner expressed it, the 'card of our negotiations' – but above all Elizabeth must produce an heir to guarantee the succession and national stability.[35]

John Yonge, writing in his New Year's gift to Elizabeth, ended with a prayer:

> I pray almighty God to prosper your Majesty's most happy reign with long continuance of love and felicity, and send fruit of your body to the comfort of your subjects, and the terror of your enemies.[36]

The members of the House of Commons had the same concern, petitioning the Queen to marry in the first week of the Parliament that was called to confirm Elizabeth's royal authority.[37]

They knew that a kingdom without an heir was a troubled kingdom, and they assumed that a woman had to be ruled by her husband. In a time when married women were unable to sue or be sued in their own right, people distrusted a woman's ability to rule. Queen Mary had done little to reassure them about female authority and Protestant divines had even argued that female rule was repugnant to God. (Elizabeth would ban John Knox from his native England for his book *The First Blast of the Trumpet Against the Monstrous Regiment of Women,* published in 1558, that called for the assassination of the Catholic women who ruled Scotland and England.)

The longer the Queen remained unmarried the greater people felt the danger to be. By mid-1561 William Cecil, the Principal Secretary of the Privy Council and one of the two most powerful men in England, wrote to the English ambassador in France a despairing letter. Reflecting on Elizabeth's giddy behaviour towards Robert Dudley, the married man who enchanted her, he wrote: 'God send our mistress a husband, and by him a son, that we may hope our posterity shall have a masculine succession. This matter is too big for weak folks and too deep for simple.'[38]

Succession, the fear of invasion, disease, economic depression and social unrest faced the realm as it celebrated the accession of Queen Elizabeth on that cold November night. She and her subjects looked for hope and knowledge about the future in the stars and other natural signs and portents. The points at which the natural and the supernatural worlds overlapped were watched carefully for the information they could provide.

Astrology allowed individuals power over their lives by providing each a profile of him or herself, defining his or her expectations, and allowing proper choices to be made. Knowing one's relationship to the stars helped take the chance out of life. No one was surprised when Elizabeth used an astrologer to fix the date of her coronation, since a wise person was expected to 'rule the stars' by knowing their influences rather than living like an ignorant beast, victim of unseen forces.[39]

The certainty that individual lives were influenced by the stars carried naturally into a belief in divination. Like the ancients, the English heard nature speak to them of future events. A disorder in the natural course was a warning of a greater disorder to come. One author summed up their belief in the correlations between future events and natural signs, asserting:

> yea . . . it is truth, there have been many monsters born, that is an extraordinary, or marvelous in their shapes, fearful to behold, and wondrous: and mark this . . . when these do come, ever commeth either the alteration of kingdoms, destruction of princes, great battles, insurrections, earthquakes, hunger, or pestilence after them.[40]

Another man noted 'many monstrous pigs with mens noses and other. It is thought to be reason of the great moisture of the last winter'.[41]

In the difficult time of the late 1550s and 1560s people avidly collected news of monsters, lightning strikes, cloud shapes and other portents that might hint at the future. The enthusiasm for interpreting natural signs gave enemies of the regime a handy spoon for stirring discontent, so that Parliament tried to regulate the interpretation of these phenomena by law. In 1563 it became illegal to publish 'fond, fantastical, or false prophecy' foretelling bloodshed or war on the basis of coats of arms or weather.[42] Needless to say, at the beginning of Elizabeth's reign the portents were being closely watched and people were gossiping about what they saw.

And what they saw need not be of much significance to cause the foretelling of trouble. Thomas Whythorne reported a prophecy current at the beginning of the reign that foretold trouble because of a change in sartorial fashion:

> When th'English do wear hats like hives and breeches like to
> bears,
> Then (it is said) they all shall be much troubled with great
> fears.[43]

These mid-Tudor people understood their lives on a grid that, on one line, revealed the power of external agents, such as God and the stars, that helped determine their future. But rather than assuming that they were predestined they believed that within the limits imposed by God's law and their astrological signs they had the free will to choose their courses of action – and to pay for those courses if they chose poorly. The nation's destiny was perceived in the same way. A sinful nation, like a sinful person, could expect to be corrected by God, but the individuals in it could influence God's determinations.

In November of 1558 people knew that a new Queen meant new courses for the nation. The troubles the nation faced might be helped by policy, but might also be helped by national repentance and the adherence to correct dogma. Thus every life made a contribution to the fate of the nation. The nation's ills came from individual greed and sin, and salvation lay along the same meridian. If Elizabeth, her ministers and her subjects would live in harmony with nature and God, all would be well. But living that way required knowledge provided by the Church, and action in individual lives.

Those actions came at all levels. The most intimate and personal – eating, sleeping, mating, dressing – were influenced by the larger frameworks of life – community, religion, local and national politics, weather, the stars and God. No one was an island unto himself or herself, and everyone's actions, in both theory and reality, reverberated to the entire nation.

The history of the 1560s is about the ways in which people sought to cope with the joys and troubles of their individual and corporate lives. There were no barriers between the personal and the political, the moral and the economic, the cosmic and the terrestrial in their vision of life.

3

The Unsettled Settlement of Religion

I

Mr Wentworth was dying. His wife and mother, despairing of his recovery, had gone down to the kitchen leaving him semi-conscious. Without warning there appeared beside his bed a stranger, a 'gentlewoman, of middle age, apparel and countenance decent and very demur' who said her name was 'God's Pity', and that God had sent her to tell him he would live long and have a son.

Taking a box of ointment from her pocket, she dipped her fingers in it and started to put her hand under the blankets but Wentworth, bashfully, held down the covers. 'I must touch thee', she said, and anointed his genitals. 'When thou art well,' she instructed, 'go to the well of St. Anne of Buxton and there wash thy self and thank God for thy delivery.' They conversed until the women were heard on the stairs, and then the spectre disappeared, having prophesied many things to come that he would not reveal.[1]

In another time Mr Wentworth would have claimed a visit from St Anne, but in 1562 his refusal to reveal the Saint's prophecies was prudent, since to do so was to risk being charged with 'superstition' by authorities of the church and state. He could go to the well of St Anne and bathe because it was a health spa, but he could no longer admit to believing in the power of the saint expressed through her well.

For religiously-minded people the 1560s were a time of fear, confusion, hope and despair as the wounds in the community opened by the Reformation and deepened by the Marian persecutions were chafed by another change. No one knew who could be trusted, and the believers, though perhaps meeting together in their parish churches, no longer had a shared religious community.

Catholics who had rejoiced to see the Marian restoration of their

faith feared persecution. Protestants who had been refugees for religion under Mary, or who had practised their faith in secret, openly
exalted that God had humbled their Catholic enemies. And for many,
if not most, people it was a time of confusion and apprehension. Their
more pliable consciences would conform to whatever the Crown chose
as the official faith, but there was a constant danger that they, along
with their more enthusiastic neighbours, would be swept into the orgy
of religious butchery that Scotland, the Netherlands and France were
experiencing in the 1560s. Religious civil war, or the vicious religious
suppression practised by the Inquisitions of Rome and Spain, were a
genuine possibility given the intemperance of the times.

Richard Allington knew that a diversity of religion was splitting his
community. Fearing death and terrorized by the demons who danced
around his bed waving the ledgers that proved him a usurer, he knew
that for the health of his soul he must make restitution to those he
had wronged, but did not know who would do it. He begged his
neighbours who had gathered around him to see to it that the usury
he had charged was repaid, even while admitting that some or all of
them might think his desire superstitious. 'I know not what religion
ye be', he said one night in 1561, but he begged them to give his soul
rest.[2]

This confusion and uncertainty about what could be done and what
should be done for salvation was particularly acute for those, like
Allington, about to face their creator. Many wills surviving from the
early days of the reign echo the sentiments of the old priest who, in
October 1559, told his executors he wanted, 'if the laws of the realm
do serve and proceedings of the high powers will suffer by the order of
the law, to have the observations and rites of the Catholic church' at his
funeral'.[3] Francis Catterick, dying in August 1559, had trouble fulfilling
his pious duty, willing twenty marks to the church 'if the church come
to the old state'.[4]

In this atmosphere many became 'jacks of both sides', disdainfully
defined in a 1562 translation of the Gnesio-Lutheran Johann Wigand,
as men who 'craftily cloak and dissemble religion', pretending to be
a Catholic or a 'gospeller' as need demands. 'And by that shift',
he complained, 'to walk as . . . in the middle and most safe way',
indifferent to both sides in order 'to keep peace, substance, honour
and dignity safe, and not altogether nor sluttishly to forsake religion,
and yet for all that to seem addict to what religion a man will'.[5] Wigand,
and the English Protestant who translated Wigand's book in the 1560s,
believed that this temporizing was devilish, concocted by the Evil One
to bury Christ. Yet he was describing that famous Elizabethan creation,
the *via media* in religion.

The translation was published because many, including the Queen, were temporizing in those early years, to the frustration of the devout. Elizabeth's dislike of religious enthusiasm heartened her Catholic subjects, though for the wrong reason. They thought Elizabeth might yet return to the Catholic fold, a thought shared by evangelical protestants, who were terrified by it. Ironically, the religious confusion of the 1560s allowed Elizabeth to gain firm control over her realm, prevented a Catholic revolt or even her excommunication until the end of the decade, and created the Puritan movement. The patterns followed by the religious history of the nation were finally established only between 1568 and 1572. Until then the prevailing mood was one of fear and suspense.

Lord Keeper Bacon had summarized the problem for the new religious regime when he urged the Parliament of 1559 to 'draw together by one line', and to beware those that would 'go before the law or beyond the law, as those that will not follow'.[6] Zealous fanatics on either side could disrupt the common peace and set off the kind of explosion that would wrest the government out of the hands of Mary of Guise, Queen Regent of Scotland, later that year, when the Protestant Lords of the Congregation revolted. Many English would have agreed with Archbishop Elect Parker's comment to William Cecil when he wrote: 'God keep us from such visitation as Knox have attempted in Scotland; the people to be orderers of things.'[7]

For the Crown the decade began with the problem of replacing the Catholic faith and leadership with Protestantism and new bishops. Once that had been done the new bishops and the magistrates of the realm had to impose the renewed Protestant order of worship and, as they would have said, 'reduce the realm to conformity' while keeping the religious peace. For individuals the problem was to discover what they could in conscience accept as legitimate religion. The range of their choices indicates the difficulty the new bishops faced. William Bullein described four sorts of religion among his contemporaries: Catholic [Henrician], Papist, Protestant and *Nulla Fidian*.[8] The papist Thomas Stapleton, whose conscience drove him to exile himself, neatly and nastily summarized the babble of theologies, optimistically expecting the confusion to cause Protestantism in England to self-destruct.

In 1564 he claimed that as long as you were not a Papist you could be a Sacramentary, an Open or Close Anabaptist, any of three kinds of Lutherans depending on one's view of grace, a new Pelagian or a new Manichean. 'All these, with a number of other doctrines professed and defended freely of Protestants,' he sneered, 'hath God now revealed for truths, faiths and gospels to recompense the darkness of nine hundred years.'[9]

Theologically these choices were available to English people, but only on the level of conscience. Legally there were no choices at all. All the English were bound to obey the Supreme Governor of the Church in England, Queen Elizabeth, and to use the form of worship prescribed by Parliament.

The Parliament of 1559 defined the religion of England and its relationship to the state in a series of statutes that began with the Acts of Supremacy and Uniformity. The Act of Supremacy declared that Elizabeth was the 'Supreme Governor' of the realm in spiritual and temporal affairs. At the same time, it repealed most of the laws made under Queen Mary abolishing Protestantism and reviving the Catholic Church as the official religion of the realm. Whereas the Marian settlement of religion had denied Henry VIII's assertion that the monarch was the supreme head of the church in England, the Elizabethan settlement chose a middle path and only claimed the right of the Crown to govern the church. In reality it made no difference whatsoever, but it did address people's scruples about a woman's right to head a church whose sacred scriptures, ordering women to keep silent in church, seemed to forbid a woman to 'intermeddle her self'.

As Archbishop Heath, Lord Chancellor of England under Mary, told the House of Lords, Elizabeth could not be supreme head of Christ's church in the realm. The chief task of a spiritual leader, he claimed, 'is to confirm his brethren, and ratify them both by wholesome doctrine, and administration of the blessed sacraments'. But because women are not called to be apostles, or evangelists, to preach or to administer the holy sacraments, a woman may not be supreme head of Christ's militant church, 'nor yet of any part thereof'.[10]

A Catholic archbishop on the verge of deprivation and imprisonment might be expected to deny the right of Elizabeth to head the church, but many Protestants were just as chary, remembering that John Calvin had said that for Henry VIII to call himself head of the church was blasphemy. Of course many, including Elizabeth, believed that the only human who called himself head of the church on earth, the Vicar of Christ and Bishop of Rome, was Antichrist in the flesh, so they considered the title to be contaminated beyond using.[11]

Head or Governor, the statute gave Elizabeth all the power over the church her father and brother had enjoyed. She would, as a Venetian diplomat remarked, 'act like the Princes of Germany, who use the power and not the title'.[12] To deny the Queen's authority over the church was treason on the third offence, punishable by death. Furthermore, anyone who held office in the church or state was required to swear this oath on the Bible or lose his job:

I A.B. do utterly testify and declare in my conscience, that the Queens Highness is the only Supreme Governor of this Realm and of all other her Highness' dominions and countries, as well in all Spiritual or Ecclesiastical things or causes as temporal, and that no foreign prince, person, prelate, state or potentate has or ought to have any jurisdictions, power, superiority, preeminence, or authority ecclesiastical or spiritual within this realm, and therefore I do utterly renounce and forsake all foreign jurisdictions, powers, superiorities and authorities, and do promise that from hence forth I shall bear faith and true allegiance to the Queen's Highness . . . so help me God by the contents of this book.[13]

The Act was designed to remove anyone who accepted the pope's claim to rule the church from places of authority in the English establishment, but it did define the limits beyond which the Crown could not go in forcing submission to its ecclesiastical authority.

The conservatives in the House of Lords managed, quite possibly with the Queen's agreement, to place some controls around the whims of the Supreme Governor and the ecclesiastics and bureaucrats who would run the new state church. The Act empowered the Queen to create the Ecclesiastical High Commissions that would function as religious police, jury and judge, empowered to discover and correct errors, heresies, schisms, abuses and offences in order to please God and secure peace in the realm. This commission potentially had great power, and it was clear that many feared that if it was given the right to define heresy Catholics and many kinds of Protestants might find themselves dying for their faiths. Moreover, some must have felt a general desire to prevent Elizabeth's Protestants from behaving as Mary's Catholics had behaved.

Thomas Brice's poem from 1559, celebrating the Protestants executed for heresy under Mary, catches the mood of those days:

> When raging reign of tyrants stout,
> Causeless, did cruelly conspire
> To rend and root the Simple out,
> With furious force of sword and fire;
> When man and wife were put to death:
> We wished for our Queen ELIZABETH.

After singing the suffering of all those martyred for their faiths he exults:

> Our wished wealth hath brought us peace.
> Our joy is full; our hope obtained;
> The blazing brands of fire do cease,
> The slaying sword also restrained.
> The simple sheep, preserved from death
> By our good Queen, ELIZABETH.

Brice was unambiguous about his hatred of the Catholics who carried out the persecution.

> When shall the faithful, firmly stand?
> Before thy face to dwell;
> When shall Thy foes, at Thy left hand,
> Be cast into hell?[14]

Luckily for the Catholics, the anger towards the Marian prosecutors was mitigated by a desire never to behave in a 'Catholic' way towards heretics. Persecutions such as those being carried out by the Inquisition were the marks of Antichrist's church, to be avoided by the Godly.

Consequently the bill was amended, forbidding the commissioners to define anything as heresy unless it was condemned in the canonical scriptures, or by the first four councils of the church. Furthermore, a second amendment guaranteed that a person indicted under the act for treason or heresy must be allowed to confront his or her accuser, and could only be convicted on the testimony of two reliable witnesses.

Another safeguard for those who had been the leaders of the Catholic restoration under Mary was the provision that established a statute of limitations of six months for those who had offended against the act by preaching against the royal supremacy. If someone had preached against it they could not be arrested for it if more than six months had passed. Since the act did not take effect until June of 1559 this clause neatly protected people like Bishop White of Winchester who, in December of 1558, had preached a sermon warning the people against the wolves of heresy coming out of Geneva into England.

The Act of Supremacy did not gain parliamentary approval easily. It was resisted by the bishops in the House of Lords who, with one exception, would never agree to the religious changes proposed in 1559. The fact that the final Act of Supremacy chose a less offensive title for the Queen while making it difficult for the ecclesiastical commission to define Catholicism as heresy indicates the strength of the Catholics and, perhaps, the moderation of a government deeply frightened by the danger of religious civil war even as it pressed forward in its plan to return to the form of Protestantism established by law in 1552.

The Act of Uniformity that required the return to the Edwardian Protestant form of worship had an even more difficult passage through Parliament. Although many members of the two houses were willing to reject the authority of the papacy as Henry VIII had done, they were less willing to reject the Catholic mass. Again, the lead was taken by the bishops in the House of Lords, where, in league with some of the lords temporal, they removed the first attempt at suppressing the mass passed by the Commons.

The bill they received from the Lower House had proposed, as far as it can be reconstructed, to re-establish the form of service used in 1552, abolishing the altars and the Latin service. Committed in the Lords, it was disembowelled. The committee, as Bishop Scot of Chester observed, had such devotion to God that they would not 'suffer the service of the church, and the due administration of the holy sacraments thereof, to be disannulled or all ready altered, but to be contained as they have been heretofore'.[15]

The men of the Catholic faith who blocked the proposed new uniformity of service were the same ones who were burning Protestants only a few months before. Their action in Parliament so frightened those who publicly supported the restoration of Protestantism that they rushed a new bill through the Commons, legislating that no one could be punished as a heretic for using the religion used in King Edward VI's last year.[16] This was a desperate attempt to protect themselves from the consequences of a failed parliamentary agenda and to give Protestantism some toleration. It might at least stop Bishop Bonner, then sitting in the House of Lords, from fuelling the fires of Smithfield with their bodies as he had done with so many other Protestants.

Elizabeth could secure her supremacy over the church, but in mid-March of 1559 it was not certain that she could also secure Parliament's blessing for the re-establishment of Protestant worship. She seems to have been left with three religious options, each of which might please some segment of the population. One, of course, was to keep the sacrificial mass of the Catholics along with their ordinal; another was to act in a Lutheran or Henrician manner, imposing Protestantism as superintendent of the church without imposing uniformity of worship by statute; the last was to try again for an Act of Uniformity. She and her councillors chose the last, staging a public disputation in Westminster between teams of Protestant and Catholic divines. The propositions to be debated reflected the Protestant objections to Catholic theology. The first asserted that it was against the word of God to use a tongue unknown to the people in common prayer – an attack on the Latin mass. The second, supporting the royal supremacy, posited that every church has the authority to change its rites and ceremonies, if the changes edify the people. The third struck at the centre of Catholic belief, arguing that it could not be proved by the Word of God that 'there is in the mass offered up a sacrifice propitiatory for the quick and the dead'.

The debate broke down in confusion during arguments on the first proposition when the parties began quarrelling about the rules and the Catholics refused to proceed. This rupture played neatly into the hands of the Council, giving it an excuse for arresting Bishops White and Watson. Sent to the Tower, their Catholic colleagues in the debate were called before the Council, fined and forbidden to leave London and Westminster.[17]

The result was that when the new bills for making the Queen supreme governor of the church and imposing uniformity of religion reached the House of Lords they were passed, but only after long debate. The Bishops, sitting as the representatives of the church in England, unanimously voted against them. The Act of Uniformity carried by only three votes, with the bishops of Lincoln and Winchester locked in the Tower and Abbot Feckenham of Westminster mysteriously absent.[18]

The difficulty faced by Elizabeth's government in reimposing Protestantism on the realm reflects the kind of ambivalence felt by many contemporaries. The bishops who so stoutly resisted the change had almost all conformed to Protestantism at one time, and it seems to have surprised the government that they were unwilling to change again – to act like the Marquis of Winchester, Lord Treasurer of England and a Catholic, who remarked that to survive one had to be more like a willow than an oak. This intransigence was matched by the fierce determination of some Protestants to re-establish their faith for the good of the realm. Lines had been drawn during Mary's reign, and those who had suffered for resisting Catholicism were determined to make Catholics suffer. If either side had possessed leaders who were willing to fight, England might have had a civil war.

The Protestants, however, placed their faith in Elizabeth, the woman God had sent to rescue them from Satan after He had chastised them for their sins by sending them Queen Mary and her persecuting bishops. Expecting great things, they waited impatiently for her to use her power to make England into a Godly state. In 1559, and for several years after, that process was going forward, and it was assumed by many of the most enthusiastic reformers that it would continue. They did not challenge the Queen's intentions, but they chaffed at her caution. As John Jewel wrote in 1559, the Queen was 'prudently, and firmly, and piously following up her purpose, though somewhat more slowly than we could wish'.[19] United against the Catholics, they were not yet ready to protest her pace or direction.

The Catholics lacked leaders who would lead them into open revolt, and suffered from internal division. Although the bishops voted against the supremacy and uniformity, they were imbued with the Tudor deference to authority that made them suffer in silence. By the same token, they had no member of the royal family to lead their resistance as there was in France. Perhaps if they had been supported by religious and political leaders on the continent they might have fought, but Pope Paul IV and King Philip of Spain were silent. Still hoping that Elizabeth might be persuaded to marry a Catholic, they did not censure her for her blatant heresy.[20]

Moreover, although the majority of the English still had traditional beliefs they did not agree on the Pope's right to lead them. Papists, as opposed to sacramental Catholics, were a minority. The votes on supremacy and uniformity had clearly demonstrated this, with the supremacy passing easily and the uniformity with difficulty.

II

By June 1559 it was obvious to the English people that religion was making another of its periodic swings. Once again the churches were being purged of their altars and the English service read. On 11 June the members of the London Grocers Company went to St Stephen Walbrook and heard 'evensong solemnly sung by note'; the year before they had heard 'the *dirige* sung by note'. The next day they went again, hearing a sermon by the Protestant Thomas Beacon in place of the requiem mass held in 1558.[21] Henry Machyn, a London draper who furnished funerals and took a professional interest in them, noted in his diary for 11 June, 'mass at Paul's was none that day, and the new dean took possession . . . and the same night they had no evening song at Paul's'.[22] Officially the new service was required throughout the realm on 24 June 1559, a date commemorated by an enthusiastic Protestant in a neat little jingle:

> St John Baptist's day,
> Put the pope away.
> One thousand five hundred fifty-nine,
> O blessed time![23]

The form of the new service was determined by the Act of Uniformity's declaration that the liturgies in the 1552 Book of Common Prayer were to be used by all the clergy in the realm. The 1559 book was identical to that enacted by Parliament in 1552 except for two changes. One was the disappearance of the denunciation of the 'detestable enormities of the Bishop of Rome' that had been in the 1552 edition. The other was more important. The words of institution, when the priest consecrated the bread and the wine, now said:

The body of our Lord Jesus Christ which was given for thee, preserve thy body and soul into everlasting life: and take and eat of this, in remembrance that Christ died for thee, and feed on him in thy heart by faith, with thanksgiving.[24]

This formula united the language of the more conservative 1549 Book of Common Prayer with that of 1552, which directly quoted Christ's words to his disciples at the Last Supper.

These changes may have been made to spare the feelings of the Catholics, and to permit the sacrament of the Eucharist to be all things to all people, allowing them to understand Christ's words at the Last Supper any way they wished. This was of great importance, because the Christian world was riven with conflicting interpretations of what happened when those words were spoken. Catholics held that the bread and wine were transubstantiated into the flesh and blood of Christ and the sacrifice of Christ on the cross was repeated, as the Lamb of God was sacrificed to take away the sins of the world. Lutherans denied that the bread and wine became flesh and blood, but insisted that the faithful ate Christ in, with and under the elements, nourishing their faith in the saving sacrifice of Christ on the Cross. Zwinglians believed that when those words were spoken the faithful were presented with a 'naked and bare' memorial to Christ's unique sacrifice, while Christ himself was not present. Calvinists held that Christ became really present in spirit when the words of institution were spoken, reconfirming the faithful in their membership in the body of Christ. Lying at the heart of Christian worship, personal understanding of the Eucharist determined much of one's world view, and people all over Europe were killing one another over which of these interpretations was acceptable. It was politically very useful to leave the issue vague.

These theological niceties were important, but probably went unnoticed by most people. What immediately confronted them was the return to English in the liturgy and the changes in the liturgical dress, space and decoration dictated by the 'ornaments rubric' of the Act of Uniformity.

This provision in the Act was to cause great trouble in the realm right up to the nineteenth century, but it looks innocent enough on the page. It orders that the ornaments of the Church of England and the dress of its clergy should be the same as those used in the second year of the reign of Edward VI, reserving any changes in ornaments, rites and ceremonies to the Queen in consultation with her ecclesiastical commission and the Archbishop of Canterbury. Probably introduced in order to forestall the kinds of disputes about church ornamentation and dress that had happened in England and on the continent before, and to prevent iconoclasm, it was interpreted by many Protestants as it was by Edmund Sandys, the future Bishop of Worcester and Archbishop of York, when he wrote 'Our gloss upon this text is that we shall not be forced to use them, but that others in the meantime shall not convey them away, but that they may remain for the Queen.'[25]

Sandys's sanguine expectations were to be dashed, but he and the other future leaders of Elizabeth's church were soon busy imposing the new settlement of religion on the realm. Visitation teams were appointed for the different regions and given their orders in the form of visitation articles and injunctions. These guided them in their work of erasing Catholicism's physical presence in the churches and remaking them in a Protestant mould, as well as bringing the clergy of the realm into conformity with the new regime.

The service dictated by the Book of Common Prayer of 1559 had to be performed in a setting cleansed of idolatrous associations. To ensure that no one mistook the new English service for anything from the 'time of superstition' the visitors were instructed to purge the churches of their altars and 'abused' idols. Just what Elizabeth intended in this regard is not clear since the Injunctions and the Articles conflict in their instructions, but she seems to have, typically, sought a middle ground.

As they progressed, her commissioners ordered the removal of the altars from the churches and their replacement with tables, decently made, and 'set in the place where the altar stood, and there commonly covered . . . and so to stand, saving when the Communion of the Sacrament is to be distributed; at which time the same shall be so placed' so that the minister could be heard by the people.[26] By keeping the tables standing in the places of the altars the church continued to look like a traditional church, even if the offending altar stone was gone.

Her twenty-third injunction directed the visitors to 'take away, utterly extinct and destroy' images. But there was added a special stipulation about the state of the buildings affected by such alterations: 'preserving nevertheless or repairing both the walls and glass windows.' The words were in agreement with the Queen's concern for preserving church buildings while shrines, monuments of 'feigned miracles', pictures and objects 'abused by pilgrimages' were being destroyed.[27]

Many of her visitors were less willing to tolerate any remnants of the Old Religion. For them the use of images in worship was akin to worshipping Christ in the bread and wine of the Eucharist. False and damnable belief, it made worship impure. The place in which God was revered had to be cleansed of all the 'scenic apparatus' that turned people's minds from God. As John Jewel wrote in his *Apology for the Church of England*, Catholic worship 'plucked away' the Word of God and replaced it with a rabble of ceremonies.[28]

In the summer of 1559 the liturgy and the very buildings of worship were cleansed, and anything that might encourage Catholic worship or be used in it was in danger of being defaced. What was available for destruction is unclear, since the Edwardian injunctions had ordered the destruction of images of superstition as well, and it is not certain how many had been taken out of hiding or newly fashioned in the time of Mary. Popular piety was in a very confused state in 1559, and local religious decoration and practice undoubtedly reflected that. Most churches had set up their altars again, acquiring new mass books and dishes, and new roods, but how much further they had gone in repairing the destruction of the Edwardian reforms depended on the wealth and enthusiasm of the parishioners. Although Mary had restored the Catholic mass she never ordered a national visitation to enforce it, leaving it to the spiritual authorities. Nor did she restore the shrines such as those of St Thomas at Canterbury and the Virgin Mary at Walsingham. There is little evidence of any spontaneous return to old cult practices such as praying to saints, and only a few chantries were re-established to pray for souls in purgatory. Nor did the Marian church introduce many of the now familiar practices of the Counter Reformation. Cardinal Pole had, however, attempted to redirect Catholic worship into more evangelical paths, emphasizing the cross and redemption and moving it away from the less focused pre-Reformation piety. The restoration of Catholicism had been too short-lived to repair fully Catholic practices, just as the Edwardian reforms had been too short to fully eradicate them, but, capping the destruction of Henry VIII's reforms, they had meant a dozen years of confusion.[29]

So when the visitation teams of 1559 set out they found varying levels of restored Catholicism, including areas in which the churches may never have been 'cleansed' and places in which their Catholic furniture had scarcely been restored. Only the records of the visitation of the Province of York survive, but we know that as they progressed from church to church they began each session with prayer and a sermon setting out the theological justification for what was about to take place. The names of clergy cited to attend were read out, and those who did not appear were declared contumacious, though they were not deprived of their livings. Then the Injunctions and Articles were read to the assembled churchwardens. After that they were sent home to prepare a written response to the orders and inventories of their church goods. Generally they had no more than twenty-four hours to prepare their returns.[30]

The visitors, equally interested in getting the clergy to subscribe to the oath, in disciplining the clergy and in detecting sin among the people, took evidence under all of these headings. If the record of the Northern Visitation is any indication the North was filled with adulterers and fornicators. But a few people, like Mistress Dutton of St Peter's Parish of Chester diocese who secretly kept a rood, two pictures and a mass book, were reported.[31]

Leaving the destruction of the images to local churchwardens meant that it was a hit-or-miss affair, but there is abundant evidence for the destruction that went on. In parishes all over the land, workers moved into the churches to remove the altars and roods and install new communion tables. In Ludlow in Shropshire, for instance, they built a table on 20 June and covered it with cloth, and then, on 23 June, they removed the altar from St John's chapel. On the first of July they purchased a Book of Common Prayer and three psalters; on the thirtieth they paid for another copy and six more psalters to be brought from London. On 27 September they took down the rood, with its crucifix and figures of Mary and John. In October they had a poor man's box built and installed, and, finally, with all the ordered changes complete, they brought in a plasterer to refinish the walls. By the end of October 1559 Ludlow's parish church had conformed to the new protestant order.[32]

In some places it is clear that the churchwardens did not carry out the changes ordered, and that many people like Mistress Dutton hid the altar stones, mass books and other furniture of worship out of devotion, because they valued their beauty or because, with frugal practicality encouraged by recent history, the parish did not want to pay for new ones when religion changed again. The laxity of the episcopal officials often contributed to the survival of what the visitors called 'trifling trumpery for the sinful service of the popish priest', since they, like the churchwardens, were often the same men who had been charged with seeing to it that these things had been acquired. In many parishes the destruction would not be completed for years.[33]

In the larger towns and Cathedral churches, however, it was much harder to protect religious objects from destruction. Henry Machyn reported public bonfires of Marys and Johns, copes, crosses, censers, altar clothes, rood clothes, books, banners, wainscotting and other 'gear'. At one fire the minister inflamed the audience with a sermon and then practised what he preached, throwing books onto the blaze and tearing down the cross in the churchyard with his own hands.[34] The glee of Protestants in this destruction is palpable in the evidence.

John Jewel, describing his participation in the visitation of the Province of Canterbury, is full of delighted horror, exaggerating the depravity of the world he was sent to destroy. 'We found everywhere,' he told Peter Martyr,

> the people sufficiently well disposed towards religion, and even in those quarters where we expected most difficulty. It is however hardly credible what a harvest, or rather what a wilderness of superstition had sprung up in the darkness of the Marian times. We found in all places votive relics of saints, nails with which the infatuated people dreamed that Christ had been pierced, and I know not what small fragments of the sacred cross. The number of witches and sorceresses had every where become enormous. The cathedral churches were nothing else but dens

of thieves, or worse, if any thing worse or more foul can be mentioned. If inveterate obstinacy was found anywhere, it was altogether among the priests, those especially who had once been on our side.[35]

What Jewel did not say was that most of the clergy were as tractable as the people, though a few resisted the changes and lost their livings.

The visitors left behind them even fewer clergy than there had been in the time of Mary. One of the chief effects of the Reformation was to create a great shortage of trained clerics, so that it was difficult for any message, Protestant or Catholic, to reach some parishes. In the first year or two of Elizabeth's reign many men were made clergy with slight qualifications.

For the people who experienced this change it was a distressing time. The rhythms of life, and psychological comforts, were once again being disrupted. Forced to attend their parish church on pain of a fine, many found it a foreign place, stripped of ornaments and liturgical music. The *Book of Homilies* read in the churches on Sundays recognized this when it allowed a woman to pose the question: 'Alas, gossip, what shall we now do at church, since all the saints are taken away, since all the goodly sights we were wont to have are gone, since we cannot hear the like piping, singing, chanting, and playing upon the organs, that we could before?'[36] By the time the year ended everyone, including the Protestants, was facing a brave new world of religion. It would take years before patterns of worship became settled and personal religious allegiances could be redefined. The religious history of the 1560s is about the process of personal definition. People needed religion, but the forms that were licit and what they could in conscience use did not rest easily together. The result was that people sought their own ways, whether by adhering strictly to what they considered to be a divine truth or by meekly following their parish priest in whatever degree of conformity he maintained.

III

With the Protestants now in the ascendant there must have been many people like William Bullein's fictitious characters Antonius and Medicus who, when they began to talk of religion, thought it best to speak of it in private. Voltaire-like Medicus, who is a confessed *nulla fidian*, will not voice his unbelief in front of the servants, warning Antonius 'beware of blabs. There are many Protestants.'[37] Keeping one's religion private meant that it became more personalized and less a matter of public worship. It was a trend compatible with both Calvinism and the emerging spirituality of the Counter Reformation, but it ran contrary to the goals of a state church.

This drift towards personal religion was encouraged by the Queen's tardiness about replacing the Catholic bishops. In late May of 1559 a commission began tendering the oath of supremacy to the Marian bishops, beginning with the hated Edmund Bonner of London, and by early November all but Bishop Kitchin of Llandaff had been deprived of their offices. They were imprisoned or placed under house arrest, and the Queen's officers began rebuilding the episcopate. Matthew Parker was elected Archbishop of Canterbury on 1 August, but neither he nor any of the other Protestant bishops were consecrated until December. Some of this delay was caused by the Queen's attempts to get the Catholic bishops to accept her authority, but royal greed played a role, too. The Parliament of 1559 had given the Queen the right to exchange property with vacant bishoprics and to enjoy their profits while vacant, and she availed herself of her rights.[38] She was not in a hurry to fill the vacancies.

Matthew Parker was consecrated Archbishop of Canterbury on 9 December 1559 and on 21 December Edmund Grindal became Bishop of London. Three others were made on the same day, and a month later four more were created. It was 1562 before twelve of the thirteen other vacancies were filled, and the last one, Oxford, had no bishop until 1567.

Business in the vacant sees was overseen by the officers of the Marian bishops and there was aimless drift for a time until the new bishops took hold. Some never took effective control of their dioceses. Downham at Chester was a poor bishop, and Horne found the powerful laymen of Winchester made his job almost impossible. In short, in the early 1560s the Elizabethan church did not have effective leadership in many dioceses. Nor did the Queen encourage vigour, preferring not to push people into open resistance.

Father Augustine Baker, a Catholic priest, described the effect of Elizabethan toleration on his own family in Wales. His parents had conformed to the Anglican faith, like most of their neighbours, in the early years of the reign, for they 'did not well discern any great fault, novelty, or difference from the former religion, that was Catholic, in this new set up by Queen Elizabeth; save only change of language, as bringing in service in the English tongue, in lieu of that which had been in the Latin'. They did not think the language of worship made much difference (many of the Welsh knew no more English than Latin), so they 'easily digested the new religion'. Slowly, unconsciously, said Baker, these people who had been Catholics in their youths became 'neutrals in religion'.[39]

By all accounts many Catholics were under the impression that they could attend the service in their parish churches and remain Catholic. No one had officially pronounced against it and, until the Council of Trent drew a clear line in 1563, their leaders allowed them to exist peacefully within the new state church, even if they were not enamoured of its theology. Nicholas Sanders reported that many, including priests, decided that if they sinned by attending church it was on the Queen's head, not their own.[40] Some, like Lady Mounteagle, even had a Protestant minister to read the service in her private chapel and a Catholic priest to say mass. She would attend both services each day.[41]

Of course many Catholics were simply returning to the way they lived under Edward VI. Devout Protestants had less trouble adjusting – they were delighted to see the removal of the mass – but the strictest had scruples about the things retained by the new church that reminded them of Catholicism. They expected the church to be purged, and they believed that the Queen would continue the reform. Certainly the bishops were of the opinion that she would take 'further orders', as the statute said. This meant that in the first few years of the reign the Godly, as they thought of themselves, were waiting expectantly and worshipping as they believed proper. The bishops, when they took office, often encouraged this behaviour, believing in the Queen's commitment to a further reformation.

In order to get a partially reformed church most were willing to live within in it for a short time, philosophically reminding themselves of the concept of 'adiaphora' that held that things unnecessary for salvation could be tolerated. According to this idea one church could vary from another in ornamentation or liturgy as long as both agreed on the essential doctrines such as salvation by faith through Christ and the Trinity. Although they conceded that adiaphora existed, their conception of the ministry led many of the Elizabethan clergy to believe that they could not tolerate any practice in ornament or dress that reminded the people of papistry. The rude, unlearned masses, unable to distinguish between theologies, might be more easily led back to Catholicism if their clergy and churches were too much like those of the Catholics. Or, just as bad for some, the church might be stranded in that terrible half-way religion of Luther.

The continental theologians to whom many English ecclesiastics looked for advice were divided on where to draw the line between tolerable and intolerable ornaments. Henry Bullinger in Zurich thought that they should not use forms of dress contaminated by popery, but Peter Martyr was of another opinion. He thought that the English reformers ought to tolerate them in order to stay within the church and reform it.[42]

Queen Elizabeth thought that her clergy ought to do exactly what she wished. What she desired was propriety and reverence. She was willing to use her power to make edifying changes in the church, but she was unwilling to allow people to follow their own theological whims or for the churches to be turned into mere lecture halls. She wanted preachers who acted like clergy and churches that looked like churches. Thus when she did take further orders for reform they did not please all her clerics.

In January of 1561 she directed Archbishop Parker to make further reformation in the church by producing a new calendar, by translating the *Book of Common Prayer* into Latin, and by seeing to it that the churches were kept clean and comely with a table of the Ten Commandments hanging on the wall where the altar had been.[43] She rested this order on her authority as supreme governor for making changes that would edify the unlearned and the laity, but her orders sent messages that disturbed some, even while they moved the church towards a more Protestant position.

The Queen's concern that churches have a reverential atmosphere – that they be clean, their windows glazed, and their communion tables covered with clean cloths – seemed to some to smack of Lutheran concepts of sanctity. The fact that she kept a cross and candles on the communion table in her own chapel did nothing to dispel this worry. At the same time, however, the order to install the Ten Commandments in the chancels was a distinctly Protestant move, concentrating the worshippers on the centrality of the Word in their lives and replacing the idolatrous images of the altar with God's commandment against graven images.[44]

She seems to have viewed her Latin prayer book in the same way, although many later scholars have used it to claim that she was trying to move the church back to a more conservative stance. The order to Canterbury told him the commissioners were to devise ways for the Latin service to be used that would not leave it open to misunderstanding on the part of the ignorant, while recognizing the desirability of using Latin in colleges where a fluency in the language was necessary.[45]

What the Queen thought was edifying and reverential was not seen that way by all of her clergy, much as they loved her. The bishops, among others, began to clamour for her to remove the cross and candles from her chapel, nearly costing the Bishop of Worcester his diocese.[46] They feared that these seemingly innocent objects were the fulcrum of the lever of idolatry that would let conservatives move the church away from purity and back to superstition. If the Queen would not purify her chapel, what hope was there that the Church in England could be purified? She had to set the example.

Thomas Sampson, a man who refused to become a bishop because of his scruples about the very existence of that popish and degenerate office, moaned to Peter Martyr that, although the altars had been removed and images banished from the entire realm, he was close to despair. 'What can I hope for,' he lamented, 'when the ministry of Christ is banished from the court, while the image of the crucifix is allowed, with lights burning before it?'[47]

The hyperbole of an over-tender conscience, Sampson's complaint had behind it a genuine theological concern that the Queen was willing to support a more Lutheran than Calvinist settlement. It was a sign that, just as Thomas Stapleton hoped, the settlement had not resolved the theological tensions within Protestantism.

Beyond the issue of adiaphora lay the distrust between the Lutherans and the Calvinists, and within the English church there were many who sympathized with each camp, although most of the clerical leaders were inclined towards Calvinism. Agreeing that people were saved by grace alone, that Scripture was the only guide for a Christian life, and that no priest could stand between the believer and God, they disagreed on the process of salvation and, most importantly, on ecclesiology. The way the church was to be formed and led put them at odds with one another. Put simply, those influenced by Calvin were interested in creating a nation ruled by God through the hearts of the people, while Elizabeth was interested in ruling the nation for God. Elizabeth and Cecil were concerned with maintaining religious uniformity and peace at all costs, using the authority of the state. Those who believed their individual consciences took priority over the community were unwilling to concede the necessity for the lukewarm mediocrity that made such uniformity possible. The temporizers were, as the quotable John Jewel wrote before he became a bishop and took the side of the state, 'seeking after a *golden*, or as it rather seems to me, a *leaden* mediocrity; and are crying out that the half is better than the whole'.[48]

At first the Queen and her ministers seemed to believe that passing and enforcing a law for uniform worship was all that was called for. They assumed that most people would obey it, even before they had appointed the bishops to carry it out in the churches. Lord Keeper Bacon solemnly lectured an assembly of nobles and justices who had charge of various local courts late in the summer of 1559, warning them that religious sects and factions were a great danger to the nation, enjoining them to enforce the religious uniformity recently enacted by Parliament. If they did not, he threatened, they would be held accountable, to their cost.[49] These stern warnings and dependence on law did not work well, since many of these men were reluctant Anglicans, and many more were unwilling to do a job that was distasteful and in the purview of the ecclesiastical courts. By 1564 the Crown had to ask the bishops for advice on which justices were 'well disposed' to religion and which were not, with an eye to replacing those who were not – though they do not seemed to have rushed to make any changes in the commissions of the peace.[50]

They wanted the religious uniformity enforced, and in the first few years of the reign one can sense an almost pained surprise at the intransigence of those who exalted their own learning over the will of the Queen in Parliament. For instance, when William Whittingham became chaplain to the troops sent to Newhaven in 1563 he introduced a rite that he personally preferred, influenced by the Genevan style of worship. Like a college dean dismayed by the idealism of his faculty, Cecil wrote Whittingham a letter that clearly expressed the official commitment to a single order of worship:

> I will not argue with you, for my part is much the stronger, and on your part small reasons can be made . . . you nor any born under this kingdom may be permitted to break the bond of obedience and uniformity. The question is not of doctrine, but of rites and ceremonies; and this I write lamentably to you; I have found more lets and impediments in the course of the gospel here, in this ecclesiastical government, by certain fond singularities of some men, than the most malice the papists can show. If you knew the crosses I have suffered for stay of religion, you might pity me, and ought, for God's cause, to yield to conformity.

God, Cecil concluded wearily, is a God of peace, not of discord.[51]

These little tempests were harbingers of troubles to come, clouds no larger than a man's hand that would grow into noisy storms later in the reign. Involving the intellectuals and the preachers, who communicated them to an enthusiastic lay audience, they had sometimes violent repercussions, but no Tudor person's relationship with the metaphysical was lived only in church. Invisible but very real forces dominated the sixteenth-century world, and English people tried to use them and protect themselves from them.

IV

The high, dry plains of theology were crossed by only a few, but the tales brought back by the scholars who travelled there were given power by people's need to know God's will in very concrete ways. Some voyagers' reports were of a judgmental God who uses fire, pestilence and war to chastise the sinners and call them to repentance, demanding that the commonwealth obey Him. Other travellers had found God to be more benign, handing out saving grace to all who asked, unwilling to swat a mite with a sledgehammer. This God required only that you love Him and act on that love. He did not need the help of human law in apportioning grace. These two images of God were warring in early Elizabethans. Most believed that God would plague them for their sins, even while some believed that they would be saved by His free grace without works. This was a tension that arose from within theological models. Other metaphysical influences were beyond the control of the theological modellers. Sorcery and witchcraft were well known, astrology was accepted by most people as a science, the fairies cured their diseases, and the Devil's help was always available to those willing to pay the high price of his aid. And by a curious twist of logic those with whom one disagreed theologically were generally assumed to be in league with the Evil One and therefore likely to practise necromancy.

One of the first important breaks with the unofficial toleration of lay Catholics practised by the regime came in 1561, and was tied to sorcery and necromancy. In Easter of 1561 a commission appointed to inquire after 'mass mongers and conjurers' arrested a group of well-known Essex gentry. Most notable among them were Sir Edward and Lady Waldegrave, Sir Thomas Wharton and Lord Hastings of Loughborough. They were charged with violating the Act of Uniformity.

The reason for the arrests was political in the fullest, most derogatory sense of the word. William Cecil, locked in a struggle with the Queen's favorite Robert Dudley for control of royal policy, admitted to Sir Nicholas Throckmorton that he was using the arrests as a weapon against Dudley and the Spanish ambassador, who were trying to manipulate the Queen. A papal nuncio was in the Low Countries hoping for permission to enter England and deliver an invitation to Elizabeth to send representatives to the Council of Trent; the ambassador was using Dudley's influence to get him admitted. So when Waldegrave's chaplain, John Coxe, arrested at Gravesend, was found to be carrying money and letters for Catholic exiles and admitted saying mass daily in Waldegrave's house, Cecil struck. Royal officers arrested the leaders of the Essex Catholics, prompting Cecil's servant Robert Jones to tell Nicholas Throckmorton 'a nest of conjurers and mass mongers here gives occasion to think that our men here had more on their minds than their old mumpsimus'.[52]

The ensuing examinations sought to discover what they knew of plots concerning the Queen's marriage, about their connections with Mary Queen of Scots, and about attempts at conjuring the death of the Queen. Eventually they were indicted in Essex on charges of denying Elizabeth's title to the Crown. Appealing on the grounds that the indictment misrecited the date of the opening of the Parliament of 1559, and insisting that their chaplain did not come under the statute because he was a private employee, they got the indictment thrown out. Eventually they were re-indicted, convicted and offered a fine of 100 marks or prison. Waldegrave died in prison, and his wife was held to be legally responsible for his fine as well as her own.[53]

By then their arrests had served their dual political function. Cecil told Throckmorton that when he saw the 'romish influence' he thought it necessary to 'dull the Papists' expectation by discovering of certain

Mass-mongers and punishing them', adding, 'I take God to record I mean no evil to any of them, but only for the rebating of the Papists humors which by the Queen's lenity grow too rank. I find it hath done much good.'[54] This episode, combined with an intercepted letter from a Marian bishop to the papal nuncio and word of Catholic subversion in Ireland, was used to create the impression of a Catholic conspiracy against the Queen, neatly discrediting the Spanish ambassador and confounding Dudley.[55]

This certainly frightened the Catholics in England, but this was not merely a question of religious persecution. This drive against papists punished not only people who broke the religious law; it also punished those who used the black arts against the Queen. One very well-informed witness reported that not only Waldegrave's congregation was arrested. The heir of Geoffrey Pole, Arthur Pole, a royal relative, was also imprisoned because in the examinations of the people arrested with Waldegrave it came out that Lord Loughborough was trying to get Pole to marry the sister of the Earl of Northumberland, creating an English Catholic claimant for the throne. The conspirators believed they needed such a claimant soon because conjurers, including one Dr Frere, had determined that the Queen would soon die and religion would return to its former state. They were so sure of this that the wedding invitations had gone out and 'many papists of the south part' meant to attend.[56]

Other Catholic conjurers were arrested, too. Leonard Bilson, a prebendary of Salisbury Cathedral and former chaplain to the Marian Bishop Gardiner, was charged with procuring John Coxe to say a mass 'to call on the Devil'. Coxe, Waldegrave's chaplain, admitted he had done it 'for hallowing certain conjurations to those of the said Bilson who practised by those means to obtain the love of my lady Cotton'. Another set of conjurers were charged with using their magic in an attempt to kill Lady St Lowe.[57]

These conjurers were paraded through the streets of London and pilloried, a grim warning to those who would use metaphysical powers, and especially to those who would use them against their queen.[58] Sorcerers and witches were perceived to be all around prompting the Bishop of Salisbury to warn the Queen in a sermon of the suffering of her subjects due to their activities. He had seen with his own eyes, he said, the manifest marks of sorcery and witchcraft in the wan color, the rotting flesh, the benumbed speech, and even the death of her subjects. He petitioned her to put the laws against them into effect.[59]

The threat from sorcerers and witches, especially when they used their powers to conjure the death of the Queen, moved the government and the church to take action against them. At the time of Waldegrave's arrest Cecil had enquired of Chief Justice Catlyn about the laws concerning sorcery and witchcraft, only to find that it was not an offence in common law.[60] The next year, when Parliament and Convocation met, Bishop Alley proposed to his fellow bishops that 'there be some penal, sharp, yea, capital pains for witches, charmers, sorcerers, enchanters, and such like'.[61] The end result was a statute entitled 'An Act against Conjurations, Enchantments, and Witchcrafts'. The Parliament refused to allow the death penalty for these crimes unless it could be proven that they had caused a death, but now the government had a weapon that could be used against such dangerous use of the Devil's power.[62]

That same Parliament revived a law against 'fond and fantastical prophecies'. Standing side-by-side with the witchcraft statute, it was another weapon against those who used or pretended to use natural phenomena in order to foretell the future that would cause political trouble.[63]

It was undoubtedly prompted by the conjurors who had foretold Elizabeth's death, and by another in 1561. That spring, in Glamorganshire Sir Thomas Stradling, found a tree blown down on his property. Inspecting the wreckage he saw the likeness of a cross in the grain of the wood and had four pictures made of it; local people began coming to see it. When word of this miracle reached the Council they appointed a commission to investigate it, committing Sir Thomas to the Tower for the offence. They feared that the 'superstitious' image of the cross was being interpreted as a sign from heaven, to be used against the regime. When Lady Waldegrave was examined one of the questions concerned who had told her about the cross found in a tree in Wales.[64]

Signs from heaven were a constant concern of the government because so many people believed in them. Events in the weather, the birth of deformed children or animals, and astrological prediction all had political implications. Astrology was a particular problem because its use was so widespread and it was so accessible to everyone through the almanacs that were published every year. Of course astrology was respectable, practised by, among others, Roger Ascham the Queen's Latin Secretary, and one could make a living at it, as Simon Forman, a young man in the 1560s, would discover. It was a learned science, too, with an international Latin literature read by scholars. The famous historian William Camden, another youngster of the 1560s, bought and carefully annotated Cyprian Leowitz's Latin book on the conjunction of the planets and the meaning of the 1563 eclipse.[65]

Astrology was a valuable science for those who believed in it because it armed them against fate. If one knew what the stars held in store, one could take actions to prevent the events forecast, which was very comforting. The greatest drawback to astrology was that it might foretell disasters that were much larger than anyone's ability to avoid.

Wars, plagues, rebellions and harvest failures could be read in the stars, and, although one could take some precautions such as storing food, one could only cower and await the coming blow from heaven. Political events were often understood with this in mind, so that astrology became a danger to the regime in the hands of unfriendly people.

To know one's own future required a personal forecast, but the pattern of future earthly events in general was available through popular publications. Almanacs, then as now, made astrological prediction their stock-in-trade, and, along with the best time to plant, harvest and breed your animals came a prognostication for the coming year. These vague forecasts were generally frightening, and to a public that took them seriously they could be very disturbing.

In 1559, for instance, 'judicial astrology' had caused great fear in the nation. The astrologers Michel Nostradamus and Richard Vaughan had both included in their almanacs for the year prophecies of great religious change and civil war. Vaughan, publishing before Mary died, saw in the stars that, due to the partial eclipse of the moon in 1558, 1559 was to be a year of strife, contention, murder, discord, disease and religious tumult. In particular he warned that the period between December and March would see 'no reverence to the ministers of religion, and murmuring among the common people. The superiority shall levy great charges upon the commons, for diverse occasions that shall happen through our naughtiness.' Then, in a passage so disturbing that he wrote it in Latin instead of English, preventing his ignorant readers from acting on it, he foretold rebellion against the monarch, mutations in the affairs of the Crown and accidents befalling the nobility.[66]

Nostradamus, enlightening his readers with prophecies so vague they are currently read as applying to today, published in Antwerp and did not specify which country would experience what he foretold, but he was taken very seriously. In January 1559, he said, many would wish they had never been born, and it was going to be a bad year for the clergy. Writing with a prescience available to nearly anyone in that Reformation era, he made a prediction that might have applied to Scotland or Holland or France as easily as to England, but which the English took to heart.

> But what misery, calamity and trouble is presaged and pronounced unto us in the rest of the year and almost all the year, 1560 and the first three months of this present year: That which is threatened, concerns more the courage and minds of the bishops and priests than of any other: although that their lives, their goods their honour and dignity depend there upon. That is to wit that there shall be difference of sects, alteration, murmuring against ceremonies, contentions, debate, process, feuds, noise, discord, discontinuance in the principal solem-

nities, seducing, and sedition of the people, especially to those that shall be subject unto them, and of them on whom all power shall depend. How many prelates shall be spoiled of their degrees? And by a greater one new chosen all shall be set up again. Also that some great monarch by extirpation and plucking up by the root . . . shall pacify all.[67]

As the events of 1559 unfolded it was obvious that the prophecy seemed to be coming true in England. Matthew Parker, protesting that he did not want to become Archbishop of Canterbury, told Cecil in March 1559, 'I pray you think not, that the prognostication of Mr Michael Nostredame reigns in my head.'[68] Others, less certain that good would come from the alteration of religion, were terrified. William Fulke, writing in 1560, recalled that some were convinced by the astrologers that twenty days after the Queen became supreme over the church the last judgement would come. He remembered how slowly and coldly the people, seduced by Nostradamus, had set up the new religious order. Even those who were convinced protestants trembled with fear and horror, frightened lest the predictions come to pass.[69] Francis Coxe, pilloried for conjuring in 1561, put it even more succinctly: 'The whole realm was so troubled and so moved with the blind enigmatical and devilish prophesies of that heaven gazer Nostradamus', that even those who wished to establish the word of God 'were brought into such an extreme coldness of faith, that they doubted God had forgotten his promise'.[70] The final proof of the serious effect Nostradamus had on public opinion is that in 1562 twenty booksellers were fined for selling a prognostication of Nostradamus printed by William Powell.

Some learned people objected to the use of 'judicial astronomy' – foretelling the future by the stars – because they said it did not work, and because it led people to ally themselves with the Devil. A spate of books attacking it appeared in the early 1560s, such as John Hall's 'poesie' against necromancy, witchcraft, sorcery, incantations and other devilish practices 'under the colour of Judicial Astrology'. A delightful little work in the form of a dream, it is terrible as a poem but charming as a piece of intellectual history. In it the narrator wanders in a delightful meadow strewn with yarrow, strawberries and 'burnet good with wine', admiring the way he could see all the signs of the zodiac both night and day. His delight, however, is rudely ended by the character Theologus, who warns him that clouds blowing there from Lethe make nothing grow that is not poisonous superstition.

Although warned, his friends continue to rush to the meadow, confusing the science of astronomy with superstitious astrology. Those who use astrology will, he avers from Scripture, be cast into Hell:

> The same may use, but that will
> to Satan his soul give:

Or if gods law observed were,
    not one of them should live
That charmers are, or conjurers,
    with witches sorcery:
Or such as choosers are of days,
    marking the birds that fly.

As well as citing Scripture to make his point against all devilish arts Hall referred his readers to John Calvin's book against judicial astronomy, assuming that the power of the Genevan's name would give weight to his own argument.[71]

The reality and accessibility of the metaphysical world meant that there were alternative sources of authority available to Tudor English people. Astrology was one of these, and the government had to work to control the messages received from the stars.

Needless to say, when a person proclaiming himself to be a prophet arrived they were very concerned about controlling him. Elias Hall was a carpenter's son from Manchester. Born in 1502, he described himself as a solitary, pious child who had been sent into service in London, turning the spit to make his living. Marrying at 27, he became a draper, an occupation at which he was so adept that he bragged that he was making five hundred pounds a year during the early 1550s. Then he began to have visions in which a man clothed in white with 'five wounds bleeding' – clearly Christ – appeared to him. After the first vision he dismissed it as a dream, but it came again and again. 'Upon a certain night, about midnight,' Hall said, 'the same vision appeared to me . . . saying "Ely thou carpenter's son arise, fast and pray for thou art elect and chosen of God to declare and pronounce unto his people his word".' Protesting his unworthiness, Hall said he was unlearned and would not be believed, to which Christ replied that he should write what he was told to write and show it to the magistrates.

After that he was carried by a whirlwind into heaven, where he saw Christ in royal estate, and then down to hell where he saw the tormented. Included in the tour of hell was the place prepared for him if he did not do as Christ had ordered. His journey lasted from the ninth until the eleventh of April 1552.

He was commanded to pray for seven years and write for three and a half. Then he was to present God's dictation to the Queen and all princes, his messenger phase lasting only a month.

Forbidden to enjoy any pleasure of the flesh he gave away his goods to his kinfolk, stopped eating fish and flesh, drank no wine, and wrote the book kneeling.

We know his story because when he tried to present his metrical revelation to the Queen he was arrested and examined by both Bishop Grindal of London and a commission led by the Earl of Bedford.

We do not know what he foretold, but clearly he was 'of the popish judgement' in religion and his revelation must have called the nation to repent its sins, probably including the Reformation.

On the 26 June 1562 Ely, Messenger of God, was taken through the streets to the pillory in Cheapside and whipped for seducing the people with false revelations.[72]

False prophecies and prognostications were obviously antithetical to the rule of God's law and the use of charms, sorcery, enchantment, witchcraft, soothsaying or any similar devilish device, was forbidden by the 1559 Visitation Injunctions. In the Parliament of 1559 a bill was proposed against their use for political ends, and in 1563 'fond and fantastical prophesying' was finally outlawed.[73]

The seriousness of interruptions of the metaphysical into the life of the realm is displayed by the way the births of monsters were treated. The arrivals of deformed humans and animals were assumed to be messages from Heaven more immediate and important than astrological messages because they were more rare. The 1560s were filled with monster births noted by everyone from the common folk to the leaders of the church and state.

In May 1562 four were widely reported, including one born at Chichester 'which was a child with a ruff about the neck, and hands like a toads foot which was brought embalmed to the court and kept in a box'. These were all 'tokens of some great thing to follow'. The next month the same writer noted the birth of pigs with men's noses. This was thought, he said, to be the reason for the 'great moisture' of the last winter.[74] By late 1562 so many monsters had been born that someone illustrated a probate roll with a series of sketches of seven prodigies born contrary to the course of nature. A ballader rhymed:

> The Scripture says, before the end
> of all things shall appear,
> God will wonderous strange things send,
> As some is seen this year.
> The silly infants, void of shape,
> The calves and pigs so strange,
> With other more of such misshape,
> Declareth this world's change.[75]

The world's change was for the worse, as these monsters proved.

Monsters were popular because of their shock value as people thrilled to hear of deformed babies (as I write this a popular tabloid carries the headline 'Bat Baby Found in Cave' complete with a photo of a baby with huge ears, eyes and teeth), pigs with horns and giant fish. But monsters were sent as warnings to humans.

Figure 1 'Prodigies which, contrary to the course of nature, saw the light, Anno Domini 1562'. The sketch was added to a copy of the will of Margaret Lane, probated and enrolled in March 1561/2.

A broadside about siamese twins born in 1565 presented an argument that was essential to the monster literature. The 'monstrous and unnatural shapes of these children and divers like brought forth in our days (good reader) are not only for us to gaze and wonder at' it argues. Nor are they only evidence of the punishment meted out by God to the monster's parents for some notorious vice or unnatural act (it was generally held that the moral quality of the parents affected the chances that a normal child would be born, and that women mating with animals caused deformed offspring). No, the births of monsters are 'lessons and schoolings of us all (as the word monster shows) who daily offend as grievously as they do' whereby God Almighty of his mercy admonishes us to amend our lives 'no less wicked, yea many times more than the parents of such misformed' children. The author concludes by quoting John 9 and Luke 13 on the necessity of amending one's life.[76]

These monsters' deformed bodies demonstrated the deformity in human lives, warning people of God's wrath to come if they did not repent. In a popular medical dialogue the wise Mr Civis assured his wife that true monsters were to be taken very seriously indeed. 'Yea, forsooth good Susan,' he says, 'there have been many monsters born.' 'And mark this Susan when these do come, ever commeth either the alteration of kingdoms, destruction of princes, great battle: insurrection earthquakes, hunger, or pestilence after them.'[77] In short monsters, like eclipses and other rare meteorological events, were warnings sent from Heaven.

When a bolt of lightning struck St Paul's Cathedral in June 1561, burning the steeple and the roof off the largest church in England, the explanation of the portent became a minor industry. Some pragmatically blamed plumbers who had melted lead to repair the roof, but many more preferred a plot using gunpowder or the actions of sorcerers and conjurors – a theory refuted by the fact that God would still have to give permission before the Devil could destroy the cathedral. A few shrugged and said the fire was the result of the unsearchable judgement of God, like the afflictions of Job. The fire made John Stowe fear God 'that so sore hath chastised us, and let us well know that he which hath not spared his own house will not spare ours, except we repent our former wicked life'.[78]

A Catholic author produced, within days of the fire, a little book in which he argued that there was a link between the end of mass in St Paul's and the bolt of lightning 'sent down . . . to burn part of the church as a sign of his wrath'. Naturally this charge could not go unchallenged. The following Sunday Bishop Pilkington preached a sermon at Paul's Cross in which he agreed that the fire was portent of divine wrath, but said it was prompted by the slowness of reform. Pilkington published a book based on the sermon.[79]

The question of who had the right to interpret the meaning of a portent was a vexing one. If a storm or monster was a warning to the community it required a political response, whether through the punishment of sin or the amendment of religion. In the world of Protestant Europe, therefore, a portent could be used by Catholics to prove that the abolition of their religion was a deformation which

Figure 2 The 'monstrous cat' born to Agnes Bowker in January 1569, sketched by Antony Anderson, Commissary of the Archdeacon of Leicester.

God would soon punish. The misinterpretation of monsters and other events so concerned the church that an official prayer printed in 1566 noted that the monstrous shapes against nature 'betoken us to *none other thing*, but thy plagues to come upon us for our degenerate and monstrous life and conversation'.[80]

That monsters would be misused as propaganda was a constant concern to the Privy Council, and when a cat was born to a woman in Leicestershire in January of 1569 a careful investigation was launched.

No one doubted that a woman could give birth to a cat. Contemporary theories of conception held that the male and female both contributed semen during conception, and that human semen could mix with animal semen. So the physical fact of a cat coming from her womb bothered them much less than the meaning of this cat's birth. It came to their attention when someone published a pamphlet describing it and, although the pamphlet does not survive, it was summarized in William Bulleins's *Dialogue against the Fever Pestilence*. He makes it clear that was a trick, a 'pleasant practice of papistry to bring the people to new wonders'.[81] Thus we can surmise that someone used it to draw the conclusion that Catholicism should be restored.

The Council instructed the Earl of Huntington to investigate. He turned to the Archdeacon of Leicester and a transcript of the interrogations taken in the case by the Archdeacon's officers was forwarded to the earl, replete with a drawing of a dark red, six-toed cat with big teeth. This in turn was sent to Edmund Grindal, the Bishop of London, for him to examine.

The story, as told in the interrogations, is confusing and it remains unclear exactly how Agnes Bowker came to be confined on a dark January evening. At first she blamed her pregnancy on a local man, detailing how they had coupled in the pea field, over the porter's lodge and in other places. But then, exhorted by the commissary with pertinent passages of Scripture, she broke down and confessed that she had been seduced by Hugh Brady, a schoolmaster. She was his servant until his wife dismissed her because she complained that Brady was committing adultery with his maids. When Agnes next met Brady, when they had both come to see the Queen on her progress, he gave her two shillings and met her by appointment in the grange yard, where he 'cast her on the ground, and had his carnal pleasure upon her and bad her be merry'.

Afterwards Brady, knowing she was an epileptic, promised to cure her. But first she had to have a child as well as do some other things. When she asked what other things he said: 'Thou must forsake God and all his works, and give thyself wholly to the Devil.' Two years later Brady sent a 'trim man' to ratify this pact. She met him in the grange yard, sealed the bargain in blood from her nose, and the man 'lay with her, and after came to her (as Brady said he should) like a greyhound and a cat, and had to do with her sundry times carnally'. The last time she had seen Brady was two years before when he, with his servants 'going softly before', met her in the porch of St Mary's church, where they made love.

Brady's parting promise was that she would have a child, and she certainly was pregnant. Witnesses testified that she was in despair over her pregnancy and tried, prompted by a mysterious bear-like creature, to drown and then hang herself, but the pool was too shallow and her belt broke.

Whether she ever had a human baby was debatable – some witnesses think she did, while others were unsure – for she gave birth to the 'cat' in the presence of a number of women. When they saw the monster emerging they fled but the midwife called them back, reciting a charm to drive away the evil: 'In the name of the father, of the son and of the holy ghost: Come safe and go safe and do no harm, now in the name of God what have we here.' The dead, skinless cat to which she 'gave birth' was carried to the innholder. The curate who dissected it found in its stomach a piece of bacon and some straw (this bacon was lost as evidence because the man who had it on his knife point unthinkingly wiped the knife on his gown).

Anthony Anderson, the commissary of the court, was a careful, scientific man and he asked many hard questions, such as how a cat without an umbilical cord could breathe in the womb. He even flayed and boiled another cat to prove that the one born to Agnes Bowker was just a flayed, boiled cat. He summed up his finding with a comment that shows his suspicions, noting that in the case 'there is great store of wares such as . . . whoredom, witchcraft and buggery, if besides there be none other [no one else], which hath tied up this fardel and given it to her to bear'.[82]

Bishop Grindal reviewed the evidence and announced, 'For the monster, it appeareth plainly to be a counterfeit matter; but yet we cannot extort confession of the manner of doing.'[83]

Although they never learned why the hoax was perpetrated (we can suspect an attempt to cover up an infanticide) this case is clear proof of the way in which the material and the metaphysical worlds meshed in the minds of Tudor people and the pragmatic measures that meshing induced in the government. First they enacted statutes against it and then they saw to it that they were enforced. Not because they did not believe in these things, but because they did, and they understood the powerful influence that portents interpreted by enemies might have. Lord Keeper Bacon made it clear that the failure to enforce laws against false prophecies were a national danger when he informed the justices about to tour the assize circuits in Hilary term of 1565 that few insurrections began without being promoted by false prophecies.[84]

As we have seen, not all Tudor people took these signs to be from Heaven, and the stamping out of superstition included attacks on them just as much as on Roman Catholicism. Leading the attacks and defining superstition in all its forms were John Calvin, Henry Bullinger and the other Swiss reformers. They had great influence with those English who were drawn to the evangelical side of religion, especially those who had spent their exile enjoying the hospitality of the Swiss Protestants.

One of the first of Calvin's books to be translated in Elizabeth's reign was his *Admonition against Astrology Judicial*, but the influence of the Genevan was felt much more heavily in the area of liturgical dress and practice. Those English who had concluded that the Genevan reform was a model reformation were impatient to import Genevan practices to the island.

The first years of the reign were a confused but quiet time in religion. Catholics and Protestants alike were waiting for the next move. For those who felt that the Elizabethan Settlement was only a half-way house on the road to purer religion, the quiet ended in what is known as the Vestiarian Controversy, but there were clear signs of tensions by 1563.

4

Protestant Discontents

'Alas what shall I do to save my life?' demands Civis in plague-stricken London, 'the daily jangling and ringing of the [funeral] bells, the coming of the minister to every house in ministering the communion, in reading the homily of death, the digging up of graves, the sparring in of windows [quarantining], and the blazing forth of the blue cross, do make my heart tremble and quake.'[1] Only God, he discovered, had the power to save him.

Thomas Whythorne made the same discovery. His employer had left him in London in charge of his son while he had gone with the army to Newhaven, where he died. From that plague-stricken town the disease came in 1563 to terrorize London, which was, Whythorne recalled, 'so sore visited with the plague of pestilence' that he was greatly troubled by the fear of death, afraid that he would be 'swallowed up among those who were devoured' by the disease. Recalling that plagues and punishments were sent by God because of our sins, he became depressed, meditating on his sins and the way the devils used fear to lead people away from God. Nonetheless, he sought comfort in Christ:

> And because that the present plague that then was in London was now grown to be so great, and in so many houses, and also so nigh unto me, as it was not only come round about me, but also into the house where I did then lie, whereby I looked every minute of an hour when I should be visited as the rest were, I doubting the worst, that is to say, to be smitten with this rod and cross, did now gather so many comfortable places of the scriptures as I could find, the which I did always think upon . . . as the chief physic for my soul, if peradventure it should please God to have laid that sickness upon me as he did on the others . . .[2]

The 'places' he collected emphasized God's love and the grace of Christ that overcomes sin. Dwelling on his certainty of election to salvation through grace, he meditated on his need to obey and worship God.

By his own account the fear of the plague was a spiritual turning point in Whythorne's life. It frightened him away from secular love lyrics towards religious music. Along the way he reached a conclusion that many others must have reached in this crisis: the True Church is not built of stone and lime. Rather it is a congregation of the faithful, where the pure and sincere word of God is preached and the sacraments are duly ministered, according to Christ's ordinances. The Church of England could not be the True Church because it was a visible church. Whythorne wrote a prayer in defence of the one, true, invisible congregation of the faithful:

> O Lord above
> Thy holy church being decayed
> Make that thereof the walls
> be kept from Satans thralls
> to be repaired and stayed.[3]

The wretchedness of Whythorne's poetry does not disguise the miserable fear he felt in the face of the plague, or the change it made in his life.

It was amendment of life that, ultimately, could take away both the fear and the plague, since both arose from alienation from God. A song published in 1563 knew where both the cause and the hope were to be found. It begins:

> The God of love, that is above
> Doth know us, doth know us,
> How sinful that we be:
> Sent his Word, the two edged sword
> To shew us, to shew us,
> Our sin and iniquity.

It ends with the necessity of following 'the true trace' of the Scripture that leads those burdened with sin to the grace of Christ. 'Lament' and 'inwardly repent' is its message. Amendment of life and response to Christ's sacrifice are required if the 'Sinner Vexed With Pain' is to find the joy everlasting.[4] Like Whythorne, this poet, William Birch, had come face to face with the necessity of the individual acceptance of grace that made salvation possible.

Apparently Whythorne never turned to the established church during this crisis, even though it acknowledged the divine origins of the plague and people's need for spiritual comfort. Bishop Grindal of London, under orders from the Privy Council, prepared a special service to be used throughout the realm.[5] It was a grim, didactic confession of sin and a plea for God's mercy in spite of the manifest guilt of the English people. It was buttressed with Old Testament allusions illustrating how God punished whole nations for their sins. England's repentance was to be signified to God by a general fast kept every Wednesday until the sickness abated. It was a corporate approach to communal guilt, and contained nothing of the comforting grace of Christ that Whythorne found so valuable. Performed by order of the Queen, it was a formulary to which 'the people shall devoutly give ear, and shall both with mind and speech to themselves assent to the same prayers'.[6]

The plague had begun to abate by January 1564, but it left many people like Whythorne with an increased sense of their own religious responsibility. For those who took comfort as he did in an invisible church guided by conscience and obedient to the will of God not princes, it was difficult to accept the order to assent to whatever was read from the pulpit. People of this persuasion could not acquiesce to something that they could not accept in conscience. They were encouraged in this by many of the clergy, who were equally unwilling to bow their heads to a royal order when they felt God required them to act in another fashion. They believed that God must be obeyed first and the magistrate after if the individual and society were to prosper here and in the hereafter.

In the first few years of Elizabeth's reign the tension inherent in this emphasis on conscience was muted. The hope that Elizabeth would eventually make England conform to God's plan was still alive, even though many could see that it was not yet fully reformed. For instance, William Fuller, who later emerged as a Puritan, was deeply disturbed when he returned to England from exile to find that 'Gods matters went so but halfly forward and more than halfly backward.'[7] Nonetheless, most believed that further reform would come, and the Queen seemed to confirm this thesis, using her statutory powers to 'take further orders' for religion. Most notably, in January 1561 she instructed Archbishop Parker to revise the calendar, to issue a Latin prayer book for the use of colleges, and to prepare new homilies 'tending more to edification'.[8]

Actions like these encouraged the bishops to believe that they could change the church's discipline in order to complete the establishment of God's purified faith. However, they were disturbed by some of the other ways Elizabeth used her authority over the church. Her vehement hostility to clerical marriage had prevented the revival of the Edwardian statute allowing it so that despite the fact that many of her new bishops were married, clerical marriage was not legal. As Edmund Sandys remarked bitterly, 'The Queen's Majesty will wink at it but not stablish it by law, which is nothing else but to bastard our children.'[9]

Sharing her dislike of married clergy with many of her subjects she used her power as Governor to ban the residence of women in collegiate communities. Any member of a college or cathedral church whose wife dwelt in or frequented his lodgings within the precincts could lose his position. She justified this by arguing that corporations created for prayer and study 'for the edification of the Church of God, and so constantly to serve the commonweal' were being disrupted by wives, children and nurses. Moreover, the women and children were using up space that should be reserved for students. Elizabeth may have agreed with a proposal made in 1561 for an Act depriving all married dons and making the promotion of married men illegal, because it was 'unfit' for women to be around so many young men.[10]

The proclamation's use of the term 'edification' must have surprised and troubled her Protestant clergy. Because one of the things that distinguished them from Catholic priests was marriage, this slap at marriage blurred the line they tried to draw in the public mind between themselves and what had gone before. The Queen's order, made in August of 1561, came at an especially bad time in this regard because the new Anglican establishment was being attacked for allowing clerical marriage. In fact, one interpretation of the burning of St Paul's Cathedral in June 1561 was that God was punishing clerical marriage, forcing the Anglican clergy to defend its legitimacy even while their Supreme Governor was demonstrating her hostility to it.[11] And we should not forget the pain this order caused the families who were threatened with the loss of their homes or incomes.

When the Convocation of the Province of Canterbury began meeting in conjunction with the Parliament of 1563 the leaders of the church approached it with the expectation that they were charged with completing the reformation began in the Parliament of 1559. It was the first meeting of the Convocation since the re-establishment of Protestantism and the first chance they had to make new regulations that reflected the needs of the new church.

What those regulations might be was unclear since not all of the bishops and clergy shared the same theological backgrounds and attitudes to pastoral care, but a document entitled 'General Notes of Matters to be Moved by the Clergy in the Next Parliament and Synod' called for four types of action by the Convocation.

First, it asked for a 'certain form of doctrine to be conceived in articles'. Designed to define the principal grounds of the Christian faith, the articles of religion were to be inculcated by a catechism and supported by John Jewel's *Apology*.

Second, it asked for further reforms to be made in the rites in the Book of Common Prayer. In particular the author wished to see the removal of anything that still smacked of popery. Heading the list was the request that the clergy no longer dress in vestments, copes and surplices when saying the service, foreshadowing the trouble that was about to erupt over clerical costumes.

Third, better ecclesiastical laws and discipline were sought. The church was still governed by the canon law of the Roman church, a fact that was repugnant to most reformers. Failing a reform of the canon law the document suggested a series of measures that would improve the quality and behaviour of the clergy. It called for grammar schools in every cathedral and insisted that ministers had to study the Scriptures. And again it was requested that ministers' apparel be made uniform and limited, especially when it came to the cap and upper garment worn on the street.

Attached to these suggestions was a list of ideas for disciplining the laity in order to bring them into conformity of action matching the conformity of worship. They ranged from fining parents and masters whose children did not know the catechism, and annually examining everyone concerning their knowledge of the faith, to seeing to it that adulterers and fornicators were punished with imprisonment and open shame. Apparently some thought no punishment was too severe for adulterers, insisting on banishment and perpetual prison.

The fourth set of concerns dealt with the poverty of the church. Much of its revenue was being diverted into the hands of secular persons and many parishes could not pay enough to support a minister.[12]

What the bishops needed from Convocation were the tools to get on with the job of educating and regulating the people in their charge – people who, for the most part, had only a vague notion of what the new church really stood for. Unless certain issues, like clerical dress, were more clearly defined they could not hope to introduce the uniformity of religion that was the official ideal. From both houses of Convocation plans emerged, some calling for a further reform more on the model of the Swiss reformation, others dealing primarily with the managerial aspects of the church, but all seeking to tighten the bolts that clamped the church onto the realm. Without the power to discipline their flocks they could not effectively implement the reformation.

By the time Convocation was ready to send proposals to Parliament to be enacted into law it was too late for most of them. A few of their bills, such as the one ordering sheriffs to arrest excommunicated persons, were passed, but most would have to wait to be introduced until 1566. Most importantly, the new declaration of Anglican faith, known as the Thirty-nine Articles of Religion, would not become the official, legal definition of faith until 1571.

The Articles prepared in 1563 were a revision and reduction of those prepared by Archbishop Cranmer in 1553, covering all the essential points for doctrine. Beginning with the being of God, they define

Anglican belief about the incarnation and atonement, the place of
Scriptures, the creeds, the fallen nature of man, the church's authority in doctrine and discipline, the sacraments, and the relationship
between the church and the state. Explaining the meaning of the
prayer book's forms, the Articles also provided official sanction for
the bishops' authority and made clerical marriage clearly legal. Importantly, they firmly decreed that the 'Church hath power to decree rites
or ceremonies, and authority in controversies of faith', while insisting
that it could do nothing contrary to Scripture. Made law in 1571, this
article summed up the problem in the 1560s: Who had the authority
to declare the meaning of Scripture?[13]

The fact that neither the definitions of belief nor the new discipline
created by Convocation acquired the force of law in 1563 meant that
the church continued to drift, its direction unclear and its superstruc-
ture weak. Worse, the debates in Convocation opened theological
rifts without empowering the bishops to deal with them. Those who
preferred a 'purer' religion began to stand apart from those who
had a more tolerant attitude towards the Elizabethan Settlement. The
Queen, however, showed little sympathy for the bishops' dilemma. She
wanted uniformity and she knew that some of her bishops and many
of her clergy were permitting and encouraging practices that were not
sanctioned by her law.

When she finally tried to force conformity on those clerics who
believed the prayer book did not go far enough she set off a dispute
that solidified the lines between moderate, conforming Protestants and
those who believed compromise with the Devil was not permissible.
From this dispute grew Puritanism and separatism. It began over what
kind of a uniform priests and ministers should wear, but, although
the vestments of the clergy triggered it, the real issues were church
discipline and ecclesiastical government.

Thomas Sampson, who would be one of the early leaders in the
resistance to 'popish' vestments, had foreseen the troubles a half-
reformed church could cause a tender conscience. A month after
Elizabeth became Queen and several months before the form of the
Elizabethan church had been settled he expressed to Peter Martyr in
Zurich his discomfort with what he assumed the new church would
demand of its clergy. If he was offered a position in ecclesiastical
government could he, he asked, accept it with a safe conscience? He
did not think he could because want of discipline made it impossible
for a bishop or pastor properly to discharge his office; because the
civil burdens imposed on bishops prevented them from acting as they
ought; and because the office of bishop had so degenerated from its
primitive purity, especially because bishops were appointed, not elected
by the people. In addition, the vanity, 'not to say the unseemliness of

their superstitious dresses', was scarcely endurable, 'even if we are to act in all things according to the law of expediency'.[14]

Martyr's reply, written in July 1559, shows that he fully understood Sampson's concern. He was, Martyr noted, afraid to reject the ministry and lose the opportunity of shaping the new church, but he also feared 'lest you should appear', by accepting office, 'to assent to those ordinances, which not only impair and weaken the pure worship of God, but also corrupt and marvelously bring it to decay'. To the ignorant his worries appear to be quibbles, but to anyone better instructed in religion his willingness to perform the service arrayed in popish vestments will seem like an acceptance of the corrupt forms. 'For he whose teaching is at variance with his actions, builds up the things that he destroys, and in like manner destroys the things that he builds up.' In a letter a few months later Martyr advised that he and Henry Bullinger were of the opinion that the wearing of garments regarded as holy, 'seeing they have a resemblance to the mass, and are mere relics of popery', was improper.[15]

Sampson turned down the bishopric of Norwich because of his scruples, as did several other prominent Protestants. Miles Coverdale and John Foxe stand out as men who would preach, but who would refuse to compromise the purity of their principles by becoming leaders of the state church. By doing so they silently reproached the new establishment.

Sampson, Coverdale and Foxe all eventually had ecclesiastical livings, but on their own terms. Sampson became Dean of Christ Church, Oxford and Foxe and Coverdale had London parishes, but they did not compromise. They and a number of others refused to wear the traditional square cap and straight collar of the clergy in the street or vestments when officiating in services.

Their reasons for being so unwilling to wear the square cap become clearer when we recall the reaction the costume evoked among the recently persecuted Protestants. The square cap was, a contemporary pointed out, the wear of cruel and popish butchers. 'If you had been,' the speaker says to his friend, 'so conversant among the gospellers in the time of Queen Mary's persecution as I was' you would not wear the square cap. 'For then all shavelings, known tormentors and massing priests wore such caps, and would you not think that all such as hid themselves in Queen Mary's time . . . would have judged all such cap men . . . to have been of the number of the tormentors and massmongers . . . ?' Though his friend protests that the square cap has been cleansed of its associations by the Queen's orders, his protest is rejected out of hand with the observation that a wolf's skin will frighten a sheep even if it is worn by a lamb.[16]

Although the bishops had agreed that article thirteen of the Queen's

Figure 3 'Faith's victorie in Rome's Crueltie', a print from the early 1570s exhorting Protestants to remember their martyrs, repent, and hate Catholics: 'Oh England, England Hate the scarlet whore, who (yet) lies wallowing in saints' crimson gore.'

Injunctions meant long clerical gown and square cap were to be worn in the street and a white linen surplice was to be worn when ministering, it was specified that it was *not* an act of holiness. Most of them sympathized with those who were offended by the Roman dress. Influenced by St Paul's argument that a Christian must abstain from actions that offend others even if they are not wrong in themselves, some, like Bishop Grindal, were sometimes willing to tolerate clergy or congregations who were too offended by the square cap and surplice.[17]

In the meantime those who abhorred the vestments tried to get the interpretation of the Injunctions changed in Convocation. Bishops like John Jewel, who had conformed to the mandated clothes, wnted to see these 'rags of popery' removed 'with the rubbish', while some members of the Lower House desired the clergy to wear the black Geneva gown. Uniformity in dress was a proper ideal, but the clergy did not wish to look like Roman Catholic priests.[18]

Attempts to resolve the problem failed in Convocation and many

Figure 4 A woodcut from Foxe's Book of Martyrs, *1563, portraying the hated Bishop Edmund Bonner of London beating a Protestant. Note the square caps worn by the clergy on the right.*

clerics wilfully disobeyed the rules concerning vestments and apparel. Finally the Queen had enough. On 25 January 1565 she ordered Archbishop Parker to stop the nonconformity in a letter that must have blistered the episcopal ears. The Queen, momentarily wishing to appear more conservative because of marriage negotiations with the Empire and Mary of Scotland's increasing strength, wanted the 'diversity, variety, contention and vain love of singularity' shown by the clergy ended. It was threatening the civil peace and making her job troublesome.

Worse, she said, she understood that the bishops themselves were at fault for the lack of uniformity. Suffering varieties and novelties they had allowed such deviation in practice that, spreading like an infection, it was destroying Christian unity. She had expected that the episcopate would stop these deviations from established order, but they had not, so she was forced to order Parker to consult with the other ecclesiastical and university leaders, identifying deviations in doctrines, ceremonies and usages in order to correct them. She wanted this done as quickly as possible, and she wanted no one admitted to office in the church who disagreed with the established forms. If anyone currently in office dissented from them she wanted to know who they were for 'we intend to have no dissension or variety grow by suffering of persons which maintain dissension to remain in authority'.[19]

Elizabeth appreciated the danger a schism among Protestants presented to her nation and feared that the Catholic critics were correct. Thomas Stapleton in that same year was arguing from his refuge on the continent that because there were so many kinds of Protestants they could not live together. The English bishops knew this too, but they were on the horns of a dilemma – a dilemma wearing a square cap but embodying all the tension over discipline and authority within the Protestant community.

In partnership with Bishop Grindal and four others Parker drew up a new set of regulations, which became known as the 'Advertisements'. They completed these within a month of the time the Queen sent her order, building on existing interpretations of the royal injunctions and clarifying a number of issues. All licenses to preach issued before March 1564 were voided. Anyone who heard a bishop or preacher stirring dissension or derogating the established church was urged to report the malefactor. Importantly there were nine articles dealing with clerical dress. They actually relaxed the rules somewhat, allowing parish clergy to celebrate services dressed only in a surplice, without the cope required in Cathedral churches. Lastly, all men admitted to the clergy in the future were to promise to conform to all external policy, rites and ceremonies of the church. Parker passed them on to William Cecil with a request that they be given royal authority.[20]

The Queen never gave her assent to the Advertisements, forcing the bishops to issue them on their own authority the next year. Although the leaders of her church were walking a fine line between upholding the legal standard imposed by the Queen in Parliament and the scruples of many, including themselves, they could not escape the blame that came to rest on them for enforcing the new standard.

Parker began the enforcement carefully and selectively. Calling Thomas Sampson and Laurence Humphrey down from Oxford, he demanded that they wear the square cap, use the surplice, and commune kneeling and using wafer bread, as required by the Queen's injunctions. They refused to conform, claiming that Scripture and church history provided no warrant for the use of the vestments. Parker, his hands legally tied, sent the matter to the Council for punishment, noting that without authority from the Queen 'we will set still'. Sampson was eventually deprived of his deanery, but Humphrey continued as head of Magdalen College.[21]

As the Oxford men were proving themselves obdurate a rumpus was beginning at Cambridge. George Withers, a fellow commoner of Corpus Christi, preached a sermon demanding the destruction

of the 'superstitious' painted glass in the University. The next month
a hot-headed young fellow of St John's, William Fulke, preached a
sermon in the University church of St Mary's in which he denounced
all 'popish trumpery', condemning those who used it as reprobates and
damned. By the autumn of 1565 Fulke, supported by the Master of St
John's, had exhorted his students into full rebellion against the surplice
and cap that all members of the University were expected to wear to
chapel each day. Students entering the chapel in their surplices were
hissed and mocked. When the Vice-Chancellor of the University tried
to curb them the students 'borrowed' his horse while he was preaching
a sermon. He came out to find it tonsured like a monk, its tail cropped
and a priest's hat attached to its head.

By the end of the Michaelmas term of 1565 the wrangling had
come to the attention of the Chancellor, William Cecil, who, after a
conference with Archbishop Parker and Bishop Grindal, discussed the
matter with the Queen. They wanted this 'lewd leprosy of libertines'
stopped for, as Parker commented, 'We mar our religion' for 'our
circumspections so variable . . . maketh cowards thus to cock over us'.
These *'fanatici superpelliciani et galeriani'* (surplice and hat fanatics) were
a distinct minority in the University and had to be controlled before
their ideas caused further trouble. Cecil sent for the Master of St John's,
forcing him to recant.[22]

In the end the Master altered his apology, nullifying its effect, and
the troubles continued. Out of them emerged a microcosm of what
was about to happen in the broader church, which was beginning
to split into identifiable groups of nonconformist puritans, a middle
party of men who sympathized with the nonconformist theology but
who accepted their duty to lawfully established authority, and people
who were Henrician Catholics. Cambridge at the time was dominated
by young men in their twenties and early thirties, many of whom
would export their theology to the broader nation as they rose in
prominence.[23] Their students, educated in the midst of the fight over
vestments, had their religious lives shaped by their experiences in the
1560s, and carried their opinions forward into their public and private
lives. Many future Puritans had happy memories of young Master Fulke
with his exciting sermons and his room full of rabbits, dogs, birds, rats
and musical instruments.

Of course his enemies took his collection of exciting pets and his
radical sermons as proof that he was corrupting the youth of the
nation. Unless something was done soon the country would slide into
the religious chaos that was tearing Scotland, the Low Countries and
France apart.

After waiting for a year for royal confirmation of the 'Advertisements' Parker finally acted on his own. He summoned the clergy of

London to appear before the Ecclesiastical Commission on 26 March 1566 to demand their conformity. Parker knew that his demand would be met with resistance, reporting drily to Cecil that they expected many churches would be without clergy to perform the Easter service and that many of the clergy would rather make their livings teaching and printing than submit. 'What tumult may follow . . . in the realm,' he mused, 'we leave it to your wisdom to consider.'[24]

On the appointed day about one hundred clergymen crossed the Thames to Lambeth Palace for the meeting. Robert Cole, dressed in the stipulated costume of a square cap 'four cornered, a scholar's gown priestly', modeled for them and they were informed that it was the Council's pleasure that they dress as he was dressed. Each man was then asked to subscribe to the order and a roll call vote was taken. Those who refused to say 'I will' when asked if they would obey were suspended for three months and, if they continued to refuse, were told they would lose their livings. Despite this threat thirty-seven of the ministers – 'of which number were the best' – refused to subscribe and lost their livings for three months.[25] 'Men's hearts,' wrote Thomas Earl who was among them, 'were tempted and tried, and many sequestered, and deposed, and deprived'.[26]

Earl, the vicar of St Mildred's, Bread Street, was one who refused to subscribe in the beginning. A committed Puritan in the making he was very bitter about the way in which Godly ministers were dragooned into obedience. Writing many years later he remembered 'Great was the sorrow of most ministers and those murmuring, saying "we are killed in the soul of our souls for this pollution of yours – for that we cannot perform it in the singleness of our hearts this our ministry".'[27] Many, like himself, surrendered in order to keep their livelihoods. Without incomes and faced with the end of their clerical careers, they had a miserable prospect. Earl recalled it made them, their wives and their children 'most miserable poor and woeful persons'. Worse, men with less precise consciences reaped the benefits of the deprivations. Earl was especially angry about the way Robert Cole was rewarded by the Archbishop for submitting.[28]

Sadly men like Earl, who gave in to political pressure and economic necessity, found that they had lost more than just the trust of their superiors. Their congregations mocked them as hypocrites while their opponents compared them to Arians, Anabaptists and other kinds of heretics.[29] Earl went back to his parish and served there until 1604, but he remained obsessed for the rest of his life with the problem of religious authority in the state church.

This attempt to reduce the London clergy to a single order of dress polarized their parishioners, and the summer of 1566 saw repeated disturbances as crowds supported their favourite preachers and terrorized those who tried to take their places or to read the services wearing the surplice.

John Stowe, a Londoner who had little sympathy for evangelical Protestants but a great interest in the history of London, watched and chronicled the tumults that, as Parker had forecast, disturbed the London churches. Stowe makes it clear that the clergy who refused to subscribe also refused to be silenced. If they could not accept the Archbishop's authority, they could hardly stop preaching on his order. Instead they attacked the vestments and other ceremonies as superstition, urging their hearers to take the side of the gospel rather than the crown.

One of the first congregations to split over the issue was Thomas Earl's at St Mildred's in Bread Street. He had been suspended and the wardens of the parish brought in another minister to do the Low Sunday service wearing a surplice. Earl and his adherents resisted so stoutly that the chief of the parish and the alderman's deputy of the ward had to stand on either side of the surpliced minister to protect him while he performed the service.[30]

On 23 April Robert Crowley, a man with a long history of bravery in the face of religious compulsion, disrupted a funeral in the name of religious purity. Vicar of St Giles, Cripplegate, he stood blocking the door of his church as the procession approached. Preceding the corpse came six clerks wearing surplices and Crowley would not let them pass. The church was his, he said, and he would not suffer 'any such superstitious rags of Rome' to enter it. The argument that ensued almost became violent, but in the end the men wearing the surplices and those who supported the Queen's position gave up and stayed outside while the burial was completed.[31]

At Little Allhallows in Thames Street the congregation came to blows over their pastor's conformity, and all over the city there were acts of resistance to the order. In one church a congregant stole the consecrated bread and wine to prevent its distribution by a man wearing a surplice; in other churches that Easter there was so much commotion that the doors were locked and no service was said. Those wishing to take the Eucharist could not, even though the service was the highest of Christian feasts.

The ministers and preachers whipped up their supporters with vehement attacks on the Queen, the Council and the bishops for their ungodly order. Not content with the spoken word they turned to the printing presses, producing a series of pamphlets. The first, attributed to Robert Crowley, declared why the ministers refused to wear the 'outward apparel, and ministering garments of the Pope's church'.[32] This was answered on behalf of the bishops and the battle was joined. The writings of the anti-vestiarians were strewn anonymously in the streets in order to avoid the official control of the presses. Nonetheless two of the printers who published them were imprisoned in the Counter for a fortnight until they admitted who wrote them – but the authors were not punished.[33]

As the financial penalties began to bite some of the men who had refused to subscribe gave in, to the disgust of their followers. One man, a Scot who had earlier provoked a riot with a sermon against the surplice, appeared wearing one early in June. Some of the women of the parish stoned him, then dragged him from his pulpit, ripping his surplice and scratching his face in what Bishop Grindal described as a 'womanish brabble'.[34]

The next day three of the stoutest enemies of the surplice were the focus of another crowd. They had been ordered to go to Winchester and spend twenty-one days with Bishop Horne, to persuade or be persuaded. As they left the city two or three hundred women accompanied them across London Bridge and through Southwark. Carrying bags and bottles to picnic with the preachers, they gave them gold, silver, sugar, spices and other gifts, urging them to stand fast against the bishop. When one of them gave in he was forced to give up his London church and move to Rye to escape the scorn of his followers.[35]

Even nine months later the troubles continued. In late January 1567 Bishop Grindal went to preach at St Margaret's in Old Fish Street, where the people, 'especially the women', 'unreverently hooted at him with many opprobrious words'. Cries of 'wear horns!' went up at the sight of his square cap, insinuating that he was a cuckold.

The following Saturday a tinker's wife was punished for this irreverence by being set on two ladders like a cuckingstool outside the church. She rejoiced, says Stowe, in her 'lewd behaviour', and so did the crowd that supported her, praising the Lord 'for that He had made her worthy to suffer persecution for righteousness, and for the truths sake (as they said) and for crying out against superstition as they termed it'.[36]

The women who were so embarrassingly vocal and such a visible part of the preachers' following may reflect the transference of the dependence on a confessor or 'ghostly father' inculcated by the Catholic Church to the clergy of the new church. They continued to seek spiritual direction, turning to a man of religious authority for it. In a society in which marriages were arranged 'intimate friendship with some physician of the soul was not seldom the result', as Patrick Collinson has observed.[37]

Whatever the cause of the attraction for the women who followed the evangelical preachers, they included some wealthy and well-educated people. Lady Anne Bacon, wife of the Lord Keeper; the countess of Sussex, the countess of Bedford, and many others sympathized with the puritan movement. Some, like Anne Locke, were so committed to

Non pater sancte, nam sic transsit gloria vestra.   Bonum est nobis hic gloriare.

Sunt mihi flauentes agri, sunt pascua laeta.
    Frumentis grauidis, horrea plena manent.
Sunt pingues vaccae, pingues tauri, pecudesque.
    Magnanimis stabulum grande, repletur equis.
Sunt pleni saltus damis, viuaria pisce.
    Atque satis faeni, florida prata ferunt.
Sunt flores hortis, sunt ortis dulcia poma.
    Prouentus multi, marmoreaeque domus.
Regua splendescit sublimibus alta columnis.
    Ingens nec cessat, fundere vina cadus.
Aurea gemmiferis, fulgescunt pocula mensis.
    Regales epulae, nectoraeque dapes.
Vestes purpureas habeo, famulosque fideles.
    Thesaurum Cresi, ferrea cista tenet.
Assidue tirijs soleo decumbere thoris.
    Ad mediam soleo, stertere saepe diem.

Figure 5 'The Secure Bishop', a cartoon with a poem attacking the wealth of bishops from a manuscript dedicated to the Earl of Leicester in 1567.

the cause that they took great risks and suffered losses to follow their spiritual guides. Locke, wife of a London merchant, left her husband and took her children to Geneva to be near John Knox. She took, Collinson speculates, a 'commanding and respected position' among the 'Godly' in the troubles of 1566, and after her husband died in 1571 she married Edward Dering, a brilliant young preacher.[38]

Bishop Grindal was the focus of the anger of Anne Locke and the rest of the Godly. Although some of the clergy in the London area answered to Bishop Horne of Winchester, Grindal, as Bishop of London, was the nearest ecclesiastical authority. When a lecturer in Robert Crowley's church was put under house arrest a crowd of sixty women occupied the Bishop's palace. Grindal refused to talk with them, suggesting that they send half-a-dozen of their husbands instead, but they were adamant. Only when another nonconforming minister, John Philpot, intervened were they convinced to go away, 'but yet so as with tears they moved, at some hands, compassion'.[39]

Philpot's authority, Grindal observed, was greater than his own, a disturbing reality that was emphasized by experiences like his interview with a preacher named Pattenson, who had publicly described his Bishop as Antichrist, a traitor to God and the Queen, and a heretic. Called before the Ecclesiastical Commission Pattenson defended his words and refused to be bound by a 'popish' preaching licence. Frustrated, Grindal told him he could stop his preaching for seven years. To which Pattenson insolently replied, '"You know not whether you shall live seven days or not."' Compounding the insult he refused a cup of wine from Grindal's men because the Bishop was '"accused before God".'[40]

Ironically Grindal had supported many of the ministers who now turned on him. Seeing himself as a friend of reform, he had tolerated men who preferred the Genevan form of worship and had winked at their noncompliance with the royal rules. Now his tolerance was returning to haunt him. In the middle of the crisis of 1566 Parker observed drily to William Cecil, 'And now my lord of London by experience feeleth and seeth the marks and bounds of these good sprights which, but for his tolerations . . . had been suppressed for five or six years ago, and had prevented all this unquietness . . . , and both his reputation better saved and my poor honesty not so foully traduce.'[41]

Slowly Grindal, like Parker, Cecil, the Queen, and many others in positions of authority, was being forced to take a harder line by the unreasonableness of these people who should have been their allies. If they were not restrained their license and disorder would, in Parker's words, 'breed a cease one day in governance'.[42]

When Parker made that remark he must have been feeling very

frustrated indeed. Not only was there a faction in the church that ignored his authority; the Queen seemed unwilling to bolster it. In letter after letter he urged Cecil get the Queen to lend her weight to the struggle for conformity, but nothing happened. It is hardly surprising, then, that when a Parliament was called for the winter of 1566 the bills for discipline in the church drafted in Convocation in 1563 were introduced in the House of Commons. If the Church was to ever establish Protestantism in its own image it had to legally define itself and acquire the disciplinary powers needed to enforce the definition. The troubles over vestments hardened the lines between the Queen, the bishops and those who wanted further, faster reforms.

Accordingly a series of bills appeared in the House of Commons in 1566. Labelled alphabetically by the Clerk of the Commons, bill A contained the Thirty-nine Articles passed by Convocation to create doctrinal uniformity. Bills B through F dealt with various aspects of clerical discipline. Primarily aimed at the clergy, these bills would have required the clergy to be better educated, to personally serve the churches to which they were presented, stopped the buying of church offices, and regulated the leasing of benefices.[43]

On the surface there was little here to which any friend of Protestantism in England could object. The bills would have, as Convocation intended, improved the church along reformed lines. But no one reckoned on the Queen's reaction to their introduction.

In a burst of anger Elizabeth stopped these bills dead. She had not been consulted about them, and, since she was Supreme Governor of the Church, she was not about to allow the bishops to take action without her permission. Archbishop Parker was taken aback by her reaction. She accused the bishops of introducing them behind her back, and, although Parker denied it, she demanded to know who had done it. She did not, he was told, dislike the doctrine in the book of Thirty-nine Articles, but she did not like the manner in which it was being put forth.[44]

The Commons passed the bill A containing the Thirty-nine Articles, but Elizabeth ordered the Lord Keeper to prevent its reading in the Lords. The Bishops wrote her a formal letter of protest, pointing out that the articles were for the greater glory of God and conformed to Scripture. Moreover – and most importantly – they also argued that the articles refuted the errors maintained by enemies of religion (Catholics) and would allow the establishment of 'one consent and unity of true doctrine', to the quiet of the realm. Finally, as the people charged with caring for God's church they begged her as governor and nurse of the church to allow the passage of the bill. She did not, forcing them to wait until 1571.

Out of the troubles of 1566 came two important revelations to

English Protestants. One was that the Queen was not going to permit further reformation, to the frustration of the bishops and all those who believed it necessary. The other was that the bishops were on the side of the established church not that of the evangelicals who put God's law above all others. From these roots began to grow Puritanism, separatism and Presbyterianism.

Although the noise of the vestments controversy slackened after 1566 the response of the Godly was, in some cases, to go underground. Bishop Grindal uncovered the first separatist congregation meeting in Plumbers' Hall in June of 1567. Ostensibly hired for a wedding, the Hall had been turned into a secret church in which the worshippers used the order of preaching and sacraments prescribed by John Calvin in Geneva.

Over a dozen of the hundred or so who were present were arrested and sent to the Counter prison. The next day they were interviewed by Grindal, the Lord Mayor, and the Ecclesiastical Commission, the body created by statute in 1559 to oversee religion. Standing before the Queen's representatives, the separatists were insolently unrepentant. They rested their case on Scripture and they refused to be overawed by the tribunal. Larding their arguments with Scripture – they had, as one said, the Word in their homes – they insisted that they had separated because Scripture forbade them to associate with those who give occasion for evil.

Met with the objection that to refuse to attend the established church was disorderly and against the authority of the prince, Robert Hawkins summarized their case:

> Why the truth of God is a truth, wheresoever it be holden, or whosoever doth hold it; except ye will make it subject to places and persons and to the authority of the prince. It had been better we had never been born, than to suffer God to be dishonoured, and his word defaced for princes' pleasure.[45]

This refusal to dishonour God carried them to avoid the established church, not because they disagreed with preaching of the Word, but because 'you have tied the ceremonies of Antichrist to it, and set them before it'.[46]

In the end they were sent back to prison, where they were visited by theologians trying to convince them to conform. They resisted until Grindal got them released about a year later. Even then they were uncowed, and several were rearrested and returned to prison for illegal preaching and assembling.[47]

Thanks to the increasingly rigorous vigilance of Grindal and other ecclesiastical leaders separatism began to wane by about 1570, to be replaced by Presbyterianism with its intense distaste for bishops.

5

Catholic Confusion

I

Catholics were not the enemies of Queen Elizabeth, said the Catholic apologists. 'There is,' insisted John Martial in 1564, 'no blast blown against the monstrous regiment of women; there is no libel set forth for order of succession; there is no word uttered against the due obedience to the sovereign.'[1] The real danger to the Queen came from English Protestants. And it is true that Catholics, officially recognized as the enemies of the Queen and the Anglican Church, condemned by law, and the bogeymen of those who feared a Catholic heir to the throne, made, until the late 1560s, much less trouble for the Crown than did the more enthusiastic Protestants. Catholic controversialists, writing from the safety of the continent, loved to point this out. Thomas Stapleton smugly claimed that no Catholic had been convicted of disloyalty 'for word or deed, concerning the prince's civil regiment' in the first eight years of Elizabeth's reign.[2]

When Stapleton made that claim he was carefully avoiding certain facts, but it is true that the Catholics of England were remarkably quiescent until the late 1560s. As discussed above, the reasons for this are in the failure of the papacy and the local Catholics to provide leadership, Elizabeth's lack of stomach for persecution, and the English people's instinctive obedience to the monarch that had given Henry VIII, Edward VI and Mary the ability to change religion without being overthrown. However, devout English Catholics were, by the mid-1560s, beginning to reach a conclusion similar to the one reached by the friends of Geneva: the moderation imposed by the Queen was not good. For Catholics it meant a slow, easy erosion of their commitment.

It would have been easier to stir resistance if Elizabeth had only martyred a few leading Catholics. But there was no early Elizabethan equivalent of St Thomas More. Although some would have willingly died for the faith, the Queen was not willing to give them that honour.

This left their apologists frustrated, for the resistance needed role models. Nicholas Sander, in exile for his faith, recognized this, as John Foxe had. Foxe, however, had the advantage of dead martyrs; Sander had to rest content with a martyrology of men who lost their positions and were imprisoned. For example Reynolds, the Catholic Dean of Exeter, told Sander that Elizabeth had been sent by God as an act of divine providence, a punishment for worldliness under Mary. Mary had to die because her presence had become prejudicial to the faithful, who were running riot. "'Then at length,'" Dean Reynolds said, "'comes Elizabeth, not destined to benefit herself but us only. For it is the privilege of the Church of God to grow by means of persecution.'" Believing that by dying for the faith he could do penance for having abjured the Pope in the time of Henry VIII, he gave his goods to the poor and went to London to '"be available to confess the faith".' Summoned before the Ecclesiastical Commission he made so glorious a confession he lost his benefices and was imprisoned. Then he died, disappointingly, of natural causes.[3]

Not even Edmund Bonner, Mary's Bishop of London and a man vehemently hated by Protestants, was martyred, despite Sander's valid assertion that he was nearest to martyrdom. Bonner had been so zealous in hunting and burning heretics that even some Catholics were disturbed by his belief that to kill one heretic was to save many lives. At his trial he was thanked, with deep irony, for having done so much to promote the Protestant cause.[4] And yet he, too, would die of natural causes.

Elizabeth, who seems to have been the architect of this policy of toleration, had succeeded in stunning the Catholics into acquiescence. They were as confused as everyone else about her true religion. Though they were certain she was not a Catholic, some thought that she could be brought to be one by a husband, a political deal or the sheer incivility of the Protestants. Domestic Catholics and Catholic diplomats maintained this hope, as did the Roman curia.

Their hopes were strengthened by her amazing refusal to persecute them as they had every right to expect. Although the Act of Supremacy and its oath could be used to find and punish Catholics, she did not allow it to be widely administered, and those people who did refuse to take it were treated with a gentleness that was truly magnanimous in the age of the Roman Inquisition.

This was a frustration to her Protestant subjects, many of whom wanted blood, but it kept much of the country at peace. No one can know for certain how many English people considered themselves

Catholic at the beginning of the reign, and thanks to Elizabeth, none of them had to decide if they were for a number of years. The Catholic apologists insisted that most people were friends of Rome, and modern studies have supported the fact that the theology of the Reformation had limited impact in much of the realm. Nicholas Sander asserted that a very large number of the nobility and the greater part of the country gentlemen were unmistakably Catholic, hating heresy. 'Not a single county except those near London and the court, and scarcely any town except those on the sea-coast willingly accepted the heresy,' he said.[5]

The mere survival of Catholicism in noble families like the Howard family indicates that Sander knew what he was talking about, as do studies of Catholicism in the counties. The north and west parts of the country had many inhabitants who were very conservative about their religion.

But were they really Roman Catholics, or just conservatives? Scholars disagree over whether English Catholicism was a continuum between the 1530s and the 1580s. Some would say that it was, while others would argue that a new Catholicism was born late in the reign out of the efforts of the missionary priests who carried the message of the Counter-Reformation to English people who had ceased to be Catholic in any meaningful way.

The truth is somewhere between, taking into account the generational differences and geographical variations that make 'Catholic' hard to define. If by it one means people who accepted the authority of the papacy, there were few left. If one means those who believed that the body and blood of Christ were in the consecrated bread and wine there were many more. If one means people whose religious practice was primarily pre-Reformation in its personal aspects there were many, many more. Certainly the reformers believed the people lived in blind superstition and ignorance, but often that meant that they still knelt at the name of Jesus, fingered their rosaries and gave funeral cakes to the poor. Though unwilling to directly resist the Reformation they continued on traditional paths until diverted from them by the authorities.[6]

Father Augustine Baker, born in 1575, described the Wales of his parents' day as existing in a kind of heathenism. The people were not Catholics as he defined them, though some Catholic practices persisted, but neither were they Protestants, since few preachers reached them and the services were read in English, a language most of the Welsh did not understand. His father recited vocal prayers out of Latin Catholic authors and used Catholic English prayer books, while conforming to the established Protestant worship. He did not trouble himself with Catholic or Protestant belief. Instead he continued reciting his daily prayers while walking in his garden.[7]

Nonetheless Baker claimed his father, had he not been burdened with thirteen children, would have fled the kingdom for religion's sake. Perhaps a piece of wishful thinking on the part of a religious son, this portrait of William Baker, steward of the Lordship of Abergavenny, a justice of the peace, and possibly sheriff of Monmouthshire, underlines the haze that obscures theological distinctions before the 1569 revolt of the Northern Earls and the resultant persecutions hardened the distinctions between Papist Catholics and Anglican Catholics.

Although most English Catholics would have recognized William Baker as a fellow in confusion, there were those who did know that their Queen was a heretic and who dedicated themselves to resisting her and perpetuating their True Faith.

Some were religious of the Marian restoration who immediately understood that the way in which they had chosen to serve God was once again forbidden. Small groups of monks and nuns fled to the continent to continue English monasticism in exile until, in the nineteenth century, it could be re-established in the home country. In the universities learned men were not fooled by the Catholic-looking Protestant service. Surplices worn in church did not make a minister a priest.

But, being human, most of those who were loyal to Rome did not flee until it began to be obvious that England was not going to tolerate Catholic practice no matter how benign the Queen was. As we have seen, the first persecution of Catholics was the arrest of the bishops in 1559. The first direct attack on the laity came in 1561 in the Waldegrave affair rehearsed above. Tied to foreign policy and the succession and compounded by sorcery it did not herald a general drive against Catholics, and until 1563 most men loyal to the old faith continued to hold offices and places of honour in their communities.

The best sign that this period of tolerant confusion was ending was the concern for disciplinary conformity in Convocation and the passage of the Treason Act by Parliament in 1563. These were foreshadowed by the outbreak of a lively propaganda battle between John Jewel and Catholic apologists in 1560 that led to the 1562 publication of Jewel's *Apologia ecclesiae Anglicanae*. His *Apology* gave the Church of England a doctrinal form that it had lacked.

The polemical battles that would give definition to Anglicanism and its Catholic resistance began on 29 November 1559, when John Jewel climbed the stairs to the Paul's Cross pulpit and delivered the first of his 'challenge' sermons. Soon to be consecrated Bishop of Salisbury, Jewel repeated it at court and again at Paul's Cross in March 1560. In the first of the sermons he had promised that if any learned man alive could 'bring any one sufficient sentence' out of the Fathers, the ancient Councils or the Scriptures to prove that the primitive church –

defined as the first 600 years of Christian history – had practised private masses, had given the laity only the bread at communion, had prayed in a foreign tongue, had recognized the Bishop of Rome as Pope, had believed in transubstantiation or that the mass was a sacrifice, he would 'give over and subscribe unto him'. When he repeated his challenge in 1560 he added to it an attack on the Catholic priesthood and noted that because no one had answered his first challenge it proved that his arguments from history and Scripture was unanswerable.[8]

Not surprisingly Jewel's smug crow of victory provoked a response. Dr Henry Cole, the deprived Marian Dean of St Paul's, wrote Jewel the day after his sermon at the court and accepted the challenge, reversing its terms and offering that if Jewel could convince him from the same sources that Catholic doctrine could not be proved consistent with the primitive church he would abandon his faith. Cole suggested that they carry on the dispute in writing with footnotes, for 'the weight of these matters more requireth learning than words'. Moreover, he suggested that it be kept on a high level, disdaining arguments – especially those of Calvin and Bucer – which might convince young folk, the simple and the unlearned, but not scholars. Jewel agreed to the duel, 'as a friend with a friend, or a scholar with a scholar'. Further defining the terms of debate he laid out the propositions to be disputed.

His response, however, had a tone that Cole found offensive. He wanted, he said in his riposte, to learn as a student, not to be put off like a beggar, warning Jewel that if he was unwilling to submit his new religion to objective tests people would believe that his silence arose from his inability to answer. Cole was stepping carefully because he could be punished by law for defending the old faith, yet he was trying to push Jewel into a full-blown scholarly debate which Cole must have believed he could win if, as he told Jewel, they reasoned as the Fathers had reasoned. For all its gentleness Cole's snide tone came through to Jewel, who summed up Cole's letter in his response: 'In your second letter I find many words to little purpose.' Slowly the gloves were coming off.[9]

Jewel had been stung by Cole's suggestion that he feared the debate because of his weak position, forcing him to suggest that Cole's failure to provide the requested single proof arose from *his* lack of reason: 'being so often and so openly desired to shew forth one doctor or council, etc. in the matters afore mentioned, yet hitherto ye have brought nothing; and that, if ye stand so still, it must needs be thought ye do it *conscientia imbecillitatis*, for that there was nothing to be brought.'[10]

The debate escalated. Cole circulated his letters among his Catholic friends and Jewel apparently decided to print his response. He wrote to Cole demanding that a copy of Cole's letters be sent to him for publication along with his response. When Cole did not respond Jewel cleverly questioned the authorship of the letters because they were too 'heaped up with taunts' and stained with choler to have proceeded from a 'sober, grave man' as he had assumed Cole to be. This nasty insinuation that the author of the reply to the challenge depended more on taunts than reason was the leitmotif of the printed reply. Jewel printed Cole's letters paragraph by paragraph, inserting his responses between each one. Abandoning reason he attacked Cole *ad hominem* at many points: 'you say much and prove nothing'; 'stout and bold asservations maketh no proof in the law'. At other points he did cite Cole's evidence, but always using the sneering tone with which he had begun. He concluded his reply to Cole by observing that although he had desired him to provide a sufficient authority to prove Catholicism true, he could not because there are no proofs, only Cole's *conscientia imbecillitatis*. *Ergo*, Protestantism is the true primitive church.[11]

Jewel's argument, resting on church history, was given much fuller scope in his *An Apology of the Church of England*. Apparently he was commissioned to write it by Cecil in May 1561, a part of the campaign against the Catholics inspired by the request of the papal nuncio to visit Elizabeth. Its audience was foreign and scholarly, a high-minded side to the effort that also included the arrest of the Essex Catholics and sorcerers who gathered around Waldegrave.

On 1 January 1562 the book was published in Latin and immediately sent abroad, where it received an enthusiastic reception from Protestants and provoked a new storm of Catholic disputations.

The *Apology* did not have official status, but it was quickly translated into English and became the touchstone of Anglican belief. Anne Bacon, the wife of the Lord Keeper and mother of Francis Bacon, did the 1564 translation, which became the standard edition, providing all English people with their first guide to their own official faith beyond the *Book of Common Prayer* and the homilies.[12]

Divided into sections, it laid out the basic creed, defined the ministry and the sacraments, defended the role of the monarch in the English church, and made a wide-ranging attack on the papacy and key Catholic doctrines using the Fathers. Short and to the point, it assumed all reformed faiths were created equal, holding that the differences between a Lutheran and a Zwinglian were no greater than those between differing Catholic schools of theology. Only extremist Anabaptists, Mennonites, Zwenckfeldians and papists were ejected from the fold that contained those who followed the true church. The critics of the truly faithful, said Jewel, could never say 'that we have swerved either from the word of God, or from the apostles of Christ, or from the primitive church', which is the true Catholic church.[13]

The religion of Christ outlined by Jewel, this church that was 'no new thing' but the restored primitive gospel church, had shaken off the yoke and tyranny of the Bishop of Rome. The Roman Catholics who taught doctrine contrary to Christ's gospel were being banished by God. 'Long since have these men's crafts and treacheries decayed, and vanished, and fled away at the sight and light of the gospel, even as the owl doth at the sun-rising. And albeit their trumpery is built up . . . yet even in a moment . . . falleth it down again.'[14]

To English women and men who were loyal to the pope, or who believed that in the mass the elements became Christ who was sacrificed again for the living and the dead, the *Apology* made it obvious that a true Catholic could not in good conscience remain within the fold of Elizabeth's church. It was an insight confirmed by the Council of Trent in 1563 and by Pius V in 1566.[15]

Even as the implications of the *Apology* were sinking in and the first small persecutions were appearing Catholic gentry were being frozen out of important parts of public life. In the Parliament of 1563 a new law was passed to protect the Queen from her domestic Catholic enemies – the adherents of Mary of Scotland – but it required anyone who held office in the kingdom to take the oath of supremacy.[16]

The bill was introduced and then rewritten, strengthening the supremacy. It made it high treason on the second offence to uphold the authority of the papacy, and a second refusal of the oath of supremacy was punishable by death. Finally, it required all members of the House of Commons to take the oath of supremacy; those who would not could not sit, a situation that did not end until 1829.

Cecil reported that the Commons 'think nothing sharp enough against Papists',[17] but there was a heated debate. Robert Atkinson, a young lawyer who would be disbarred by the Ecclesiastical High Commission in 1569, attacked the bill on the grounds that supporting the pope was an offence in religion, not treason, noting that excommunication, not death, was the appropriate penalty. In Mary's time, he remarked with conscious irony, the Protestants had claimed that faith could not be forced by law. Now they were proposing to do just that. Besides, did they think that men, threatened with loss of their goods and incomes for the first offence, would refuse the oath? No matter what they believed in conscience, they would swear and then, angry and disenchanted but still in office, they would become even more dangerous. In his conclusion he warned of what did indeed come to pass. Remember, he told them, the trust their country placed in them and, having the sword in their hands, be careful who they struck 'for some shall you strike that are your near friends, some your kinsmen, but all your countrymen and your even [equal] Christian'.[18]

Atkinson was given the answer that a refusal of the oath of supremacy was a temporal matter and it was the duty of every subject to recognize the Queen's sovereignty. Anything else was treason. The bill passed the Commons on division, 186 for it and 83 against it.

In the Lords it was attacked by the Catholic peers. They knew they could not defeat it, but they did try, with some success, to mitigate it. The Earl of Northumberland remarked to the Spanish ambassador that the temper of the bill was such that when they had beheaded the clergy they would go after the lay nobility. Viscount Montague, a devout Catholic, argued that his co-religionists were living quietly. But, he asked darkly, what man would receive a new religion by force? 'It is to be feared, rather than to die, they will seek how to defend themselves.'[19]

The bill passed, but, even though the Queen had given her assent, she was not anxious to have it enforced. Cecil helped Archbishop Parker draft a letter to his bishops instructing them not to offer a second oath to anyone without archiepiscopal approval. The Archbishop was careful to affirm his dislike of subjects who 'bear a perverse stomach to the purity of Christ's religion', claiming he felt a fatherly care for all men. But lest people believe they would not be molested by the bishops he instructed them to keep his letter secret.[20]

The Act was used against a few recalcitrant clergy in the next few years, but no one was executed. The failure to use it is in part directly attributable to the Queen, but it was so legally flawed that it was very hard to use in court. In April 1564 Bishop Horne of Winchester, backed by Parker and Grindal, offered the oath a second time to Edmund Bonner. The hated former Bishop of London refused to swear, and he was arraigned in the Queen's Bench. It is clear from a letter to Cecil that Bishop Grindal, and most likely his brethren, wanted Bonner to die, but the case blew up in their faces.

Bonner's defence was to question the form of the indictment and to challenge the legality of Bishop Horne's consecration. The justices found that Bonner's case had some merit – at which point the proceedings were suspended. Bonner remained in prison until he died of natural causes in 1569, and the government, in order to protect the bishops from further challenges to their legitimacy, turned to Parliament.[21] When it met in 1566 the first statute on the book declared the consecration of the bishops 'good, lawful and perfect'.[22]

Although Bishop Horne had ignored the Queen's injunction against using the Act there were many men of law who were reluctant to enforce it. It would mean, as Atkinson warned, punishing their friends, neighbours, families and even themselves. If Nicholas Sander is to be believed (and on this point there is much external confirmation) the Inns of Court were conservative in their religious sentiment. Few lawyers, he reported in 1561, were heretics, but most of them were willing to put Caesar before God. The innate conservatism of the senior judiciary was a problem, but an even greater one was the reluctance of the justices of the peace to take an active role in enforcing the religious settlement.

Just as they had been excluded from Parliament by the act of 1563, so in 1564 Catholic gentry found their places in the commissions of the peace being threatened. In October 1564 the Privy Council wrote to the bishops requesting them to identify the justices of the peace in their dioceses who could not be trusted to defend the religious regime. In consultation with trusted gentlemen in their regions the bishops returned lists of the sitting commissioners of the peace and recommended new appointments. The justices were classified according to their religious enthusiasm. In Berkshire, for example, Sir Henry Neville was noted as a 'furtherer earnest' of religion; Richard Warde of Hurste as 'no hinderer', of religion; and Edmund Plowden the famous Catholic lawyer as 'a hinderer'. In the diocese of Hereford Bishop Scory reported that in Radnor 'none of the justices of the peace . . . are counted favorers of this religion but the best of them is judged but a neuter', and complained that the resident canons at his cathedral were all 'rank papists'. More cheering to the Council was the news from Durham that all the aldermen of Newcastle would enforce the new faith.[23]

Many of the bishops took the opportunity to offer the Council advice on how to make the realm more conformable to God's will and to denounce people who were not on the commissions of the peace. What emerges from their observations is a very rough picture of the distribution of Catholic gentlemen around the country. There appears to have been a strong Catholic presence in Chichester, Winchester, Hereford, and all of the north – though one has to use their reports with care since the Bishops themselves varied in their approaches and attitudes, not to mention their local connections.[24] Nonetheless, the survey showed that only about half the justices in the country were enthusiastic about the new religion. Of the approximately 850 in the study some 150 were noted as committed Catholics.

The Privy Council cannot have been happy with what they learned from the bishops. Their fear that Mary of Scotland and her new husband Henry Stuart would produce a Catholic heir to the English throne, giving England's Catholics a focus, was not assuaged by the information, but what could they do about it? In some areas removing the Catholics from the commissions would alienate the local leaders from the government at a time when they could not afford to lose their support.[25] What few changes the Privy Council made in the list of justices of the peace were made apologetically. John Scudamore of Home, the Keeper of the Rolls for Herefordshire and a member of the Council for the Marches of Wales, was denounced by Bishop Scory as opposed to the religious settlement. When Bacon sent him the 1565 commission of the peace for the county he told him that the changes in the commission had been made by the Privy Council, acting on the information provided by the bishops, not by Bacon's own authority.[26]

The messages sent to Catholics by the government response to the attempt of the Papal Legate to enter England and its fears over Mary of Scotland's claim to the throne, the new treason law, and the increasingly clear distinctions between Anglicanism and Catholicism began to undermine the fragile religious peace that had allowed Catholics to remain unmolested. By the middle of the decade the number of committed Catholics who went into exile began to increase and the plotting in support of Mary grew.

The exiled community centred in the Low Countries where they could remain in close communication with England while practising their faith. Among them were some of England's leading intellectuals, refugees from the universities who would use their scholarship in the defence of what they believed to be the true faith. Among those who fled 'fearing the contagion of schism' were Thomas Stapleton and Edmund Campion. Stapleton was born in July 1535 and was named, he liked to believe, after Thomas More, whose martyrdom inspired him in later years. Educated at Canterbury and Winchester, he went up to New College, Oxford and took a degree in 1556. In 1558 he was ordained a priest and given a prebend in Chichester Cathedral.

Stapleton left England in autumn 1559 in the train of the Count de Feria, the retiring Spanish ambassador. Once he was in the Low Countries he acquired a license from Elizabeth to remain abroad and study, doing linguistics at Louvain and theology at Paris before making a pilgrimage to Rome.

For reasons that are unclear, but which prove that he did not fear a savage persecution, Thomas's father called him home to England and he dutifully returned. He would not be burned, but as soon as he arrived, he recalled, 'I was called before the mock tribunal of the heretic jester to whom fair Chichester had become subject.' Bishop Barlow offered him the oath of supremacy, Stapleton refused, and he was deprived of the income he received from his prebend at Chichester.

In 1563 the entire Stapleton family chose to leave England for Louvain and life as religious exiles. Once there Thomas's anger, frustration, and pain were used to stoke the fires of his polemics. Between 1565 and 1569 he poured out challenges to Anglicanism.

Stapleton made it his job to prove that history could not be used, as the Act of Supremacy claimed, to prove that the king of England had the right to rule the church in his realm. In 1565 he published a monumental book entitled *The Fortress of the Faith*. At its heart was his translation into English of Bede's *Ecclesiastical History of the English People*, but in the almost 500 pages of commentary he used Bede to demonstrate that the primitive church varied from the Protestants in forty-six ways.

As if the labour of translating and commenting at such length warmed him to his work, he became involved in answering Jewel's Challenge, an industry that had become so large that several exiled scholars divided the work among themselves.

The last of his books in English attacked the Bishop of Winchester. In *A Counterblast to M. Hornes vayne Blaste against M. Feckenham* he spent over a thousand pages demonstrating that Horne had told 'six hundred, four score and odd' lies in his defence of the royal supremacy.

Stapleton demonstrated himself to be among the first rank of English historians of his generation with the breadth and quality of his work, a fact recognized by the University of Louvain when he was elected Regius Professor of Scripture. Before that, however, he taught at the new English College at Douai founded by William Allen in 1568. There Stapleton and his fellow exiles prepared themselves and their students to return to England when the Elizabethan regime finally collapsed. They knew there would be a terrible shortage of priests when it came and they wanted to be ready. By 1574 they gave up on the collapse and turned their attention to preparing missionaries, making Douai a centre of intellectual resistance and political agitation.[27]

Many of the faculty of the English College at Douai had been colleagues at Oxford. Although the visitors of 1559 had sought to purge the colleges there of Catholics, they had not carried out their job with thoroughness – in part because the removal of all the Catholics would have emptied at least two colleges. Marian Catholic reformers had succeeded in purging most of the Protestants from the University, and the establishment of Trinity and St John's colleges in Mary's time had created pockets of devout Catholic theologians. The result was not only the indoctrination of undergraduates, but also the conversion of formerly Protestant scholars to Catholicism. Thomas Harding, one of John Jewel's great opponents, had been an active Protestant preacher, but by 1561 he was described as 'stiff in papistry'. Thomas Neale, appointed Regius Professor of Hebrew by Elizabeth, abandoned his chair in 1569 in order to follow his Catholic convictions, finally convinced that they were correct.

Many Catholics continued to teach in the University for years after Elizabeth's accession and a steady trickle of scholars ran out of Oxford towards the continental havens of English Catholics. Among them were the founders and leaders of the Catholic resistance. Besides Thomas Stapleton and Thomas Harding there were William Allen, Edmund Campion and Robert Persons. Allen would found the College at Douai, while Campion and Persons would be the first missionary priests martyred by the Elizabethan regime.[28]

Edmund Campion joined Stapleton and Allen in Douai in 1571. Campion was an outstanding student. As a child of thirteen he had been chosen to represent the students of London by making a speech of welcome to the new Queen Mary, an act he repeated in 1566 when he welcomed Elizabeth to Oxford University. The speech was so eloquent that Elizabeth noticed him and recommended him to the Earl of Leicester, who later became his patron. By the time Edmund Campion left Oxford in 1569 he had been appointed both University Orator and Junior Proctor.

On becoming a master of arts in 1564 Campion took the oath of supremacy, and he remained for a long time within the Anglican fold. He was increasingly troubled in conscience about it, but Bishop Cheyney of Gloucester, who was himself sympathetic to conservative theology, assured him that he could find a place in the established church. Convinced, or fearing the consequences of admitting his qualms, Campion was ordained a deacon in the Anglican faith, gaining him the right to preach and seek preferment.

His ordination, however, seems to have precipitated a crisis. His doubts about the establishment were well known and the Grocers' Company of London that was supporting him on a scholarship demanded that he come to London and preach in favour of the Anglican faith or lose his exhibition. Campion resigned rather than preach.

Tortured by his doubts, he was urged by his exiled friends to flee to the continent and openly embrace Catholicism. Gregory Martin, a fellow member of St John's and a brilliant classicist, herbalist and poet, had already moved to Douai and joined the new foundation. He encouraged Edmund to imitate him, but he was not yet ready.

Instead Campion decided to leave Oxford and go to Ireland where the moribund university at Dublin was to be revived by James Stanihurst, the Catholic father of a former student. When his term as proctor ended on the Feast of St Peter in Chains, 1 August 1569, he delivered an account of his term of office in his best academic Latin and left the University.

Suspicions about his loyalties pursued him to Ireland where he lived openly as a Catholic. Warned just in time, he fled Dublin in the middle of the night, crossing the channel to be lost in the London crowd. There he seems to have witnessed the execution of Dr John Story for the treason of supporting the Pope's authority and stirring political trouble, an event that galvanized Campion to go to Douai and commit himself to the Catholic cause.

In 1573 he became a Jesuit, and in 1581 he was executed for

his underground work against the Queen's supremacy and the new
religion.[29]

II

To many folk less subtle than an Oxford don the distinctions between
their Catholic faith and the Queen's church remained comfortably
vague until the end the decade. As in Oxford, the visitation of 1559 had
failed to remove many conservative priests, and in the remoter parishes
of the North of England these men conspired with their parishioners
and often the gentlemen of the commission of the peace to continue
rituals that did not conform to the prayer book.

In Lancashire the vicar of Farnsworth was accused of hearing confession and lighting candles of Candlemas Day in honour of the
purification of the Blessed Virgin. His neighbour at Huyton was said
to use holy water and encourage people to pray in the old way. All over
the diocese of Chester there were reports of images still being used, the
holy water still in the fonts, and the prayer book service altered at the
whim of the vicar. The people were praying the old prayers using Latin
prayer books and they prayed for the dead in Purgatory. Lancashire
was so attached to the old religion that in 1567–8 there were fears of
a Catholic revolt in the shire.[30]

Yorkshire was similarly intransigent. For instance, in 1566 the Commissary of Richmond, carrying out an order from the High Commission to search for 'monuments of superstition', found that in Aysgarth
the rood images, a pyx, a chrismatory, oil-stocks, a corporax and a latin
hymnal were concealed within the parish church. The churchwardens
claimed that they had destroyed them after they had been uncovered,
but they were still there in 1567. In their wills some testators were
still asking for prayers for their souls, and rosaries were still in use in
places.[31]

In the rural parishes it took the slow disappearance of the older
clergy – of 98 Lancashire priests in 1563 only 53 were in service in
1565 – and changes in administrative personnel before much would
change.[32] That and the crackdown on Catholics that followed the revolt
of the Northern Earls in 1569 that forced a distinction between the
merely conservative and those willing to become recusants and remove
themselves from their parish churches.

The City of York was the administrative centre of the shire and there
the picture is one of slow, creeping conformity. The city government
had followed the Queen's orders about changes in the services of the
churches, but not enthusiastically. Many of the leading families of the
city were identified as unsympathetic to the new religion. Archbishop

Young reported in the 1564 inquisition on the commissioners of the peace that only two of the thirteen aldermen favoured the newly established faith.

The quarrel over whether York would continue its ancient Corpus Christi play proves the conservatism and caution of York's citizens. In 1561 the plays were retained by judicious editing. All the references to the Virgin Mary were expunged and the feast was not honoured even though the play continued. In 1563 a determined group of Protestants demanded that the plays be ended, but the aldermen refused and they continued until 1568. A majority of the citizens were attached to the traditional festival, even though they were unwilling to take a staunch stand in defence of Catholicism.[33] The revolt of the Northern Earls would finally galvanize the city into a greater interest in conformity.

At the other end of the nation, in Sussex, a similar pattern was visible. The 1560s were a time of uneasy peace when Catholics continued to participate in parish life without supporting the faith by law established. The county had pockets of Protestants in ports like Rye, but it also had the staunchly Catholic family of Anthony Browne, Viscount Montague, living in Battle and controlling local politics. He and his family followed a pattern familiar across the nation. Slowly retreating into their private chapels, the Catholic gentry were beginning by the late 1560s to establish the pattern of worship that would characterize English Catholicism.

As in Yorkshire, although the prayer book was used in the parishes, the men performing the service were usually priests who had served Queen Mary, too. Preaching, so necessary for re-educating the parishioners in the new theology, seldom occurred in many of the churches of the diocese of Chichester. In 1569 the Bishop complained that 'many churches . . . have no sermons, not one in seven years and some not one in xii years'.[34] In its absence, and with many churches still held but not served by men who had exiled themselves rather than use the new service, Sussex was drifting in a religious vacuum made worse by poor administration. In 1564 Bishop Barlow confided to the Privy Council that of the upper clergy only two holding benefices in his diocese could be trusted as commissaries or vicars general – as, that is, enforcers of the religious settlement. Lacking preachers and administrators the Bishop could do little to convert his people, even if he succeeded in making certain that the right service was used.[35]

Bishop Barlow would have found sympathy from Bishop Parkhurst of Norwich who lacked the personal skills to be a good administrator as well as enough officers dedicated to the task of imposing the reform. Some 172 of his 510 Suffolk parishes lacked incumbent clergy in 1563, a lack compounded by the shortage of suitable ministers to preach. Worse, some he allowed to preach got out of hand with their evangelical enthusiasm, refusing to wear the surplice or conform to the prayer book. Their behaviour was so flagrant that the Queen noticed their nonconformity during her progress in 1561.[36]

Meanwhile Parkhurst was unable to deal with the unruly conservatives, in large part because officers of the church like Archdeacon John Spencer allied themselves with powerful gentry to retard the reform. Key among the better sort who protected Catholicism was the Howard family. The Duke of Norfolk's clientage formed a conservative network protected by his power and influence until his execution in 1572 for plotting with Mary of Scotland. Until he and men like John Spencer died the East Anglian gentry maintained an attitude of cautious compromise, impeding the spread of Protestantism.[37]

As the decade wore on the conditions for Catholics were changing. Sporadic persecution and marked hostility from some parts of the government combined with the increasingly loud propaganda battle began to threaten the tenuous truce that Elizabeth's moderation and the inability of the bishops to effectively impose their will had permitted in the early 1560s. By the middle of the decade it was becoming apparent that the Elizabethan Settlement was not going away soon and so some devout Catholics went away themselves. Flowing into the Low Countries they began to build a religious resistance based on words.

Some went to Ireland, too, where it was easier to avoid the eyes of the authorities and where there was some resistance in the name of Catholicism – though English Catholics in Ireland found themselves defined as the enemy by anti-colonial Gaels, even if they shared a religion.

In June 1569 James Fitzmaurice attacked the new English plantation near Cork, proclaiming the rebellion in defence of the old faith and calling for the expulsion of the 'Huguenots'. In spite of this pious appeal Cork resisted, perhaps sensing that this was, in the end, a feudal revolt, not a religious one.

It took the English until 1573 to suppress the revolt, which was done with the same gentleness displayed against the English rebels of 1569: by April 1573 some 800 Irish rebels had been hanged.[38]

But for most committed Elizabethan Catholics the turning point in their relationship with their government was 16 May 1568 when Mary, Queen of Scots, fled into England. Exciting anti-Catholic hysteria, she became a natural focus for disaffected English people and especially for Catholics. Possessing a strong claim to the throne of England, she was a Catholic princess who might give England a different, Catholic government. Intimately connected with Mary, the Northern Rising of 1569 appeared to contemporaries to be a religious revolt.

When Mary entered England she rode into a volatile situation.

The conservative prejudices of the northern nobility had made them untrustworthy and Elizabeth's government had been protecting its border from Catholic Scots and Frenchmen by removing the traditional rulers from their places and sending southerners to replace them. The Earl of Northumberland, Thomas Percy, was deprived of his office of Lord Warden of the Middle March and the Dacre family lost control of the West March when the fourth lord died. Lord Hunsdon was appointed commander of Berwick and Sir John Forster, an enemy of Northumberland, took control of the Middle March. Naturally the loss of their offices and honour was bitterly resented by men who considered themselves to be the rightful rulers of their home territories.

Their dissatisfaction was enhanced by their Catholicism. Northumberland had reconverted in 1567, and the Earl of Westmorland was deeply influenced by his priest, his devout mother and his Catholic advisors.

But it was an attempt to use Mary in a game of court intrigue that triggered the anti-Catholic turn in policy. The game being played around the Queen centred on attempts to remove the power of William Cecil and throw the succession to Mary. An aristocratic and semi-Catholic group, the players included the Duke of Norfolk, the Earl of Pembroke, the Earl of Arundel, and Lord Lumely. Their goal was to marry the Queen of Scots to Norfolk, England's most important peer, guaranteeing the succession and the removal of the commoner Cecil as chief minister. Westmorland, Norfolk's brother-in-law, and Northumberland backed the plot, and Mary herself was interested.

In the end the affair was bungled. All secrecy lost, Norfolk found himself confronted by an angry Queen who commanded him on his allegiance to give up the idea of marrying Mary. Confused, Norfolk was pressed by Mary's adherents to take action. Some wanted to seize the Tower and his allies in the north stood ready to raise their troops, while he suffered from migraines and indecision. Finally he fled for his country home in Norfolk, but he agreed to return to the court when the Queen commanded it, sending a message to the Northern Earls not to revolt. If they did he feared it would cost him his life.

Within a week he was in the Tower and Pembroke, Arundel and Lumley were held at court, where news had come that a rising was about to break out in the North Riding and Durham. The Privy Council informed the Earl of Sussex, Lord President of the Council of the North, ordering a general review of the political and religious state of the North. Northumberland was commanded to appear before Sussex at York, but it was too late. The messenger Sussex sent to Northumberland's seat at Topcliffe was awakened around midnight by the bells being rung backwards to raise the country in arms while the earl slipped away to meet Westmorland at Durham. There, on 14

November, they ordered the celebration of mass. Sussex, hearing of their flight, declared them traitors and ordered the mobilization of the forces of Yorkshire.[39]

Thomas Percy, Earl of Northumberland and Charles Neville, Earl of Westmorland proclaimed the revolt on 16 November 1569, calling on all true Catholics to take up arms and save the Queen from her evil counsellors who were oppressing the realm and persecuting the true church. They were essaying, they said, to remedy every disorder in the realm by restoring the ancient freedom of the church of God and of the realm. 'If,' they announced, 'we do not this of ourselves we risk to be made Protestants by force.' After the proclamation a mass was celebrated and they marched under the banner of the five wounds of Christ, dressed in crusaders' armor.[40]

Although it is clear to historians that Neville and Percy were manipulating the religious sentiments of the northerners in order to escape financial troubles and assuage their own hurt dignity as nobles, it is also clear that they took what they assumed to be the popular line. They expected the people to rush to the defense of the Catholic faith. Certainly 'Simple Tom' Percy and the young Neville had been assured that they would by their advisers, who included Richard Norton a member of the Queen's Council of the North and Sheriff of York.[41]

Using their own extensive powers as feudal lords in a region that was more loyal to a Percy or a Neville than a Tudor, they raised an army and marched towards Tutbury, intending to rescue Mary of Scotland. When her keepers quickly moved her they retreated back north, stopping to besiege Sir George Bowes in Barnard Castle. Poorly victualled and lacking canon, the triple-walled Castle might have been held against the rebels, who lacked siege equipment. But the garrison deserted. Bowes reported that in one twenty-four hour period 226 men leaped off the Castle wall and went over to the enemy. He noted with some satisfaction that thirty-five broke their arms, legs and necks in their escape, but he had to surrender.[42]

As the rebels marched they made clear their feelings about the new religion. In the churches they overturned the communion tables, ripping up the English bibles and books of homilies and trampling or burning them, and then celebrating mass.[43]

By the beginning of December it was becoming clear to the Earl of Sussex who was in command of the loyal forces that the revolt was unravelling. The earls had failed to get further support from their fellow nobles. The Earl of Cumberland arrested their messenger and sent him to the Queen. The frontier fortress of Berwick and York, Carlisle, and Newcastle remained loyal, too, so that by mid-December it was obvious that the rebel cause was hopeless. The earls disbanded their men on 15 December and ran for the Scottish border, hotly pursued by Sir John Forster and his horsemen from the East and Middle Marches.

It seemed as if the revolt had ended by early January, but there was one more twist in the story. The Scots borderers, ardent Catholics and always enthused about plundering English property, made common cause with Leonard Dacre and the rebels. A force of 1,500 men under Henry Lord Hunsdon was sent to arrest Dacre and was attacked in the only full-blown battle of the revolt. Dacre's men shattered themselves in a charge on Hunsdon's arquebuses in what he later described as '"the proudest charge upon my shot that ever I saw'." Dacre fled, leaving three hundred of his men dead on the field.[44]

Although the revolt quickly lost momentum the rebels were not forgiven and forgotten. The Queen's army pillaged the region. The Earl of Sussex complained that the Earl of Warwick and the Lord Admiral, the field commanders, were seizing the property of the rebels and that their troops were pillaging the country. Against his orders they drove off the cattle 'and ransomed the people in such miserable sort, and made such open and common spoil, as the like . . . was never heard of, putting no difference between the good and the bad'. Sussex issued a proclamation to stop their depredations and save the plunder for the Queen, to whom the goods of traitors escheated.[45]

In the meantime Sussex was methodically setting about the punishment of the region. He informed Cecil that he intended to use martial law to execute all the constables and other local officers who had supported the revolt, as well as some men from each town that had sent troops to the rebels, in order to make an example. George Bowes was appointed Marshal and charged with carrying out the judicial slaughter according to a formula. Gilling West sent 141 rebels to the earls, so 30 should be hung there. Hang West sent 241, so 42 should suffer. Bowes was instructed to use his discretion to decide who among the commoners would die but he was forbidden to execute any freeholders or wealthy people '"for so is the Queen Majesty's pleasure, by her special commandment".'

Bowes carried out his orders with dispatch, sending his horsemen to round up the fugitives and hanging them on the spot. To his credit he tempered the Queen's wrath by refusing to leave the widows and children of the executed men destitute when he seized their forfeited property. His kindness was calculated: he wanted the wives and children to have no cause to complain. In all he hanged some 800 men in the first two weeks of January 1570.[46]

The people of the North paid a terrible price for this revolt predicated on religion. Pillaged, killed, executed, widowed, orphaned and terrorized they had cause to complain, but they had learned not to.

Moreover, the Catholic leadership in the North had been shattered, left dead or in hiding. And all over the nation the hunt for Catholics was intensifying as it became ever more certain that they were enemies of the Queen.

To compound the ill effects of the revolt came the papal bull excommunicating Elizabeth. Protected for years from excommunication by Philip II and the Emperor Maxillian as they waited for her to marry a Habsburg, the anathema finally fell in an attempt to help the rebels. The earls had written to Pius V in November 1569 asking for his help. The letter reached him three months later and the excommunication was promulgated on 22 February 1570, by which time the gibbets were laden with rebels. Its chief effect was to prove to Protestant England that Catholics were an intolerable danger to the realm. Their loyalty could not be trusted. A ballad summed up the frightened, bitterly anti-Catholic mood of many:

> Between Doncaster and Perth,
> Be many popish hearts,
> Would their heads were in carts,
> And their bodies in graves:
> Rebels are thieves and knaves.[47]

It was a mood fueled by the rumor mill that churned out reports like the one that 15,000 Scots had invaded and the Duke of Alva, Spanish commander in the Netherlands, had sworn that he would pay his soldiers their wages in Cheapside and force Elizabeth to hear mass in St Paul's on Candlemas (2 February).[48]

The plots, fears and rumors that Mary of Scotland's entry into the country had set afoot had caused the government to begin, for the first time, a systematic crack-down on Catholics. The rebellion lent it wings. In early November 1569 the commissioners of the peace in the realm were all ordered to subscribe to the 'book and statute' for the uniformity of common prayer as a test of loyalty in the face of Norfolk's plot. This forced the Catholic gentry who held positions of authority to make the hard choice of offending their consciences and lying or of making themselves self-confessed enemies of the regime. Most of the men took the oath, but a few refused it.

In Berkshire, Edmund Plowden, who had been reported by his bishop as a Catholic in the 1564 survey, unsuspectingly attended a meeting of the bench, discovering to his surprise that he was expected to subscribe on the spot. Brilliant lawyer that he was, he refused to sign until he had read the fine print, explaining to his fellows that he needed time to examine the prayer book and the Act before saying he could support it. When they met again on 25 November in Reading he was prepared with his answer.

He could not, he said, subscribe. Although he was a regular church-goer, more regular than any lawyer he knew in term time, he had carefully examined the prayer book and the statute and found that he could not agree 'generally to all things in the act and book'. Some things in them gave him a scruple in conscience and he just could not promise to believe them, for 'belief must precede his subscription' and 'great impiety should be in him' if he pretended to 'full assurance or belief of those things in which he is scrupulous in belief'. He hoped they would not take his refusal as resistance to the Queen, to whom he swore love and obedience, but he simply could not betray his conscience and pretend belief. As was required in cases of refusal, they made Plowden give his bond to appear before the Privy Council if summoned.[49]

In Hereford, John Scudamore of Fenchurch, named by his Bishop in 1564 as a justice 'not favourable to religion', did not attend the meeting of the bench, writing instead to say that he would not subscribe, though he would keep the peace. He would do anything except for 'coming to church or not coming, and saving matters of religion, or any manner [of] thing touching . . . my poor conscience therein'.[50]

There were not many who had such tender consciences, or such courage to refuse to subscribe while a Catholic rebellion was occurring. In London a crack-down was aimed at the Inns of Court, known to harbour many sympathetic to the Roman faith even though most, as Sander observed, 'submitted to Caesar and went with the times, giving the second place to God'.[51] When members of the Inns were questioned about their reasons for being absent from church few took the high road marked out by John Scudamore. They waffled, knowing that outright recusancy could blight their careers. Robert Atkinson, who made the powerful speech in favour of religious toleration in the Parliament of 1563, claimed that he went to church in the country and that the press of business often kept him away. Thomas Greenwood was too busy to attend, but prayed privately in his chamber. Thomas Bonde insisted that he was usually in the Temple church on Sundays and holy days, but walking in the round western end rather than coming into the body to be counted.

Pressed as to whether they had heard mass or matins in Latin, or confessed their sins 'after the popish manner', Atkinson indignantly said he had not offended in that way since he was hauled before the Ecclesiastical Commissioners eight or nine years before. Bonde said the same. Greenwood insisted he could not be compelled to answer because it amounted to self-incrimination.

On a third question they had more difficulty. Asked if they had received the Eucharist three times a year since the first year of the Queen's reign they were forced to admit their delinquency. Bonde and Greenwood said they had only done it once, when the ecclesiastical commissioners forced them to. Atkinson said he had taken it twice, once when forced to and the year before at Easter.[52] In 1570 Atkinson was disbarred.

These moves against Catholics in influential places marked the end of the period of confusion that had allowed them to live unmolested since the beginning of the reign. The rebels in the north and in Ireland had risen in the name of the old faith, aiming their attack at both the Queen and her religion. From now on Catholics were to be trusted less and less. Patriotism, if not religious conviction, demanded that all good subjects of the Queen look upon them as the enemy.

6

Marriage

Thomas Dampart denied that he had taken a knife to bed intending to harm his wife. She could not prove otherwise, he said, and if there was any such event it was her fault, not his. He took his oath on it, knowing he would be damned if he lied. After eight years of cohabitation she had left him without cause, at the behest of her father, and he did not know where she was. And no, he had not used the company of other women in Werington parish 'suspiciously'. There were no grounds for the divorce she was requesting, even if he was under ten when they married.[1]

Thomas Dampart's wife Elizabeth was pleading an acceptable reason to be divorced from her husband: consentless marriage when they were children. The fact that he had threatened her with a knife might influence the court into believing that she had not given consent or that he was the kind of husband who might have affairs, but violence towards her would not be grounds enough for a divorce – though it might explain her refusal to live with him.

Elizabeth's and Thomas's miseries illustrate the way in which the familiar outlines of family life in all ages are nuanced by attitudes and ideals that are vary enormously from era to era. Family virtue as preached and lived in other times is often alien, even though the biological realities are the same. Then as now courtship, marriage, birth, education, ageing and death set the parameters of individual experience, but in the 1560s they were lived in very different ways, made understandable only because we all live the same general patterns.

Elizabethans patterned their lives according to the roles assigned them by God as reified in society. Bound by class expectations, their choices were shaped by where they were born, the social rank of their parents, and, most importantly, by their genders. For Elizabethan women sex was destiny, and Elizabethan men, although given slightly more variegated roles, were expected to fulfil the duties of their sex as well.

When Queen Elizabeth responded to Parliament's 1559 petition that she marry – the first of many – her response was radical and baffling. Refusing to fulfil the expectations people had of women, let alone a female ruler, she announced that she had happily chosen to remain single. Placing herself in God's hands, while insisting her spinster state was not displeasing to God, she stunned her auditors when she said: 'And in the end, this shall be for me sufficient, that a marble stone shall declare that a Queen, having reigned such a time, lived and died a virgin.'[2]

The men and women around Elizabeth did not take her seriously and it would be many years before they accepted that she did not intend to marry and fulfil her appointed purpose, producing children. That she was Queen magnified the expectation and the need, since her children would guarantee a peaceful, Protestant succession to the throne, but it was assumed that she, as a woman, should accept that role. In a world where sterility was a legal ground for divorce her refusal to marry and bear children set her apart from normal people in the same way celibacy aimed at keeping the parish priest above the local fray.

The roles of men and women in marriage were usually described by contemporaries as 'duties'. William Cecil was a strict father with a dour seriousness that made him the perfect bureaucrat, but his conception of his duty in marriage was clear and it began with the man. He was the responsible guardian of his wife, bound by God to care for her as a part of his own body. Quoting Colossians 3:18 he wrote in Latin what the Geneva Bible of 1560 translated as: 'Husbands, love your wives, and be not bitter unto them.' From 1 Peter 3:7 he copied 'ye husbands, dwell with them as men of knowledge, giving honour unto the woman, as unto the weaker vessel, even as they which are heirs together of the grace of life . . .'. Cecil summarized the husband's duties with another Latin paraphrase of 1 Peter 3:8, 'be ye all of one mind: one suffer with another: love as brethren: be pitiful: be courteous.' As Cecil put it, man and wife must 'consent well' together.[3]

Edmund Tilney, who, as Master of the Queen's Revels, must have been known to Cecil, summarized man's duties in both positive and negative ways in a little book entitled *A Brief and Pleasant Discourse of Duties in Marriage, called the Flower of Friendship*. He must, especially when newly married, be pleasant to his wife, not chiding or grudging, so she grows to love him. If he does not she will make his life miserable 'for if she once fasten her eyes on another he shall enjoy her in despite of her husband's beard'. But while the husband must procure his wife's love by gentleness, his ultimate intent is to rule his private commonwealth more efficiently, attaining to that biblical ideal of 'consenting well together'. The husband should 'gently procure that he may ... steal away her private will, and appetite, so that of two bodies there may be made one only heart, which he will soon do, if love reign in her ...'. In return the wife could expect the husband to, as the gloss in the Geneva Bible said, nourish her, govern her and defend her from perils.

If the husband is to make his wife's will and his own the same he must avoid certain kinds of behaviour. Obviously adultery is a weed that will overgrow the flower of friendship that maintains marital love, and so will gambling which wastes the family's substance. Riotousness and drunkenness that reduce a man to a beast and make him unlovable must be avoided, too. Sober in demeanour, thoughtful in speech, courteous and gentlemanly in conversation, he should deserve his wife's trust and give her wise counsel. He takes care to provide for his household and is diligent in looking after his property, suffering the importunities of his wife tolerantly. Accepting her peccadillos with affable patience, he is 'dangerous and circumspect' in matters touching her reputation but not jealous of her. Lastly, he is careful about the education of his children. Tilney's observation about the duty of educating children bears repeating in this century: it is better that children were unborn than untaught.[4]

In his list of manly duties Cecil underlined the injunction from Ephesians 5:28: 'so ought men to love their wives, as their own bodies: he that loves his wife, loves himself.' When he compiled his list of duties of wives to husbands he underlined its sister passage: 'Wives, submit yourselves to your husbands, as unto the Lord.' And he underlined a quotation from Ecclesiastes 26:1, 'Blessed is the man that hath a virtuous wife.' One wonders what private misery led Cecil to conclude his list of wifely duties with 'what God has joined together no man can separate. Fornicators and adulterers will be punished by the Lord.'[5]

Cecil's summaries of the duties of marriage, ending with the jarring note of divine vengeance against those who fail to perform their responsibilities, catches the contradictions within the impossible ideal of Tudor marital relations. A man had the awesome and impossible position of being king of his own home, ruling his wife as a benevolent, loving despot. She was to return his care with worship and devotion, surrendering her discretion in obedience to him. This surrender was described in detail in contemporary books of advice, though it was all too difficult to obtain. As the Geneva Bible explained to women, being subject to their husbands would pay in the end, for if they were obedient they would be trusted with more liberty, and their husbands would more willingly provide for their needs.[6]

This advice is the familiar obverse of the women's movement, but in its particulars it was concerned with unfamiliar concepts of wifely duty. Tilney informed his readers that the great safeguard of a happy marriage, in which the wife patiently suffered her husband's corrupt nature, ugly face, ill conversation, and rash, inconsiderate behaviour, was shame. A woman with a lively sense of shame had, like Rome's Lucretia, the weapon that would preserve her reputation, her chastity, her honour and her praise.[7] If she combined 'shamefastness' with good housekeeping, and was never idle, plying the needle in her spare time and dressing well, she would deserve the love of her husband and become like the great matrons of Roman history.[8]

Obedience was the greatest virtue, followed by the wisdom to take good care of her husband, never contradicting him while smothering him in comfort. If she did this she might achieve bliss in her assigned role and in the hereafter.

Love, as talked about in the theoretical discussion of marriage, came after marriage and was earned through proper deportment on the part of both parties. It was the love of brother and sister, born of shared responsibility, growing little by little until it was rooted in the heart. As the Geneva Bible said, a man 'ought to love his wife because they lead their life together'. Romantic love certainly did exist, but it was a dangerous acid that undermined good marriages.

As Romeo and Juliet discovered, marrying for love meant trouble with families and it was not considered to be a sufficient ground for a happy marriage. William Painter, who first published a translation of the familiar story in 1567, told his readers, 'Julietta and Romeo disclose . . . what danger either sort incurs which marry without the advise of parents.' Entering the 'amorous labyrinth' of passionate love Juliet found herself torn between desire and duty, her eyes giving off 'lively sparks and violent fire' that fiercely inflamed 'all the most sensible parts' of Romeo, moistening 'the sweet amorous venom' that would kill him. Surrendering to desire Juliet made Romeo her 'only Lord and Master' by marrying him, but they still paid a heavy price. Lady Fortune, 'envious of their prosperity, turned her wheel to tumble them into such a bottomless pit, as they paid her usury for their pleasure past'. If she had only consented to marry the Count of Paris as her father wanted she might have lived to a ripe old age, but instead the lovers died by their own hands.[9]

Passionate love meant, as hundreds of Elizabethan poems attest, suffering that unhinged the mind. Marital love had the opposite effect, soothing, calming, stabilizing, long-lasting. As a 1569 ballad put it,

> Love that is too hot and strong
>> Burneth soon to waste . . .
> Constant love is moderate ever,
> And it will through life persevere . . .
> Love me little, love me long,
> Is the burden of my song.[10]

For most humans these temperate ideals of sanguine marriage run contrary to their natures, and the passion of erotic love had a disturbing tendency to rear its attractive head in spite of all the moralizing that was done. The fallen nature of humankind meant they were victims of their gross bodies, made unreasonable by their passionate appetites, living under the divine injunction to the unmarried and the widows to remain chaste unless they cannot control themselves, for 'it is better to marry than to burn' with unrequited lust.

Like so many things in the mid-sixteenth century individual responses to the Word on marriage varied enormously, confusing the nature and even the desirability of marriage. A significant portion of Elizabeth's nation still believed that men who served God could not be trusted to serve a wife at the same time. Hundreds of years of clerical celibacy and the exaltation of chastity as the highest ideal of Christian life prepared people to be scandalized at the sight of married clergy. The monks and nuns had been expelled from English cloisters in 1540, but the ideal they represented was hardly dead – in 1563 there was a case attempting to overturn a court decision holding that an ex-nun's vow of chastity made it impossible for her to marry.[11] For a few years under King Edward the clergy had been permitted wives, but Queen Mary had repealed that permission and forced them to put away their spouses or leave the clergy, so when Elizabeth's clerics brought their wives home from exile or chose to marry there was scandal.

The Queen herself, living the life a virgin dedicated to God and her subjects, was not sympathetic with the desire of the clergy to marry. Her dislike of marriage may have stemmed from the traumatic effects of her father's marital history – a daddy who has your mother's head chopped off and then goes on to dispose of other wives in the same way cannot have been a good role model for a little princess – but it may have also stemmed from her innate conservatism or watching her sister's experience with Philip II. Whatever the cause, married priests offended her by their existence.

And there is no doubt that her stand was supported by subjects who felt the same way.[12] We do not know why Parliament failed to sanction clerical marriage in 1559, but even Protestants who no longer believed in clerical celibacy had trouble stomaching priests' weddings, and they were never legalized in her reign. Nicholas Sander, writing with hatred

of the new regime but accurately, noted that even Protestants thought
it was disgraceful for their daughters to marry priests.[13]

The end of clerical celibacy made it difficult for some English people
to accept or respect the new, married clergy. Moreover, it was generally
feared that married clergy would divert the income of the church to the
support of their families. Because it was generally believed that women
were greedy, grasping and manipulative, and that fathers were prone to
look after their children, they accepted reports like the one attacking
the clergy of Worcester Cathedral. Sir John Borne complained, with
wild exaggeration but with conviction, that the prebendaries of the
Cathedral, having imported their families into the close, had divided
the Cathedral plate among their wives, melted the pipes of the organ
into dishes, leased the Cathedral's lands to their own children, and
– worst of all in a status-conscious age – diverted the income of the
Cathedral to support their wives' fancy clothes. They 'deck their wives,'
he complained, 'so finely for the stuff and singular fashion of their
garments, as none are so fine and trim in that city.' And then these
women thrust themselves into the places of greatest honour at service
time. Even the Bishop had been suborned by his wife and children,
pulling down a fine chapel in order to build a nursery, 'his wife being
of good fecundity and a very fruitful woman'.

Accused by the Bishop of harbouring papists, hiding the altar stone,
and other offences against the religious settlement, Borne denied them
all but one. 'I must confess,' he said, 'my continual misliking of priests'
marriages . . . as the thing that showeth their covetousness, wantonness,
and carelessness, to do in their office that they are chiefly bound' to
do.[14]

Borne was forced to recant his accusations against his Bishop, but his
fear that wantonness was at the heart of the matter was echoed in high
places. The Queen, and others, feared that the presence of women in
places of education would destroy discipline. Scholars, who had been
required to be celibate before, might not pay attention to their books if
women were too visible. Their communal identity would be destroyed,
and their collegial atmospheres ruined by the presence of children and
wives who expected husbands to dine at home. And those same families
were occupying spaces that should have housed students. So the Queen
issued an edict in August 1561 banning wives, or any other women,
from dwelling in, frequenting or haunting the precincts of colleges
and cathedrals.

Transmitting the edict to Archbishop Parker, Cecil sought to soften
the blow by pointing out that it could be much worse. The Queen,
he said, was so evilly affected towards clerical marriage that she had
threatened to forbid it, only dissuaded by Cecil's stiff resistance.[15]

It is doubtful that Parker's wife appreciated the Queen's order. One can imagine the bitter smile she returned to Elizabeth's famous, and probably apocryphal, thanks for her entertainment: 'Mistress I may not call you, madam I will not call you, but I thank you.' Sander reported that the Queen would never receive even the archbishops' wives at court, counting them as unmarried women with no right to the reverence due their husbands.[16] It was, as Bishop Cox of Ely told Parker, a miserable situation. Writing about a prebend in his Cathedral whose family was going to be ejected from their home he expatiated on their misery and then made a bitter attack on the idea that the clergy should not marry, saying it was against Scripture. Marriage was a natural thing enjoined on priests and bishops and they had the duty to have a wife, keep hospitality, and raise their families in virtue, proving themselves worthy of higher government in Christ's Church. In short, to live as an example to their flocks.[17]

Cox had Protestant theology on his side, but the Queen was the Supreme Governor of the Church and did not relax the rule. The arrival of the Reformation has been hailed by some historians as the beginning of a new kind of familial relationship, in which wives were accorded more respect that before, but the people of the mid-sixteenth century did not know that this was happening. They only knew that yet another stable piece of their world had been blown up.

II

Whether celibacy was a higher state or not, marriage was a social relationship and a process participated in by the community of the espoused. It marked the married couple off from others in society and imposed a set of responsibilities upon them. Because of this families, the church and the state all resisted the idea that individuals could marry themselves to whoever they wished by the very simple expedient of promising to live together as man and wife, exchanging tokens and copulating, even though such behaviour made a legal marriage.

It could be done, and perhaps was done frequently, by people who had no property, but it was preferable that the formal routine be followed that made them into a social unit. And it was preferable that the marriage be arranged by the families, who could pay proper attention to questions of age, wealth, social connection and rank in choosing a partner for a child. It was approached in a calculating way by fathers, mothers, daughters and suitors that left little room for romance and even less for the exciting passions of lusty attraction. Marriage was for the perpetuation of the family name and property and the couple were expected to recognize their duties in this.

Grace Mildmay's story of her betrothal represents a common

approach, with the father of the groom selecting the bride and presenting her to his son. Meditating in old age on the lessons life had taught her she bethought herself of the love Sir Walter Mildmay had for her when she was a teenager. 'Which love was such that he desired me of my father, to marry with his eldest son.'

Sir Walter's son Anthony did not share his father's love of Grace. He wanted to travel and see the world, not marry. His father, however, put an end to any notion of independence by informing him that if he did not marry Grace he could never bring any other woman into the house. Faced with an ultimatum Anthony began negotiating the terms of his surrender, demanding to know what jointure (a gift of property to the bride) he would provide, and how much support his father would give the couple until he died. 'I speak before God,' his father declaimed, 'if thou marry with this woman I will give thee all that I have; and whatsoever else I can procure, shall be thine.'[18] Grace and Anthony Mildmay were dismayed years later to find that his father had broken his word and left half his estate to Anthony's brother.

The negotiation of marriage frequently began with the parents and friends of the girl approaching the parents and friends of eligible men. Their motives were complex, for although marriage was a matter of serious economic and political business, it usually concerned the future of a person who was dear to the negotiators. They had his or her welfare in mind, but often they assumed that an advantageous marriage was the best for their welfare. If they could find a wealthy, well-connected spouse for their child, their solicitous concern was justified.

When William Cecil, despairing of his 'wild' behaviour, decided to marry off his eldest son he found him a wife thanks to Henry Percy. A future Earl of Northumberland, Percy belonged to one of the most powerful families in England, a fact that he did not overlook when he sought to arrange a marriage for his wife's little sister. In January 1561 he offered Cecil the chance to 'advance your house' to much greater honour by marrying Thomas Cecil to Dorothy the daughter of Lord Latimer. At fifteen she was wise, sober, womanly, and as temperate as a woman twice her age. Her brown hair and clear, fair complexion promised that she would grow into a tall beauty.

Offering Dorothy was an enormous favour to Cecil, Percy said, because his family was common and not very wealthy. How could William turn down the chance to ally himself with 'a great house' and see his son 'planted in some stock of honour', enjoying Dorothy's fortune? Of course all parties recognized that William Cecil's enormous power in the realm would be valuable to the Percys, so Thomas was worth acquiring. If, Percy said, Cecil thought the marriage was a good idea he should tell no one until his brother the earl was brought into the plot.

Once William Cecil and the Percys had settled the arrangements Dorothy Latimer and her mother would be told what they had in mind 'for women be willful if not first sought unto'. Thomas Cecil married Dorothy in 1564 and did indeed become a gentleman of estimation in the North.[19]

Occasionally some soft-hearted father tried to match his daughter with a man she actually desired to marry, unwise though it was. Mary Darrell's father did this, creating great confusion.

The man Mary liked was the son of a Mr Leonard. It appears that she convinced her father to approach Leonard and commence negotiations. Leonard's son Sampson was not home at the time so he assumed the task of interviewing his potential daughter-in-law. He tested her, raising all the objections to the match he could think of, but 'so far was she from a nay that she never offered any delay to be my son's wife'. At last, Leonard recalled, hearing her 'mild and loving answers with full consent to have my son who I knew loved her entirely' he concluded that they should marry. 'Nature wrought in me for him to lay my right hand on her breast and to speak to thus effect: Then I see that with God's help the fruits that shall come of this body shall possess all that I have and thereupon I will kiss you. And so indeed I kissed her.' As a token of his goodwill he gave her silk for a gown and she gave his son a handkerchief.

Formal permission soon came from Mary's father, Thomas Darrell from Kent. He reported that he, too, moved by Leonard's Godly admonitions to be sure her consent was genuine, had questioned her intentions, and he was satisfied. She was most willing and desirous to match with young Sampson Leonard. Darrell promised she would make a 'loving and obedient' wife and a nearly perfect daughter-in-law.

It seemed all that remained was the reading of the banns and the nuptials before Sampson and Mary could enter into connubial bliss, but there was a serpent in their garden. Barnaby Googe, a perfectly-named villain, wanted Mary for his own. He had made his suit and been rejected in no uncertain terms by Mary herself. She wrote him a letter in which she coldly informed him that he had no hope of marrying her. A dutiful daughter, displaying her piety to perfection, she told him that her mother and father would never consent for them to marry and she would never dream of disobeying them. She added at the end of the letter a more personal note: 'I heartily beseech you gentle Mr Googe, if every any true love or goodwill you have borne toward me, cease and leave off from all further suit or means to me in this matter . . . I will in no wise match with you.'

Mr Googe did not take his rejection well. He flew into a rage and, acting like a 'wheat head and a sick brain', denounced Leonard for having bought Mary away from him. Googe was a lawyer, a gentleman

pensioner to the Queen, and, most importantly, a cousin of William
Cecil, and he did not accept his dismissal. Googe harassed the Leonards
with 'saucy letters sent with ruffians' and threatened to tell the Queen
and have Mary carried away by royal men-at-arms. He wrote to her
cousins, who were his friends, and accused Leonard of fabricating 'a
pretty laughing toy as touching a precontract', fit to make Democritus
laugh more than at anything done in Greece. He spoke darkly of the
martial furniture prepared against him and the 'Italian inventions'
menacing him, threatening that when the Privy Council heard about it
they would be not approve – meaning his cousin William Cecil would
not approve.

Googe appealed to Cecil, who asked Archbishop Parker to investigate
whether there had been a precontract. In the meantime, however,
Leonard was backpaddling. He withdrew his son's consent, blaming
the girl. He accused her of being inconstant and without steadfastness:
'And so I knit up that though she would, my son says he will not have
her. I say that he shall not have her.'

Mary's hope of marrying Sampson Leonard was shattered by the
pressure Googe brought to bear on the families. On 5 February 1564
she married Barnaby Googe, bearing him seven sons and two daughters
before she buried him in 1594.[20]

For those who were not members of powerful, wealthy families the
process of courtship was less formal, though families and friends still
took a lively interest. Others had worse fortune and more difficult
searches, resorting to marriage brokers to find a spouse of suitable
income and lineage. These brokers charged for their services, though
people also found that friends of friends were willing to play the
matchmaker. Thomas Whythorne, who had escaped the 1563 plague
in spite of his terror, was approached by an acquaintance who knew
a widow in need of a husband.

Whythorne, a music tutor and composer, was in his late thirties,
having never been married even though he had, by his own account,
been the object of marriage of a number of women. Taught to distrust
women and all their works he often found them to be as inconstant as
he expected, and his experience with his 'twenty pound widow' confirmed his misogyny and is presented entirely from his point of view in
his memoirs. Nonetheless this courtship between mature, middle-class
adults, negotiated face-to-face, is as crass as those conducted by parents
of the upper classes.

Whythorne's friend offered to 'help him to' a widow of his acquaintance who was of worshipful parents and had twenty pounds a year
in jointure. She was childless and five or six years younger than
Whythorne, and it was natural for people to expect her to remarry.
Since marriages in the sixteenth century lasted only ten to twelve years

Figure 6 Thomas Whythorne at age 40, about the time he was courting the 'Twenty Pound Widow'. A woodcut copied from a painted portrait made in 1569, possibly by George Gower.

on average there was a plentiful supply of widows and widowers, and three-quarters of the widows would marry again, especially if they were of the age of Whythorne's prospective bride.[21]

Whythorne's friend took him to meet the widow – who remains nameless in the account – and after a formal introduction that included

the information that Whythorne was there to propose, Whythorne and
the widow discussed the possibility of marriage.

As they walked away Whythorne told his friend that he 'misliked her
not' and hoped to marry her. The friend used further enticements
to increase Whythorne's enthusiasm, arguing that she was the kind
who would increase his income by her good management. To that
Whythorne offered a jointure of ten pounds when he inherited his
mother's property.

After two more visits to the widow that week she accepted his offer
of marriage. They exchanged tokens and began negotiating the date
of their marriage, with Whythorne setting it at the beginning of the
next legal term when his brother-in-law, a lawyer, would be in town to
attend.

All seemed well until the next visit, three days later. Suddenly she
seemed cool towards him, chiding him for not visiting her for three
days after their engagement. They argued and she offered to return
his pledge, which he refused and withdrew. A deeply introspective
man, Whythorne was disturbed by what had happened and he began
to suspect that the friend who had introduced them was a con man, in
collusion with the widow, hoping he would give her extravagant gifts.

These qualms were allayed by his friend and the negotiations continued. Whythorne courted more enthusiastically, calling every day.
He was guided by the folk wisdom of the popular proverbs he took
so seriously. As the negotiations drew out he mused that it was true
that 'blessed is the wooing that is not long adoing'. His widow was a
demanding woman, proving the truth of the proverb 'He who doth woo
a maid shall not be the worse welcome though he come but now and
then to her, as in 3 or 4 days, but he that wooeth a widow, must ply her
daily.' Experience had also confirmed that 'he that wooeth a maid must
go trick and trim, and in fine apparel, but he that wooeth a widow must
go stiff before'. (This proverb has another form quoted by Whythorne:
'He that wooeth a maid must be brave in apparel and outward show,
so he that wooeth a widow must not carry quick eels in his codpiece,
but show some proof that he is stiff before.') He intended to continue
his wooing, but he consoled himself with the reflection that the market
for wives was open all year long.

The widow's 'inconstancy' had to be overcome and so her brother,
with whom she lived, was brought in to add his voice to his suit.
Whythorne called on him and was invited to breakfast, but the widow
refused to join them – it was her custom to remain in bed until ten –
but her brother finally ordered her to get up and come down.

She walked in and sat down at the table without embracing or kissing
Whythorne. There was a desultory conversation during the meal, after
which the brother slipped away and Whythorne renewed his suit. He

charged her with inconstancy and breach of promise. She responded by saying she had wanted to marry quickly but because he put it off and did not visit her enough she was convinced that he was not serious, and now she was determined never to marry. Whythorne left 'intent never to travail in that matter with her again'.

Nonetheless he was with her again a week later, urged on by his friend who said she had changed her mind again. Indeed, she asked him to have a wedding ring made of some old gold she had. Reasoning that she would not have a wedding ring made with his help unless she intended to marry him, he told her to choose a date for the wedding and gave her a ring of his to wear until the new one was made.

Hurrying excitedly to a goldsmith he had the ring made, engraving it, as was the custom, with a posy: 'The eye doth find, the hart doth choose, and love doth bind, til death doth lose.' During the four days it took to make he went daily to visit the woman he now described as 'his widow', bringing a lute to her brother's house so he could play for her.

To his dismay, when he gave her the new ring she complained that its design was out of fashion. Whythorne stiffly, and justifiably, declared it was the best fashion he knew but she did not repent her judgement. As her 'glumming, pouting, and sighing' continued he offered to have it remade but it did no good. She sullenly said 'I must content me with it as it is seeing it is my fortune.'

Her passivity convinced Whythorne that she had consulted an astrologer who had told her to have the ring made as a test. If she liked the ring, so her husband would like her. Unable to cheer her he took his leave.

Once again his friend became involved, arranging another meeting with the widow and her brother. Demanding a decision, Whythorne was informed that she had decided never to marry. Her brother and the friend took her aside and reasoned with her. When they returned Whythorne offered to get a handsome house if she would only have him, but she still refused.

She explained that she was frequently depressed and that she feared that if she remarried she would displease her husband, and he would not bear with her quietly. In that case there would be trouble and unhappiness between them. Whythorne swore that he would always be patient, but she dismissed his claim saying, 'I do mean to prevent the worst, and therefore I will never marry.'

Returning to his chamber he remembered that they still had one another's rings, so one more meeting was required. In preparation for it he composed four verses to match those he had engraved on the wedding ring:

For reason now
Hath broke the band
Since to your vow
You would not stand.[22]

Whythorne's experience with the widow demonstrates that although courting took hard-headed negotiation, it always involved strong emotions. Fears of rejection, of being tricked, of external manipulation, and of marriage and remarriage underline the emotional content of actions. Individuals feared for their personal futures, and marriage largely determined those futures. It was a time when irrevocable choices were made about money, family and domestic tranquillity.

This was as true for the lower classes as the upper, but for most people marriage was more a matter of acquiring a 'helpmeet' than of marrying land, money or influence. The domestic scale of production that characterized most manufacturing, and the extra income generated by another pair of adult hands in the field and farmyard, encouraged the choice of mates for the skills and work discipline they could contribute to the union. Women, of course, had their own sphere of activity, and it was widely recognized that a wife was the economic underpinning of her husband.

The lower down the social scale one was, the more it was likely that both spouses worked to produce income. A survey of the poor in Norwich made in 1570 showed 86 per cent of the women over twenty-one employed. Few of the women, however, worked at tasks associated with their husbands' occupations. They made buttons, embroidered, spun, picked chalk, washed clothes, turned spits, filled bobbins, made lace, distilled aqua vitae, and many other things, often in combination. That same survey indicated that their children worked, too, as servants, weavers, guides to the blind and even running a bowling alley.[23]

The necessity of marrying someone who was prepared to provide part of the family income meant that most Tudor people delayed their marriages until they were in their mid-twenties, even though the age of consent was fourteen. Again, there is a correlation between age at marriage and social class, since the upper classes tended to contract marriage – even if they did not consummate it – much earlier than the lower classes. They used marriage to secure land and advantage. The lower classes waited until they could afford to marry.

The necessity that drove them to late marriage was exacerbated by the law. The Statute of Artificers passed in 1563 prescribed that no one could be released from his apprenticeship until he was twenty-four. Reasoning that young men could not be trusted to make wise decisions, the framers of the law apparently feared early marriage. 'Some,' says a gloss, 'take wives and before they are 24 years of age have three or four children, which often they leave to the parish . . . to be kept.'[24]

In this case reality enforced the law, since apprentices, living as legal children within the households of their masters, had little opportunity and less money for marrying. Among the 413 apprentice carpenters of London enrolled between 1560 and 1569 only half a per cent were dismissed from the Company for marrying during their apprenticeships.[25]

When little property or power is involved history does not speak loudly so it is hard to know how courtship proceeded among the lower classes, although it is clear that the sexes mingled freely. Gilbert Clerke, a servant of William Staunton, Underkeeper of the Receipt of Exchequer, deposed in court in 1571 about his daily activities, showing that in that household the men and maids mixed openly and in a friendly way. They attended church together, they worked together in the kitchen, and they played together. Their familiarity is caught in a lively miniature: Clerke had gone to his room, which he shared with another servant, and was in bed when 'mistress Ann Dorytie and the nurse and my fellow Edmond Dedd all came running into the chamber and was merry, letting down a window that doth look into the palace and there they did stand beholding the young folks that there were a playing until it was dark night.'[26]

Alessandro Magno, an Italian merchant who visited England in 1562, was struck by this un-Italian freedom between the sexes. He reported that Englishwomen had great freedom to go out without their menfolk and that many women served in shops. 'Many of the young women gather outside Moorgate and play with the young lads, even though they do not know them. Often, during these games, the women are thrown to the ground by the young men who only allow them to get up after they have kissed them. They kiss each other a lot.' He went on to say that at banquets the English slapped men or the shoulder, or patted women on the belly, and cried 'frolic!' At dances this familiarity was even greater. The men 'hold women in their arms and hug them very tightly, and for each dance they kiss them in a very lustful way'.[27]

Thomas Whythorne, tutoring in households, was bedevilled by women high and low who sought his attentions. One girl left a poem expressing her desire in his gittern strings. Terrified and bashful, he put a quick stop to her passion, but the other servants talked. Her master and mistress, 'finding that she was so loving without provoking or enticing thereunto' discharged her 'out of that house and service'.[28]

In the country there were more chances to be familiar in private. Agnes Bowker, under investigation for giving birth to a cat, detailed the trysts she had with various men and animals. She made love with Randall Dowley, a fellow servant, in the porter's ward, in the malt mill and in the fields.[29] It was the beginning of what can only be described as a peculiar sexual career.

Free to meet, presumably they were freer to marry whoever they chose, but they were still curbed by economic reality and by their masters and mistresses, if not by their parents and families. Marriage, therefore, remained a matter of negotiation, not happy enchantment.

In these negotiations the women had fewer choices than the men – and sons had few enough choices when Father had declared his love for a maid – but the canon law did demand that women give their consent. A woman could not be forced to marry against her will. That did not prevent men from trying, though, because with a woman's hand came her property. In the normal course of things a father might buy the guardianship of an orphan from the Court of Wards and bestow the child's property and person on his son or daughter. This was legal because as guardian he stood in place of a parent, though the child still was expected to give consent of some sort, but of what sort was problematic. In the child divorce cases from Chester in the early 1560s the court was always careful to look for signs of nonverbal consent, such as kissing and exchanging gifts. In child marriages this was doubly important because the children were often too young to speak the matrimonial pledge, but consent was a necessity.

A true marriage consisted of three things: consent, exchange of gifts and consummation. Once there had been consummation a marriage was nearly impossible to undo, consent or not, which gave rise to the despicable practice of kidnapping and marrying underaged women in order to acquire their estates. There were enough instances of this that the royal law tried to stop it, as much for the protection of property as for the protection of the girls. A statute of Queen Mary declared that 'the taking away of a maid under sixteen . . . without the consent of her parents or governors, or contracting marriage with her, or deflowering her, is no felony, but yet shall be punished by long imprisonment without bail, or with grievous fine.'[30] A statute of 1598 finally made it a felony without benefit of clergy. It says maidens, widows and wives, having moveable goods, real estate or inheritances, were being carried off by 'saucy misdoers' and married. This displeased God, disparaged the women, and caused great heaviness and discomfort to their friends, and the authors of the law did not want the perpetrators to escape hanging by reciting the 'neck verse' that made it impossible to execute them.[31]

The imputation of marriage for personal gain and the question of consent were at the heart of the most infamous marriage of the 1560s. While the nation was preoccupied with the question of when Elizabeth would marry and produce an heir to the throne, the Earl of Hertford and Katherine Grey married and had a son who might have been an heir to the throne. In retrospect what happened between them can only be described as a love match, though to many at the time it seemed a crassly political marriage. Katherine Grey had a strong claim to the throne through her grandmother, Henry VIII's sister Mary, the late Duchess of Suffolk. According to Henry's will if his children died without issue the throne should pass to Mary and her descendants.

Katherine was the eldest descendant and stood to inherit if Elizabeth died – and if Mary of Scotland's claim through Henry's sister Margaret, Queen of Scotland, her grandmother, was ignored. It was this connection that led Katherine's unfortunate sister Jane to be made Queen in 1553 in a desperate attempt to keep a Protestant on the throne and preclude Mary. It failed and Jane lost her head, leaving Katherine in direct line for the throne. This made her a prize for any man who wished to elevate his social standing and, perhaps, become king of England by acquiring her.

Edward Seymour, the Earl of Hertford, was a handsome young man who was well connected in his own right, with impeccable Protestant credentials. His father had been the Duke of Somerset, Lord Protector of England, running the nation for Edward VI and imposing the first Book of Common Prayer on the country before he lost his head.

Together Hertford and Grey had a formidable claim to the throne; their child would have an even better one if it was male. Naturally any rumour of an alliance between them would be seen as a play for the throne, so when they fell in love they had to step cautiously, meeting in secret.

If they were to marry there was another bar, too. Not only would Elizabeth pitch a royal tantrum at the mere rumour of their marriage, but Mary had already married Henry, Lord Herbert, the son of the Earl of Pembroke, in May 1553. Part of the plot to guarantee the Protestant succession, the unconsummated marriage was dissolved, but Katherine and Henry seem to have assumed that their future lay together.

But then she met Hertford in the spring of 1559. The Spanish ambassador, who kept a close eye on her as a possible royal heir and marriage partner for a continental prince, noticed in March that she no longer talked about Lord Herbert.[32]

Herbert himself got wind of the developing liaison in July. In a furious letter he announced that it was not in his gentle nature to be cuckolded and demanded his tokens back. If she would not send them he would seek them from 'that companion's hands of yours, by whose practice to cover your whoredom and his own knavery and adultery you went about to abuse me'. He promised to never write to her again, protesting that he had only written this time because he was forced to by her own 'detestable and abominable living whereat all the world speaks not a little shame'.[33]

For his part, Hertford was smitten. Verses, probably in his hand and dated 1559, complained of wounds from cupid's arrows.

> She stood in black said Troylus he,
> That with her look hath wounded me.
> She stood in black say I alas,
> That with her eye, hath bred me woe.[34]

How much woe they would breed together was beyond their knowing. Katherine was a lady in waiting to Elizabeth so she and Hertford could only meet when the Queen was away. Hertford's sister Jane was their go-between, and they tried to keep their budding romance from his mother. She noticed nonetheless, and warned him to stay away from Katherine – but he huffily replied that well-meaning young folks could keep company anywhere they liked.

Once they had decided to marry they began plotting how to do the deed. They had to wait until the Queen went hunting or to some other place that did not require the attendance of her ladies, so they could not fix a date. Finally a chance came and they seized it. Katherine slipped down river from the Court, alighted at the water stair of Hertford's house, and was spirited up to his bedroom. A bearded priest wearing a black Geneva gown married them, using the service in the Book of Common Prayer. Hertford slipped a ring of five golden links on her finger and the priest left, carrying a ten pound tip.

Jane, the only witness, soon left, too, and they proceeded to the third and final step of making a legal marriage. Having exchanged promises and tokens they immediately 'went into naked bed' where, as Hertford chastely put it, he lay sometimes on one side, sometimes on the other, and sometimes in the middle for the next two hours.

He was naked, but she was not. She wore on her head a silk scarf she had brought expressly so that her head would not be uncovered during the consummation. Apparently this was expected of all chaste matrons, since it was a major point of interrogation at their trial.

Katherine had to be back at the Court before Elizabeth returned, so she slipped away again. They met when they could, and Hertford admitted that they had sex in the King's Chamber at Court.[35]

With their marriage still a secret Hertford went on acting as if he was a carefree young aristocrat pursuing his education. In May 1561 he was licensed by the Queen to cross the channel 'for the sight of other countries and commonwealths whereby he desires to come to knowledge of things meet for his estate' to better serve Her Majesty.[36] He went to Paris where he met Thomas Cecil who was travelling for the same reasons. Perhaps they went together to see the fight between a lion and three dogs that thrilled Thomas, but young Cecil's tutor and his father soon agreed that Hertford was to be avoided. The tutor hinted at a certain turpitude that was a bad influence.[37]

Perhaps Hertford did not know that Katherine was pregnant when he left the country in May, but in August Francisco the courier delivered to Sir Nicholas Throckmorton, the English ambassador in Paris, an order from the Queen demanding Hertford's immediate return to England. The Queen was, as Cecil told Throckmorton, 'much offended'. Apparently Katherine had kept her pregnancy secret until she was eight months along.[38]

The baby, named Edward like his father, was born on 24 September 1561. His parents were clapped in the Tower and the affair became a matter of common gossip in London, with some people arguing that they were married and others that they were not.[39] By October the rumour that Elizabeth was intent on having little Edward declared illegitimate had reached Rome, and it was true.[40] Unfortunately for the couple, although they both declared they were married, they could not produce any witnesses. Hertford's sister Jane was dead and they had no idea where to find the priest who had performed the wedding.[41]

Once they were safely locked in the Tower, preventing Katherine and her baby from being seized and used as the centre of a revolt – there had been rumours of a Spanish plot to kidnap her and now that she had a son the risk was increased – Elizabeth issued her letters patent to the Ecclesiastical High Commission for an investigation to determine the legitimacy of their child.[42]

By sending the matter to trial in a religious court the Queen was following the legal form, so the judges had to prove the marriage invalid in canon law. They concentrated on discovering if the marriage was legally contracted, how and by whom were they married, what tokens were exchanged, when and where consummation occurred, what Katherine wore on her head during the consummation, if Hertford assigned Katherine any income from his lands, and if anyone talked them into marrying. Underlying this questioning was the issue of whether they were married by a Catholic or Anglican ceremony, by a priest or a minister.

Although these interrogatories stayed within the legal requirements of the case, it is clear that Elizabeth was afraid that their marriage was part of a plot to throw the succession to the Suffolk line, evidence of the Catholic plot she had been warned against. Ironically Katherine would become the centre of Protestant hopes in the succession debate.

The Ecclesiastical High Commission found baby Edward Seymour to be a bastard, unable to inherit from his parents. To the Commission's credit, a marriage without witnesses performed by a mystery priest gave the judges all the legal grounds they needed, but they must have been under intense political pressure to find against the child's legitimacy. Certainly no one questioned the fact that Katherine and Hertford believed they were married, but they were not nonetheless. Hertford was fined fifteen hundred pounds for having 'illicit and illegitimate carnal copulation' with Katherine and left in the Tower.[43] Katherine remained imprisoned there, too.

True love is not easily thwarted, however, and Hertford began a series of legal appeals to get the verdict overturned. A surviving letter from one of his attorneys shows them plotting to plant evidence to improve his chances of success. He should, the lawyer said, acknowledge to everyone he met 'by some petty means' that Katherine was his wife, creating witnesses who could depose that they believed her to be his 'lady wife'. They were going to instruct Katherine to do the same. Hertford's reply, scribbled on the same letter, made it clear that he was already doing this. 'I have said (as truly God knoweth) she is my lawful wife as likewise she may truly affirm me to be her lawful husband.' Nonetheless, if they could not get the decision overturned he was willing to marry Katherine a second time. He asked the lawyer to show Katherine his letter 'hoping that afore it be long, for all that is already past, God's strength is able shortly to bring us together again, who he has already joined and united'.[44]

The same letter indicated that the Lord Lieutenant of the Tower was sympathetic to their cause, and perhaps it was his sympathy that made it possible for Hertford to 'escape' from his cell into Katherine's where their second son, Thomas, was conceived.[45]

They were both released into house arrest because of the danger of the plague in August 1563, but they were kept strictly separated. Perhaps Elizabeth might have permitted Katherine more freedom over time, but in 1564 John Hales, a member of Parliament and Clerk of the Hanaper, published a pamphlet challenging the sentence of the court and announcing that Katherine's sons were the true heirs to the throne, not Mary of Scotland. For his pains he was tried under the Act of Supremacy, imprisoned in the Tower for a year, and then kept under house arrest until he died in 1571.[46]

Marrying for love could cause pain and confusion for the couple and the extended family, even if they were not so exalted as Hertford and Grey. Better, most people believed, to see to it that couples were well matched, in the most literal sense of the word, than that they loved, or even knew, one another. That would take care of itself if they were lucky.

III

All the various forms of courtship had one thing in common: they were intended to end in marriage, but marriage was detached from weddings in a way foreign to the modern mind. Attitudes varied according to class – and the amount of property involved – but sexual union and cohabitation were permissible as soon as the couple had contracted to live as man and wife. A wedding in a church was public confirmation of something that may have been long since agreed upon and acted upon by the couple. Thus you could overhear, as someone did one Somerset night in 1562, a conversation between a man and his bed companion:

> 'Be you not my wife? Why should you refuse me?'
> 'I am so . . . but what will folks say, because I am not married.'[47]

These 'clandestine contracts' were legal in England until 1753, and many people of the lower classes were married in this way, even though the church was bitterly opposed to them. The Convocation of 1563 wanted such contracts outlawed, though it failed in the effort.[48] For the classes whose marriages involved property, however, there was more need for a church wedding. It was an act of social significance and therefore was expected to be a public one.

In order to be married according to church law it was prescribed that the couple's intentions be announced three times in their respective parish churches (the 'reading of the banns') on separate Sundays. After that they could be married, coming into the body of the church (not at the west door in the old manner) where the minister recited words that are still familiar to the English-speaking world: 'Dearly beloved friends, we are gathered here in the sight of God, and in the face of His congregation, to join together this man and this woman in holy matrimony, which is an honourable estate, instituted by God . . .' The groom then promised to love, comfort, honour, and keep his wife in sickness and in health until she died. The bride promised obedience and service in the place of the comfort promised by her husband and was given away by her father or a friend, transferring responsibility for her from father to husband. The troth plighting came next, with the groom presenting the bride with a ring, as a token of the contract they were entering, making it 'vested' in law and therefore binding. After this they were pronounced man and wife, although the prayer book service does not instruct the minister to announce 'you may now kiss the bride'.

There followed prayers, including one for fecundity and long life, which was omitted if the woman was past child-bearing. The congregation then took communion and listened to a sermon designed to drive home the divinely-ordained marital duties, a gloss on what the couple

Figure 7 A marriage feast at Bermondsey, c.1570, by Joris Hoefnagel. The banqueting, dancing, and even the glove giving that went with a wedding celebration are visible here.

had just promised to perform.[49] In 1565 Robert Crowley preached a sermon in which he explained that Paul taught the duty of husbands towards their wives, of wives towards their husbands, and of the duty of everyone to do his or her duty. He elaborated a chain of command, beginning with the 'weaker vessel' who had to obey her husband as the congregation had to obey Christ. Men were responsible for keeping the commandments too, and for seeing to it that their wives did. If they disobeyed they would be punished by God, just as a master would punish his servant for disobedience. The man, he said, 'hath no more liberty though he be her head, than the woman which hath no power over her body'.[50]

The principle behind the prayer book was that the lessons of the marriage service should be engraved on everyone's heart through repetition. It would work very well, since the very words of the marriage service are still common parlance in the English-speaking world, but in the 1560s it was still new and people were still learning. The education, however, was sugar-coated by eating, drinking and dancing.

Once the service was done the rejoicing began. Weddings are times for expressing family position, cementing the new solidarity between

families, and for welcoming the new household into the community.
The feast was where this serious social work was done. Even the poor
celebrated as best they could, while the wealthy families provided lavish
entertainments.[51]

Henry Machyn delighted in pageants, noting impressive weddings in
his diary along with the elaborate funerals he loved so well. Five days
after Katherine Grey gave birth to her second son in February 1563
Machyn reported a double marriage at Baynard Castle, London seat
of the Earl of Pembroke, in which a Talbot daughter and son were
married to Lord Herbert (Katherine Grey's jilted fiancé) and his sister.
For four days after 'was a great dinner as has been seen' and every night
mummers performed and the guests danced at masked balls.[52]

The Earl of Pembroke was expected to throw such a party, but
gentlemen of the City did their best. When three daughters of Mr
Atkinson, a scrivener, were married in a triple ceremony Machyn
was impressed: each wore a head dress with chains of pearls and
precious stones, and each had a gilt communion cup. Scenting the
scene were bouquets of flowers and rosemary, the herb of love and
fidelity. Naturally there was a 'great dinner' after the service.[53]

The father of the bride usually paid for the celebration, and he
was expected to give gifts to the people who attended. Besides food
and drink, ribbons, gloves and scarves were handed out in token of
friendship. Done well, this too could make a good impression. Machyn
reports that when James Sutton's daughter was married in 1559 he gave
away 100 pairs of gloves.[54]

Then as now couples entering into marriage were taking an enormous personal risk, but more than now marriage in the 1560s was
seen as a permanent, until death do you part, proposition. Divorce as
presently conceived was not possible, but annulment was under very
specific circumstances. If a technical flaw prevented a legal marriage,
annulment could be granted. Thus a pre-existing engagement would
be grounds for annulment, as would lack of consent (this is the
ground used in child divorce cases). Marrying within the forbidden
degrees of consanguinity – marrying too close a relative – was also a
ground for annulment. The legal rules governing consanguinity were
extremely complicated, even stretching to forbid marrying relatives
of a deceased spouse. In 1563 Archbishop Parker tried to clarify the
allowable degrees of relationship between partners by issuing a table
of sixty specific sorts of kinship that made marriage impossible. His new
rules, however, did little to stifle the imagination of lawyers who kept
the courts busy with unforeseen cases, causing Parker to lament that
the lawyers continued to explore the sea of perplexities surrounding
marriage law.[55]

Legal separation was a better possibility for the couple who were incompatible. Separation 'from bed and board' could be granted in cases where adultery or cruelty had damaged the relationship, but the couple remained legally attached and could not remarry. The reformers sought to abolish this kind of separation as contrary to Scripture, but because the reform of the ecclesiastical law prepared in 1552 was never made law the separations continued to be granted.[56]

The desire to escape a difficult marriage led people to search for loopholes in the law. One was that divorce was allowed if one partner could not fulfil the divinely-ordained purpose of marriage – procreation. If the couple had no children, and if they could pass examination by a panel of physicians, the church might grant a dissolution for the marriage 'by reason of natural frigidity'.

Willma Gifford sued for divorce from her husband Henry because he, she claimed, had been unable to consummate their union. Upon examination by doctors and 'wise, honest and expert matrons' it was found that Henry was impotent and the marriage was nullified. What was wrong with Henry is unclear, since the judges noted it was 'not decent to record'.[57]

Henry Blagburne tried to escape his marriage by charging that his wife had 'an impediment in her body' that made it impossible for her to conceive. Married for twelve years, he had certainly tried to have a child by her – in fact, he claimed, he had married her because she said was carrying his child – and he had used her body, loving her well, until four years before he filed the suit in 1562. At that point they had separated, but the justice of the peace ordered them back together again until a church court ruled on their case.

Living together under orders from the justice must have been very difficult because Blagburne was willing, in order to use the excuse of 'natural frigidity', to admit to being an adulterer and father of at least one and possibly two bastards. The first he had taken into his home and was raising; the second child he said was not his, but he admitted having sexual relations with its mother. Clearly, he wanted to prove the failure of Mrs Blagburne to conceive was her fault, not her husband's, and he faced the penance required for adultery and fathering bastards in order to prove it.[58]

If Blagburne succeeded in obtaining an annulment *ab causa frigiditatis naturalis* he could put his wife away, but only so long as she did not have children with another man. Any proof of her ability to conceive could undo the annulment. Thus when Thomas Sabell's wife secured a divorce on the grounds that he was impotent they were both free to marry again. But when they both remarried and had children by their new partners they were forced back together by an indignant court which declared that 'the Holy Church was deceived' and annulled the second marriages.[59] The pain and horror of such a finding must have been intense, and one suspects that most people ignored it – but it meant that their first spouses, not the children or spouse of the second marriage, had the right to inherit all their property.

Lacking ready remedies for unhappy marriages people took the Church's injunction to grow into marital love very seriously. While the making of marriage seems cold and mercenary by our standards, to marry in the 1560s was to accept the job of making the best of the marital hand dealt by one's family, friends and circumstances. Thomas Whythorne could propose to a stranger because he expected affection to grow out of acquaintance, rather than expecting affection to precede marriage. This ideal, however, was as flawed as the romantic ideal of marriage for love, and caused just as much personal stress. Marital bliss and bitter misery were both possible outcomes of marriage, as well as life-long companionship born as much of habit as inclination. The evidence, fragmentary though it is, indicates that unhappy marriages were more common than ones in which both partners enjoyed their estate.[60]

But measured as a social institution sixteenth-century marriage had a stronger chance of success than twentieth-century marriage because it was seen as an economic and social partnership with clearly defined, dependent roles. Sir Thomas Smith's 1560s classic *De republica Anglorum* neatly delineated them: 'The man to get, to travail abroad, to defend: the wife, to save that which is gotten, to tarry at home to distribute that which comes of the husband's labour for nurture of the children and family of them both, and to keep all at home neat and clean.' Each, he believed, had characteristics that made them excel in their distinct offices, so each governed his or her own proper sphere.[61] If each partner fulfilled his or her role the institution provided security and comfort, if not happiness, and the human race was perpetuated. It was when the woman or the man failed to meet the terms of the marital contract that bitterness came in, and the shame and frustration of a failed partnership began to canker.

The words of the marriage service recognized that it could not be dissolved by human agency and that marriage was 'for better, or for worse'. The evidence of the 'for worse' is much greater than for the 'better', but certainly there were many loving marriages in the mid-sixteenth century. The evidence of wills and epitaphs allow us to impute them, but sometimes, in their private reflections, we get little glimpses of contented spouses. Nicholas Bacon, Lord Keeper of England and father of a large family, wrote a poem of thanks to his second wife, Ann Cooke. An ardent Protestant, translator of the *Apology* for the Church of England, and the mother of Francis Bacon the philosopher, she was to her husband a paragon among wives. Remembering her care during a long sickness in 1558 he wrote

Calling to mind my wife most dear
How oft you have in sorrows sad
with words full wise and pleasant cheer
my drooping looks turned into glad,
How oft you have my moods too bad
Born patiently with a mild mind
Assuaging them with words right kind

Remembering to mine own good name
A tired mind with cark and care
How oft you have how well you came
With modest mirth of wit not bare
Refreshing me, and how you are
Glad by all means like a good wife
To breed and keep a pleasant life

Thinking also with how good will
The idle times which irksome be
You have made short through your good skill
In reading pleasant things to me
Whereof profit we both did see
As witness come if they could speak
Both your Tully and my Seneck

Seeing also daily at eye
In my sickness both great and long
Your care of mind pain of body
Seeking always to make to strong
So as except I should say wrong
I must needs say and with good hart
You have well played a good wife's part . . . [62]

The affection Bacon had for his wife takes an unusual form in his poem, but the affection inspired by a caring wife or husband is evident in many sources.

Much of a wife's time was spent caring for her husband, children, and – if her husband was moderately well off – their servants. As long as she played her role in her proper sphere she earned the praise of the busy bee, never idle, always pleasing. If she failed in her womanly duties, or demanded her own way too directly, her husband might have to rein her in. Sir Francis Willoughby found this necessary when, four years after his marriage in 1565, his wife, depressed after more than one miscarriage, became less and less tractable. The fact that her father had reneged on her dowry and Sir Francis was contemplating suing him did not help, but it was his wife's rages that bothered him the most. His sister, Lady Arundel, suggested that the cure was to bring in her father. Between them they could cause her to lose her 'wilfulness'

Figure 8 Marriage disputes were tried by the ecclesiastical courts. Here Archbishop Parker is surrounded by the judges of his Prerogative Court in 1559.

and teach her that her duty was to please him.[63]

A troubled wife had to rely on the aid of her male relatives and friends in dealing with her husband. Lady Ormond's brother requested the Earl of Sussex's help when he heard that the Earl of Ormond was mistreating her, hoping Sussex would report Ormond to the Council if the rumours were true.[64] Similarly Sir Peter Carew wrote to the Bishop of Exeter in 1563 requesting an investigation of John Parker 'for his naughty froward [sic] dealings towards his wife'. The result was an order to the Mayor of Exeter for Parker's arrest. He had already fled Exeter, apparently because 'he hath almost killed his wife diverse and sundry times' and 'hath not been at church almost these 12 months and regards neither God nor man'.[65]

Brutality towards the person one was expected to comfort was tolerated as long as it was proper correction of the weaker vessel, but the community might step in if there was an inversion of order. John Stowe reported that a man was ridden on two staves born on four mens' shoulders accompanied by nearly 300 armored men with guns and pikes in St Katherine's parish. This spectacle was organized because 'his next neighbour suffered his wife to beat him'. In short, the men of the parish had to make an example of this fellow for allowing a woman to invert the natural order, threatening the authority of men everywhere.[66]

Adultery was the most common form of inversion in marriage. When one partner or the other broke his or her vow of fidelity there was bound to be trouble, even though the onus was greater on women than on men. Because adultery was illegal a wronged husband might sue the man who cuckolded him in the secular court, or a wronged partner might sue for a separation in the ecclesiastical court. In all venues the pain, anger and betrayal involved in adultery is apparent, even though the Church encouraged the offended spouse to forgive and go on.

The inability of the church courts to allow divorce and remarriage in the face of adultery could lead to tragic, frustrating results. John Stowell suffered a good deal before finally suing for divorce from Mary Portman. After their marriage in 1556 his wife carried on an open affair with one of his servants for several years, 'using him too familiarly . . . putting her arms around his neck in a meretricious manner, and visiting his couch early and late'. Sir John warned her, 'Wife, if you will not leave these light toys with my man, you shall not find me to be your husband', but her behaviour continued, to the outrage of the other servants. Finally, in 1561, after she had become pregnant (in her husband's absence) and induced an abortion using an herbal compound, he separated from her.

Stowell soon found in one Frances Dyer a woman who would be the wife he had hoped to have when he married Mary Portman. But in order to marry Dyer, the daughter of Sir Thomas Dyer, he needed a dispensation from the Church courts. He approached his bishop in Wells, where he was given a sympathetic hearing, but Portman's family blocked the suit. He then sued in the Archbishop's Court of Delegates, which granted his separation from bed and board, but did not dissolve the chains that bound the couple in marriage. In the meantime he and his intended new wife began living together.

By 1572 John Stowell was wild with frustration, appealing to Archbishop Parker, complaining that he had no legitimate heir and needed to marry. Parker granted him a license, but Portman sued in the Court of Arches to be reinstated as his wife, and he was charged with cohabiting contrary to the law of God in the Court of Audience. He refused to answer the suit in the Court of Arches and was imprisoned for contempt, but he was adamant. He would not take Portman back and lose the woman he considered to be his real wife.

The measure of his desperation is found in the bribes he offered members of Parker's household to get the Archbishop's favour. Parker was incensed, complaining that the use of bribes would undermine the commonwealth and give the Puritans ammunition against him and his courts. Nonetheless, he was sympathetic to Stowell, and, after Sir Edward Dyer bribed Mary Portman with £600 to give up her suit, Stowell was allowed to keep Frances Dyer as his wife. However, when Stowell died in 1604 Mary Portman sued for recognition of her marriage and her right to her dowry, and she won.[67]

Frances Dyer Stowell and Sir Edward Dyer were the children of Sir Thomas Dyer, whose own marital history is distressingly grotesque. His first wife, their mother, had died and in 1556 he married a widow, Joan Poyntz, when he was in his mid-fifties. By 1564 word of his abuse of Joan had spread and William Cecil asked the noted physician, herbalist and Protestant controversialist William Turner, Dean of Wells, to look into the case. His investigation combined piety and hard science, the first expressed in English, the second in Latin.

'Grace, mercy and peace be unto you from the Father of our Lord Jesus. Amen', Turner began his letter, piously observing, 'I am loth to meddle with matters pertaining unto man and wife, lest I should breed hatred whereas love ought to be.' However, he found by common report that Dyer's treatment of his wife was 'barbarissime' and that when she died the entire cause of her death could be attributed to Dyer, whose blows had damaged her liver, causing an incurable tumour and 'intolerable pain'. Before he summoned a bearer to deliver the letter he had further news of Lady Dyer: 'this present Wednesday about seven of the clock at after noon, my lady Dyer departed from us in steadfast faith, and marvelous memory, without any sudden pangs and pains of death as other men and women commonly use to have. The Lord showed great mercy unto her for her breath went out like a candle.'[68] There is no evidence that Thomas Dyer was prosecuted for his wife's death. He died a year later.

Although Thomas Dyer was not prosecuted and his daughter's husband could escape his adulterous wife only through the greatest efforts, a good lawyer might find ways to punish his adulterous wife's lover. In 1566 Chief Justice James Dyer made a note of a case that he found unusual because it raised questions about venue and the correct wording of a writ. He was presiding in the Court of Common Pleas when an action of trespass *de uxora rapta et abducta cum bonis viri* was brought by a husband who claimed that his property had been violated because one Martin had carried off and violated his wife, unjustly detaining her. Martin, the defendant, denied the charge for it seems that the plaintiff's wife ran away from her husband in Middlesex to join Martin at her sister's home in Surrey of her own free will. He, naturally, claimed he had not carried her off against her will, but the jury in London did not believe that she was guilty of choosing adultery; she must have been seduced. They fined Martin £300 and £3 6s 8d in court costs.[69]

A jury's willingness to believe the woman a victim in such a case is part and parcel with the view of gender relations that would punish a man for allowing a woman to beat him. But adultery in a woman was considered a more serious offence because it threatened the security of patrilineal descent. If the woman had sex with a man other than her husband her children might not belong to her husband's family. Security of descent was an important issue, and it was wrapped up with family honour and the honour of the husband. To be a cuckold was to be the laughing stock of the village. A man was less than a man if he failed to rule his wife's lust.

The man who could not rule his wife, whether in bed or in the home, was a failure. Sometimes he threw up his hands in exasperation and walked out, as Thomas Bennett did when, after drawing up covenants for the separation, he left his wife 'for that they could not agree and for that she would not be obedient'.[70]

Most, however, simply carried on their feud with one another until they died. Simon Forman recalled that his mistress used to demand that his master beat him without cause. His master would dutifully deliver the blows, even though he knew that she was a 'wicked, headstrong, and proud and fantastical woman' who wasted his money. When Simon and his master were out of the house together they would commiserate and his master would say 'Simon thou must suffer as well as I myself. Thou seest we cannot remedy it as yet; but God will send a remedy one day.' Simon added that his master twice became so angry with her that he threw a pair of tailor's shears at her so hard that they pinned her dress to the door. At such times he swore he would cut her out of his will.[71]

Most couples stayed together until death did them part. Staying together, however, did not guarantee personal happiness and men and women found ways to be revenged upon one another in the on-going war for personal honour and self respect. Thomas Harman's fictitious tale of how a wife and her 'gossips' punished her lecherous husband must have caused an appreciative chuckle among women and served as a warning to men. Her husband had demanded sex in exchange for pulling a pregnant vagrant (described as a 'walking morte') out of a tide pool into which she had fallen while gathering oysters. Forced to choose between sex and death, she promised to meet the man in his barn that night. Recognizing him because his wife had given her alms, she confessed to her the forced bargain with her husband.

The wife and the 'walking morte' agreed that the rendezvous should be kept, plotting that the man should be urged to unlace his hose. As soon as they were around his knees the morte was to cry 'fye, for shame, fye!'

In the meantime the indignant wife complained to her friends 'what a naughty, lewd, lecherous husband she had, and how that she could not have his company for harlots, and that she was in fear to take some filthy disease of him, he was so common a man, having little respect whom he had to do with . . .' Hearing this a neighbour informed them that he had made advances on her virtue, too. They devised a remedy 'that I may live in some surety without disease, and that he may save his soul that God so dearly bought'. Arming themselves with birch rods they hid in the barn.

When the morte gave the signal they grabbed him, tied him up, and whipped him until he was bloody, warning that if he did not mend his ways this beating was but a flea bite compared to what would follow. When a hired hand found him bound, bleeding and mortified he refused to explain what had happened.[72]

Marriages unhappy and happy were measured by expectations established by scriptural definitions and cultural expectations. An estate created by God for the procreation and rearing of children, for the preserving of chastity, and so that man might have a helper, not a hinderer, in his life, marriage contained explicit sexual roles. It demanded that men be responsible for their wives and that wives be obedient to their husbands; that women safeguard the honour of their husbands, and that husbands discipline their wives.

It was these explicit expectations that made Queen Elizabeth, the most eligible woman in Europe, so difficult to understand. Throughout the 1560s Europe was atwitter with rumours of her suitors and possible marriage, while England agonized over her failure to marry and produce an heir. It was part of her political skill that she understood and refused to perform the role that people believed had been assigned her as a woman. The men with whom she worked found themselves in a confusing position, mistrusting her as a woman without a master while fearing that she would accept the wrong master. Worse, she might die without an heir, leaving the kingdom to Mary of Scotland, practically guaranteeing the return of Catholicism and its professional persecutors. In short, Elizabeth's refusal to act like a woman made marriage the central political issue of the decade.

7

Royal Marriage

I

In April 1566 Robert Dudley, Earl of Leicester, went to meet 'secretly' with Queen Elizabeth. He came into London with 700 lords, knights and gentlemen, accompanied by the Queen's footmen and his own in their rich coats, marching from Temple Bar through the City and down New Fish Street to London Bridge, over into Southwark and on to Greenwich. Elizabeth came 'secretly into Southwark, taking a wherry with one pair of oars for her and two other ladies', rowing to the Three Cranes in the Vintry, where she entered a blue coach. Leicester and his army met her in the highway and, deigning to come out of her coach, she embraced and kissed him three times. They rode together into Greenwich. Leicester, reported John Stowe from his vantage point at the bars without Algate, returned before the Queen, lighted home by the northern lights.[1]

This description of Elizabeth's meeting with the man who was assumed by the world to be the leading candidate for husband and king, is reminiscent of the way tabloids watch the royal family today, underlining the popular fascination with Elizabeth's marital prospects. The Queen's possible husbands were the subjects of intense speculation by all levels of English society and by Europe's diplomats. Beyond the romantic excitement of a royal marriage, however, were the much more serious issues of who would rule Elizabeth and what impact he might have on domestic and foreign policy. Intimately linked to those questions was the urgent issue of an heir to the throne. In order to preserve the peace after Elizabeth died an heir was assumed to be necessary. The man who fathered that child would, through its birth, tie England to a dynastic course that could not easily be changed. Elizabeth's marriage might determine peace or war, religion, domestic tranquillity or turmoil, artistic taste, and a host of other things of

Figure 9 The 'Coronation Portrait' of Elizabeth Tudor when she was about 26 years old.

great import to the English, so it was natural that they speculated about it.

It was also natural that many had strong opinions about who she must marry. They agreed that she would – that was a foregone conclusion since she was a woman – but nationalists preferred an English husband for her; Protestants hoped fervently for a match with someone who would not interfere with their faith; Catholics were equally ardent in their hope that her husband be a man who could protect them; those who believed that the continuation of the Habsburg alliance was all important sought a husband for her in those lands, while those who wanted an alliance with the Lutheran powers looked to the Baltic for her mate.

Elizabeth quickly understood the political importance of her marriage and used it as a negotiating card in dealing with her powerful neighbours. Although a brilliant diplomatic policy this made her subjects so frustrated they could hardly believe that she truly cared for them.

Certainly she had plenty of opportunities to marry. Almost before Queen Mary's body was cold her husband, Philip II of Spain, offered himself to Elizabeth as a possible husband, and, failing that, one of his nephews, sons of the Emperor. The King of Sweden began paying ardent court to her, and various domestic candidates emerged. By late 1559 it was obvious that her heart, if not her hand, was going to Robert Dudley, her Master of the Horse. There was talk of a French marriage, too. The diplomats were sure that she had to choose one of these men for a husband for, as the Emperor was told, 'I find no reason why the Queen should thus protract the affair. For in the natural course of events the Queen is of an age where she should in reason and as is a woman's way, be eager to marry and be provided for.'[2]

Meanwhile Parliament and her ministers kept pressuring her to marry and to either bear or declare an heir so the succession to the crown could be established. Unless she did there might be a civil war with Mary of Scotland and her Catholic supporters aligning themselves against Protestant claimants, most notably the Suffolk line represented by Katherine Grey.

The fear engendered by Elizabeth's single state was magnified by the marital history of her cousin Mary of Scotland. The men she married – she would have three husbands in the 1560s – had direct implications for England, too. Her first, Francis II of France, made her the Queen of England's arch enemy by allying France and Scotland. Her second marriage, in 1564, to Englishman Henry Stuart, Lord Darnley, gave her – and England – a male heir who would become James VI of Scotland and James I of England. After Darnley was murdered in 1567 she married her third, James Hepburn, Earl of Bothwell, who was widely believed to be Darnley's murderer. This time she married by a Protestant service, but her subjects, prompted by disgust at the marriage and by religious partisanship, drove her into exile in England in May 1568. There she became the magnet for English people who desired a Catholic succession and for magnates who sought to rise in the world through marriage to her. The Duke of Norfolk's attempts to marry her contributed to the Northern rising in 1569 and caused his execution in 1572.

Elizabeth, if she reflected on the marital histories of members of her house, had reason to fear marriage. Henry VIII's behaviour towards his wives was infamous, and her half-sister Mary's relationship with Philip II was hardly inspiring, since she was used in a calculating way by the Spanish, deluding herself into believing that Philip had fathered a child upon her. It is not surprising that Elizabeth seems to have had a deep personal distaste for marriage.

When Queen Mary was alive her counsellors and the Spanish had planned to marry Elizabeth to some conveniently distant foreigner and get her out of the realm, but they did not act fast enough. After Elizabeth inherited the throne the speculation about her possible husbands went into a fever pitch, but among the suitors discussed there were three who showed themselves to be serious in their pursuit of her hand in the 1560s: Eric XIV of Sweden; the Archduke Charles of Austria, son of the Emperor Ferdinand; and Robert Dudley, Lord Dudley, created Earl of Leicester in 1564. In addition James Hamilton, Earl of Arran and Duke of Chatelherault, former regent of Scotland, leader of the Scots Protestants and heir presumptive to the Scottish throne until James was born was believed by diplomats to be a serious contender, and Philip II, King of Spain and the Spanish Netherlands, toyed briefly with the idea of marrying her. There was a motion to marry her to Charles IX of France, after the death of Mary of Scotland's husband Francis II. In short, Elizabeth, could have had the pick of the royalty of Europe if she had been so inclined.

The sweepstakes for Elizabeth and England began as soon as she took the throne, everyone assuming that her first duty was to marry. In early February 1559 the House of Commons sent her a petition requesting her to do so with all convenient haste. They did not specify who or when, but made it clear that they felt that it was in the best interest of the realm if she married quickly. Her reply was the first of her many responses to their petitions, though gentler than some of the later ones. She told them that, since she first had consideration of herself as 'born a servitor of Almighty God', she had happily chosen to live a single life, 'which I assure you for mine own part hath hitherto best contented my self and I trust has been most acceptable to God'. She pointed out that neither the opportunity to acquire high estate by marrying some great prince (like Philip II) nor the chance to escape the threat of death that marriage would have provided under Mary, had persuaded her to marry. However, if it pleased God to incline her heart to marriage, she would; and if she did marry, she promised her choice would not be prejudicial to the realm. If God did not prompt her to marry and allowed her live singly He would, she assured them, 'so work in my heart and in your wisdoms as good provision by His help may be made' for an heir more beneficial to the realm than any offspring of hers would be.

She ended her speech of 10 February 1559 with the famous declaration: 'And in the end, this shall be for me sufficient, that a marble stone shall declare that a Queen, having reigned such a time, lived and died a virgin.'[3]

In hindsight there is little reason to believe she was lying. Her subsequent statements about marriage generally follow the same pattern, but Parliament kept reminding her of her duty as a woman and a queen. In 1563 they again urged her to marry and have children. The fact that God did not incline her to marriage surprised and frustrated her subjects, for by 1563 Robert Dudley had apparently won her heart and serious marriage negotiations had been carried on with the Archduke Charles, while the Swedes spent money lavishly hoping to attract her affection.

It could be said that the Swedes were the first onto the matrimonial field, since they had been considering an English marriage for a long time. Although Elizabeth herself did not seem to care much for the Swedish king or kingdom – she once described Sweden as 'barbaric' – her subjects watched the courtship with enthusiastic interest.[4]

In an audience in late May 1559 she had rejected the Swedish ambassador's proposal of marriage but it was too late to stop the coming to London of a magnificent embassy from the Swedes. In early July they began impressing the Londoners with Swedish wealth. The Bishop of Valence wrote to Count Helfenstein in Germany that the embassy made fine show with many noblemen, good horses and numerous servants. The servants wore, pinned to their red velvet coats, hearts pierced by javelins, symbolizing the passion of their sovereign. Moreover, the ambassador spent money lavishly, tipping one of the Queen's maids-of-honour with a 'trinket' worth 300 crowns. His carefree spending was the talk of the City, where he spent, it was rumoured, more than 40,000 crowns on presents for important people.[5]

Although Elizabeth did not encourage the match others in the court were more enthused, a feeling increased by the arrival of John, Duke of Finland, in October 1559. The second son of King Gustavus, he was pleading the suit of his brother Eric, who, by the time John left England the next easter, had become Eric XIV. Principal Secretary Cecil liked him well enough, noting he was well-spoken in Latin, but he might have liked any prince who married Elizabeth. As he remarked at the time, contemplating the field of suitors, 'I would to God her majesty had one [for a husband], and the rest honourably satisfied.'[6] Elizabeth does not seem to have been as impressed. Perhaps she did find him to be, as she had heard, a very odd man.[7]

Odd or not, he spent money like water before he went home, making a Swedish match popular with the crowd. Living at Winchester Place in Southwark, Duke John kept a great house. It was noted with wonder that he gave the poor the leftovers from his table, having fresh food prepared for his own servants, who would have been expected to eat their master's leavings. When he departed he gave the poor households of Southwark gifts of six, eight, twelve, or twenty dollars 'which made him well spoken of'. By report he spent 20,000 dollars in England, coined out of the bullion he had brought with him, giving part of it to the Lords of the realm to secure their good will. The Earl of Hertford became a good friend and tennis partner, undoubtedly to his financial improvement. The courtier who recorded these details summarized his impressions, which echo those of his master William Cecil: 'He was a very proper man, well learned, well nurtured and had the commendation of all men.' And he was a Protestant who brought his own preacher with him.[8]

In the summer of 1561 someone was printing portraits of Elizabeth and Eric together, which the Queen ordered suppressed, but his popularity continued.[9] The rumour spread in September of 1561 that the King of Sweden was coming himself to England with waggon loads of 'massy bullion', exciting the businessmen. It had been a year of bankruptcies and bad harvests and the Swedish King offered hope for a more profitable future. A contemporary observed that there was 'great desire of the king of Sweden's coming of the merchants and Londoners, because they thought he would bring great treasure' with him. In the event he was prevented from arriving by a storm that drove him back to port, but three of his ships did reach London. One was loaded with eighteen great pied horses, which were stabled at the Cross Keys in Gracechurch Street where they could be admired. The other ships were, at least in rumour, laden with £100,000 in bullion, which was unloaded at the Tower.[10]

With the English people convinced that Sweden was paved with gold – and that Swedes were good for business – the Swedish ambassador made another proposal of marriage in December of 1561. Included in it was a stipulation that if Sweden and England had a child Elizabeth would agree to live in Sweden. The proposal was rejected out of hand as preposterous, and the diplomats at the Court speculated that it was purposely unacceptable in order to break off the negotiations, freeing Eric to woo Mary of Scotland who was now a widow.[11]

Although Elizabeth may have believed she had rebuffed the Swedes some of her subjects did not give up so easily on the idea of a Swedish marriage. In the summer of 1562 Catherine Ashley, the Chief Gentlewoman of the Privy Chamber and Elizabeth's old nurse, along with Dorothy Broadbent of the Privy Chamber, wrote to the Swedish ambassador urging Eric to come to England. If he did, said another person writing to a gentleman of Eric's privy chamber, Elizabeth could not refuse him because of the popular enthusiasm for the marriage. When this correspondence was discovered in August 1562 Ashley and Broadbent were confined to their chambers and their servants who had carried the letters were sent to the Tower. It was rumoured that there were members of the Privy Council as well as the royal household involved in this plot to further a Swedish match.[12]

Elizabeth's last contact with the Swedish royal family came in 1565 when Eric's sister Cecilia arrived in September. She became a friend of Elizabeth's and was treated royally at first. As her debts mounted, however, her Swedish extravagance began to make her less welcome. When she colluded with Elizabeth's alchemist, who, having failed to make the gold he promised tried to escape England under Cecilia's protection, Elizabeth lost her patience. Cecilia's husband had a pension from Elizabeth but he fled the realm in order to avoid his creditors. When he came back to visit his wife he was arrested and thrown into debtors prison. Elizabeth had him released, but must have sighed with relief when her royal guests fled the country, their debts unpaid, in April 1566.[13]

Eric XIV was overthrown by his brother Duke John in 1569.

II

The enthusiasm for the Swedish marriage was expensively bought, but it reflected a strong element of wishful thinking, too. Here was a Protestant prince who seemed tailor-made to provide England with a consort and a child. The Bishop of Aquila, the Spanish ambassador, caught the popular mood when he reported in 1560 that he was convinced that the entire kingdom, and not just the Catholics, 'would rather that the realm should come under the sway of any man than that it should be ruled as it is at present'.[14] Any man would do, but by 1560 it looked more and more as if one particular man had a strong chance of becoming king. Robert Dudley was emerging as the Queen's favourite. She had lost her heart if not her virginity.

Her enthusiasm for her tall, dark, handsome and married, Master of Horse first became apparent in April 1559, although they had known one another for years. It was then that the Count de Feria told his master Philip II of the scandalous familiarity Dudley was allowed. He reported that Dudley had so risen in Elizabeth's favour that she visited him in his chamber day and night. People were saying that Dudley's wife, Amy Robsart, was ill and that as soon as she died Elizabeth intended to marry Lord Robert.[15]

Her enthusiasm for Dudley was so apparent by the summer of 1559 that it was gossip fodder not only in England but in foreign courts. Baron Bruener, writing to the Emperor Ferdinand, said that he had, in response to the Emperor's questions, investigated the 'calumnies' heard everywhere about Elizabeth. Employing a spy who was friendly with the ladies of the Queen's privy chamber he tried to discover the truth, but he could learn nothing definite. The women swore by all that was holy that the Queen had never forgotten her honour.

Breuner did, however, report a scene that proves that Elizabeth's intimates were well aware of the damage being done to their Queen's reputation by her familiarity with a married man. Catherine Ashley had thrown herself at the Queen's feet and 'implored her in God's name to marry and put an end to all these disreputable rumours' about Dudley before she sullied her honour and lost the respect of her people. Ashley entreated her to marry someone, 'lest God, to punish her, call her away from this world before her time'.

Elizabeth's response was petulant. Insisting that there was no cause for the rumours because she was always surrounded by her ladies and because she was only giving Dudley the treatment his gracious nature deserved, she lamented that 'in this world she had had so much sorrow and tribulation and so little joy'.

Breuner added to his letter the news that Dudley was married to a fine lady, but since Elizabeth became Queen he had not dwelt at home, living at Court in the same house as the Queen. This proximity fed suspicion.[16] By September this suspicion so weighed on some that one Drury was imprisoned for planning to assassinate Dudley because of his behaviour with the Queen.[17]

By the spring of 1560 there were rumours that Dudley might divorce his wife and marry the Queen, and worse. In Devon, John White confessed that 'Drunken Burley had said to him in his own house that the Lord Robert Dudley did swive the Queen'.[18] Across the country, in Essex, commissioners were ordered to stop the slanderous rumour spread by Mother Dowe of Brentwood that Elizabeth was pregnant by Robert Dudley.[19]

Clearly many of the common folk assumed that Elizabeth and Dudley were but human. Courtiers began to see Dudley as a power in politics. He might become king, and he certainly was the favourite. In mid-1560 Dudley precipitated a severe political crisis in England, emerging as a power in opposition to Cecil in the court. As his strength increased he sought to enlarge his power base, turning to the Catholics and their friends for support. He even became involved in the marriage negotiations, sometimes seeming to favour the Archduke Charles and at other times King Eric.[20]

By late summer his wife's health was declining and as it declined his boldness increased, to the despair of many. William Cecil, finding his power slipping away from him and into Dudley's hands, began to talk of resignation. On 6 September 1560 he told the Spanish ambassador that he was going to retire because Elizabeth's intimacy with Dudley was ruining the realm, begging him in God's name to warn her against the course she was taking. Twice he repeated that he wished Lord Robert was dead, and then said that Lord Robert, who kept claiming his wife was ill, was thinking of killing her.[21]

Cecil feared poison, but the next morning Elizabeth informed the ambassador that Lady Dudley was 'dead or nearly so'. In fact, she had died the day before, of a broken neck. Her body was found at the foot of a staircase at Cumnor Place near Oxford.

The news of her death electrified the nation. Few doubted that she had been murdered, and the assumption severely damaged Elizabeth's already tarnished honour. De Quadra told his Spanish King, 'The cry is that they do not want any more women rulers, and this woman may find herself and her favourite in prison any morning.'[22]

Rumour at court told the popular version. All of Lady Dudley's gentlewomen had been lured away from the house by a fire, giving a servant of Sir George Verney a chance to push her down the stairs. The people watching the fire had overheard Verney talking to his man:

> 'Thou knave, why tarry thou?' asked Verney.
> 'Should I come before I had done?'
> 'Hast thou done?'
> 'Yea,' was the reply, 'I have made it sure.'
> Whereupon Verney spurred for the Court.

A coroner's jury viewed her body and brought in a verdict of suicide, but few believed it. The foreman of the jury, it was reported, was 'the Queen's man' and a shady character. Besides, a flight of only eight steps was hardly enough to kill her in the popular mind.

'The people say,' reported the anonymous courtier, 'she was killed by reason he forsook her company without cause, and left her first at Hide's house in Hertfordshire, where she said she was poisoned.' Hide asked her to leave after that accusation and she went to stay with Sir George Verney in Warwickshire, moving on to Foster's house, Cumnor Place. 'Many times before it was bruited by the Lord Robert his men, that she was dead. And P. [his informant] used to say that when the Lord Robert went to his wife he went all in black, and how he was commanded to say that he did nothing with her, when he came to her, as seldom he did.'

Verney and others of Leicester's servants, he continued, 'used before her death, to wish her death, which made the people to suspect the worst'. Although Dudley, his family and supporters left the court wearing black and weeping dolorously, no one believed them. 'Great hypocrisy was used', summed up the chronicler.

Dudley did not spend long mourning in the country; he returned to Hampton Court in the first week in October. The courtier, who was a minor diplomat and Cecil's man, recalled: 'Mr Danett and I met him, and it was reported to the Queen, that we in despite would not do him reverence, but we put off our caps. And for my self I knew him not, for I never saw him before, me knew not it was he, til he was past.'[23]

That a minor court official could be reported to the Queen for slighting Dudley indicates the tension within the Court, and confirms how aware it was of the popular assessment of Lady Dudley's death. Her lavish funeral, complete with four Heralds of Arms and a great dole of money to the poor, did not convince the public that Dudley really mourned for her.[24]

Neither did it convince foreigners. Nicholas Throckmorton, resident in Paris as ambassador, was miserable about the affair. In the French court things were being said about Elizabeth 'which every hair of my head stareth at and my ears glow to hear'. People were laughing at and reviling his Queen, asking 'what religion is that that a subject shall kill his wife, and the Prince not only bear withal but marry with him?' He feared that if the reports were true it was the undoing of England.[25]

Throckmorton was so upset with the damage Elizabeth was doing to her reputation and the nation that he sent Robert Jones from France to England with a verbal message for her, bluntly urging her not to forfeit the world's respect for Dudley's highly suspect hand in marriage. As a result Throckmorton, Jones and Jones's patron Lord Paget all suffered Elizabeth's displeasure.[26]

If Robert Dudley murdered his wife, or if she died of a degenerative disease, or if she killed herself, or if she accidentally fell down those stairs, the result was the same. Elizabeth could not marry him and retain her honour as a woman or a prince. That Elizabeth came to understand this is clear now, but it was not clear then. Between the summer of 1560 and the summer of 1561 the Court and the country was full of speculation about whether she would or would not marry Dudley.

This speculation left its tracks in literary productions by leading intellectuals, even giving rise to the first tragedy in the English language.

Sir Thomas Smith, best known for his description of English government *De Republica Anglorum*, wrote a long dialogue on the Queen's marriage that concluded that she ought to marry one of her own – clearly Dudley. It combined the popular arguments for and against marriage in general with large measures of English and ancient history, and theory about the function of princes and women's roles. His character Spitewed, who argues for the value of a single life, stressed the danger that Elizabeth might die in childbirth, to no one's benefit. Moreover, if she married a subject she would be ridiculed for marrying beneath her station, like a duchess who married her servant. If she married a foreigner the laws of marriage made it even worse:

> If she marry a stranger, then must he needs by God's laws be her head, and where she was highest before, now she hath made one higher than her self. If she study to please him, then is she in subjection of him: if she mind not to please him, why should she then marry him?

To those who said that a male prince was needed to lead the army, able to carry spear and buckler in the front of the charge, he answered that not all princes led their own troops. Moreover, there were in history many examples of queens who led armies, but it was more in their womanly natures to practise peace, a thing much better than war. All in all, it was preferable to have a single, peaceful Queen ruling the nation than to have her dead in childbirth or dominated by a warlike man.

Lovealien responded to Spitewed. He argued that though virginity was a less troublesome state than marriage, it was necessary for a prince. 'But for a Prince, upon whose quiet succession a great part of the commonwealth doth hang, whose family is the root and foundation of inward peace within the realm, to live sole is to be an author of such mischief, as no man can wish to a realm a greater.' The dangers of childbirth, he argued, were negligible, matching Spitewed's portrait of the agony of childbirth with one of easy labour in feather beds, giving women a maternal bloom that makes men even more enamoured of them. Irish and gypsy women bore their children in barns and fields, going on with their work before and immediately after, proving that childbirth was not as dangerous as Spitewed said. And what if it was painful? The pain was the just punishment God inflicted on Eve for her transgression.

Rather than seeing the Queen's subjection to a husband in a negative light, Lovealien sees it as positive. As a woman she needs someone to manage her affairs, and who better than a husband? Especially since as a man he is free to go out of the house and to places a woman could not, hearing and seeing and returning to give good counsel.

A royal husband would not be as warlike as was implied, either. As a husband his first care would be for his wife and family. Just as merchants face raging seas, lawyers 'cry in the day' until they are hoarse, and all men toil for their families, so a king would labour to provide ease for his family, and by extension the realm. He would not make war his priority, but domestic tranquillity.

Attacking Spitewed for his failure to speak out against Parliament's petition for the Queen to marry, Lovealien warns that even if things are going well in England now a storm can be expected. In preparation for trouble ahead, and in order to guarantee the prosperity of their posterity, it was best if the Queen married and had a child, the sooner the better. Women were created and ordained to bear children and Elizabeth's biological clock was running (she was 28 years old at the time). She should not hesitate to do her duty and become the mother, the schoolmaster, the nurse, the bringer-up of a future king (it does not seem to have occurred to those who argued this way that she might bear only daughters).

Lovealien earned his name with his final soliloquy, arguing that Elizabeth should marry a powerful foreign prince. Such a match would bring greater honour, wealth and power with it, giving England a protective ally in the world.

The last speaker was nicknamed Homefriend and embodied Thomas Smith. He argued that Elizabeth should marry an English nobleman. Whereas Lovealien had said that a foreigner and an Englishman were equal when it came to fulfilling the essential duties of marriage – tempering lust, begetting children, and providing comfort and joy – Homefriend was adamant in his insistence on the superiority of all things English and all English men. As the proverb said, English smoke was warmer than French or Italian fires, or the horrible stoves of Germany. An English consort would be dedicated to England alone, and could please the Queen because he was not a foreigner. Besides, foreigners had foreign attitudes towards women and marriage. An Italian, for instance, would lock up his wife like an English hawk in a mew and then resort to courtesans, while a Spaniard would sin against his wife and then, to make amends and salve his conscience, would whip his naked body at Lent. To marry an Englishman was to marry a known quantity: English men and English women understood one another, and English men were the best on earth. To marry a foreign prince was 'to buy a pig in the poke'.

With a fine sense of equality Homefriend took up the question of whether it would dishonour Elizabeth to marry one of her own subjects. Of course it would not, since an English noble was more noble than a foreign noble and besides, why was it a disparagement for the Queen of England to marry an English man when it was not for the King of England to marry an English woman? (Here he deliberately avoided the issue of a Queen's subservience to her husband.)

Musing on the Parliament's petition to the Queen to marry he asked Spitewed if he remembered how all the members of the Commons 'ran all one way, like the hounds after the hare, high and low, knights and esquires, citizens and burgesses, such as were of the Privy Council and others far and near' in voting for marriage. And who did they prefer, a foreigner or an English man? Clearly, to argue against marriage, or for a foreign match, was contrary to the will of Parliament.

Summing up, Homefriend sang a paean to an English marriage. 'I say and see,' he said,

> that it is ENGLAND alone that shall make her Highness strong; ENG-LAND, and no other, her true patrimony, riches, power, and strength, whereto she must trust; ENGLAND, her Highness's native country alone, being well tilled and governed, shall be better to her Majesty in the end, than all those empires, kingdoms, dukedoms, and marchionates, and other rabblements of gay titles, which are but wind and shadows, and makers of cares and costs.

The most joy, comfort, pleasure, honour, and strength are to be found in a native husband for their native Queen: 'it were better for the Queen's Majesty . . . to marry an Englishman, than any other stranger whatsoever he be.'[27]

Smith's dialogue reflects the nature of the debate over Elizabeth's marriage, but it carefully never mentions Dudley, or any other suitor, directly. The reader was expected to know the contenders without hearing their names.

As her people debated who she should marry, Elizabeth was indecisive. She was clearly infatuated with Dudley, but whether she would, like her cousin in Scotland, allow herself to marry a man so disliked by so many powerful people was an open question.

Cecil began to sense that the tide was turning in December of 1560 when he received the plum of Master of the Wards, proving that the Queen, in spite of Dudley, still supported him. But it was Dudley himself who continued to undermine his own position.

He began to plot with the Spanish ambassador, seeking Habsburg and English Catholic support for his marriage with Elizabeth. In order to be king, rumour reported, Dudley 'would procure the banishment of the Gospel'. Word was out in the streets 'that religion should not long continue', a report traced back to the imprisoned Catholics. When one of them, Dr Frere (imprisoned for sorcery) was questioned about his sources he admitted he had heard it from the Bishop of Aquila, the Spanish ambassador. The Bishop, he said, had been promised by Sir Henry Sidney (father of the poet) that if King Philip could get Elizabeth to marry Dudley the Pope's authority over England would be restored. Philip II was persuaded to write a letter urging her to marry a subject, but Elizabeth soon saw through it and the matter cooled. In the meantime, the Spanish ambassador tried to use Dudley's influence with the Queen to get a papal nuncio carrying an invitation to the Council of Trent admitted to England.

Anxious to keep the Pope's messenger out of England for fear that he would stir Catholic resistance and encourage Dudley, Cecil and his allies found a way to spike his guns. In April 1561 Cecil had the chaplain of Sir Edward Waldegrave seized as he tried to leave the country carrying letters that incriminated a number of Catholic gentry in a plot to replace the Queen, and perhaps to murder her through sorcery. It was the first persecution of Elizabethan lay Catholics, and it was enough to convince the Queen that admitting the nuncio would be a bad idea, though not enough to disgrace Dudley.[28]

Dudley's attempt to use the Catholics as supporters had backfired, leaving Cecil the most powerful man in the Court. Dudley, however, did not go away. Nor did the fear that Elizabeth might yet marry him.

Writing in July 1561 Cecil told Throckmorton that if Elizabeth did not marry soon great evil would come to the state and 'to the most particular persons'. Explaining to the ambassador that a secret plan had been hatched to make Mary of Scotland heir to Elizabeth if Mary would resign all claims to the English throne until Elizabeth died Cecil moaned, in a moment of true candour, 'God send our mistress a husband, and by him a son, that we may hope our posterity shall have a masculine succession. This matter is too big for weak folks and too deep for simple.'[29]

Cecil's frustration with unmarried female rulers probably went beyond the politics of the moment, for it was common knowledge that there was something unnatural about a woman ruler. Weaker vessels in need of management, women in positions of command inverted the natural order instituted by God. In England and elsewhere women were ineligible for every public office except that of reigning monarch, an irony that was not lost on contemporaries. Denied legal authority over their own children, unable to sue in court in their own right, they were 'weak' and 'simple' by definition. Nature proved women to be weak, frail, impatient, feeble and foolish, said John Knox in his *First Blast of the Trumpet Against the Monstrous Regiment of Women* published in 1559. Experience proved them inconstant, variable, cruel and lacking the 'spirit of regiment and counsel'.[30] The book got him banned from England by its Queen, but in 1561 anyone raised with such prejudices who meditated on the behaviour of Mary of England, Mary of Scotland and Elizabeth might have concluded that Knox was right.

Unknown to contemporaries, Elizabeth seems to have concluded by mid-1561 that she could not marry Dudley, but he remained in the Court and played an important role in national politics as a counsellor and patron. The public discussion of Elizabeth's possible husbands continued, however, and there were many who were willing to take Dudley's side because of the power he could wield. And there were also many who assumed Dudley and Elizabeth were married in all but name. In Suffolk, in early 1564, there was a report that Lord Robert 'kept' the Queen, and that when she was at Ipswich 'she looked like one lately come out of childbed'.[31]

Seemingly untouched by the suspected murder of his own wife and his plot to subject England to the pope, he seemed to have boundless power. One story, told by the man who had been reported for not showing him enough deference, hints at his behaviour. It seems that one Mr Brewton, a servant of Dudley's, had been sued by a Cheshire gentleman and forced to pay a forty-pound debt. Brewton paid it, but swore he would 'get his pennyworth' in the end. One day when the gentleman and his wife were walking over their grounds, Brewton and his servant ambushed them. The servant slashed his face with a sword while Brewton smashed his skull. Captured and condemned to death they were pardoned by Elizabeth at the behest of her darling 'Robin' Dudley.

The widow appealed to a higher court in Westminster, which confirmed the condemnation of the servant, but left a decision in Brewton's case pending while he roamed the streets with Dudley's men. Meanwhile 'great suit' was made to the widow to abandon the appeal. On 13 June 1562 Lord Robert and the Lord Chamberlain came from Greenwich to London to speak to her, but she refused see them. She was then peremptorily ordered to appear at the Court in Greenwich the next day, where she was 'both enticed with fine words and rebuked with foul words' to give up. She would not, stoutly asserting that she would never sell her husband's blood. Whereupon she was placed under house arrest at the Court, unable to leave until she capitulated. This, says our courtier, 'caused the people to speak very evil of the Queen and of the Council that justice should be thus stayed'.[32]

Just how much justice Dudley could stay is illustrated by his relationship with the Inner Temple. The lawyers there curried his favour in a dispute with the Middle Temple over the control of the Inns of Chancery. The Inner Temple had three of the chancery schools, Cliffords Inn, Lyons Inn and Clements Inn, while the Middle Temple had only New Inn. The Lord Keeper and the Chief Justices (who were all Middle Temple men) had decided that legal training would benefit if Clements Inn was administered by the Middle Temple. Faced with a *fait accompli* the Inner Temple begged Lord Robert's aid. Against the wishes of the leading lawmen of the nation Dudley went to Elizabeth who, at his request, ordered Lord Keeper Bacon to stop the transfer. In appreciation the members of the Inner Temple declared that none of them would be counsel in a suit against Lord Robert or his heirs.[33] A mark of their friendship was the fact that he was Lord Governor at their Christmas celebrations in 1561–2 when a special play was produced by Arthur Broke in his honour.[34]

Dudley was never named in *Gorboduc or Ferrex and Porrex,* written by Thomas Norton and Thomas Sackville and performed on a scaffold in the hall of the Inner Temple on twelfth night, 1562. Characterized by Vita Sackville-West, a descendant of one author, as the first and most boring tragedy in the English language, it kept the attention of those in attendance that January night because it was so topical.

An anonymous courtier was present and wrote what may have been the first theatre review in the English language. His attention to the dumb shows [pantomimes] suggests that he found the text as boring as Sackville-West had. He writes:

> There was a tragedy played in the Inner Temple of the two brethren Porrex and Ferrex K[ings] of Britain between whom the father had divided the realm, the one slew the other, and the mother slew the man killer. It was thus used. First wild men came in and would have broken a whole fagot, but could not, the sticks they broke being severed [*sic*]. Then came in a king to whom was given a clear glass, and a golden cup of gold covered, full of poison. The glass he cast under his foot and broke it, the poison he drank off. After came in mourners. The shadows were declared by the choir. First to signify unity, the 2. how that men refused the certain and took the uncertain, whereby was meant that it was better for the Queen to marry with the L[ord] R[obert] known than with the K[ing] of Sweden. The third to declare that civil dissension breeds mourning. Many things were handled of marriage, and that the matter was to be debated in Parliament, because it was much banding [bandied?] but that it ought to be determined by the Council. There was also declared how a strange duke seeing the realm at division, would have taken upon him the crown, but the people would not of it. And many things were said for the succession to put things in certainty.[35]

The reviewer certainly caught the central message about the succession, but he failed to note that the duke who invaded and seized the realm was Fergus, Duke of Albany, a thinly-disguised Scotsman (when he married Queen Mary Henry Stuart became Duke of Albany and King of Scotland), who proclaims:

> If ever time to gain a kingdom here
> Were offered man, now it is offered me . . .
> No issue now remains, the heir unknown . . .
> Is not my strength in power above the best
> Of all these lords now left in Britain land? . . .
> Ours is the scepter then of Great Britain.[36]

An understudy for Mary, Queen of Scots, Fergus delivered a clear warning that if the succession was not settled England would be left to Scotland. The closing speech, spoken by Eubulus, the Secretary to the King (the grave William Cecil in the flesh) was a meditation on the ills that had befallen England and how they might have been prevented. His conclusion is hardly a surprise when we remember that Thomas Norton was a leading member of Parliament:

No, no; then parliament should have been holden,
And certain heirs appointed to the crown,
To stay the title of established right
And in the people plant obedience
While yet the prince did live whose name and power
By lawful summons and authority
Might make a parliament to be of force . . . [37]

Subtlety was not the authors' strong suit, but apparently the play was well received. The gentlemen of the Temple were called to do a royal command performance in Westminster Hall a week later.[38]

The Christmas revels at the Inner Temple may have been an artistic triumph but the Queen refused to accept the moral. She kept Dudley at Court, but she did not marry him. He was slowly transforming from lover to courtier, though still a favourite.

If Elizabeth refused to do her duty Parliament did not, especially after their Queen, the only person standing between them and the dreaded Catholic woman in Holyrood Palace, nearly died of smallpox in October of 1562. When they assembled in January 1563 her safety and the succession were uppermost on their minds.

They took her near death as a warning from God to establish the succession. 'We fear,' said the Commons, 'a faction of heretics in your realm, contentious and malicious papists' who 'most unnaturally against their country, most madly against their own safety, and most traitorously against your Highness' hope for the Queen's death, laying in wait to 'renew their late unspeakable cruelty, to the destruction of goods, possessions and bodies, and thralldom of the souls and consciences of your faithful and Christian subjects'. They did not dare name a husband for her, but they begged her to take anyone, swearing they would love and support him.

The Lords' petition was weightier, using the Queen's duty to God as an argument for her marriage. Elizabeth herself had declared that she knew she was responsible to God for her kingdom, so the Lords reminded her of what God expected. Her duty was to prevent the civil wars that would arise from a disputed succession, so she must marry. Moreover, the spirit of God pronounced by the mouth of St Paul that 'whosoever makes not due provision for his family is in danger to Godward'. Elizabeth's response to these pleas was to put them off. 'The weight and greatness of this matter might cause in me, being a woman wanting both wit and memory, some fear to speak, and bashfulness besides, a thing appropriate to my sex', she averred, evoking from them sheltering paternalism. But she also occupied a kingly throne and as a prince she was not about to make a quick answer in so important a matter as the succession.

To the Scripture quoters she said, 'There needs no boding of my bane. I know now as well as I did before that I am mortal' and aware duty must be done to God.

Although she refused to give them an answer she reassured them in a warm, maternal fashion that their concern for her and for the realm was welcome. 'I will discharge some restless heads, in whose brains the needless hammers beat with vain judgment that I should mislike this their petition,' she said, assuring them 'though after my death you may have many stepdames, yet shall you never have any a more natural mother than I mean to be unto you all.' She had no child but they were all her children.[39]

In her speech at the closing of Parliament, read by the Lord Keeper, she returned to their petitions for her marriage and gave them some small glimmer of hope that she might yet marry. If they believed that she was 'as it were by vow or determination' bent on never marrying they should put that heresy out of their heads, for 'though I can think it best for a private woman, yet do I strive with myself to think it not meet for a prince'.[40]

Once again Parliament had failed to convince Elizabeth to either marry or declare the succession, but they had at least wrung from her a confession that as a prince she ought to marry. In the meantime the law-makers re-enforced their Queen's security by passing a new treason law denying professed Catholics the right to sit in Parliament and declaring the first attempt by the Protestant leaders to punish Catholics for being Catholic.

As we have seen, Elizabeth refused to enforce this law but it did reflect their heightened fear that if Elizabeth was overthrown or died, their Protestant nation would be left in the hands of the Catholic Scot.

Elizabeth's personal confusion and misery seems to have been well hidden from her subjects, even though they knew she was infatuated with a man who might have murdered his wife and who she knew she could not marry. Her Scots cousin's misery and confusion was more apparent, for in this period she became a widow, was rejected by her own nobility, and was defeated in a war with the English. Throughout these troubles, however, she clung to her insistence that she was the rightful heir to Elizabeth's throne, even though Henry VIII's will seemed to give the right of succession to the Suffolk line and Katherine Grey.

III

Although 'Mary Queen of Scots' rolls off the lips like a single word she had seen little of Scotland before she arrived there, a widow at

nineteen, in August 1561. She had spent the previous thirteen years
in France, living for a decade in the French royal household before
marrying the dauphin, Francis, in April 1558 when she was fifteen. He
became Francis II in July 1559 when a splinter from a jousting lance
slipped through the eye slit of the royal helmet and drove into the
brain of Henry II. Francis died of a brain tumour – in John Knox's
pungent phrase, he was 'stricken with an aposthume [abscess] in that
deaf ear that never would hear the Truth of God' – on 5 December
1560.[41]

France at the time was not a stable kingdom. It was tottering towards
a forty-year civil war provoked by religious fanaticism and family ambi-
tion. Mary, Queen of France and Scotland, was a member of the
Catholic Guise family and therefore an enemy of the Huguenots (Protestants led by the Bourbons). There had been an abortive Huguenot
attempt, supported by the Scots Protestants, in 1560 to overthrow and
kill the Guise, Mary included. The experience must have confirmed
Mary in her Catholicism and dislike of Scots Protestants, but after she
was widowed she found herself at loose ends in a nation now ruled by
the Queen Mother, Catherine de Medicis, in the name of her young
son Charles IX. Catherine was a political moderate – a *politique* – who
sought to find a path between the rival fanaticisms.

Her experience with politics in France made Scotland's political
world familiar to young Mary, even if she was not well acquainted with
its people. Scotland was ruled in her name by her mother, the Queen
Regent, Mary of Guise. She and her French troops were intensely
resented by the Scots for both their French manners and their Catholic
religion. Protestantism had made serious inroads into Scotland by
1559, despite persecution, and in May of that year the Queen Regent
declared the Protestant ministers outlaws, triggering the beginnings
of a revolution. The movement was helped by the caustic sermons
of John Knox, whose contempt for Catholic woman rulers was well
established.

The rebels, known as the Lords of the Congregation, tried to force
the Queen Regent to abolish Catholicism, but her answer was to send
for more troops from France. In response the Lords sent Maitland of
Lethington to England soliciting Protestant English help against the
French Catholic occupation force.

For the English this was a pleasant, if ironic, twist of history. England
had fought three wars with Scotland in the 1540s, and the Scots had
been allied with the French against England and Spain in the war that
had just ended with the treaty of Cateau Cambresis in April 1559. Much
of the spring of 1559 had been spent preparing to defend England
against an invasion of Scots and French troops that was expected,
but already it was apparent that many of the Scots preferred English

Protestants to French Catholics. James Hamilton, the Earl of Arran and Duke of Chatelherault, with a strong claim to the throne of Scotland, even proposed in early 1559 that the English invade Scotland and help them destroy the French in an alliance for the maintenance of the Word of God.[42]

Elizabeth was reluctant to intervene in Scotland, to the enormous frustration of Cecil, who believed that religious division was a god-given chance to keep England's enemies off balance. By October 1559 the Lords of the Congregation had temporarily occupied Edinburgh and their movement looked more and more like it might succeed – but if it failed French control of Scotland was assured.

Meanwhile Francis and Mary had ordered a new set of dinner ware. Painted on their new dishes were their coats of arms, including those of England, pronouncing to the world that Mary believed herself to be the rightful Queen of England. Her claim rested on the argument that Elizabeth was illegitimate. Henry VIII's divorce from Katherine of Aragon had never been recognized by the Catholic Church so, after the death of Henry's legal heir Mary of England, the Queen of Scotland, as a descendant of Margaret Tudor, was next in line to inherit. This propaganda coup enraged Elizabeth, not least because it gave Catholics a 'legitimate' alternative to her as queen and encouraged the idea of a Franco-Scottish invasion to put Mary on the throne of England.

The pleas of the Lords of the Congregation and English resentment over Mary's insistence that Elizabeth was a bastard, illegitimate queen had, after intense pressure from the Privy Council, convinced Elizabeth to send money to the Scots rebels – in French coins – in the autumn of 1559. Nonetheless she was deeply troubled by the idea of encouraging subjects to rebel. She hated John Knox, too, since he had insisted that a woman could not rule. Finally, however, English troops were committed in order to drive the French out of Scotland. Known as The War of the Insignia in England because of the misuse of England's arms, it saw English soldiers besieging the Queen Regent and her French army in Leith in early 1560.

Mary of Guise had died, defeated, of dropsy at the end of the siege in June of 1560. That physician of souls John Knox reported that shortly after she had exalted over the Protestant dead at Leith, 'began her belly and loathsome legs to swell, and so continued till that God did execute his judgment upon her'.[43]

By the Treaty of Edinburgh of July 1560 Mary and Francis were expected to abandon their claim to the English throne and to withdraw their troops from Scotland. Although Mary did not ratify the treaty, the French left on 15 July. On 11 August the Scottish Parliament promulgated a Protestant confession of faith and on the 16th it passed a law abolishing the pope's jurisdiction and making celebration of mass a capital offence.

In November 1560, as a French invasion of Scotland was being prepared to revenge the loss of Leith and punish the rebels, an embassy came from Scotland to Elizabeth. Their purpose was to propose a marriage between Elizabeth and the Duke of Chatelherault, uniting the two crowns in one couple, depriving Mary of Scotland, and assuring that the entire island would remain Protestant. Elizabeth put them off, and the threatened invasion was stopped by the death of Francis II in December.[44]

The parliaments of both the sovereign nations of Britain had declared their realms Protestant, but the Scot's law needed the assent of the Queen of Scotland before it became binding. She would never give it. Therefore when Mary returned to Scotland in 1561 she found herself suspected by her own people, tarred by the brushes of Guisean France and papal Rome. She was, however, the second most eligible Queen in Europe. A widow with a kingdom of her own with close ties to the French crown, the man who married her might expect to receive England, sooner or later, as part of her dowry.

English policy became obsessed with the dual issues of Mary's possible marriage and the threat presented by those who wished to put her on England's throne. Elizabeth and Cecil hoped to play the matchmakers for Mary in order to ensure her neutralization. Mary, who practised a tolerant religious policy in Scotland, only asking that she be allowed to have mass in her household, may not have been the Catholic threat the English believed, and she was certainly conciliatory towards England. She seems to have hoped for an accommodation between the two queens – an accommodation made more necessary by the fact that when Mary arrived in Scotland, Elizabeth mobilized 2,000 men on the border.[45] Mary's principal secretary, William Maitland of Lethington, sought an agreement with the English that would recognize Mary's right to succeed Elizabeth in return for Mary's recognition of Elizabeth's right to the English crown during her lifetime, thus securing the peace.

In order to accomplish this Maitland, helped by Dudley and France, tried to arrange a meeting between the two queens. In spite of the resistance of her Council Elizabeth accepted the invitation and plans were laid for a rendezvous in the late summer of 1562. The plans went forward, with orders sent to purveyors and magnates in the north to prepare the coming of the two queens and with the careful planning of the masques that would be danced when their courts were together in York or, when the venue changed, in Nottingham.

As the negotiations for the meeting went forward Katherine Grey bore her first child in the Tower of London. She and Hertford had recently been joined there by Matthew Stuart, the Earl of Lennox, because of another twist in the succession drama.

Lennox, a Scot living in exile in England, had been entangled in the plotting of his wife, Margaret. Margaret Douglas, the Countess of Lennox, was the daughter of Margaret Tudor by her second marriage and was pushing the claim of their son, Lord Darnley, to both the throne of England and of Scotland. When Lennox was silly enough to admit before the Council that he believed his wife was the next heir to the throne he was imprisoned.[46]

It is safe to speculate that the rumours heard in London that the Countess of Lennox was the bastard daughter of a bigamist marriage may have been started in high places, a pre-emptive attack on the Lennox claim. Certainly the Spanish ambassador heard the Privy Council was secretly gathering evidence to prove her illegitimate and unable to inherit the throne.[47]

The meeting between Elizabeth and Mary never happened. Both sides seemed willing enough, but in the end French politics intervened. By the spring of 1562 the Protestant Prince of Conde had summoned the Huguenots to his standard and war seemed imminent with the Guise. When the fighting started in June the Huguenots did not fare well and turned to their co-religionists in England for help. Dudley, waxing stronger and stronger in English politics, took the lead in urging English intervention in France. Elizabeth, once so hesitant about intervening in Scotland, readily agreed, perhaps because she saw a chance to recover Calais, previously lost to England's shame in 1558. In exchange for their intervention the Huguenots ceded Le Havre (Newhaven to the English) to England until Calais was returned. An English army was assembled and sent to France in October 1562. Commanded by the Ambrose Dudley, Earl of Warwick, Lord Robert's brother, it had scarcely arrived before the Huguenots were defeated and changed sides. The English found themselves besieged in Newhaven by all of France.

They would be defeated by plague and siege craft in July 1563, bringing disease home to England instead of honours, but their presence in France made it impossible for Elizabeth and Mary to meet.[48] English intervention on the side of the Huguenots against the Guise was too offensive to Mary. Worse, it almost threw Mary into the arms of Don Carlos, the heir to the Spanish throne. A union between Spain and Scotland would have put England in as tight a vice as the union between France and Scotland had.

Most of the men who had tried to marry Elizabeth were considered as husbands for Mary. The Archduke Charles of Austria and Charles IX of France were prime candidates, while Eric of Sweden, ever hopeful, set his cap at Mary. The English worked hard to prevent her from marrying a Habsburg (either the Archduke of Austria or Don Carlos) and Elizabeth told the Scots that such a marriage would carry with it her enmity.[49]

In a long despatch in cipher the Bishop of Aquila told Philip about these various negotiations and reported Elizabeth's reactions. William Maitland, Mary's representative at the Court, told him of a conversation with Elizabeth in which they had discussed the candidates, and she made an astonishing proposal that confirms that she had decided against marrying Dudley. Elizabeth told him that if Mary would take her advice and wished to marry safely and happily she should marry Lord Robert, a man implanted with so many graces that Mary would find him preferable to all the princes in the world.

Maitland, with great presence of mind (one can imagine his surprise), thanked her for being so willing to give to Mary something she valued so much herself. He doubted, he told her, that Mary, knowing how she loved Lord Robert, would deprive her of the joy and solace she received from him. This provoked Elizabeth to muse that she wished to God that Robert's brother Ambrose had Robert's grace and good looks. Then there would be one for each of them.

Maitland 'could not reply for confusion', but Elizabeth continued to follow her thoughts, saying Ambrose was not ugly, but his manners were a little rough and he lacked Robert's gentleness. Nonetheless, he was a worthy husband for any great princess.

Profoundly uncomfortable, Maitland sought to escape the conversation by raising the issue of the succession, knowing it would 'shut her mouth directly'. So he made a joke that might have landed him in prison had he not had diplomatic immunity. He told Elizabeth that, since Mary was much younger than she was, she ought to marry Dudley and have children by him. Then, when Elizabeth died, she could will her kingdom and her husband to Mary. That way Lord Robert would have children by one or both of them; either way his children would become kings of both countries.[50]

Elizabeth's response is not recorded – we can be sure she caught the humour and the barb – but she seems to have been serious about offering Dudley to Mary. The next August she sent a representative to Edinburgh urging Mary to marry an unidentified English aristocrat. When pressed to name that aristocrat the ambassador could not, and a game of diplomatic charades began that lasted until March 1564 when Elizabeth finally told her she could have Lord Robert. Mary and her Council took the proposal coolly but they did not reject it out of hand. If Elizabeth would guarantee that Mary was the heir to her throne it might be worth accepting her cast-off lover as their royal consort.

In order to sweeten the offer Elizabeth finally ennobled Dudley, making him Earl of Leicester in September 1564, but that was not enough. Maitland and Murray, Mary's chief counsellors, concluded that in these negotiations the English were dishonest, treating Scotland as a toy. 'If we misconstrued your advice,' they wrote to Cecil, 'might we not suspect that it is not merely for friendship that you make this match, but you also hunt for a kingdom, and go about under that pretence to make an Englishman a king of Scotland?'[51]

By the time the negotiations over Dudley, now Leicester, ended in early 1565 most of Mary's other matrimonial hopes had evaporated, too. The Archduke Charles had been dismissed as too poor. Don Carlos became increasingly insane and was ruled out as a candidate. Charles IX of France was an impossibility because his mother so distrusted the Guise. As these suitors departed, however, another, much more attractive one arrived: Henry Stuart, Lord Darnley, the son of the Earl of Lennox.

Elizabeth had imprisoned Lennox because he supported his wife's claim to the English throne, but when Mary restored his Scottish lands and invited him to return to Scotland, Elizabeth allowed him to leave in September 1564. Following him came his son, travelling on a three-month passport. Inheriting Tudor blood from his grandmother Margaret, Queen of Scotland, he had a claim on England's throne that made him, along with Katherine Grey, the object of much speculation. It was probably a mistake for Elizabeth to allow him to visit his father in February 1565 for Mary married him in July 1565, changing the nature of the succession debate and quickly creating new crises in England and Scotland.

It would seem that Mary had forgotten what everyone knew in the sixteenth century: never marry for love. She had fallen head over heals for the handsome, egotistical and silly young man during Easter 1565, nursing him through what appeared to be measles but may have been syphilis. By May she was probably secretly engaged to him, and she was in such a hurry to wed that she did not wait for the arrival from Rome of a papal dispensation allowing the two first cousins to marry. She not only married him, she proclaimed him king without seeking support from the Scottish parliament. It was an unwise thing to do, but they did produce an heir to the throne in short order.

With Mary wed the royal marriage game refocused on Elizabeth. The men in the Court who hated Dudley, which meant most of Privy Council, were determined to marry their Queen to anyone but the Earl of Leicester and in 1564 things seemed to be running their way. Elizabeth's offer to let Mary marry her favourite had set a new tone. The man they now chose as the most eligible was Charles, Archduke of Austria. There had been negotiations on his behalf in 1559, but then few in England liked the idea. By 1565 everyone but Dudley thought it was a fine notion to see Elizabeth linked with the Habsburgs through

Charles. They were so anxious to have her married they even forgot or reasoned away the fact that he was Catholic and likely to remain so.

The opening moves of this game were made in 1563 when Cecil contrived with the Duke of Wurttemberg to begin pressing her to marry Charles. Cecil admitted to him that it was going to be a difficult negotiation because Elizabeth 'has such an aversion to marriage that she would rather have her throne occupied by an alien after her demise than hear a word about marrying'. Nonetheless, 'Everyone must recognize that this is folly' and the English nation would be eternally grateful to the Duke if he added his exhortations to their entreaties that she marry.[52]

In January 1564 his entreaties arrived in the form of an ambassador who exhorted her in the name of the Protestant states of Germany to marry. As far as they were concerned, Elizabeth needed a reminder of her duty to God. Ahasverus Allinga, speaking for the Duke of Wurttemberg and other Lutherans, had been warned by Cecil to proceed cautiously because Elizabeth had dedicated herself to celibacy – he knew too well the rages which sometimes possessed her when the issue was raised. Consequently he kept the address on a high theological plain. He asked her to consider what would happen to God's true religion if she died without an heir. He invoked the image of an international papal conspiracy prowling around England's borders. He told her that if she did not provide for the succession 'your realm will so to speak be motherless, and this prosperous kingdom and its loyal subjects will by reason of their creed be exposed to dire evils, cruelties, tortures, and threats of death'.

These dangers, he intoned, could be averted if she obeyed God and married. All Protestants, he confessed, were 'amazed and pained' and that she had not married, 'the more so as the state of matrimony was consecrated by God at the beginning of Creation, and marriage can bring your Majesty and your realm nothing but advantage', especially if she had children. Running down a well-worn track he told her that 'there is among mankind no state so honourable as that of the lord and husband'. 'In the beginning of Creation this state was created . . . confirmed and its subsistence established in matrimony.' He warmed to his work, thumbing through ancient sources for precedents of happy marriage and pointing to the sad histories of nations that lacked heirs. Once he called marriage 'a desirable evil', provoking Elizabeth to interject with a sarcastic laugh, 'Desirable?' When he finished she modestly claimed a lack of learning to answer his arguments, but went on to make it clear that no appeal to reason could induce her to marry. Political necessity was the only logic that could convince her, and if she married it would be as Queen not as Elizabeth.

After she had rehearsed all the attempts already made to marry her the ambassador summoned his diplomatic suavity and announced that he was pleased that she was so friendly towards marriage. Raising the subject of the previous negotiations concerning a marriage with Charles he fell into a pit that was hard to escape. He gave Elizabeth the impression (a correct one) that the Emperor believed that the negotiations had failed because she did not want them to succeed. That provoked her to blame both the emperor and the his representatives, all the while admitting that she had not wanted to marry and that she would never marry a man she had not met – remembering too well the disaster that resulted from Philip and Mary's lack of previous acquaintance.

When Charles did not come – she did not know, she said with a grin, whether he thought it undignified to 'come at first call' or if he thought her shameless to invite him – the negotiations collapsed. So their failure was the Emperor's fault, not hers.

She told the ambassador that if the Emperor renewed the suit of the Archduke there might be some hope of a marriage. He pressed for a quick decision about her willingness to entertain the suit, warning her that there were strong efforts being made to arrange a marriage between the Duke and Mary of Scotland.

Elizabeth made a superior reply. '"I am aware of that," she said, "for I write to her every two or three weeks, and but a short time ago jokingly congratulated her on her marriage with the Emperor's son, adding that I was going to marry the father."'

Urging her to give him some hope that she was willing to marry the Duke she laughingly said, '"I do not know how the affair will end"' and walked away.[53]

In the next conversation, encouraged by Cecil, Allinga pressed harder for a positive answer to the proposal. Once more she told him that she did not wish to give her consent to a marriage to a man she had never met, even if that was not the common way among princes. Moreover, she told him stiffly, '"You have heard from my own lips that I do not of my own free will consent to a marriage, but only under compulsion; and to invite anyone to marry me is not in my nature."' Allinga was convinced that she had little interest in marrying Charles, but when he met Cecil he was told that he had misunderstood Elizabeth. The Principle Secretary insisted that she was inclined to the marriage and encouraged him to tell the Emperor so.[54]

The Emperor Maximilian sent Adam Zwetkovich to London in May 1565 to continue the negotiations and Elizabeth allowed him to see Cecil, Norfolk, Leicester and her other inner advisers because of the intense pressure she was under from the Court. A friendly welcome would also allow her to repair her relations with the Habsburgs after the trade embargo of 1563–64 had stopped trade with the Spanish Netherlands.

However, there were three serious impediments to the marriage: religion, the role of Charles in England's government and the cost of his household. In all of these the Habsburgs demanded more than Elizabeth could give.

She took a very hard line on religion. Charles demanded the right to practise his devout Catholicism. Elizabeth would not allow this – by the middle of 1565 she was beginning the drive against evangelical Protestants that led to the Vestiarian Controversy and she could hardly afford to appear sympathetic to Catholics even if she was, which is doubtful. As for the Archduke himself, he had the same problem. He told his brother, 'Most illustrious and most puissant Emperor! . . . I have most carefully weighed the matter and find that I must earnestly beg, and that not alone for the sake of my Christian conscience, but also because of the marked contemptuous attitude adopted towards the true Catholic and Apostolic religion' that a separate church be set aside for him in England in which he could hear mass.[55]

He also wanted to be King of England, and to remain King if she predeceased him. Elizabeth countered by offering the same powers Parliament had given Philip II when he married Mary. He could not accept her refusal to make him a ruler in his own right.

The negotiations stalled in late 1565 and Zwetkowich went home. Then, surprisingly, Elizabeth sent an ambassador to Vienna to ask Maximilian to reconsider the match. Why is unclear, although the reasons seem to have been political. Although she still did not want to marry, keeping the negotiations alive protected her from public pressure to marry.

When Parliament met in September 1566 it became a willing instrument of Cecil and some other councillors – but not Leicester, who favoured Mary, or Norfolk who supported Katherine Grey – as they increased the pressure on Elizabeth. As in many less important marriage negotiations, more of her 'friends' were being called upon to make her see reason about an arranged marriage.

The issue was raised in the Commons by Robert Molyneux, a client of Cecil's, and supported by Sir Ralph Sadler, a diplomat and ally of Cecil's on the Council. Both of them talked about the subsidy and marriage, leading some scholars to believe that they were threatening to deny Elizabeth taxes unless she settled the succession. This interpretation has been shown to be incorrect – Cecil would have been cutting-off his nose to spite his face to develop such a strategy – but once the succession had been raised as an issue the members took their bits in their teeth and ran. They could not agree on which claimant had the right to succeed Elizabeth, and they could not agree on who she should marry, but they could all agree that this reluctant lady should be forced to do her duty and accept a husband.

There were two issues involved that could be, but were not necessarily, separate: marriage and the succession. If Elizabeth married she made a start on solving the succession question, but what if she did not? And what if she did, but did not bear an heir to the crown? So they could ask her to marry, but many wanted her to go a step further and declare who should inherit the throne if she died without issue.

Elizabeth was always willing to avoid the marriage question with soothing words and vague promises, but she adamantly refused to name a successor. She knew that as soon as she did that person or family would become the focus of all dissent and that the temptation to remove her by one means or another would grow geometrically. The anonymous courtier who chronicled the early 1560s encapsulated her argument when he wrote that she was persuaded that if there was

> any heir apparent known the people would be more affectionate to him than to her, because the nature of Englishmen is variable, not contented with the state present but desirous of alterations. And that the people in hearing never so little fault in the prince would, if the successor were known, exaggerate it.[56]

The Queen, Cecil knew, would be enraged if Parliament dared talk about her marriage, but would be doubly enraged if they also asked her to name a successor, and he tried to head them off. But they would not listen to his subtle logic. The Commons would have an answer from her, appointing a committee to confer with the Lords on a petition asking her to settle the issue by marrying and by limiting the succession.

No doubt their willingness to face her anger was tied to the scares given by her close bouts with disease. In 1562 they had been frightened by her near death from smallpox. In December of 1564 she had an attack of diarrhoea that lasted a week and 'made the Court sore afraid'.[57] These reminders of her mortality heightened the already powerful concern for the stability of the government felt high and low. An anonymous treatise on the succession, probably written just after the close of the 1566 session, was hostile to what Parliament had done but it catches the mood of the time. 'I marvel,' says its author, 'at the blind boldness of the common lawyer, that in the last parliament so rashly moved the establishment of succession to the Crown.' What furies moved the lawyer he knew not, but he was not surprised that 'the nobility and commons did so well like of the matter that with one voice they all commended the motion'. The nation was in such danger from the lack of an established succession that all honest and loyal hearts were frightened, praying God to protect the realm.[58]

Before they could deliver the petition, however, Elizabeth went on the offensive. Ordering thirty members of each house of Parliament

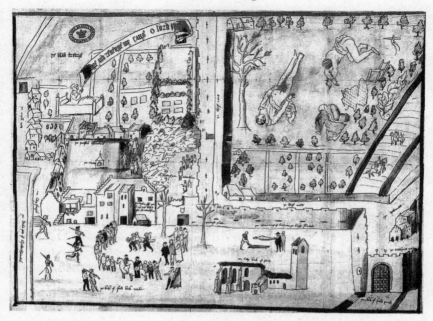

Figure 10 Vignettes concerning the murder of Henry Stuart, King of Scotland, at Kirk o'Fields, Edinburgh, 10 February, 1567. Stuart, in bed on the upper left, prays, 'Judge and revenge my cause O Lord'; on the upper right he lies dead.

to appear before her she blistered them for daring to touch her royal authority by talking about the succession. When she thought about their behaviour, she told them:

> how far from dutiful care, yea rather how nigh a traitorous trick, this tumbling cast did spring, I muse how men of wit can so hardly use that gift they hold. I marvel not much that brideless colts do not know their rider's hand, whom bit of kingly rein did never snaffle yet. Whether it was fit that so great a cause as this should have had his beginning in such a public place . . . let it be well weighed.

It was monstrous, she said, that the feet should direct the head, and she was pained that they valued her so little that they had forgotten all that she had done for them. To ask her to name a successor was to bring division into the realm and danger of death to herself. Did they care so little for her and for the realm that they would advance their own fear in front of good policy? She had a mind to name a successor just to enjoy their discomfiture when it brought suffering to the kingdom. She only wished that the men who had raised the issue 'may before their deaths repent the same, and show some confession of their fault, whereby the scabbed sheep may be known from the whole'.

But because she was an anointed Queen she could not abandon her duty. Though a woman, she had the courage to do it, and she would never 'by violence be constrained to do anything'. If she was turned out of her realm in her petticoat she knew she could live anywhere in Christendom. All their petitions were not going to force to her to budge. Nonetheless, they could be assured she knew her job and would look after the realm.

The representatives of the two houses were told to take her message back to their members.[59] As reported the speech lost some of its sting, but the moral was clear: they were not to talk about the succession any more.

If she thought her intervention had brought the matter to an end she was wrong. William Lambarde (not the famous antiquary) rose the day after the Commons heard her order and introduced a bill for nominating an heir. He answered her objections to appointing the succession point for point, going on to argue that it was their duty to settle it. If she did not allow the heir to be known she would lose the love of her subjects and they would know no peace.

> If God should take her majesty, the succession being not established, I know not what shall come of my self, my wife, children, lands, goods, friends or country; for in truth no man doth know what. And therefore every man hath great cause to meditate hereof, for it concerns everyone. I say that this meditation being gravely, maturely, and wisely pondered to remember that [if] her Majesty will not settle the succession, [it] will . . . cool the heat of love in any, how fervent so ever it be.[60]

His bill does not survive and it is unclear what it would have done, but Lambarde said in his speech that it offered the Queen a tax if she would settle the succession.[61]

Lambarde's speech was enthusiastically received and a motion was made to go that very afternoon to present the Queen with a petition for settling the succession. Conveniently, there was one available, already prepared by Lambarde.[62] They soon thought better of using his, however. Another, drafted by Cecil and presumably much more conciliatory than Lambarde's defiant patriotism, was presented to Elizabeth.

It was, given her temper and position, appropriately cringing, representing them as coming on their knees with hearts full of humility, begging her, in all manner of lowliness, not to mistake their love for her in requesting her to fulfil her earlier promise to marry. There was no mention of establishing the succession. It closed by invoking the maternal image that she herself had used in 1563, begging her, out of her motherly love, to care for her subjects, who obey her 'like children'.[63]

In the meantime more trouble had arisen. In the Commons some believed that their right of free speech in counsel to the Queen had been infringed by her order not to discuss the succession. Already sensitive, they were given another reason to suspect that they did not possess immunity for whatever was said on the floor of the House. James Dalton, speaking on a bill to ban seditious books, used the opportunity to attack a book that called the baby just born to Mary of Scotland, Prince of Scotland, England and Ireland. Dalton was outraged. '"Prince of England"', he sputtered, 'and Queen Elizabeth as yet having no child.' The mouths of those who wrote such books ought to be stopped, and, even though the Queen had forbidden them to talk about the succession, to let such a book pass without revenge would make the heart of a true Englishman break in his breast. Filled with righteous indignation, his mouth ran away with his head as he attacked the Scottish Queen, forcing the Speaker to interrupt him. But he had not been stopped in time. James Melville, the Scottish ambassador, protested that Dalton had declared himself against the succession of any Scot or foreigner, so Dalton was examined as to what he had said. He denied having intended to deal with the succession, claiming to have been enflamed by his own rhetoric.[64] His hasty retreat from his speech earned him the nickname Dalton 'The Denier' in a lampoon of the members.[65]

Elizabeth moved to reassure the House of its right of free speech in a message that stated that, because they had obeyed her and not discussed the succession, she was lifting her ban on discussing the succession.[66] It was a curious piece of political justification, but it did restore the right she had infringed, quieting the dissent.

This stormy Parliament had achieved little except a tax bill. 'The succession not answered.' 'The marriage not followed.' 'The bill of religion stayed to the comfort of the adversaries', Cecil wrote gloomily in his notes.[67] Not even the bills for religious discipline had been enacted, since Elizabeth had concluded that the alphabetical bills for reform, introduced without her permission, contravened her prerogative. As she had said, she was an independent prince and would not do anything against her will.

Perhaps in expectation that the pressure exerted by Parliament would work, the Privy Council drew up instructions for the Earl of Sussex who was to lead an embassy to the Emperor. In the end he did not leave for Austria until June 1567, empowered to promote a marriage with the Archduke, but unable to define what religion Charles was expected to use in England. Sussex was told to claim that 'no quiet Catholic' would be offended by worship in England, where only the very words of Scripture were read and spoken in church.

These naïve arguments did not deceive the Germans and the negotiation collapsed. The Archduke told an English envoy that he would not
deny his conscience and abandon his religion. He wrote to Elizabeth
that the impediment of religion stood in the way of the marriage, and
that to go contrary to their consciences in such a matter 'would spell
eternal death for Your Highness and for me'.[68] His conclusion can
hardly have surprised Elizabeth, since she had already decided that her
conscience would not permit her to make an exception and permit the
Duke to hear mass in England.

There is little doubt that she felt great relief at the outcome. Her
repeated insistence that she would only marry for reasons of state
were too frequent and vehement not to be true. And perhaps she had
found a way to trump those who wished her to marry a foreign prince.
Although she had announced that she was willing to marry for the good
of the realm in 1564, she made it clear then, and she continued to
insist, that she would never marry a man who would not practise her
religion. It was this objection that foundered the negotiations with the
Duke of Anjou that began in 1571, too. Refusing to marry a Catholic
also pleased those hard-to-satisfy devout Protestants who would never
tolerate any toleration of Catholic worship in the realm.[69]

IV

The negotiations with the Habsburgs collapsed in the first months of
1568. Elizabeth, now thirty-six, was still not married, still insisting that
she was willing for reasons of state but unwilling personally to let a
man in her life. While negotiations had continued her cousin Mary of
Scotland married, bore a child, witnessed the murder of her secretary,
lost her husband to assassins, was abducted and raped, and then
married her abductor. Is it any wonder that she has been a mainstay
of the historical romance market?

When Mary chose to marry Darnley in July 1565 her eldest half-
brother, the Earl of Moray and one of her chief councillors, withdrew
from Court and raised his forces. Mary answered with decisive action
in the Chaseabout Raid, chasing Moray into exile in England. She could
not, however, chase away the resentment that the marriage and other
things had raised in the breasts of the Scots nobility, who opposed
her use of commoners for advisers. Others, including John Knox,
feared – incorrectly – that her success in defeating Moray threatened
Protestantism, believing that she would try to restore Catholic worship
in the next Parliament.

These dissidents made the naïve Darnley their tool. Convincing him
that Mary was having an affair with her Italian secretary David Riccio,

they persuaded him to believe that they preferred him for their king but that Mary would never allow him to be crowned, thanks to Riccio. Drunken and violent, Darnley was rapidly slipping from his wife's affections, and the Riccio story made sense to his muddled mind. He fell in with a plot to murder the little secretary.

They did the deed in the presence of Queen Mary, who was six months pregnant. She and Riccio were dining in her private apartments, surrounded by servants, when Darnley and his co-conspirators appeared. Denouncing Riccio, they pried his hands from her skirts and dragged him, screaming 'Save me, Madame, save me!', from the room and stabbed him to death.

Mary, with astonishing coolness, managed over the next day to win her treacherous husband back to her side, convincing him that the conspirators were going to kill them both unless they escaped. Riding all night to Dunbar Castle she raised the country, returning to Edinburgh a week later at the head of a large army.

Mary gave birth to James Stuart on 19 June 1566.

She had won this round, but Darnley had not. She no longer trusted him, and neither did her enemies. The events of the next few months are confusing, but it was suggested that she divorce him. The need for a divorce, however, was obviated when he was murdered on 10 February 1567. Sick in bed in a house in Kirk O'Fields in Edinburgh, he was probably strangled before the house was blown up.

Why he was killed is disputed. He might have been killed in order to free Mary of his presence. Or he might have died in a plot to kill Mary, since she had been expected to sleep in the room below his on the fatal night. Perhaps it was Protestants, who feared that his recent friendly relations with the Catholics boded them ill. But at the time the most popular explanation was lust. Mary, it was rumoured, was having an affair with the Earl of Bothwell, who, conniving with her, had blown up the King in order get him out of the way.

Within days there were placards in the streets of Edinburgh accusing them of the murder and within weeks it was rumoured in Europe's courts that she intended to marry Bothwell. Although Bothwell was tried and acquitted for the murder, later events gave impetus to the rumours.

On 24 April Bothwell and 800 men abducted Mary when she was out riding, taking her quietly to Dunbar Castle. There he raped her. Three weeks later they were married. In the interim between the abduction and the marriage Bothwell obtained a divorce from his wife. It appeared to most of the world that the entire episode was a charade designed to save the Queen's honour in the face of her disreputable behaviour. The fact that Mary ordered the ministers of the Kirk to read the marriage banns after they refused unless they had it from her in writing that she wanted it done seemed to prove the case.[70]

'All Scotland cried out on the foul murder of the king', recalled Sir James Melville, who had been abducted along with Mary. In their disgust and embarrassment over the murder and marriage many of the lords raised their men and 'went out of Edinburgh on foot, with great earnestness and fierceness to fight'. They met Bothwell and Mary, whose troops, says Melville, had no heart for the quarrel, at Carberry. The French ambassador attempted to mediate between the sides, urging Mary to give up Bothwell and return to Edinburgh, but she angrily refused. In the end, however, she surrendered and was placed under arrest. As she was taken back to the city she was taunted by the soldiers and the crowd.[71]

In the midst of this turbulence Elizabeth wrote Mary a letter neatly summing up the view many took of her actions, though it may also reflect on Elizabeth's own decision about Dudley. 'Madam,' she wrote, 'to be plain with you, our grief hath not been small that in this your marriage so slender consideration has been had . . .' 'For how could,' Elizabeth demanded, 'a worse choice be made for your honour than in such haste to marry such a subject who, besides other notorious lacks, public fame has charged with the murder of your late husband.' Especially since 'he hath another wife alive, whereby neither by God's law nor man's yourself can be his lawful wife nor any children betwixt you legitimate?'[72]

Shortly afterwards the victorious lords forced Mary to abdicate, appointing her half-brother Moray the regent for Prince James, who was crowned King of Scotland on 29 July.

Mary spent the winter in the custody of George Douglas, Regent Moray's half-brother, on the island of Lochleven. He was fatally attracted to her and, on 1 May 1568, he helped her escape to Hamilton, where the clan of Hamilton and the Bishop of St Andrews welcomed her. Technically a married woman, that did not prevent the Hamiltons from seeing their opportunity to make one of their own king, and it was rumoured, and feared by Mary, that the Bishop intended to marry her to Lord John Hamilton.

Mary wished to withdraw, but the Hamiltons prepared to fight the Regent. Outnumbered, they were also victims of superior strategy when they met his forces. Forced to attack uphill, the leaders of the Hamilton vanguard were dropped by culverin fire as they panted upward, meeting the pikes of the Regent's guard already out of breath.

After the defeat, says Melville, Mary 'lost all courage, which she had never done before, and took so great fear that she never rested till she was in England'.[73] She was not a welcome refugee, presenting difficult problems for Elizabeth and literally opening a new chapter in the political history of the reign.

The English acted with unusual despatch to secure her person. The Catholic Earl of Northumberland raced to take her, but the officers of the Lord Warden of the West March were ahead of him. She was kept under guard while Elizabeth toyed with the idea of letting her visit her, and with sending troops to put her back on the throne, but choosing to proceed with care. Outraged that the Scots would treat an anointed monarch as they had, Elizabeth had the sense not to rush in.

The situation, as ever, was complicated by religion. Moray and baby King James quickly emerged as the leaders of the Protestant party in Scotland, while their opponents, led by Elizabeth's erstwhile suitor the Duke of Chatelherault, claimed Mary as the rightful sovereign. This placed England in the position of supporting Moray for ideological reasons, and in a few months *de facto* recognition was extended to his government.

While Elizabeth waffled, uncertain but sometimes wishing to restore Mary, her Council was working hard to keep her. England's most dangerous foe was in their hands and they had no intention of sending her back to Scotland or letting her go abroad. In Scotland she would provoke more civil war; in France she would renew the old alliance against England. Nonetheless, as Cecil knew well, keeping her in England was fraught with danger, too. She would plot with dissatisfied English people to get the English throne, an especially sweet idea to English Catholics.

Mary appealed to Elizabeth for a meeting, but instead she was forced to agree to a hearing of her case. Convened in September of 1568 at York before the Duke of Norfolk, the Earl of Sussex and Sir Ralph Sadler, it was purposely designed to have but one outcome: Elizabeth would become a controller of Scottish affairs, either by continuing to hold a 'guilty' Mary, useable at any time against Moray, or by restoring Mary to a puppet throne. In the process it would be nice if her reputation was so sullied in English eyes that her claim to England's throne became untenable.

The question at issue was Mary's involvement in the murder of Darnley, which Moray tried to prove with the famous Casket Letters, forgeries intended to prove that Mary and Bothwell were lovers and had planned the murder. After three months of intense negotiations and posturing Elizabeth issued a 'sentence' summed up in the Scottish verdict 'not proven'. Although she did not find that there was evidence that Mary had murdered her husband, she also did not find reason to believe Moray and his supporters had done wrong.

Both sides were found to be innocent, but only Moray was allowed to return to Scotland. It had been concluded that English interests would be damaged if Mary was sent back. Meanwhile the civil war in Scotland between Mary's supporters and the Regent intensified. Her followers now alleged that they were fighting the English when they fought him.

When, in January 1569, Mary was moved south to Tutbury Castle she knew that she could not expect help from her cousin Elizabeth, but she was already turning elsewhere in England for succour.[74] Ambitious nobles and disgruntled Catholics naturally turned to her with enthusiasm.

The last phase of Mary's marital history is her attempts to marry the Duke of Norfolk, rehearsed above. She became the darling of the northern Catholics who hoped to remove that upstart commoner William Cecil and his Protestant queen, replacing them with Mary, a rightful Queen of England, and Norfolk, the greatest nobleman of the realm. It seems to have been a purely political arrangement and it failed almost before it began, but the northern earls rose in revolt and died for the idea.

The central fact of the political history of the 1560s is that the gender of the rulers of England and Scotland created a situation impossible to imagine if they had been men. The assumption that they would and should marry, and that through marriage their power would be passed to their husbands, made them the centre of repeated attempts at marriage. Because of this assumption any man to whom they were attracted acquired through the possibility of marriage inordinate power in the realm; the sort of power no mistress could ever achieve, since men were allowed to be out in the world. Lord Robert Dudley, in all fairness a man of great talent, acquired a place in the inner circle, a puissant following, and much wealth because Elizabeth fell in love with him.

Elizabeth, to her credit, understood the assumptions about the proper place of a married woman and refused to assume it. The only way to avoid surrendering her singular power was to avoid marriage. Had she been someone other than the queen she might have married Lord Robert, but she knew she could not be fully queen and a dutiful wife at once. Like a celibate priest, she dedicated herself to her parish, foregoing the pleasures of a family in order to better serve her people.

She was open and blunt about her preference to remain single, but no one wanted to believe her. At first her courtiers and the foreigners who came to court her assumed she would marry. Did not all women? Later, as the fear grew that there would be no heir and no successor chosen when she died, people were less inclined to think about her marriage in terms of what was expected of a woman, recasting it in terms of her royal duty. This change was largely her fault, for they seized on the leverage she gave them, but it was a change in nuance only. At bottom it rested on the certainty that children were needed to preserve the peace of the realm and Elizabeth was the only woman who could bear them.

For all private families children were the guarantee of a decent old age; for the generation of the 1560s only royal children could guarantee a quiet old age.

8

Family Values

I

In the deep dusk of a January evening in 1569 the women of the village of Harborough in Hertfordshire were called to attend Agnes Bowker's labour. In the dense gloom of the room the servant girl was giving birth to a bastard of uncertain paternity. As her delivery progressed Elizabeth Harrison the midwife demanded the name of the father, as was the custom at illegitimate births. Bowker, kneeling on the ground and leaning back into a neighbour's arms, confessed that Randal Dowley had 'borne her company'. She fainted when Harrison began to pull the baby out. As it emerged all bloody the women present saw it had a tail and panicked. They snatched up their children and began to run, but Harrison, with great presence of mind, invoked the Trinity against evil and called them back. One of the many witnesses, Margaret Harrison, reported that 'the wives willed her to fetch a candle, and when she came with it she saw the monster', a cat, lying on the ground.[1]

Except for its outcome the witnesses to Bowker's labour were describing a familiar, and absolutely universal, human drama. Childbirth, and its consequent responsibilities, are at the centre of human life biologically and socially since the care for one's immediate and extended families gives meaning to life. In the 1560s, as at any time in human history, raising children occupied a significant portion of people's lives since the little ones had to be nursed, disciplined, morally formed, educated, and, in the end – if they lived – married in order to start the process over again. To a certain extent child-rearing in the 1560s was identical to child-rearing in any other time, but it was a more deadly era in which to be a child or a mother, and it was an era in which education, disturbed by the reformation of religion, was in a state of confusion. New educational theories were being tried, too, and more children needed more education than they had formerly, all of which meant that parents found themselves in a landscape that was not entirely familiar. As for the children, their chances of being orphaned were almost as high as their chances of dying before reaching their majority, so it was a society that expended a great deal of effort coping with children who had lost their biological parents.

As we have seen, Agnes Bowker survived the birth of her bastard cat to be interrogated by the law. Her interrogation suggests that no one doubted that she could have conceived a cat, or that the conception was the work of the Devil. The investigators became convinced that her cat–child was a fraud, but their theories of conception made such a child possible.

Conception, it was believed, was the result of the mixing of female and male seed in the two chambers of the uterus. Learned from Aristotle, this meant that a 'monster' could be conceived if the male seed was not human. Galen had taught that the chances of conception and the sex of the child might be affected by atmospheric conditions under which the seed was planted, so that Thomas Raynalde, the most popular author on conception and birth in the 1560s, could argue that conditions for conception were the same as those for a successful crop of wheat. The seed, the sower and the condition of the soil all influenced not only conception, but also the sex and normality of the child.[2]

One corollary of this theory of conception was the belief that the woman had to reach orgasm before procreation could occur. Her desire had to match the man's, so sexual pleasure was a necessary concern of those seeking to conceive. Thomas Raynalde chided those who did not think that the woman's pleasure was important in making children. Those who suppose this should rethink their belief, for, if they would consider further, they would find pleasure to be part of God's plan. Without 'vehement and ardent appetite and lust . . . neither man nor woman would ever have been so enticed to the works of generation and encreasement of posterity . . .'[3]

Contemporary theories of conception were relevant whenever a couple wished to conceive but could not, or when they wished to avoid conception. The reasons and cures for sterility were mysteries attacked with a number of weapons, most of which had to do with diet and careful attention to the preparation of the 'seed bed'. The latter had much to do with the proper form of intercourse that allowed the commingling of the seeds of the male and the female, with the 'missionary' position receiving medical sanction as that best suited to the business.

The dietary and herbal remedies for sterility were built around the belief that the four humours of the body greatly affected all bodily processes. Since the 'matrix' of the woman had to be properly prepared for conception – neither too hot, cold, humid, or dry – her diet directly influenced her fertility.

The medical community, and folklore, provided information on what to eat and not eat if one wished to be a lusty and fertile mate. For instance, Thomas Hill, who published his first gardening manual in 1563, warned that the eating of the female blades of parsley made men and women barren. Eaten during pregnancy it caused the child to have epilepsy, and stopped women's milk. In spite of (or perhaps because of) its effect on fertility, parsley also 'procureth the eaters of it unto the venereal act'. Hill further observed that it was an excellent cure for stinking breath, information important to maidens and widows wishing to decive their wooers by disguising their fetid exhalations. If a male child was desired artichokes were recommended, and men should not eat lettuce because it harmed the venereal act.[4]

There were also charms, ointments, pills and other cures for sterility available, although it was recognized that identifying the defective partner was useful. Raynalde told his readers that to determine the sterile party each should soak a seed in their own urine for twenty-four hours, plant it and water it every morning for eight to ten days with their urine. If the seed grew the person was fertile. However, he recognized that this was folklore, not science, commenting that it was a far-fetched experiment.[5]

The stress caused by infertility in a society that believed the aim of marriage was procreation could be great; but the stress caused by conceiving unintentionally or too often could be even greater. Raynalde and the other medical experts were careful not to explain contraception or abortion, holding them to be morally repugnant, but the information in their books could be used to prevent pregnancy as well as encourage it. Unmarried people, woman exhausted with child-bearing or families with too many mouths to feed, and women whose lives were in danger of another pregnancy, were all interested in them.

Of course the most certain method of contraception was sex without full coition. Failing that, Raynalde admitted that there was a folkloric tradition about contraception and abortion of which no woman was ignorant.[6]

When Mary Portman Stowell aborted her child fathered by her husband's servant she used an herbal compound, most likely one of those available from apothecaries. Rue, or herb of grace, was available to combat witchcraft, ward off diseases, and as an insecticide, but it also could cause abortion. The berries of the savin-tree were used to make an oil that drove off insects and cured skin complaints, as well as helping urinary complaints, but they were also a popular abortifacient.

Along with these, which do work, there were undoubtedly many other compounds and cures peddled by the ignorant or the unscrupulous, but the rate of infanticide suggests that most were not too effective. A desperate woman might also try jumping off tables, physical exertion and the other means of abortion that still exist in the folkloric pharmacopoeia, as well as bleeding her foot.

For a girl like Agnes Bowker, unmarried and unemployable if she had a child, the alternative to abortion was suicide. She tried both drowning and hanging herself before she gave birth to her cat.

Perhaps one of the strongest reasons for contraception or abortion was the danger of childbirth. It was so common that pious women prepared themselves for death before their labour. A leading cause of death, roughly one hundred times more women died annually in childbed in the sixteenth century than in the mid-twentieth century in England.[7] Sir Thomas Smith, arguing in favour of Elizabeth's safe spinster state, painted a picture of the dangers of childbirth that is tame in comparison to the medical manuals of the day. Insisting that women giving birth were in as much danger as any man could ever be, he noted 'we see by common order, they are wont to take the Communion, to take their leave of the Church, and prepare themselves even to it as persons that were neither alive nor dead, but betwixt both.' The seriousness of childbirth was proved, he said, by the number of women 'every hour, [who] even in their travail, or shortly after, be dispatched, and sent from their childbed to their burial'.[8]

The reasons for this danger were both natural and human-caused. Then as now factors such as the age of the mother influenced her chances of surviving unscathed, as did her general health. Any obstetric complication, such as twins, sharply increased the risk to the mother during the birth, and infection – often caused by the unwashed hands of the midwife and the general lack of sanitation – frequently set in after birth.[9] If any complication arose the woman laboured until the birth finally occurred or she died. If the child was dead in the womb the midwife might use hooked instruments, saws and anything else at hand to remove it bit by bit, cutting off limbs and crushing skulls. The accepted practice of the midwives added to the danger, since they often interfered in deadly ways, increasing the danger of tears, ulcers, sores and haemorrhage. Nor did the custom of giving the mother 'birth pills' containing ingredients such as eels' livers decrease the risk. For the pain there was the universal stupefacient, alcohol.[10]

If the mother survived the birth she had every reason to thank God for her safe delivery, as did her husband and family. The tense fear that surrounded the labour gave way to thanksgiving with the 'churching' of the mother and the baptism and christening of the child. As soon as she could after the birth the mother went to be churched, a Christian variant of Jewish purification rituals.

Kneeling near the communion table with the priest standing over her the woman gave thanks for surviving. As the prayer book service proceeded the priest and the woman recited a liturgy ending: 'O Almighty God, which hast delivered this woman thy servant from the great pain and peril of childbirth: Grant . . . that she . . . may both faithfully live and walk in her vocation, according to thy will in this present life . . .'[11] The woman then made her thanks offering and took communion. Afterwards she might have done as Mistress Bacon, the wife of the Sergeant to the Catry under Queen Mary, did. Her father gave a dinner for 'a great company of gentle women'. Because it was Lent of 1563 they only had fish, but the thanksgiving and joy were still present at the party.[12]

The christening often occurred before the churching for it was popularly supposed to be done as soon after the birth as possible, even though the Book of Common Prayer denied this. Thomas Hoby's diary tells us of each birth and christening in his family. His first child was born on 20 March 1560; on 4 April his son was christened Edward with Lord Windsor, Lord Darcy and Lady Williams of Ricot standing as godparents. After their first child the Hobys shortened the interval between birth and baptism to three or four days – perhaps because arranging godparents for girls was less important than for a first-born son. Thus when his wife was delivered of a 'wench' on 27 May 1562 they had the child baptised on 31 May with Lady Frances Gresham, Lady Elizabeth Nevill and Mr John Doylie, esq. standing as godparents, naming her 'Elizabeth'.[13]

Like so much else in the mid-sixteenth century, the traditions surrounding baptism and godparents were changing under the impact of the Reformation. Although baptism was still necessary for a Christian, the legal abolition of purgatory and limbo meant that Protestants did not believe it was absolutely necessary to baptise as soon after birth as possible. Nor was the godparent quite as responsible for the salvation of a child who bore the name chosen by the godparent. But in the 1560s these traditions were in flux, somewhere between the late medieval customs and what would emerge in the late-sixteenth century as a Protestant tradition. The Book of Common Prayer reflected that suspense neatly with its questions and exhortations at baptism.

The baptismal service still contained many traditional elements. Godparents were asked on behalf of the child, 'Dost thou forsake the devil and all his works, the vain pomp, and glory of the world, with all covetous desires of the same, the carnal desires of the flesh, so that thout wilt not follow, nor be led by them?' Making the sign of the cross on the child's forehead after washing away the child's original sin by dipping or sprinkling (depending on the health of infant) was another traditional element.

The church discouraged baptism at home. Nonetheless, it was so widely practised that the prayer book provided a service to be used by those present at the birth. The language of the instructions reflect the desperation that prompted these do-it-yourself baptisms, instructing those present to say the Lord's Prayer 'if the time will suffer' before naming the baby, and dipping or sprinkling while saying, 'I baptize thee in the name of the Father, and of the Son, and of the Holy Ghost. Amen.' The rubric exhorted the parents to believe that such a baptism was legal and did not need to be repeated. Nevertheless, 'if the child . . . do afterward live' they submitted to a catechism to prove that the baptism was legal. If it was, the priest swore the godparents to their duties of raising the child as a member of the body of Christ.[14]

The forms of baptism prescribed in the Book of Common Prayer came under attack in the early 1560s as Protestant bishops began to chafe under the book's compromising conservatism. Many found the crossing of the child's forehead in baptism 'very superstitious' and it became a favourite object of Puritan attacks on 'popish remnants' in the Church. Asking questions of the child during baptism was found to be another Catholic remnant, too. Most of all, however, allowing private baptism at birth horrified the ardent reformers. They wanted baptism to be performed only by ordained ministers. Part of the impetus for this was their aggressive clericalism – they simply did not want the laity trespassing on their turf – but they had a theological reason as well. Calvinists took St Paul's order that women should keep silent in church seriously, automatically denying the ability of a woman to perform a sacrament. Since emergency baptisms at birth were performed by women they were, by definition, wrong (Catholic priests agreed). Moreover, they urged that there was an element of superstitious magic in these baptisms, with their assumption that the innocent would not be allowed into heaven unless the mechanical forms of baptism were observed.[15]

The net effect of these attacks on the form and meaning of the ceremony was confusion for the parents and godparents. The ceremony itself was an ingrained and important social event, one of the milestones of life that not only introduced the child into the body of Christ but also into the patterns of social connection embodied by the godparents. So much so that when a child was christened without godparents in 1561 it caused Henry Machyn to make a note of it.[16] The argument over the proper form threatened this comfortable custom and, for those who took theology seriously, raised difficult matters of conscience. How should a child be baptised? And what were their duties towards their godchildren?

Even as scruples of conscience crept into some minds the traditions of christening continued, and, like weddings, they included a party. Henry Machyn tells of a high-society christening for the daughter of William Harvey, Clarenceaux King of Arms, in July 1562. Sir William Cordell, Master of the Rolls was godfather. The sisters Lady Bacon and Lady Cecil, wives of the Lord Keeper and the Principal Secretary, were godmothers. Harvey's banquet impressed Machyn by the volume and quality of the alcohol served: 'wassail of hippocras, French wine, Gascon wine, and Rhenish wine, with great plenty, and all their servants had a banquet in the hall with diverse dishes.'[17]

Christenings and godparents were for children who were rooted in their communities, not for the illegitimate and the unwanted. Agnes Bowker may well have killed the human infant she bore, replacing it with a cat to cover her crime. Alice Wood, a 'spinster' of Little Horstead in Sussex, was not so clever. She was indicted and found guilty of drowning her baby. Pleading pregnancy to save herself from hanging she was examined by a jury of matrons. They brought in a verdict of not pregnant and Wood was hanged.[18]

In Cambridge in July 1562 the justices tried a case of infanticide in which the mother, the midwife, and the father were indicted. George Parker, a married man, and Helena Millesent, a widow, had produced a baby daughter. After it was born the midwife cut the child's throat with a knife (valued at 1 penny) in the presence of its mother. The mother and the midwife were convicted of murder and hung. Parker was convicted of 'feloniously' counselling and procuring the murder, and hung on the evidence of Alice Biby, another spinster who had comforted the mother after the murder. The Crown became the owner of the knife, since all murder weapons belonged to it.[19]

The next January a man and a woman found a French maid burying the body of her pretty baby girl in Holborn Field. She had broken its neck. The two forced her to dig it up again and took her to the alderman's deputy, who locked her in the Counter prison.[20]

These murders reached the courts and were enjoyed by the horrified public, but many babies died in accidents that may not have been accidents. In particular many infants died of 'overlaying'. When a baby was born it was wrapped in swaddling clothes, bound tightly in order to ensure that its limbs would grow straight – deformities were often blamed on negligent swaddling.[21] Thus bound the child could not move, and could even be hung on the wall to keep it out of the way of danger. In theory it was supposed to be unwrapped and washed two or three times each day, though it is unclear how realistic this was. Placed in the family bed – it was customary for many people to use one bed – these infants were sometimes smothered when their bedmates rolled over on top of them.

This was such a common cause of death – 19.9 per cent of all deaths reported in three London parishes in the early modern era were attributed to 'overlaying' – that it is suspected that it was a safe and efficient way of getting rid of unwanted children. Its safety, however, was a direct result of the fact that it was such a common accident.[22]

Not all mothers had the will to kill their unwanted babes. Abandonment was widely practised, as the foundling hospitals attest. Giving the child to a foundling hospital such as Christ's Hospital in London, however, was tantamount to a polite form of infanticide. The death rate for infants left at Christ's in the 1560s and 1570s was almost one in two.[23]

The incidence of infanticide and abandonment is hard to measure, and most children were raised by their parents or relatives unless they were completely orphaned. Nonetheless the chances of a child surviving to adulthood were poor. Demographic historians estimate that as many as half the people born in early modern England died before they reached the age of ten.[24] This meant that if a person survived until age thirty he or she could expect to live another thirty years, but surviving to thirty was not to be expected.

The causes of these deaths run a long gamut beginning with birth defects, through malnourishment and all the childhood diseases, to all the dangers of a world full of open fires, wells and large animals. There is no doubt that the deaths of children took a heavy emotional toll on the adults around them, but their ways of coping with that toll has disguised it. In a society imbued with Medieval Christian concepts of life and emotion, and one in which the deaths of little ones was so common, the losses were met with both more stoical resignation and greater expectation. The concern for rapid baptism underlines this outlook. With even still-born children and abortive births recorded in the parish registers and given proper burial there is no doubt that people cared about their children even if they did not show it with elabourate public grief.[25] The longer a child lived, the stronger the ties of affection grew, even as the risk of loss diminished.

II

The longer a child lived the greater the responsibilities it imposed on its parents and guardians. The child had to be cared for, but, more importantly, formed into a human being, purged of as many of its evil habits as possible. Knowing that children were contaminated by original sin – they were the 'natural men' so feared by the righteous – Elizabethan society made it its business to form and reform them. The primary task lay with the parents, but often they were expected to carry out the will of the state and the church in order to mould the obdurate child into a useful citizen of the commonwealth. The desired result was a pious, obedient, hard-working Christian subject of Her Majesty, possessed of no evil habits and properly respectful of his or her betters, be they husband, parents, aldermen, the Queen or the Lord Jesus Christ.

Sir William Cecil believed that children had duties to their parents, just as their parents had duties to one another and to God. As he had done in his reflections on marriage, he compiled a list of biblical precedents to describe these duties. From Ephesians he cited Paul's instructions: 'Children, obey your parents in the Lord: for this is right. Honour thy father and mother (which is the first commandment with promise) that it may be well with thee, and that thou may live long on earth.'[26]

From Ecclesiasticus 3 in the Apocrypha he took a series of quotes The first was, 'who fears God, honours his parents'. He underlined the next two: 'Who so honours his father, shall have joy of his own children' and 'My son, help thy father in his age, and grieve him not as long as he lives.'[27] After quoting the poet Terence, Socrates, Chrysostom and the book of Proverbs he concluded with this summary: children should obey their parents in everything because it is pleasing to God.[28]

Strict raising and careful educating were the ways to secure the obedience to authority that they so prized. But the very loftiness of this goal meant that it was seldom met. The troubles of the nation were often blamed on the way in which young people drew God's wrath on the nation and refused to undertake their responsibilities, so child-rearing was much on the mind of the men who led the Tudor state.

The general belief that the world was decaying towards the last judgement was confirmed by the disrespect children had for their parents and masters. The young everywhere, wrote Roger Ascham, had lost their innocence. They were assertive and presumptuous, giving no reverence or authority to their elders, neglecting their duties to such an extent that 'disobedience doth overcrowd the banks of good order, almost in every place, almost in every degree of man'.

Teenagers were a special problem. Ascham was disturbed by their light-minded pursuit of fashion and their rude slang, repeating a generational complaint as old as parents:

> And, if some Smithfield ruffian take up some strange going; some new mowing with the mouth; some wrenching with the shoulder, some brave proverb; some fresh new oath, that is not stale, but will run round in the mouth; some new disguised garment, or desperate hat, fond in fashion, or garish in colour, whatsoever it cost, how small soever his living be, by what shift soever it be gotten, gotten must it be, and used with the first, or else the grace of it is stale and gone.

This behaviour was causing God to send 'just plagues' upon England. The cure for these liberties was not only the making of good laws – though they were necessary – but private discipline. Every person had to exercise it in his own house, and teach his children obedience, keeping them from 'ill things' and ill company and providing good schoolmasters to train them. He did not, however, believe that you could frighten children into becoming educated in obedience and civility.[29]

Thomas Whythorne, a professional music teacher until he entered Archbishop Parker's service in 1571, agreed with Ascham about juvenile corruption, but his solution was more traditional. Citing the same scriptural references as Cecil, he concluded that too much cherishing, coddling and permissiveness was breeding 'great incurable vices, the number of the which may be both infinite and strange, when . . . unbridled liberty is suffered in them to reign'. The cure was fear. Children had to be held in awe of their parents and guardians.[30]

The feeling that the nation's youth were running wild meant that education preoccupied English people in the 1560s in both the religious and political spheres. According to their gender and station children had to be taught the skills necessary for making a living and the proper worship of God (if their master did his duty). It was a decade in which many of the great names of English letters began their educations. Shakespeare, Jonson, Sidney and many other luminaries were children at the time, receiving something from their educations that their fathers, a notably unpoetic generation, lacked.

For most people moral education was the most important part of raising children. Their definition of 'moral', however, was much broader than the modern one. Seeing the spiritual and secular spheres as inextricably linked, they placed the duty of obeying God, and thereby fulfilling one's role in society, at the heart of all education. Instilling a sense of place and responsibility in God's world was essential if children were to be successful adults. Station and gender were nothing more than the markers that indicated the nature of the education required for the moral formation of the child. The literate gentlemen – and a few literate gentle ladies – were most concerned with the formation of the 'gentlemen' who ruled society. They had great responsibility and had to be both equipped to undertake it and taught to accept it. The lower orders of society had to be taught their duty to their masters and be prepared to work hard and carefully for them.

Girls had to know the skills appropriate to the tending, nurturing sex while being taught obedience to men and chastity. Boys had to be taught to control their dangerous passions, to avoid the snares of women and to rule over their families. Ultimately all these behaviours meant that the child was prepared for salvation, a salvation explained by the sing-song repetition of the catechism that all children were supposed to master.

Catechisms were a Protestant invention that became popular across Europe in the sixteenth century. Taking the form of a question and answer dialogue, they required children to memorize the correct answers to a set of questions designed to give them the foundations of their faith and their role in society. The basic English catechism was built into the Book of Common Prayer and it was the responsibility of clergy, godparents and parents to see to it that the children memorized it before confirmation. The youth had to be able to recite the Lord's Prayer and the Ten Commandments, and explain their meaning and the behaviour they demanded.

The partnership of clergy and parents for religious education was a new one, born in the Reformation and first fully expressed in the days of Edward VI. The 1549 prayer book contained a catechism, and the *Primer* of 1553 – reprinted by Queen Elizabeth in 1560 – contained explicit statements of parental responsibility for religious education. Father and Mothers were instructed, in this replacement for the medieval books of hours, to pray for the grace to train children in God's doctrine and holy law, teaching them to fear, love and obey Him. Householders were taught to pray for the grace to avoid God's curse by making the children and servants in their charge live Godly lives, avoiding vice, embracing virtue and living in fear of God, avoiding idleness and diligently exercising themselves 'every one in his office, according to their vocation and calling'.[31]

Parents and masters could not, however, be trusted to explain the new Protestant faith to the young. That was the job of the clergy. The prayer book instructed 'all fathers and mothers, masters and dames' to send their children, servants, and apprentices to the church 'to hear, and be ordered by the curate, until such time as they have learned all that is . . . appointed for them to learn'.[32]

What they were appointed to learn was their creed and their duties, enshrined in a gloss of the Ten Commandments. From the decalogue they knew their duty to God and to their neighbour. Their duty to God was to believe in Him, to fear Him and to love Him with heart, mind and soul, keeping his commandments. Their duty to their neighbours was to love them and to keep the golden rule:

> To love, honour, and succour my father and mother. To honour and obey the king and his ministers. To submit myself to all my governors, teachers, spiritual pastors, and masters. To order myself lowly and reverently to all my betters. To hurt nobody by word nor deed. To be true and just in all my dealing. To bear no malice nor hatred in my heart. To keep my hands from picking and stealing, and my tongue from evil speaking, lying, and slandering. To keep my body in temperance,

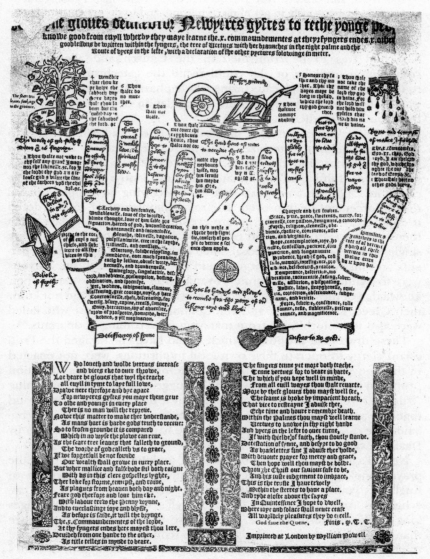

Figure 11 'Some fine gloves devised for New Year's gifts to teach young people to know good from evil', printed by William Powell (1559–67). The left glove lists sins on its palm; the right lists virtues. Each finger is a new year's resolution. The Ten Commandments are written around the tops of the fingers. Man's hard heart is illustrated by a plow on frozen ground.

soberness, and chastity. Not to covet nor desire other men's goods. But learn and labour truly to get mine own living, and to do my duty in that state of life, unto which it shall please God to call me.[33]

No child was to be confirmed in the Church and allowed into communion until he or she could recite the catechism by memory to the bishop. Although catechizing was haphazard in practice, its ideal was to instill in the young people a foundation of Christian morality that would guide their lives.

The re-established reforms of Edward VI required Elizabethans to have their children catechized, but the earnest leaders of the new Church did not find the instruction contained in the prayer book sufficient to fulfil God's commands. Bishop Sandys came to Convocation in 1563 with a proposal that the catechizing be stepped up and that enforcement be improved. The royal Injunctions of 1559 ordered it done every other Sunday before evening prayer, on Sundays when there was no sermon and on holy days; Sandys wanted it done every single Sunday. Another proposal called for ten shilling fines against parents and masters whose charges could not say the catechism. Parsons were to examine their parishoners over age fourteen every year on their knowledge of the catechism, excommunicating those who did not know their Creed, Lord's Prayer and Ten Commandments. Those who failed were also to be forbidden from marrying or becoming godparents.[34]

These draconian proposals, which would have encouraged the Protestant clergy to operate their own local inquisitions, were not enacted by the Convocation. Another part of the reform of children's education proposed in 1563 was embodied in the suggestion that the Thirty-nine Articles, a version of Jewel's *Apology*, and a new catechism be bound together and published as the official doctrine of the Church of England. The catechism they proposed to use had already been written by Dean Alexander Nowell of St Paul's.

Nowell's *Catechismus Puerorum* was an ambitious expansion of the prayer book catechism, designed to introduce Calivist doctrine to England's young. In the modern edition of the prayer book the catechism is four pages long; Dean Nowell's catechism is 108 pages long in the modern edition. Too massive to memorize, it was more than just a catechism in design; it was conceived as a text central to children's education by a man intimately associated with St Paul's School. Children learning Latin were to use it as their Latin primer, imbibing reformed theology along with ablative absolutes.[35]

Nowell's *Catechism* was approved by Convocation but not licensed by the Queen, so, like the Thirty-nine Articles, it survived in a limbo, an unofficial but approved text. It was published in 1570 in both its Latin and English versions, eventually becoming the official catechism, but in the 1560s it represents the ideal towards which the sculptors of the newly-reformed world aspired. Here, at much greater length, they made it clear that obedience to God and the prosperity of the state were intimately linked. Moreover, it emphasized that every person was to obey: obey God, obey the monarch, obey the clergy, obey their school masters, obey their social betters, obey their masters, obey their parents, obey their elders. In glossing 'honour thy father and thy mother' Nowell explained that honour meant 'love, fear and reverence' in obeying, saving, helping and defending them.

When the student in the dialogue asks for a definition of 'parents' they are defined as anyone to whom any authority has been given by God, since all authority comes from that single source. These authorities are all constituted for the single purpose of training people's minds, which are naturally puffed with pride. This obedience to magistrates expected of all laid on those in authority a heavy responsibility for those under them. They had to be 'fatherly correctors' of the people.[36] From the love and fear of God grew obedience and responsibility, two sides of the same coin.

The Protestant nation the reformers sought to build was an ideal commonwealth in which every part of the body politic worked harmoniously with every other. Regarding God's law with care, they would guarantee the peace and prosperity of the nation, bathing in God's blessings. The ideal they wished to teach children had the double benefit of creating a strong nation and ensuring salvation. In order to reach that ideal, however, they had to win the younger generation over to the ideology of the Reformation state and church. Inspired by the same educational theory and Christian idealism that moved Ignatius Loyola to use the Jesuits so effectively as schoolmasters, Elizabeth's Protestant leaders knew, in the words of Solomon, 'Teach a child in the trade of his way, and when he is old, he shall not depart from it.'[37]

The first and most important part of education was religious. It was mandated by law that every child be instructed in the faith and the duties that went with it. Instruction in reading, writing and arithmetic was less common and certainly not ordained by the authorities. Nonetheless many adults in the 1560s were concerned about improving the opportunity and quality of education for the children. Caught up on a wave of religious instability, broken families and changing educational theory, they were interested in improving the way children were prepared for life.

Perhaps the flowering of English culture in the next generation has to do with the confusion besetting education in the middle of the sixteenth century, whether we talk of grammar schools or apprenticeships. Like so many other things, the ideals and the institutions of education were undergoing important changes that had not ended by 1570. The impact of humanistic educational ideals and the attempts of the Church to educate young Protestants were clashing with the destruction done to educational institutions by the Reformation and by the changing economy. Many of these changes were viewed with dismay by parents and rulers, who did their best to shore up the system in the interests of both their children and themselves.

One indication of the concern of adults for better education is the explosion of school foundations in the mid-century, leading to an 'educational revolution' between about 1560 and 1580. In the 1560s, 42 new school foundations were added to the 47 founded in the 1550s. Literacy rates improved sharply for people who were children early in Elizabeth's reign. University enrolments jumped, too. Cambridge matriculated about 160 students a year in the 1550s; by the 1570s the number had vaulted to 340 a year. It was an era of educational vitality with sharp increases of literacy. This enthusiasm for learning to read, as David Cressy has observed, created an audience that could appreciate the literary achievements of authors of their generation, like Shakespeare.[38]

The boys of the 1560s were likely to know how to read and cipher, especially if they apprenticed in occupations in which those skills were valued. While William Shakespeare's father John was illiterate, he saw to it, as did thousands of his contemporaries, that his son learned to read and write as a necessary business skill. By the 1580s a majority of the London craftsmen and tradesmen – many schooled in the 1560s – were literate, while all merchants, vintners, scriveners, apothecaries and grocers appear, in one sample, to have learned to write. On the other hand, men engaged in outdoor trades, such as thatchers and bricklayers, fishermen and shepherds were less likely to be able to write. Yeomen farmers had a moderate level of literacy throughout the country, while 'servants in husbandry' were mostly illiterate. Women in general were as likely to be illiterate as field labourers since they had less economic need of writing.[39]

Children of the 1560s were, as a group, the most literate in English history to that time thanks to economic imperatives, humanistic enthusiasm for the value of education as a formative process, and Protestant enthusiasm for personal study of Scripture.

How they got that way remains unclear. Certainly there were tiny schools, run by clergy as a by-line or by people who had enough literacy to teach reading. Reading came before writing, since, lacking paper and pencils, children had little opportunity and less need for writing. As anyone who has studied a foreign language readily admits, writing is a different skill than either reading or speaking, and the hardest to acquire. Thus John Hart, expounding his method for 'all unlearned to read English' in 1570 advised that the unlettered 'first learn to read before they should learn to write, for that is far more ready and easy'.[40] In practice this meant learning by saying the letters of the alphabet aloud. Children were taught to say the letters and then to join them together in the elements of spelling, after which reading could begin. The sing-song recitation of letters and words following the teacher's pointer was hardly an exciting curriculum, but it matched the methods pioneered by the Church with its question–response catechisms. Arithmetic followed the same techniques, often using number tables like the one still visible on the wall of a chapel in Long Melford church. In all cases it was assumed that the function of education in English was the imparting of basic skills.[41]

Simon Forman started his formal education under the tutelage of William Rider, a literate cobbler who, because the early Elizabethan church was desperate for more clergy, became a minister in the early 1560s. A short, dark man, he could, Forman says, read English well, but what Latin he knew he learned from his sons, who went to the local free school. His school met in the former lepers' hospital of St Giles in Wilton, Wiltshire. Rider had settled there as a refugee from the plague in Salisbury.

Forman, who became a voracious reader, had trouble learning to read his prayers and, 'because his capacity could not understand the mystery of spelling', he wanted to quit school. His master's answer was normal for the time: he beat him. The beating, he recalled, 'made him more diligent to his book', and he shortly mastered spelling so that his master 'never beat him for his book again'. Stimulated by the rod, Forman made rapid progress so that within a year he had learned basic grammar and the rules of spelling. (The rules of spelling were a mystery that most Tudor people must have had trouble mastering because there was no standard orthography.)

In order to ensure that 9-year-old Simon learned his letters his father had arranged for him to board with Rider. It must have been a miserable experience because in the winter he made Forman sleep naked, 'which kept him in great fear'.

After his year at Wilton, Forman was moved to the free school in the close of Salisbury Cathedral kept by 'Doctor' Bowles. Matriculated from Clare College, Cambridge, Bowles was in charge of the choristers of the Cathedral, taking into his school any suitable boy who wished to study there. Forman describes him as a very furious man, but without explaining his meaning.[42]

Presumably he was following the traditional educational theory that demanded frequent beatings of the boys to whet their appetites for learning Latin. Roger Ascham reflected on the assumption that only fear would induce a child to learn Latin. In common schools, he wrote, the child was forced to learn Latin by first memorizing the parts of speech, followed by basic grammar. Then things began to go wrong. Poor vocabulary, ill-framed sentences and bad word placement marred the child's ability to advance in the language. But even more damage was done by the rod:

> There is no one thing, that hath more either dulled the wits, or taken away the will of children from learning, than the care they have, to satisfy their masters, in making of latins.
>
> For the scholar is commonly beat for the making, when the master were more worthy to be beat for the mending.[43]

To Ascham's pacific objections his colleagues could answer with the violent, irrefutable logic of Scripture: 'Withhold not correction from the child: if thou smite him with the rod, he shall not die. Thou shall smite him with the rod, and shall deliver his soul from Hell.' Or 'He that spares his rod, hates his son: but he that loves him chastens him.' Or, 'Foolishness is bound [he is naturally given unto it] in the heart of a child: but the rod of correction shall drive it away from him.' Or 'Beat down his neck while he is young, and beat him on the sides, while he is a child, lest he wax stubborn, and be disobedient unto thee, and so bring sorrow to thine heart.' In short, *Qui parcit virgae, odit filium* – Who spares his rod, hates his child.[44]

This belief in beating to ensure learning encouraged teachers with vicious natures to express their violent inclinations, but there were limits. In July 1563 a teacher named Penred beat a student with a belt buckle 'that he left no skin on his body'. Penred was pilloried at the Standard in Cheapside, his neck, hands and feet fastened to a stake with iron cuffs while the Beadles of the Beggars whipped him. Sometimes as many as three were striking at the same time, striving to see who could hit him the hardest for what he had done to the child. The Lord Mayor came to see the punishment and the injured boy was displayed on the pillory, his bare torso gashed and bruised from the beating. Henry Machyn said the sight of the child was the most pitiful he could imagine.[45]

In the free schools and the grammar schools the curriculum stressed Latin because it was the language of the universities and therefore the professions. Without it a boy could not hope to rise in church, state, medicine, law or teaching.

Simon Forman's attempts to acquire it indicate how aware he was of its importance – although he seems to have been born with the temperament of a scholar. Unlike his contemporaries who, as Shakespeare recalled, crept like snails unwillingly to school, he desperately wanted knowledge. Unfortunately his father died on New Year 1564 after a night of dancing and sport. His mother, who, he claims, never loved him, took the 11-year-old from school and 'set him to keep sheep and to plough, and gathering of sticks and such like'. At fourteen he ran away and apprenticed himself, but that did not lessen his desire to learn Latin.

His master, who seems to have been a decent man, chided him for spending so much to 'with his book' and finally took all his Latin books away from him, but Simon found another way to learn. A Devonshire boy was boarding with his master in order to attend the free school in Salisbury, and he was Simon's bedfellow. Each night Simon tried to learn from him what had been taught in the school that day. In retrospect Forman concluded he learned little this way, but it kept what he had learned from evaporating.

At age seventeen he left his master after a dispute with his master's mistress, returning to his mother's house and the free school. He attended school every day for eight weeks – until his mother threw him out. At seventeen Simon was so anxious to learn that 'if his master would not have beaten him if he could not say his lesson well, he would have wept and sobbed more than if he had been beaten'. Nonetheless, poverty forced him to hunt for some way to make a living.

He found it in the little school at St Giles where he began his own education. He became, as he later boasted, a schoolmaster before he was eighteen, teaching thirty boys. Their parents paid him mostly in room and board while he saved whatever money he received. When, after a year and a half, he had amassed two pounds he resigned his post and left for Oxford 'for to get more learning'. He went, however, as a servant to two boys he had known at school, not as a student, apparently hoping that he could further his education by being in the presence of learning. His two friends spent their time drinking, hunting and wenching while Simon ran to fetch bottles and bags, struggling to find opportunities to attend the Magdalene College free school and follow his book.[46]

Forman was unusual in both his thirst for education and the fact that he got it, but another aspect of his life reflected the lives of thousands of English boys. He became an apprentice. Apprenticeship prepared most English youths for a productive life in all trades, whether as farm labourers or great merchants, being, as Margaret Davies has remarked, an institution so widespread in Tudor England that its nearest analogue is modern compulsory formal education.[47] According to the terms of the indentures for an apprentice, however, this was not just an education in a trade; it was also a way of controlling and providing moral formation for young people.

The apprentice went to live with his master and was in return raised by him through his difficult 'adolescency'. The first age of 'man', 'infancy' lasted until age fifteen, following which came 'adolescency', which lasted until age twenty-five, Thomas Whythorne tells us. It was an age much troubled by Cupid and Venus, when young people were in danger of the shafts fired by the winged messenger of love, so they needed careful looking after to keep them on the straight and narrow while learning a useful trade and a place in their community.[48]

Therefore any attempt to cure the nation's troubling youth was likely to start with the nature and length of apprenticeships. Given the tenor of the times it is not surprising that dozens of local efforts in the 1550s and early 1560s came together in a national law controlling apprenticeships, the great Statute of Artificers that set the basic terms for labour contracts for centuries to come.[49]

The statute was concerned with setting wage rates and controlling the labour market at a time of rapid inflation, while protecting the social hierarchy by suppressing competition and keeping people in their ordained places; but contained within it was a comprehensive restructuring of apprenticeship, the source of much labour and the origin of workers in skilled trades.

The genesis of the Act was the national concern over the numbers of 'masterless' vagabonds (often nothing more than unemployed people seeking work) who were appearing in large numbers in the towns. The Act sought to control these people by apprenticing adolescents in a trade for at least seven years. Since apprenticeship seldom began until the late teens, it meant in practice that a young man would not be free to rule himself or start a family until he was at least twenty-four, keeping him from 'the riotous and licentious life' to which young men are prone while giving his master his services for a time after he had become proficient.[50] Even apprentices on the farms had to be kept until age twenty-one, even though they could begin their apprenticeships as early as age ten.

Proof of the statute's draconian enthusiasm for social control was the provision that a young person could not refuse to be an apprentice if a householder of sufficient income demanded it. The justices of the peace were empowered to imprison the disobedient youth until he chose to submit. The Act was careful to forbid the apprenticing of young people of the 'wrong' social classes – children of persons worth less than three pounds a year could not be apprenticed in market towns, while those of parents who were not forty-shilling freeholders could not be apprenticed in cities and corporate towns – in order to ensure an adequate supply of agricultural labour and stop social climbing. One of the complaints often heard in those hard economic times was that men who did not belong were encroaching on the rightful trade of the craftsmen, taking bread out of their families' mouths. Moreover, by limiting access to skilled trades to people of substance it was hoped that gentlemen would give their younger sons a useful skill that would allow them to support themselves. The inability of young scions of the gentry to make a living, said one commentary, made gentlemen 'more mindful to gather for their children than to regard the state of the commonwealth'.[51]

Masters who disregarded the Act were to be fined ten pounds for taking illegal apprentices. The act was enforceable by *qui tam* actions – that is, private informers or 'promoters' could turn in offenders and be paid half the fine. Often this meant demanding protection money from the master rather than bringing a case in court, but that made the Act even more terrifying than if the legal fine was adhered to.

The impact of the Act, which also set wages, is hard to gauge since it codified what had been the standard practice in many parts of the country. In fact, it was a solution to tensions that had been growing as changing economic conditions altered the needs of employers and created stress between them and their employees. But for the young men who were eligible it formalized relations in a way that had not been done before and gave their masters greater coercive power, even while making it possible for them to appeal to the Justices against cruel masters.

Robert Miller, a 16-year-old apprentice tanner, discovered what the seven-year apprenticeship could mean when he had a quarrel with his master's wife in February 1563. She rebuked him for his work and he replied: 'I am sorry that I cannot please you, but if my service may not please you, if you and my Master will give me leave to depart I shall provide me of a service in some place, I trust.' She instantly went to her husband with her complaint. He called Miller in and told him that if he and his wife could not get along he was free to depart. Miller accepted the offer, but he was not as free as he thought. His master informed him that he would not let him leave the Hundred and proposed that he be bound as an apprentice in husbandry to one of two local farmers. The youngster protested: 'Master, I have served these three years in your occupation and can [know] no skill in husbandry and I will be loth to lose all this time that I have served in the occupation [of tanning].'

Miller was set to leave for Norwich to find a new job when his master offered him a new pair of shoes if he would stay until the next Sunday, which he agreed to do. But on Tuesday he discovered that a warrant had been issued to force him to work on the farms, so he fled to Norwich and apprenticed himself to another tanner. The catch was that he now had to bind himself for seven years, adding it to the three he had already served. When he met his old master at a fair the man jeered at him for having been caught in such a trap.[52]

Living as an intimate of his master's family might guarantee that the apprentice learned his trade, but it transfered all the troubles of adolescence away from his biological family and into the workshop.

When Simon Forman ran away from his mother after his father's death in 1564 he apprenticed himself to Matthew Commins of Salisbury, who 'used many occupations'. The terms of their agreement were that Forman would serve ten years, and that Commins would send him to school for three years. Forman learned to make and sell hosiery, and to sell cloth and hops, salt, oil, pitch, rosin, raisins, apothecary drugs and groceries.

Master and apprentice got along well, but young Simon fought with the other youngsters in the house and quarrelled with his master's wife. One of his great enemies was Jean Cole, the daughter of his mistress's sister, who Commins had taken in. Naturally his mistress favoured her in their quarrels.

She favoured Mary Roberts, a maid, too. The youngest of the four apprentices in the house, Simon was picked on by the others. Mary, he recalled, often hit him so hard the 'blood would run about his ears'. The bad blood between the two grew until one day, when Simon was in the shop alone, he turned the tables. They were busy and he needed Mary's help, but she refused. So he carefully shut the door and went after Mary with a yardstick. She attacked his ears, but he got the upper hand, beating her black and blue, leaving her 'crying and roaring like a bull'.

He was proud of his victory, but he was also frightened. If his mistress came home first he knew she would beat him. Luckily, Commins arrived from the garden ahead of his wife. He listened to both sides and then delivered a verdict, telling Simon he had his permission to beat her again if she refused to help in the shop. When Mistress Commins returned Mary howled out her complaint to her, sending her storming into the shop in full cry, but Master Commins prevented the beating she intended to give Simon. Simon recalled that after that he and Mary got along well, and that she often saw to it that he had butter for his breakfast.

Matthew Commins not only had to deal with combat in his house between his servants. Simon told of an episode in which he took on two boys who were throwing rocks and threatening their wares at a fair. The journeyman who was helping in the stall sent him out to stop them, but they taunted him and he 'being somewhat fearful, stood abashed' until the journeyman 'fleshed' him and convinced him to attack. He beat both of them, after which he 'would not shrink for a bloody nose with any boy'.

These combats were matched with another parental problem for the Commins family: young love. Simon, who chronicled his sexual adventures in later life with great care, was a shy boy but he attracted the attention of Anne Young, the daughter of a well-to-do townsman. She loved Simon 'wonderful well and would surely see him once a day, or else she would be sick'. She would come round and beg for Simon to be allowed to see her on holy days; she sought his company at 'pastimes'; and she would stand with Simon and his master and mistress whenever she could. Commins would often tease her: 'Mistress Anne, you love my boy well, methinks.' She did, but Simon did not love her in return – yet. But later she was a part of his life for many years.

Battles and young love could be met with worldly tolerance but it was different when Simon rebelled against his mistress. She had accused him of stealing flax from their market stall. Intending to beat him for it with a yardstick, 'as she was wont to do', she found, as her servant before her, that Simon could be dangerous. He seized the stick, shoved her behind a door and closed it on her. His master had no alternative but to beat him.

After the beating Simon declared that he was leaving. Commins had promised to send him to school, which he had not done, and so Simon had grounds for dissolving their contract. Commins gave him his indentures and told him he was free, 'At the which his mistress took on mightily and they all wept, some for joy and some for madness and rage.'[53]

Simon Forman had lost his father when he was eleven; his mother cared little for him, and he had to look after himself. If he had been the child of a man who had the freedom of a corporate town or of a man who owed feudal service to the Crown his life would have taken a different course. An orphan in a town was generally under the protection of the aldermen, who 'inherited' the children of freemen and were bound to care for them. In London and Bristol this was done through the Court of Orphans, an institution being copied by Exeter, Worcester, Northampton, Gloucester, Rye, Leicester, Newark-on-Trent and Lincoln in the 1560s.[54] An orphan of a man owing the Queen service became a ward of the court, governed by the Court of Wards. In either case, the property of the child was supposed to be managed on his or her behalf until majority or marriage ended the period of tutelage.

Given the strong odds that a child would be orphaned, parents had an interest in seeing to it that someone would protect their children in their minority, but there were other reasons for these courts. They made the property of the children available for use by others until they came into their own. Their charge was to take control of the orphans' estates so their property could be 'faithfully and justly kept without spoil or division . . . and . . . employed or disposed to the best use and profit' of the orphans.[55] The court took over the property, renting the real estate and lending out the money in order to generate an income to support the child without destroying his or her principal. They charged one to four per cent on the money lent, making it the cheapest money anywhere at a time when a loan normally cost between fifteen and thirty per cent, and lending at interest was illegal. Thus a comfortable cross between filial piety and sound capitalism was created. In theory everyone benefited, though sometimes the coffers of the court of orphans proved too tempting for the oligarchs who managed them.

The Court of Wards worked on a similar principle, but with less honour. There the guardianships of children of powerful people were sold to the highest bidders, who in turn tried to maximize their income from the children's property. Besides keeping the rents for themselves, the guardians might sell the child to a secondary market or marry him or her to the person of his choice – perhaps his own son or daughter, guaranteeing that the property came permanently into their own hands. There was a good market for wards, allowing the Crown the opportunity to sell them immediately rather than manage them itself.

In selling the wardship the Master of the Court of Wards – William Cecil for almost all the 1560s – estimated the annual revenue of the property, established the value of the 'exhibition' or child support the purchaser had to pay each year, and sold it for some multiple of the income. The price of the sale varied enormously as political and economic factors were taken into account on both sides. Sometimes the Queen made a gift of wardship to a mother or other relative, or to some favourite. When John Vaughan's father died in 1562 he inherited lands worth £16 9s. His mother was allowed to buy his wardship for the same amount, but she was bound to spend seven pounds a year on his support.[56]

Although the guardian had acquired control over property, he or she had also become responsible for the rearing and educating of the child. However, if the child had been purchased in order to make money the guardian had little incentive to take his or her responsibility seriously. It was popularly believed that wardship ruined the property built up by the father, so the child came out of his wardship with 'woods decayed, houses fallen down, stock wasted and gone, land let forth and plowed to the bare [sic]'. The only reason some guardians kept their wards alive, said Sir Thomas Smith, was for their own gain. If the child died before he had 'married his daughter, sister or cousin, for whose sake he bought him' his investment would be lost.[57] Of course Smith was right, in that the risk of purchasing a wardship lay in the mortality tables. If the child died before one recouped one's investment it was lost. On the other hand, a wardship was a possession that could be willed to one's heirs.

Not all children who became wards of the Crown suffered for it. If they were bought by a decent person, and especially if they became part of a great household with its schoolroom and opportunities for acquiring sophistication, their chances of marrying well and rising in the world may have been considerably improved. For instance, William

Cecil, Master of the Court of Wards, seems to have been a caring though strict guardian. When the young Earl of Oxford became his ward he devised a curriculum for him to follow in order to ensure that he was properly educated for his station in life.

Oxford's exercises in 1562 had him studying by seven a.m., learning dancing before breakfast and French, Latin, writing and drawing before lunch. Afternoons were devoted to 'cosmogrophie', Latin, French and exercising his pen. He attended the common prayers of the household twice a day, and on holy days he read the epistle of the day in French and the gospel in Latin, along with a commentary. The remainder of the day (after 4.30 p.m.) he was instructed to spend in riding, shooting, dancing, walking and other exercises – never forgetting to pray on schedule.[58]

Edward, Lord Beauchamp, the officially 'illegitimate' son of the Earl of Hertford and Katherine Grey, was also being raised beyond the control of his parents, but his education was rigorous. When he was nine he wrote to his father an account, in Latin, of his day's studies. On the evening of Friday, the fourth of February, he said his evening prayers, and then recited Xenophon's oration of Cyrus to the Homotimi. He does not make it clear if he did this in the original Greek, but certainly Greek was considered an important language for a child to learn. The next day he wrote a composition in imitation of Cicero (in Latin). He also told his father about his studies in geometry, sending him a copy of his working of a problem in calculating area. It used the question–response formula of the schools and was neatly illustrated with a diagram. Beauchamp's younger brother, Thomas Seymour, the fruit of his parents clandestine union in the Tower, informed his father (who wrote to him in French in 1571 when he was eight) that he was studying, among other things, the *Institutes* of the law from the *Corpus Iuris Civilis* and, mysteriously, 'things corporal' and 'things incorporal'.[59]

As in the basic skills education that many children received, this learning did not demand that the child learn 'critical thinking'. It assumed that the child should not be invited to think, but to imitate. The net effect of this kind of education by rote is summed up with intentional irony in the story of the Parrot in Thomas Blage's *School of Wise Conceits* (1569).

> A parrot dwelling in a king's court was asked of other birds, why she was so highly esteemed? Who answered, because I have learned to speak as a man.
> *Moral*: We must learn good and liberal sciences if we will be had in honour and estimation.[60]

This curriculum reflects what it was believed a gentleman of the upper classes needed in the way of an education. Beyond reading and writing English were the essential foreign languages, but within those languages was the entire world of humanistic learning. To learn Latin was to read the classics, so that the mere presence of the language in the curriculum meant that the student imbibed the civic humanism of Cicero and the didactic morality of Livy. Combined with religion, this knowledge of classical history and philosophy equipped the young man to become a member of the ruling classes, to enter a learned profession, and to exercise authority with dignity and gravity.

Moreover, it gave him the necessary intellectual shorthand for participating in the pan-European dialogue. The necessity of a knowledge of Roman language and law as the ground upon which policy discussion could rest is visible on all sides, as when Sir Thomas Smith tried to explain England to his French hosts. Rome became the control against which England was measured. Thus, when explaining the place of children in English society, Smith wrote 'Our children be not *in potestate parentum*, as the children of the Romans were: but as soon as they be *puberes*, which we call the age of discretion,' they can buy and sell land independently, 'and therefore *emancipatio* is clean superfluous.'[61] Although the book had been translated out of Smith's original Latin, these terms and concepts of Roman law were left in Latin, both because it was expected that the reader would understand them, and because they had exact legal meaning.

That this kind of multilingual discourse existed outside of books is proved by the debates in Parliament. There members not only used classical allusions freely, but seem to have used them in the original language. They also tended to quote the Bible in Latin, since well-educated people had read it in Latin. Thus Thomas Norton could tell his colleagues to remember the 'true old saying *quod dubitas ne feceris*, and for that *quod non ex fide est, peccatum est*'.[62]

The modern languages in the curriculum, which were French first and Italian second, had a different kind of use. They, especially Italian, gave English people access to the most sophisticated literature in Europe and made them useful as diplomats and merchants. After all, no foreigner could be expected to know English. By all accounts there was great enthusiasm for Italian literature in England in the 1560s, but among businessmen and merchants French was their first language, more important than Latin in dealing with other merchants. A trickle of textbooks appeared in England and abroad designed to help them learn the tongue. In 1563, for instance, there appeared in Antwerp *Familiar Communications no less proper than profitable to the English Nation desirous and needing the French Language*. It was explicitly aimed at merchants, factors and apprentices. Multilingual dictionaries made their appearance, too.[63]

Probably the most popular self-help guide to French was prepared by

Claudius Hollyband, a Huguenot refugee who moved to Lewisham and opened a school in which the children of tradesmen were taught French in large classes. His students learned through the 'natural' method of question and answer dialogues pioneered by the great humanist Juan Luis Vives in 1539 and used in schools across Europe. Hollyband published some of his dialogues in 1566 giving us a glimpse of his methods, which combined entertaining conversation with alternative vocabulary. In his dialogue 'In School' a boy is asked why he is tardy. The response, memorized in French by the students, was 'Master, I met him by the way which did leap, did slide upon the ice: which did cast snow: which fought with his fist, and balls of snow: which did scorge his top: which played for points, pins, cherry stones, counters, dice, cards.'

Meanwhile 'Tell Tale' Nicholas is whining to his master about another boy's sins: 'William hath spitted on my paper: torn my book: put out my theme: broken my girdle: trod my hat under his feet: marred my copy: spoken English.'

Later on the children have their school lunch, with ample instruction on etiquette built into the dialogue. They learned, in French, never to take their caps off at the table lest their hair fall in the food, not to pick their teeth with their pen knives or forks, never to lean on the table, and to scrape the ashes off their bread with their knives. Of course they had prayer in school, but the school also served them ale.[64]

The dramatic quality of Hollyband's dialogues make them a delight to read; perhaps they also taught children workable French. The alternative to buying one of these little (4 " x 2 ") books and studying at home was to travel abroad. Many young men did, either as apprentices learning their trades or as the sponsored sons of wealthy men who were being sent to acquire the polish of foreign languages and courts. These *Wanderjahre* were considered important experiences for apprentice courtiers, but they gave their fathers and guardians heartburn. To send a young man to the cultured lands of France and Italy meant exposing him to the devilish wiles of the Catholics who lived there, with their corrupt foreigner morality. The boy needed their languages and a knowledge of their lands, but Heaven protect him while he was acquiring them!

William Cecil's eldest son Thomas was sent to France to learn the language and see the world, leaving in May 1561, laden with paternal advice and accompanied by a tutor, Thomas Windebank. They were projected to spend a year on the continent, their destinations to be determined as time wore on. Sir William tried to run his son's life as he ran the kingdom, drawing up detailed instructions and demanding reports. At their parting he gave Thomas the kind of advice that Prince Hamlet would have recognized. While he was away Thomas was to

keep God before him in thought and word, praying every morning
in private on his knees and attending common prayer, using the
service of the Church of England in Latin. He should always pray
for preservation from the horrible sins and bodily harms that he
was prone to, and to pray from the heart. A year gave him enough
time to read the Psalter twelve times, the New Testament four times,
and the Old Testament once – and he should attend every sermon
preached by men who 'accord with our persuasion here'. He was
not supposed to eat or drink too much, or enjoy lewd, filthy tales
or 'enticements of lightness or wantonness of body', asking God for
forgiveness if he did. Sir William, as his earthly father, committed
him to his Heavenly Father, 'remitting you again by education of you
from childhood to this state wherein you are and from ignorance to
knowledge, to the hands of God from whom I have received you as
a gift.'

But the lecture was not over. He was to obey his tutor as if he was
his father. If he did not, he would call him home in shame. So he could
recall what he had observed, Sir William said, Thomas was to keep
a journal of his travels. Knowing Sir William as we do, he probably
wanted to see the journal, just as he told Thomas that he wanted to
see the annotations in his biblical commentaries that would prove that
he had studied them.[65]

At nineteen Thomas must have felt a great sense of liberation when
he took ship for France. His father's strictness and severity were
left behind in England and, as his distressed tutor's letters quickly
told, the young man was intent on having a good time. Despite his
father's intentions he was more interested in girls and theatricals than
improving his French. He wanted horses and fine clothes more than
he cared about education.

They took up their residence in Paris under the eye of ambassador
Sir Nicholas Thorckmorton and Sir William began receiving regular
reports on his son's activities – though Thomas himself, to his parents'
distress – seldom wrote (perhaps because Sir William insisted he should
only write in Latin or French and sent back his letters corrected). Sir
William chided him about this, ordering him to include messages to his
stepmother whenever he wrote.[66] With Windebank, Throckmorton, the
employees of the embassy, foreign ambassadors and several merchants
reporting on Thomas' behaviour we have a clear picture of how he
spent his time, and of his father's stern anger about it.

Sir William already knew his son was slow to rise, a spendthrift,
careless in his dress and a gambler who did not care for study, but
he hoped maturity and travel would cure these things. Meanwhile he
ordered Windebank to report his son's behaviour. If he continued in
such a dissolute life he would be brought home.[67] Thomas, on the other

Figure 12 Sir William Cecil in the 1560s. By or after Arnold von Brounckhorst.

hand, expressed his wide-eyed enthusiasm for Paris in postcard length letters written in stiff Latin and clumsy French. In one he wrote that he was sightseeing more than studying, admiring the beautiful buildings, and listening to famous men without saying where, which or who. The most interesting thing he had done was to go with Ambassador Throckmorton to a nobleman's house where they saw (a 'thing rare and unheard of!') the terrible combat of three dogs against a lion. The dogs won. After that burst of excitment he concluded, 'Nothing more occurs to me to write at this time.'[68]

He had other causes of excitement, however. He was spending money quickly, breaking into Windebank's chest to get more when he needed it.[69] And, in spite of all the watchers, he was conducting a seduction. By April 1562 it was becoming clear, as Windebank told Sir William, that his 'inordinate affection' was transporting him towards a young gentlewoman living in an abbey near Paris. Windebank urged him to write Thomas and warn him against this 'since she is a maid, and her friends will hardly bear the violating of her'.[70]

That was the version Windebank sent his employer. To Nicholas Throckmorton he was more open: Thomas had seduced a nun with a promise of marriage. Luckily for him, the promise had not been made before witnesses, even though she had urged him to get some Englishmen to witness it. Unluckily her brother knew about it and they had to get him out of France 'lest the friends of the nun should seek the performance of his promise'. Apparently the girl was not actually a nun, but in an abbey school, but that meant that a marriage was a possibility and Thomas was depressed by the thought of having to fulfil his promise.[71] So he and Windebank fled France secretly.

Sir William was increasingly outraged. Like a father in melodrama he postured and roared. One of his letters to Thomas, dictated to a secretary rather than written in his own hand, was signed, 'Your father of an unworthy son.'[72] To Windebank he wrote: 'I am here used to pains and troubles, but none creep so near my heart as does this of my lewd son . . . The shame that I shall receive to have so unruled a son grieves me more than if I lost him by honest death.' 'I could best be content,' he continued, if Thomas was secretly 'committed to some sharp prison.'[73] Too embarrassed to have his son in England, he asked Windebank to take him into Germany 'for indeed the wound is yet too green for me to behold him'.[74]

Thomas's year abroad was turning into an exile. December 1562 found him in Strasbourg begging his father to let him return to France to see the war over religion beginning there and asking that his past follies be forgiven.[75] Unbeknown to him events at home had conspired to move him back into his father's affection. Sir William scribbled a note to Windebank on 15 December:

Windebank, I am so tired with writing that I must write to you but words . . . My young son is dead, and I have no more but your charge there. Fain I would he see Italy and loath to object [*sic*] to hazard. God do his will with him. Fare well good Windebank; and direct him as you think best. I thank you for your good letters.

Your Loving Master, William Cecil[76]

Polonius' mask had slipped. Although Sir William was a scrupulous, demanding father he still cared about 'lewd' Thomas. He brought him home in January 1563 and gave him a seat in the Parliament of 1563. In 1564 he gave him Dorothy Latimer, daughter of Lord Latimer, for a wife and his travelling days ended.

Thomas Cecil had already been to Cambridge before he went to the continent, making him one of the tiny elite who had attended one of the nation's two universities. Like most Elizabethan institutions, the universities were caught in the confusion caused by the successive waves of religious change. Essentially religious institutions designed for training clergy, they had seen their teachers purged and their coffers raided. New colleges had been founded by pious men of both Catholic and Protestant persuasions, so that even the foundations' charters could put them at odds with the government. As we have seen, the visitation of 1559 had paid careful attention to them, and there would be a slow leaking away of dons during the 1560s as Catholics were removed or decided to flee. Ardent Protestant dons disrupted the colleges with their radical teaching, too, so that Oxford and Cambridge were in a period of exciting ferment.

At Oxford new statutes governing degrees were passed in 1565, tightening the standards that had been relaxed under Edward VI, but this made it so uninviting to take a bachelor in theology degree that it seriously compounded the shortage created by the purges. There was, the Lady Margaret Professor of Theology remarked in 1565, a 'remarkable scarcity of doctors'.

These new statutes, like so many other reforms of the decade, had been made in part to create a new Protestant world by bringing the rules governing the University into agreement with the new religion. With the conservatism so characteristic of universities the new rules simply redefined some terms. Where the candidates were ordered by the old statutes to lecture in Latin on Peter Lombard's *Sentences*, a Roman Catholic biblical commentary much despised by the reformers, the new statutes instructed that all references to the *Sentences* be construed to mean 'a book of Holy Scripture'.[77]

The life of a serious student in one of the universities was arduous. Robert Jones, who had gone up to Trinity Hall, Cambridge in 1563 as a mature student felt, like most 'non-traditional' students, that he had to work hard to make up for lost time, and he worked harder than most students by his own admission, but he gives us a taste of the curriculum. Jones rose at four or before every morning, praying and doing light reading until five. From five until six he read the *Digests* of the civil law; from six to seven he attended lectures on the *Institutes*. From seven until eight he read glosses on the civil law, followed by a lecture on the *Digests*, which he 'diligently' heard and wrote down. In order to refresh himself after all that law he spent from nine until ten reading either Terence or Cicero to his boy. The rest of the morning he spent dining, talking or playing the lute.

After lunch he revised and then went to the Schools to hear a disputation. The late afternoon was given over to Cicero, Livy or 'some French story' (he was fluent in French already). The hour from four until five was reserved for reading in the law. After supper he practised Latin conversation with his acquaintances. 'You see,' he wrote a friend, 'that though I may seem to have great leisure yet I have no more than is requisite.'[78]

III

Very few boys had the opportunity for the breadth of education received by Thomas Cecil or Robert Jones. What would Simon Forman have done with the chance to go to Cambridge, attend an inn of court, and travel with a private tutor like Thomas did? But boys, literate and illiterate, shared another form of education. They learned to be male. In a society with very clear ideas about the differences between male and female roles this education came through example, but it gave their world rigid boundaries. Thomas Whythorne helps us understand the way in which boys were taught to view women in order to learn how to use their authority over them, and how to avoid the silken snares women laid in their paths.

Equipped with a mind that gathered proverbs like lint, Whythorne lists those he heard used by his acquaintances in Oxford and London about women when he was a young man first confronting his attraction to women. The resulting compound of folk wisdom, classical pronouncements and biblical observations had at is base fears of sexual sin, loss of authority, loss of autonomy and loss of honour reminiscent of Rabelais' search to avoid being cuckolded in *Gargantua and Pantagruel*. What Whythorne heard from his friends was mostly proverbial, and many of their warnings against women are familiar to men in English-speaking cultures today, just as they were to Roman men.

First of all, women are, he was told again and again, false, fickle and manipulative. Proverbially a man should 'like all women, but love none of them; 'laugh and be merry with them, but love them not, for they be like unto pitch and tar, the which one cannot handle very much, but his hands shall be defiled therewith.' They entice men and then torture them with their fickle, grasping natures. 'A woman's first enticing will give a man cause to love them, so will they after trifling, and misdeeming force him to undo it again.' 'Yea,' said another, 'they be as slippery as eels, and will turn as the wind and weathercock.' Finding a wife who could be trusted was as hard as finding an eel in a barrel of snakes blindfolded. One of Whythorne's friends quoted Chaucer's Wife of Bath: 'Deceit, weeping and spinning was given to women from the beginning.'

Their deceitfulness explained why they were generally the opposite of what they appeared to be. Though they were the weaker vessel, one woman's lust could overcome two, three or four men, they were so sly. The proof of both their lecherous, proud hearts and their subtley was how they 'deck and attire themselves so flaunting and gloriously like peacocks, together with their paintings [make-up] and frowsing of their hair'. A man must beware their beauty if he was to escape destruction at their hands, for as Plutarch said: 'It is a thing most sweet, and most joyous to behold beautiful persons, but to touch and lead them with the hand is perilous.'

Some men, went the tales, were so besotted and controlled by their wives that they accepted their adultery and tyranny rather than have them carted and whipped or set in the cucking stool. Whythorne, reflecting on this, thought he might do the same, since the shame and ignominy of having one's wife's misdeeds publicly proclaimed would be too great. Better to turn a blind eye.

As a young fellow hearing these warnings, Whythorne recalled, they pleased him very much. And they confirmed his own bashfulness – a trait probably acquired from lack of acquaintance with women, raised as he was by his celibate priest uncle in Oxford. Reflecting on his fear of women, he concluded that it was a good thing. It protected him from the moral decay and 'horrible, filthy, and incurable' disease that followed those who carelessly pursued sex – syphilis was rampant in the sixteenth century.

Whythorne credited his bashful nature and these warnings against women with saving him from 'the evils that I might have gotten by the following and keeping company with *Venus* darlings'. For when he remembered the proverbs about them it caused him 'to give no heed to the allurements, enticements and snares of women, and if I did spy them, yet I would despise and shun them as much as I might'. The cautionary wisdom encouraged him to strive with his frail nature 'for I must confess that I am not made of sticks or stones, but even of the self-same metal that other men be made of, and for that I would not lose the late liberty and freedom that I had gotten'.[79]

Male folklore, biblical warnings against sexual temptation and the misogyny of classical authors all made the same point: a man had to beware becoming enslaved to a woman and used for her own ends. He must be careful not to lose his independence and even his soul by answering the siren songs of sex and beauty. Whythorne, and presumably most of his fellows, knew that these strictures did not apply to particular women, but until they found the 'right' one, the one that was not like other women, they had to be careful.

Women, of course, were receiving a similar education. They were being taught to fear and mistrust men's intentions just as much as men were taught to fear and mistrust their intentions, but with one important difference. They had to learn to obey and fear men as they obeyed and feared the Lord, while guarding their virtue from the assaults of men who had no virtue in order to protect the honour of themselves and their husbands. Of course if they lost their honour before marrying they might never have a husband. It was so important that a woman's honour was considered in law to have economic value, which gave her the right to sue in order to protect it. If she lost it through libel she deserved to be paid damages to replace potential income lost with the chance for a good marriage.

This placed the protection of honour at the heart of what girls were taught. Presumably they learned to protect themselves from men in the same way men learned to beware women, but since they were under the tutelage of men their educations in sexual politics were more overt. They learned to value honour from parents who had to find them husbands, they learned it from the clergy, and they learned it from their teachers and role models. In a negative way they learned it through their friends – the Tudor word 'gossip' meaning a close friend – who pronounced judgement on one another, helping to reinforce men's expectations of women.

Grace Mildmay, né Sherington, reflecting on her education in the 1550s and 1560s at the end of her long life, wrapped her reminiscences in didactic meditations on the Bible but left us a picture of how a girl's mind was formed in a wealthy home. Her role model was a cousin on her father's side who had been raised by her own mother and had become her governess. She was 'very religious, wise and chaste, and all good virtues that might be in a woman were constantly in her'. She was smart, too, educated enough that could set her mind down in writing 'as well as most men could have done', and she had a good knowledge of medicine and surgery. A witty woman, Grace and her sister loved her.

The lessons they learned from this governess helped guide Grace's life. She scoffed at dalliance, idle talk and wanton behaviour and was so concerned to keep her charges from falling into immoral ways that she

> counselled us when we were alone, so to behave our selves as if all the world did look upon us, and to do nothing in secret whereof our conscience might accuse us, and by any means to avoid the company of servingmen, or any other of like disposition, whose ribald talk, idle gestures, and evil suggestions were dangerous for our chaste ears and eyes to hear and behold, lest the innocence and virginity of our tender hearts should be stained thereby.

She advised the girls to deal honestly in matters great or small, to avoid gossip, and to hear much and speak little, 'seeming to be ignorant in some things rather than to boast of the knowledge which we have not'.

The curriculum Grace followed under the direction of this lady was rigorous. She had to cipher with her pen, practising accounting. She had to write 'supposed' letters of various kinds. At times she had to study medicine by reading in Dr Turner's herbal or in Vigo's books on surgery and health.[80] In lighter moments she had to sing songs and work with her needle. Idleness was impermissible.

When she was away from her governess the good woman would be on her heels, checking on where and with whom she was and what she did and said. If she did not approve of her companions she warned her about them. One gentlewoman who frequented the house was marked down as improper company because she was 'of a subtle spirit, full of words and questions, and of an undermining disposition, a busybody, and a meddler in matters which concerned her not'. To be seen with her was to bring into question one's own reputation, so Grace was supposed to avoid her, even though this lady often sought her company.

Observing that two of their guests, a married man and a married woman not married to each other, were impudent in their behaviour together, the governess taught Grace a lesson against licentiousness by helping her compose a ditty on it.

In the battle for chaste deportment anything could be the Devil's prybar so the governess warned her about accepting gifts, such as a book in which might be written words 'whereby I might betray myself unawares'. Gloves and apples given by admirers were also suspect, 'for that wicked companions would ever present treacherous attempts.' In time, Grace noted, she found this to be true, but she does not tell the story.

Her governess's aim was to ensure that she always had a modest eye, a chaste ear, a silent tongue and a considerate heart. Wary and heedful of herself and all her actions, Grace was sent 'furnished into the world'.

The governess was carrying out the instructions of Grace's parents. Her father had very pronounced opinions on female propriety. He 'could not abide' to see a a woman who lacked a demure carriage and comely countenance. He liked them graceful, pretty and well behaved. These outward signs of a virtuous disposition drove away wicked men and attracted the respect of good men. He was also of the belief that a woman seen with evil companions could not have any virtue in her. Censured by all good men, she would come to destruction.

To ensure that no lewd companions had access to his children he fired servants who did not meet his standards. Her father scourged one young man 'naked from the girdle upwards, with fresh rods, for making but a show . . . of a saucy and unreverent behaviour towards us his children'. Grace noted piously that the girls could not stand the lad because they had been taught to detest all shows of evil from their tenderest youths.

Lady Grace Mildmay ended her reverie on her childhood with the observation that parents have much to answer for before God if they neglect their duty in raising children. The children will be spoiled and the parents will suffer for it unless the youngsters are brought to God and taught to forsake the vanities and follies of the world.[81]

Of course parents then and now could only do so much in preparing their children for life. Spoiled or not, children and the adults they became faced a hostile natural environment. In the 1560s parents high and low were faced with the hidden dangers of disease, famine and violence which threatened life with unpredictable regularity. Sent by God for their sins, these calamities often struck the innocent more mightily than the guilty, but they sent everyone searching from religious, legal and medical remedies.

9

Carpe Diem

I

In July 1564 news came from France that two men had been hanged in Lyon, part of a gang suspected of smearing the 'matter and villainy' that ran from plague sores onto people's door latches and door rings. Opening their doors they would catch the plague and die, murdered in revenge for their inhumane abandonment of the sick. After the hangings the bourgeoisie of Lyon could be seen purifying their latches, smeared with something like old grease, with burning wisps of straw.[1]

The Englishman who made this report suspected that the story was invented out of fear in the face of the plague, a fear that English people knew well. The decade between 1555 and 1565 was the worst in the century for disease. Blaming the spread of the disease on gangs of criminal poor would not surprise English people, either, since England in the mid century was racked with fear of vagrants, masterless criminals who wandered the country committing crimes. But of course the thrill of fear, horror and disgust the story evokes makes it entertaining as well. For some perverse reason people have always enjoyed contemplating terrible events from a distance, perhaps because entertainment is a way of mitigating the grimness of life. Elizabethan poets summed up the unpredictability of life and the necessity of enjoying every day with pithy advice: *carpe diem*.

Sudden death and suffering made people in the 1560s acutely aware of how few days they might have. It is estimated that 6 per cent of the English population died in the epidemics of 1556–9. In the famine that followed the disastrous harvests of 1555 and 1556 'burning fevers', 'spotted fevers', and typhus spread over the country, softening it for the deadly punch of the influenza epidemic of 1558–9. Striking at all classes all over the country these diseases were in general more deadly than outbreaks of the plague, which usually struck the poor more than the rich and was more particular in its geographic concentrations.[2]

Plague, however, was a more public way of dying than influenza, and in 1563 there was the worst outbreak of the century. It struck with such force that whole families and neighbourhoods were decimated, making it a political problem. Civic leaders and the royal government had to face not only the disease itself, but the repercussions of the pestilence as it disrupted community life. The beast was always lurking among the rats in the walls, and with the coming of each summer came the spectre of plague. As the heat increased so did the danger. As infected people moved from place to place the disease spread. Fear ran before the illness, calling for tough laws to prevent the infected from moving among the healthy.

By the 1560s responses to plague were well established in the popular, medical and civic minds. Three hundred years of close communion with its various forms had given people explanations and responses so that when it struck the besieged English army in Newhaven in 1563 people knew what to do and what could not be done.

The troops in Newhaven [Le Havre] had been sent to aid the Huguenots in their fight against Catholic France in October of 1562 only to find that their allies made common cause with their enemies against them, bottling them up in the port town. All through the winter and spring the Earl of Warwick and his men held the attackers at bay. Short of food and munitions, sleeping in their armour, they held the town. The men, Warwick reported, 'fight like Hectors, labour like slaves, are worse fed than peasants, and are poorer than common beggars', but the French by themselves could not break into the town. Plague could. On 7 June 1563 Warwick reported to the Privy Council that a disease had appeared 'whereof nine died this morning and many before very suddenly'.[3]

Meanwhile the government was struggling to raise more troops and supplies. Running past the French guns to supply Newhaven was dangerous, but without food and reinforcements defeat was inevitable. Throughout the country magistrates were receiving orders for more men to be sent.

William Stanton collected the money raised in St Margaret, Westminster, for equipping and transporting the twelve new men supplied by the parish to the Queen's army at Newhaven and for paying the wages of the men pressed in June. Two hundred twenty-three parishioners contributed two to four shillings apiece to the effort and the men were sent to risk the French guns and take the places of the dead and the maimed, the victims of plague and the shot.[4]

In Newhaven itself the siege was tightening. In early July French pioneers dug a new trench closer to the port and began building

Figure 13 A broadside in the tradition of the Medieval danse macabre, teaching that Death, and his minstrel Sickness, is coming for everyone (1569).

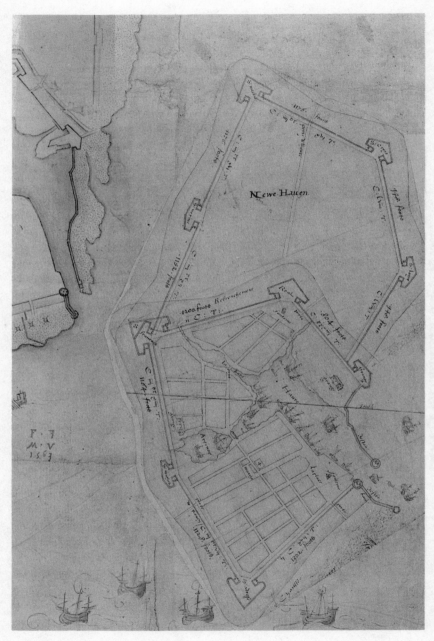

Figure 14 A map of the fortifications at Newhaven during the seige of 1563.

a new gun mount. Several hundred women were employed in the construction, bringing in bundles of wood to increase the height of the gun platform. Once it was done it would threaten the ships in the harbour.

Meanwhile other works had crept so close to the town that shots from small arms were striking the defenders.[5] Warwick lacked pioneers to build counter works and the plague was biting harder and harder. By mid-July the garrison was losing a hundred a day by death and double that number by sickness. Food was desperately short, especially biscuits, since the flour mills had been lost and the ovens destroyed by the shelling. Besides, most of the bakers were dead from the plague.[6]

On 11 July the Council was informed that the men were dying so fast that no one had time to bury them. Warwick feared that the plague would reduce his remaining 1,500 men to 300 within ten days unless reinforcements came.[7] By late July the French guns were covering the haven and Warwick's men were almost out of food. Pleading desperately for bread and beer he complained bitterly that the reinforcements he was getting were unskilled. The raw countrymen could not handle the arquebuses and the veterans were almost all dead. The carpenters he had been sent turned out to be unskilled in their supposed trade, but that mattered little. Within two weeks they were all either dead or sick. As the French trenches crept nearer and nearer and the plague raged in the town it became increasingly clear that an assault would be unnecessary. Plague would take the town for France.[8]

By the last of the month Newhaven was lost. Its defences were in tatters, its defenders were decimated and starving. Out of bread and beer the troops were threatening mutiny from hunger. Warwick, wounded in the thigh defending a breach, had no choice but to surrender the town.[9] The army in Newhaven was allowed an honourable withdrawal by the French, but their other enemy was already waiting to attack them when they returned to England. The plague had come home with men invalided out and by early July was making itself felt in London.

On 3 July Lord Mayor Thomas Lodge ordered 200 blue crosses made and distributed to the aldermen to mark the doors of houses in which there was plague. By 6 July he had to order another 200 crosses made 'with speed' as the plague burgeoned.[10] The custom of marking infected houses with the blue cross and a sign pleading 'Lord Have Mercy Upon Us' was well established, based on the contagion theory of the plague.

Those who subscribed to this theory believed that the disease was spread by human contact. Therefore they sought to keep people away from one another. Experience had proved that the plague was most virulent in crowded towns, and especially in the poorest parts, where the people were crammed together. William Bullein said the people most likely to catch the fever pestilence were those sluttish beastly people, that keep their houses and lodgings unclean, their meat, drink, and clothing more noisome, their labour and travail immoderate, or to them which lack provident wisdom to prevent the same by good diet, air, medicine, etc. and these bodies do infect other clean bodies, and whereas many people do dwell in heaps together . . .

The other popular theory was the miasmatic one, which held that infected air caused the disease. The Roman physician Galen had advanced this theory, arguing that some people's life-styles made them susceptible. Avicena had expanded upon it in his book on the fever pestilence. When putrefied vapours, carried, perhaps, by the wind from plague graves, battlefields, dead cattle, or stinking fens met with clean air they corrupted it, causing the pestilence. It could also be taken in through the pores when a person ate too much, made love, bathed, worked hard or did anything that made him or her sweat.

The most dangerous time of the year for plague was harvest time; the safest the spring. An approaching epidemic was often heralded by eclipses of the sun and moon, but it was certainly induced by the meteorological changes that came in September with its cold nights and hot days. Another sure sign of a coming plague, said William Bullein, was a food shortage (like the bad harvest of 1562).[11]

Following these theories the authorities sought to purify the air, cleanse the streets and keep infected people away from the healthy.

On 9 July the Queen ordered every London householder to lay a fire in his or her street or lane and light it at seven in the evening 'that they should thereby consume the corrupt airs, which otherwise might infect the city with the plague'. They were instructed to do this three times each week.[12] At the same time the aldermen began cleaning the streets. The bailiff of Finsbury received his blue crosses along with an order to remove the filthy dunghill in the highway near Finsbury Court.[13]

The churches were cleansed and their windows opened to let out the bad air, and the Mayor instructed that the 'pits and graves' for the plague victims should be properly sealed so 'no manner of evil exhalation or air may . . . break out'. Orders were issued to prevent the airing of the clothing and bedding of victims in public air.[14] Believing that dogs spread plague the Mayor appointed a dog killer to dispose of any running loose.[15]

The Queen's ministers knew the source of the infection and immediately after Newhaven surrendered, before any of the troops had returned, the Queen issued a proclamation informing the country that they had been defeated by the hand of Almighty God who sent the plague. She warned her subjects against associating with the soldiers. The men who had fought for Queen and country were pariahs and the people should 'forbear for some season to be conversant' with them.

This did not mean that they were to be neglected. Elizabeth 'earnestly' required in God's name that the magistrates

> provide some remote places where the same poor and sick persons [soldiers] may be separated from conversation with other beings whole, and have relief by common provision and alms to be ministered and given by the richer. Which, beside that Christian charity requireth it, the same is also requisite and expedient to be done by them which be whole and rich for their own preservation, for otherwise they may feel the sharp hand of God over them for their unmercifulness.[16]

Nonetheless, the survivors who were traveling back to their home parishes carried the plague along the roads and it began to appear in the countryside as well as in London. Along with them came a stream of people leaving London, heeding the old German proverb about the plague recalled by Bishop Grindal: 'fly quickly, fly far off, return late.' [17]

The belief that contact with other people spread the disease led, in February 1564, to the banning of all 'interludes and stage plays'. Bishop Grindal explained that nothing was more likely to have kept the contagion raging than the 'practice of an idle sort of people, which have been infamous in all good commonweals; I mean these *histriones*, common players'. There daily productions drew many young people who were infected. Besides, the players were irreverent and 'God's word by their impure mouths is profaned and turned into scoffs'.[18] Any Londoner staging a public performance could be imprisoned because 'the great and frequent confluences, congregations and assemblies of great numbers and multitude of people pressed together in small rooms' was very dangerous.[19]

When the bonfires began on 9 July the weekly toll of plague victims in London and its suburbs was forty-four, up from twenty-three the week before. Three weeks later the weekly toll had reached 289. In the last week of August the weekly toll was 963. In the last week of September the weekly body count was 1828. It was not until the first week of January 1564 that the weekly death count fell below one hundred again, to the jubilation of the citizens.[20] By the time it ended in April as many as one in five of London's people had died.[21] At its height the deaths came so thickly that the aldermen abandoned their attempts at marking infected houses. Thomas Cooper recalled that 'the citizens were crossed away so fast, that at length they were fain to leave their crosses and to refer the matter to God's good merciful hands'.[22] Henry Machyn was an early victim. His invaluable diary ends on 8 August 1563, just after he recorded the return of troops from Newhaven.[23]

When the sickness struck it struck hard. William Bullein said victims swooned and vomited yellow choler, their stomachs swelled and they broke into a stinking sweat. In intense pain, they boiled with fever. Their heads ached, their noses bled and their voices changed. Some went into feverish deliriums. As the poison air was drawn into their hearts by their arteries their blood, putrefying in the feverish heat, swelled into buboes or carbuncles. The appearance of these lumps was a sign that death was imminent and that they were past helping.[24]

In the presence of massive, rapid death people turned to personal reform, medicine, government and religion for protection. Physicians, applying their Galenic theories, advised that people avoid bad air and get into a good soil. If one could not escape the infected area it was recommended that one use a diet that drew from the body superfluous moisture, diminishing hot and dry humours. This meant eating tart food, sharpened with vinegar. Consumption of wine was to be reduced and pottage, milk and green fruits were to be avoided, along with hot spices, dates, honey, sweet meats and wine with sugar.

Along with the diet a person was urged, with unintentional irony, to avoid worry, 'specially the passion called fear'. By drawing blood to the heart worry increased the risk of infection. Making love and bathing were forbidden because they opened the pores and let in the disease, as was hard work. Following this same logic it was urged that one be bled every month, giving four ounces of blood.

It was important to keep a quiet mind so music, pleasant stories and good food helped. A clean room lit with a soft fire, clean clothes, perfumes and 'no privies close to hand' was prescribed, too. Lastly, south winds and mists were to be avoided so one's south windows had to be kept shut.[25]

Along with these improvements in life-style it was recommended that people take plague medicines, either triacles, pills or powders. The medical books are full of recipes for these. William Bullein's plague pill consisted of:

> 2 oz. yellow aloe
> 1 oz. myrrh
> 1 oz. saffron
> Beat together, add sweet wine, and make a pill, taking one daily.

A powder against the plague could be made by grinding together the leaves of *dictamnus albus* ['burning bush'], gentian, bittony, pimpernel, aloe, myrrh, saffron, mastic, ammoniac and clay. This was mixed into four to six spoons full of rose or sorrel water, and drunk in time of danger.

The most popular treatments turned around the ancient triacles described by Galen. Theriaca 'of the making of Andromachus', also called the 'Great Triacle'; triacle salt; and the *antidotari* of Mithridatis. Mithridatium was a key ingredient in plague remedies. Generally imported from Venice (though William Turner claimed London apothecaries could make it) it contained opium, rue and vipers' flesh among other things, making a bitter, nasty compound that may have relieved some symptoms because of the virtues of both the opium and rue.[26] Rue was one of the ingredients in 'four thieves' vinegar' which supposedly was drunk as a prophylactic by robbers who plundered plague victims. Rue was also an active constituent of Thomas Gale's *aquae balsami*. Soaked with wormwood, marigolds and other bitter leaves in pure rain water for three days it became a plague remedy.[27]

The poor, who could hardly afford to buy theriaca, could fall back on drinking bitter syrups of violets, sorrel, endive or sour lemons mingled with borage water. Or, as some physicians recommended, they could drink their own urine.[28] All of these remedies depended on the theory that hot, dry humours caused the plague and had to be decreased.

As desperate people searched for medical help against the disease they became the victims of charlatans – though the expensive physicians with their medical degrees offered very little more than psychological solace. The inefficiency of most medical remedies was recognized in a collection of remedies copied out between 1564 and 1569. Its medicine against plague is another mixture: 'Take a pound of good hard penance, and wash it well with the water of your eyes . . .'[29]

Of course penance was prescribed. Since God sent the scourge of plague God could take it away if He was convinced that people had repented. The special prayers instituted by the Church in 1563 for relief from the plague were accompanied by a special homily 'Concerning the Justice of God'.

Written by Alexander Nowell, it minced no words about the people's sin. Like a loving father God tried to entice people to righteousness, only threatening violence in order to convince them to repent their evil ways. When they refused, however, he had to punish them for their own good, smiting his 'most stubborn and rebellious servants' with the rod of correction. If therefore people gave over their wickedness the Lord would relieve them of their terror. 'For if, as God by affliction goeth about, as our heavenly schoolmaster, to teach us thus to flee from sin, and to follow righteousness . . . so we . . . do well learn the same.' Then 'we shall not need much to fear this plague . . . '.[30]

Just who God's anger was punishing was open to interpretation. Preaching at Paul's Cross in January 1564 before an enforced audience of the Lord Mayor, the aldermen and the members of the livery companies, Archdeacon Cole said that the plague was caused by the 'superstitious religion of Rome . . . so much favoured by the citizens.' If they did not turn away from this false religion, he warned them, God would send fire and sword as his next plague, slaying children at their mother's breasts. Cole fared better than one Baldwin who preached at the Cross that a gallows should be set up and all the Catholics hung: Baldwin himself died of the plague a week later.[31]

The fear and confusion that entered individual homes and hearts in plague time was made worse by the disruption of civil society it caused. The fear of crowds led the authorities to close the law courts as well as to quarantine houses and the shops they contained. In September 1563 Elizabeth announced that to preserve her loving subjects from the danger of the pestilence she was canceling Michaelmas term in the law courts at Westminster, delaying all the business of the courts of Chancery, Star Chamber, Exchequer, Wards and Liveries, and the Duchy of Lancaster until Hilary term. Unfortunately the plague had not abated by December so Elizabeth adjourned Hilary term, which begins in early January, to Hertford Castle.

Even though they had moved out of the city the courts attracted large numbers of people, many of whom had been exposed to the infection. Accordingly Elizabeth ordered that any infected person, or anyone who had plague in his or her house, had to inform the authorities of their situation and carry a white rod one yard in length wherever they went. All officials in the area were warned that they must take steps to see to it that a *cordon sanitaire* was maintained for eight miles around the Castle.

Although litigations were suspended and then moved, no one owing money to the Crown could use the plague as an excuse for non-payment. Instead the receipt of the Exchequer and those of the other courts were exiled up the Thames to the former nunnery at Sion.[32]

The court terms had to be adjourned again in 1569 and 1570 because of outbreaks of plague.

Elizabeth and her Court fled to Windsor in September 1563. There a new pair of gallows were built in the market square to hang anyone who came from London. Even passing up or down the river through Windsor could be punished by hanging without benefit of a trial.[33] The leaders of society were cut-off from one another by the fear of contact. Bishop Grindal of London wrote to William Cecil in July 1563 'Because some have died lately near my house here I dare not come to the court to speak with you.'[34]

In the 1569 epidemic the Court entered into a slightly less draconian protective quarantine. No one was allowed to enter Windsor or Eton, where the Court was, who had been in London or its suburbs. Nor could any goods be imported from London. Inhabitants of Windsor going to London could not return. Access to the Court itself was by special warrant only, and even messengers could not enter until they had received special permission. The Knight Marshal and his men were watching the roads between Windsor and London, empowered to arrest people attempting to pass between them. Anyone who broke the quarantine could be imprisoned and 'whipped and punished like a common vagabond'.[35]

The quarantining of the Court, the adjournment of the law courts and the evacuation of the Exchequer meant was that the national government had abandoned its capital city and nearly stopped conducting business. When the Exchequer moved it moved its employees, too, disrupting a source of London income and inconveniencing hundreds.

The flight of the royal government left the leaders of London to deal with the plague on their own, but they were no more willing to face the plague than the Queen. In August 1563 the London Court of Aldermen, the City's legislative council, ceased to meet because of the absence of 'a great number of my masters the aldermen from the said city, for the eschewing of the great danger and peril of the said plague yet fiercely reigning'.[36] By October the contagion was so bad that the corporate feast of the officers of the livery companies in the Guildhall had to be cancelled.[37]

Most of the civic actions taken during the plague were attempts to protect the healthy from the sick; once people fell ill they could expect little help from church or government. Even though the price of food skyrocketed as the plague kept frightened farmers and merchants from delivering food and the usual outlets were disrupted, few parishes had the will or the money to help those who could not help themselves. The London parishes in 1563-4 hired extra gravediggers and bought copies of the official prayer against plague, but they did not increase their expenditures on poor relief. The suffers were left to depend on individual charity, just like the returning soldiers. By contrast the Dutch church in London hired physicians, collected money for the care of members who caught the disease, and appointed people to visit them.[38]

The plague scenes acted out in London in 1563-4 were repeated around southern England as the infection moved slowly into Reading, Salisbury, Bristol, Exeter and Worcester, and smaller towns and villages, finally petering out in 1565. In 1569-70 the plague arrived in Newcastle, probably carried there on a coal boat. Exeter suffered, too.

In any place touched by the plague economic and social disruption followed. Certainly the suffering of southern England in 1563-4 deepened the economic crisis that had already begun. Among other things epidemics created labour shortages. After the terrible years of 1558-9 the annual enrolment of apprentices in London almost doubled; after the plague of 1563 the enrolments were 30 per cent over the average, pointing to a heavy loss of apprentices from death or flight.[39]

Archdeacon Cole, preaching at the end of the epidemic, called on the citizens to rejoice because life was returning to normal, expatiating on the ways plague had disrupted economic life:

now should the lawyers be frequented and set a[t] work, now shall the schools be opened, now should the merchants have free traffic into all countries and nations, where as before all nations did abhor them, now shall you artificers rejoice, for you shall now sell your wares abundantly, and now shall you be set a[t] work even thoroughly, where as of long time you have had no work but lived in great penury. Now, O you artificers, shall you make money abundantly. O you apprentices rejoice, for now shall you have your bellies full of meat, which of long time have been starved through your masters scarcity.[40]

II

The chances of dying of bubonic plague were high if one was poor and lived in a crowded urban parish, but there were plenty of other diseases to worry about if one was so inclined. Among the common ones were smallpox, syphilis, flux, typhus, diphtheria, tuberculosis, ague and new ague (probably influenza), and the sweating sickness. Health was a constant problem for most people and the illnesses they were most accustomed to were chronic ones that brought pain and inhibited their activities without killing them.

Sore eyes, stomach-aches, the burning pain of kidney stones, colds, coughs, chilblains, arthritis, misaligned spines, pulled muscles, ear worms, sinus infections, tooth-aches and a host of other problems assailed them. In a world in which aspirin was only available by chewing elm bark these pains were hard to escape, and the cure was often worse than the pain.

People were constantly trading advice about how to relieve these bothersome ailments. For instance, Frances, Lady Winchester passed on a cough syrup recipe with the comment that she had bestowed it on several people and they had all found it useful. The person with the cough or his nurse was to take a pint of weak ale and add two spoons of honey 'which came from the combs without forcing'. One should boil this over the fire, skimming it until it is clear, and then add grated elecampane and sliced ginger. Once it has simmered awhile strain it through a cloth and administer two or three spoonfuls at a time. Another of her recipes was heavy with horehound.[41] The recipient of this recipe presumably went to her garden and gathered the elecampane and horehound; the ginger would have to be bought. Most established households devoted a large amount of garden space to medicinal plants.

Perhaps Lady Frances's syrup was what the Court needed in the winter of 1563 when Elizabeth, Cecil, and many others had an affliction called 'a pooss [sic]'. Cecil had it so bad that he could hardly see, and Elizabeth complained of pain in her nose and eyes. It was blamed on the intense cold that froze the Thames so hard people played football on it.[42] Elizabeth and Cecil were lucky; this 'new disease . . . of the cough' killed many people that winter.[43]

Back pain was chronic, too. William Cecil's attack in the autumn of 1563 brought a sympathetic letter from Bishop Grindal, who had suffered from a similar ailment. Grindal said that when he had once had back pain he thought he had the stone and so tried to cool the place by slashing open his doublets and petticoats at the back and going without a belt. Unfortunately, he said, the cold got into his back, causing recurrent attacks of a stitch 'which beginneth under the point of one shoulder or both, and suddenly claspeth on the small of my back', lasting fifteen or twenty days. Since Cecil had shown him his doublet and petticoat cut open the year before, Grindal was sure that he had cooled his back too much. His advice was to keep the back warm, sending Cecil a hermetically sealed jar of Thomas Gibson's balm that was so hot that he should not use it without a physician's counsel.[44]

Sir William Petre, the other secretary to the Privy Council, did have the stone and he spent large amounts of money trying to find some relief. His account books show payments for clysters, purges, urinals, barley water and almond milk, syrup of succory [chicory] with rhubarb, and many other ingredients and sick room implements purchased in 1559. He had another serious attack in 1560–61, and he consulted Thomas Vicary, a famous physician who had written *The Anatomy of Man*. What he needed from Vicary was instruction on how to make a plaster of white lead, known as Ceres plaster, so he could treat himself if he became ill while at his country house.[45]

Petre did not submit to the horribly painful operation for the stone, but he might have. A 1566 Norwich agreement for 'cutting for the stone' stated that a surgeon would operate on a man's son for ten pounds, including room and board for himself and two assistants while the child recovered. However, the contract specified that the surgeon did not guarantee that the child would survive the operation.[46]

Petre's need to treat himself was magnified many times over among people who could not afford the huge fees of doctors, who charged Petre five or six shillings for a single visit. This was as much as a skilled London journeyman goldsmith was paid in a week, while a journeyman barber only earned a shilling a week.[47] It is hardly surprising then that there was a ready demand for medical self-help books like Thomas Raynalde's *Birth of Mankind*. Raynalde not only explained childbirth, he offered cures for dandruff, blemishes, hair in unseemly places on maidens and women, warts, freckles, rough skin, pimples, stinking breath, pungent arm pits, flux, eye troubles, fever, stomach-ache, insomnia, nightmares, worms, epilepsy, goggle eyes, and consumption.

William Bullein's dialogue on the fever pestilence had the same purpose: to put medical knowledge into popular hands in an easily understood form. William Turner's books on wines, triacles, medicinal baths, and herbs were also aimed at a wide audience, written in English to help the medicine go down.

The medical establishment of the era was, like so many other things, in a state of transition. New medical ideas, such as Paracelsian medicine, were just beginning to penetrate from Italy into the young College of Physicians and new techniques were being pioneered in the fledgling Company of Barber Surgeons. The apothecaries were also active practitioners. Members of the grocers' company, they made and sold remedies but they often diagnosed and treated as well. These people, with their practical knowledge of herbs, were perhaps better physicians than the university-trained physicians.

Much of the medicine practised in the land, however, was done by unlicensed individuals, to the intense annoyance of the physicians, who often prosecuted them. Simon Forman became a highly successful but illegal medicine man later in his life. Others were more specialized. Thomas Gale reported that over sixty women were curing illegally in London in the 1560s. 'These women,' he said, 'be called wise women, or holy and good women, some of them be called witches, and useth to call upon certain spirits, and some of them useth plain bawdry, and telleth gentlewomen that cannot bear children how they may have children.' Others had more prosaic specialties, 'as some for sore breasts, some for the stone and strangurie, some for pain of the teeth, some for scald heads, some for sore legs, some cunning in Mother Tomson's tub, and some to help maids when they have lost their maidenhead, when their bellies are grown too great, to make them small again, with a thousand more'.[48]

Full of indignation at these unlicensed practitioners, Gale reported that in 1562 alone he had seen over three hundred people in St Thomas' and St Bartholomew's hospitals who had been injured, maimed and even killed by witches' charms and women practising herbal medicine.[49] He was afraid that the surgeons were being blamed for these failed cures, but it was common knowledge that witches hurt people.

Margaret Robinson of Southwark was convicted in 1568 of bewitching Sarah Caldwell, age two, so she fell from her mother's arms into the fire, lingering from April until September before she died.[50] Alice Latter was indicted for murdering the children of a Tonbridge butcher, but the jury found her not guilty, while Cecily West was convicted of bewitching a girl who was not yet dead.

The judge followed the statute and sentenced West to a year in prison and the pillory.[51] Clearly people believed, though Gale might have disagreed, that witchcraft, like other medical practices, could be used to good or ill effect.

Gale, Master of the Barber Surgeons in 1561, tried to raise the educational standards and professionalism of his Company. Surgeons, he complained in his *Enchiridion* of 1563, were not respected like the university-trained doctors, and the fault was their own. Surgeons were poorly trained, exercising their art rudely and blindly, inflamed with greed for filthy lucre. Consequently they had no more respect than cobblers, joiners, women or horseleechs [veterinarians] – and they got paid like them.

Most surgeons were not educated enough to read the learned medical authorities in Latin. Gale therefore wrote in English to provide his fellows with a pragmatic guide to their trade of curing wounds, setting broken bones, and fixing dislocations. His books are manuals for surgeons full of dry, stomach-turning descriptions of their art.[52]

Parts of his books were delivered as lectures to the members of the Barber Surgeons' Company required to attend dissections at their hall. The famous John Caius was a regular lecturer, and in 1567 the Venetian Julio Borgaraucci was appointed lecturer in anatomy for four years. They were given their choice of the hanged felons for their anatomical lessons, so when eighteen men and two women were hanged in February of 1562 one of the bodies was sent to their hall.[53]

Gale had learned much of his art as a military surgeon, becoming expert at the amputations that almost always followed the shattering, crushing wounds of musket balls. He and his colleagues, however, had plenty of opportunity to see other kinds of wounds. When a maid dropped a candle wick into a barrel of gunpowder in the garret of a house in Bucklersbury, blowing the backs off three houses and mortally wounding herself, the surgeons would have been called.[54] When William Smith was swept off his cart horse by a tree branch and died of his injuries the surgeons would have been called.[55] Whenever a bone was broken or a head punched the surgeons might be summoned.

Therefore Gale's books were full of basic treatments. He taught how to immobilize a joint or broken bone with a cast of linen cloth soaked in oil of roses and egg whites, and how to reduce swelling by 'refrigerating' the wound. 'Small' diet, purging and blood-letting could, he said, help with the pain brought on by a flood of humours into the wounded part. If, however, the pain could not be controlled by these methods a 'stupefactive' was needed such as oil of poppies, opium or oil of mandrake.[56]

Gale provided detailed instructions on how to treat various troubles, but when it came to gunshot wounds he was a leading expert. He had written a treatise on them after serving with the army of Henry VIII in France and with Philip II at the siege of St Quentin in 1557. In his lectures to his Company he took the opportunity to expatiate on the cauterizing powder he had invented and put into use in the Hospital of St Thomas in Southwark.

If the surgeon had the time, Gale explained, he should prepare the patient for amputation by feeding and purging until humours were balanced. The day before the operation the limb to be removed should be bound very tightly, preventing heavy bleeding and reducing the pain of the operation. When they were ready to cut the surgeon should 'put the party in good comfort, declaring unto him that the fear is much worse than the pain'.

When the patient had been reassured three assistants held him down, while a fourth was detailed to hold the limb that was to be removed. Quickly an incision was made to the bone (do not forget, he warns, to sever the nerve between the bones in the leg – if the saw frays it there will be spasms, pain and possibly death) and a sharp saw was used to cut through the bone.

Now cauterization was needed if it was a major limb. Traditionally this meant the application of a cauterizing iron heated to a white heat. Applying the iron often killed the patient 'as you that be hospitallers of London' could testify, so he recommended his powder instead. A mixture of alum, turpentine, arsenic and quick lime, it sealed the wound chemically without the shock of the burning iron.[57]

Gale claimed that he had invented his cauterizing powder for the benefit of the Company and for the poor. Certainly the poor were his patients in the hospitals, but did the poor have access to other medical facilities? If the spa at Buxton is any indication, they did.

Modern people who drink bottles of Buxton Water are the unwitting descendants of the medieval folk who went to the well of St Anne in Buxton, Derbyshire, to be cured of their illnesses. When Thomas Wentworth was visited by St Anne *manqué* in 1562 he was the end of a long line of people who had gone there to bathe in the miraculous power of the Saint's well. The destruction of holy well in the Reformation did not, however, stop the flow of people coming through its baths.

Buxton became a well-established spa with a four-storey building equipped with galleries, exercise equipment, airing rooms, 'most decent' privies and lodging for all classes, including a dormitory for the poor. It took in rich and poor alike. The Warden charged 4d for administering the bath to everyone who came, plus a fee according to rank. A yeoman or minister was charged 12d; a gentleman paid 3s 4d and his wife 2s; a doctor or serjeant at law paid 10s; a duke paid £3 and a duchess £2. At the top of the scale was an archbishop, who paid £5. The money raised was divided into two parts, half helping the poor who came to be treated and the other half supporting the resident physician, Dr John Jones.

The regimen Jones recommended was to bathe morning and evening, exercising hard in between. The exercise promoted the evacuation of excrement through sweat and increased one's temperature, helping digestion and hardening the body. This vehement exercise was only to be undertaken after an examination of one's urine to determine if the digestive system was ready for a work-out. Patients at spas tended to become obsessed with their urine, which was a prime diagnostic tool, drinking the water and observing their urine's colour, smell and even flavour to determine if their humours were coming into balance. Doctors could make a diagnosis based only on an examination of urine.

Jones's patients, who included Leicester and Cecil, had a number of exercises available to them, depending on their sex and rank. Ladies, gentlewomen, wives and maids walked in the galleries and played Troule in Madame, a game in which balls of lead were rolled down a bench into eleven holes. The weights of the troules could be changed to fit the constitution of the person. Bowling alleys were available, both in full length and half length, for 'fine and gentle' exercise. Shooting at the garden butts with a long bow was highly recommended, but the crossbow was discouraged, since it did not stretch the muscles.

Three or four people could get up a game of 'wind' or 'yarn' ball, with the violent stretching and swift movement that accompanied it. Or a person could walk up and down carrying lead weights until he became heated. Hanging by the hands from a 'bow line' was good, too. Dangling a couple of feet off the floor one's 'intern panicles' and waist were stretched, preserving one from 'apsotumes, obstructions and pains'.

People went to Buxton for health, either to be cured or to preserve what they had. It was widely respected as a place of healing, and all classes were welcome. The City of York occasionally gave money to the poor to support their visits to the spa. The baths at Bath had a similar reputation. William Turner wrote a book celebrating them, along with others in England and on the continent, and providing specific medical advice, including how one could make an imitation spa by adding chemicals to one's bath water.[58]

III

Wherever people gathered to take the cure they also sought entertainment as part of their regimen. Staying in a good humour was taken literally in those days, since worrying was considered to draw blood to the heart, where it might be thickened, sickening the patient.[59] Music and theatre could be therapeutic, as were athletic sports, but early Elizabethan mirth could also be provoked by the violence of

bear-baiting, cock-fighting, executions and other blood sports. Any sport
was made better by gambling, to which the generation was addicted, to
the distress of the church and, more hypocritically, the state.

Parliament had prohibited the operation of gambling dens for playing
and betting on bowling, quoits, closh, kails, half-bowling, tennis, dice,
tables or cards drew apprentices, servants, husbandmen and artificers
away from socially valuable activities, such as archery.

Every man of seventeen or more was expected to own a bow and
know how to use it; if he did not his master would be fined. The
linkage between gambling and national defence was underlined by the
fact that in 1569 the Commissioners for Musters were asked to enforce
the laws against unlawful games and for archery.[60] Every commoner was
expected to have a bow and the statute of 1542 had required bowyers
to make three cheap elm and ash bows for every yew bow. The price
of these cheap bows was fixed. By 1566 this law had created a surplus
of junk bows priced at below cost, forcing a new statute to raise the
price and change the regulation so that every bowyer had to keep only
fifty cheap bows on hand.[61] In times of national stress these laws were
taken seriously, so that in 1569 a commission was appointed in Exeter
to suppress unlawful games and to discover if each master had enough
bows and arrows for himself and his servants.[62]

Shooting at the archery butts was required on festival days, and
villages which failed to maintain their butts were supposed to be fined
by the Justices. People worth a hundred pounds a year were exempted
from the gaming laws because they could afford to gamble, and from the
archery requirements because they were expected to use gentlemen's
weapons.[63]

Blood sport was the hallmark of a gentleman, and social status was
measured by the amount of venison on a man's table. Hunting with
greyhounds and hawks was enthusiastically pursued by the upper classes,
the Queen among them, and draconian laws were passed to protect deer
parks and hawks' nests from poachers. In 1563 a new statute punished
'unlawful taking of fish, deer and hawks' from gentlemen's parks, adding
to all the laws guarding the 'King's' deer. Mixing issues of class and
property, this statute protected the supply of gentlemen's food being
raised in their living larders.

That the right to hunt and eat venison was a mark of social status is
proved by a curious note in the biography of John Isham. Chosen Warden of the Mercers in 1567, he was expected to give the members a feast.
In order to impress his colleagues he used his extensive connections to
find venison for the company. 'Having had great good will and liking of
gentlemen', recalled his son Thomas, he assembled thirty-three 'fat and
large' bucks. Putting them on display in a gallery of his house he invited
his friends to see the bounty and be awed by his connections. They were

appropriately impressed, wrote Thomas Isham, 'as by their speeches I might perceive, being then a youth [and standing by as others did]. Yea it was thought, that not one man before his time nor since . . . had the like by a great many'.[64]

Hawking provided wild birds for the table, taking them in a sporting manner rather than with the nets and limed twigs of the commercial hunters and poachers. Nicholas Bacon, a son of Lord Keeper Bacon, wrote to his brother Nathaniel when his hawk Denice 'did strike a heron stark dead the last flight . . . and every flight . . . [she] did kill every foul stark dead, that ever I was afraid she should have killed herself'.[65]

Hunting and hawking were for the upper classes, whereas everyone could enjoy the blood sports and gambling together at animal fights. Bear and bull-baiting, in which the large animals fought with packs of dogs, were extremely popular and some bears had national reputations for their ability to wipe out whole packs of hounds. The centre of these sports was Southwark, London's wild neighbour across the Thames.

Alessandro Magno attended the Southwark baiting and left a vivid description. There were, he said, two hundred dogs kept in individual kennels and separate buildings for bears and bulls. In the centre of the complex was a ring surrounded by wooden stands covered against the rain and the sun. Every Sunday afternoon 'everyone' paid two pennies to stand, or four pennies to sit, around the ring.

> First they take into the ring . . . a cheap horse with all his harness and trappings, and a monkey in the saddle. Then they attack the horse with five or six of the youngest dogs. Then they change the dogs for more experienced ones. In this sport it is wonderful to see the horses galloping along, kicking up the ground and champing at the bit, with the monkey holding very tightly to the saddle, and crying out frequently, when he is bitten by the dogs. After they have entertained the audience for a while with this sport, which often results in the death of the horse, they lead him out and bring in the bears.

Singly or in groups the bears fought the dogs, 'but this sport is *not* very pleasant to watch'. Finally a fierce bull was tied to a stake in the middle of the ring with a rope two paces long. 'This sport,' said Magno, 'is the best one to see and more dangerous for the dogs than the other: many of them are wounded and die.'[66]

Men participated in all sorts of outdoor games, such as football, while women were less likely to join in these exercises, which were often accompanied by heavy drinking and fights.[67] Both sexes could attend theatricals and enjoy music.

In the wealthiest households professional players made regular visits. The records of Sir William Petre's Ingatestone Hall show that Lord Robert Dudley's Players (later Leicester's Players that employed

William Shakespeare) were paid twenty pence in November 1560 for a performance, though little is known about what these professional companies performed.[68] As we have seen, the 1560s were the twilight of the religious play cycles sponsored by various towns and companies. These religious dramas were being killed off by the Reformation and the changing taste that came with the introduction of classical concepts of theatre. Undoubtedly, however, when there was a performance there was a crowd since entertainment was at a premium.

The plays and interludes available to the general public were acted in taverns and were less polite than those performed in country houses and civic halls. Certainly they had satirical and political content, for Elizabeth issued a proclamation in April 1559 prohibiting unlicensed performances 'wherein either matters of religion or of the governance of the state of the commonwealth' were portrayed. A report to Rome said Elizabeth had stopped the 'comedies and other diversions by which in taverns on feast days the corrupt populace used to make mock and scorn of the Catholic and true religion'. The Spanish ambassador said that the comedies in the taverns ridiculed Philip II.[69]

In the more controlled settings of College halls, guild halls, stately homes and churches, theatre flourished. Although, as we have seen, the medieval play cycles like the Corpus Christi at York were dying in the 1560s, their secular brethren were thriving as entertainment and teaching tools. The Twelfth Night plays in the Inner Temple, such as *Gorboduc*, are representative, as were the ones performed for the Queen at Oxford when she visited in 1566 or those played by the children of Windsor for the Queen on Shrove Tuesday, 1566.[70]

These plays were frequently in Latin for heuristic reasons, as well as snob appeal, even though their matter was not high-minded. *Bursa Basilica seu Regale Excambium* [*Church Purse, or The Royal Exchange*], written by J. Ricketts and dedicated to Sir Thomas Gresham, who built the Royal Exchange between 1566 and 1571, was low comedy, couched in classical Latin. In one exchange of insults a character says, 'You have the understanding of a ship of fools.' To which comes the reply, playing on *Aeneid*, book I, 80–5, 'And you, Huff-puff, your stomach breeds winds like those born from the womb of Aeolus.'[71]

Music was another way of maintaining one's humours in balance. It was so valued that young people were taught to play, and young women seem to have improved their positions in the marriage market by their abilities to perform – Robert Jones' praise of his fiancé for her ability on the virginals is typical.

It was a time of changing musical fashion. The madrigal, then popular in Italy, had not yet entered the English musical scene. John Dowland, Thomas Campian and Thomas Morely were boys at school in the 1560s, but they were in the midst of a shift in taste and venue. The only person

publishing newly composed secular music in the middle of the century
was Thomas Whythorne, whose *Triplex of Songs, for three, four, and five
voices* appeared in 1571, just before he abandoned teaching to become
Master of the Music in Archbishop Parker's chapel.[72] Reflecting on the
condition of music in his day Whythorne lamented its decayed state.
In the church it was so poorly supported that 'when the old store of
musicians be worn out the which were bred when the music of the
church was maintained . . . ye shall have few or none remaining'.[73]
Ironically he wrote this while Thomas Tallis and William Byrd, two
of the greatest Elizabethan composers, were writing. Their style of
music, however, was best suited to the chapel royal where they worked.
There professional performers could sing the elaborate polyphonic
compositions like Tallis's *Spem in allium*, which required forty voices
divided into eight choirs singing antiphonally. Their talent was enough
to protect them even though they were Catholics.

In the cathedrals and parish churches of England, however,
Whythorne's observations were correct, especially in those dominated
by men committed to thorough reform of religion. Religious music
performed by choirs and organs was suspect because it sounded papist
and because it could not be easily understood by the congregation.
Music that did not teach theology was of no use in a reformed church.

During the battle over vestments Bishops Grindal and Horne wrote
to Heinrich Bullinger and Rudolph Gualter in defence of the establishment. Among the things they discussed was whether they had retained,
as was accused, Papist music. 'We do not assert,' they commented,
'that the chanting in churches, together with the organ is to be
retained; but we disapprove of it, as we ought to do.' When shown
their letter by Bullinger, George Withers sneered, 'They say that they
disapprove,' 'Nevertheless they all adopt them in their churches, and the
archbishop of Canterbury especially has caused an organ to be erected
in his metropolitan church at his own expense.'[74]

Professional choral music in church was definitely on the decline, but
the organ Parker installed did have an edifying use: it could accompany
congregational hymn singing. Parker himself had translated the psalter
into English in the 1550s, publishing it in 1567 with four-part settings
by Thomas Tallis.[75] In the reign of godly King Edward psalms were set
to popular tunes, rivalling ballads in popularity.[76] At the beginning of
Elizabeth's reign people were still singing them and their Archbishop
was trying to harness their enthusiasm and use it as a part of the service,
as was being done on the continent. Perhaps the Dutch Church in
London set the example in this, since Parker's printer, John Day, had
issued *De Psalmen Davidis in Nederlandischer sangs-ryme* in 1566, possibly
following up on the Dutch psalter he had published in 1561.[77]

Naturally the singing that drew people to church also drew them to taverns where religious themes could be perverted into happy drinking songs like 'A Religious Use of Taking Tobacco', written sometime before 1568. It plays on popular sermon themes of contempt for the world and meditation on sin:

> The Indian weed withered quite,
> Green at morn, cut down at night,
>   Shows thy decay;
>   All Flesh is hay;
>   Thus think, then drink tobacco . . .
> But when the pipe grows foul within,
> Think of thy soul defiled with sin.
>   And that the fire
>   Doth it require:
>   Thus think, then drink tobacco.[78]

Singing in taverns was, of course, accompanied by food and drink. Sixteenth-century English people were very interested in food, so much so that dour Puritans like William Harrison complained of their decadent feeding and drinking, a sad decline from the austere days of their fathers. Of course eating was a primary way to balance one's humours, so attention to diet was medicinally important, but Harrison thought that the English were so fond of feasting that it was very beneficial to the physicians, 'who most abound where most excess of misgovernment of our bodies do appear'.[79]

The amount of attention he lavished on the drink of the English indicates that he liked it, even as he complained about the quantities of food and ale consumed at 'bride ales', the churching of women, church ales and other celebrations enjoyed by the common folk. He himself preferred the beer that had recently become fashionable, pushing out the traditional ale ('now taken with many for old and sick men's drink'). He illustrated the alcoholic power of both by reciting the names of some of the brews: 'huffcap, the mad-dog, father-whoreson, angels'-food, dragons' milk, go-by-the-wall, stride-wide, and lift-leg.' 'Our maltbugs,' he wrote, 'lug at this liquor, even as pigs should lie in a row lugging at their dam's teats till they lie still again and be not able to wag.'[80] Alessandro Magno's Italian palate had a less flattering impression of the beer. It was 'healthy but sickening to taste. It is cloudy like horse's urine and has husks on the top.'[81]

IV

Singing, eating and drinking was entertaining, but it could not rival an execution for excitement. For felonies, such as murder, rape and robbery, English law had a single punishment: hanging. A speedy trial and quick execution in a public place was the ideal of justice, and contemporaries assumed that the death had to be public in order to dissuade the public from further crimes.

The conviction that enforcement was not sharp enough, however, was widespread. In the 1560s people were worried by what they perceived as a dangerous upsurge in the population of 'vagabonds', a criminal class by definition. They feared thieves, too. Violence in the streets was not uncommon in a society in which most men carried knives, and the roads were unsafe because of highwaymen.

One day in 1562 Alessandro Magno became a victim of this widespread fear of criminals, even though he never met any. He and seven other merchants had hired horses and gone from London up the Thames to see Hampton Court, Richmond Palace and Nonesuch Palace. They had a lovely day, admiring the palaces and delighting in their ride through the countryside. Their pleasure was cut short, however, when the realized that evening was drawing in and they were far from London. 'As it was dangerous to go on at night because of robbers, when we found ourselves some miles from the city, one of our companions who was afraid of danger said "he who can follow me, follow me. I do not want to stay out at night".' Therewith he spurred his horse and galloped away. Magno and one other were left behind because their horses were too slow. Only vaguely aware of the route, they got lost in a swamp. Finally, knowing that London was to their east, they rode towards the rising moon.

It was a terrifying ride. Magno says he and his companion were sure that the hooting owls were the robbers calling to one another. Even after he had realized that they were only owls, Magno could not convince his friend, who was 'overwhelmed by fright'. Eventually they came to a village, where his companion wanted to stay, pointing out that they were travelling a road on which people had been murdered only a few days before. Magno, young and excited about the banquet to which he had been invited in London, insisted that they go on. They hired a guide and 'having armed him sufficiently', they proceeded.

At last they came into a large field near the City gate. There in the moonlight they could just discern two horsemen. His companion panicked and wanted to run, fearing that there were more than two, but Magno bravely claimed that since they outnumbered these shadows they should proceed. As they advanced they recognized the horsemen as their friends, who thought *they* were robbers. Magno let them beg for mercy before identifying himself.

At last Magno reached his party, where he danced with two fine-looking women until well after midnight. His host gave them torches to light them home and as they passed through the dark streets they kept meeting bands of the watch. Several let them pass unchallenged but one, commanded by elderly captain who could not understand their language, arrested them as suspicious characters and marched them off to prison. Luckily the commander of the watch understood their vigorous Italian protests and sent them home with an armed escort.[82]

While Magno and his friends met no robbers, their experience illustrates the popular fear of highway robbers. The roads leading into London were unsafe. Highwaymen concentrated in the rural areas just beyond the City and anyone approaching them ran the gauntlet. In Kent, robbers worked the roads from Canterbury and Tonbridge into London, but most of the robberies occurred around Shooters Hill within sight of the City. At Shooters Hill on 28 February 1565, Thomas Freeman, John Duffield and Henry Whitehead robbed Robert Marberey of his money, boots and sword; they then stole Francis Goldsmith's money and two horses. In 1563 Robert More robbed Henry Lane at Shooters Hill and then, three days later, he robbed his servant. Sixteen per cent of the indictments in Kent between 1559 and 1579 were for highway robbery.[83]

Magno's experience with the watch underlines the suspicions that unexplained movements in the streets and unknown strangers were dangerous. William Bullein gave Civis, his honest London householder, a speech about London's night-walkers:

> Good night, God save the Queen say the constables, farewell neighbours. Eftsoons after their departing creepeth forth the wild rogue and his fellows . . . with picklocks, handsaws, long hooks, ladders, etc. to break into houses, rob, murder steal, and do all mischief . . . to maintain their harlots, great hose, lined cloaks, long daggers, feathers . . .

The cause of this evil doing was 'want of punishment by the day, and idle watch in the night'. Civis feared that the watch was colluding with the thieves, as were servants. If something was not done to improve the watch no one would be able to keep a penny, or even their lives. If the rogues did these things in London with its watch, what horrors might happen in isolated rural places?

Civis knew the cause of this crime: fancy clothes. Even though many criminals were executed 'it helpeth not: it is the excess of apparel. Hose, hose, great hose, too little wages, too many serving men, too many tippling houses, too many drabs [whores], too many knaves, too little labour, too much idleness.'[84]

The belief that conspicuous consumption causes crime is a tradition in Western civilization. Cato 'the Censor' told the Roman Senate about it in the third century BC and English kings had been trying to stifle it since the thirteenth century AD. Tudor rulers associated it with the dangers of human greed and social climbing. The 1560s saw a series of royal proclamations ordering the enforcement of the statutes of apparel that were designed to keep people dressing within their social degrees and incomes.

William Harrison recognized the enthusiasm for clothes as another sign of the end of time, another proof of moral decay. Puritan that he was he wanted people to dress somberly, as they had done in the good old days when every man contented himself with clothes of 'sad tawney' or black velvet, 'without such cuts and garish colors as are worn in these days and never brought in but by the consent of the French, who think themselves the gayest of men when they have most diversities of jags and change of colors about them'. Merchants, he said, continued to dress gravely, if expensively, but the 'younger sort of their wives' were out of control. The colours of cloth devised to please their 'fantastical heads' were astonishing: 'goose turd green, pease-porridge tawny, popinjay blue, lusty gallant, the devil-in-the-head (I should say "the hedge", and suchlike.' He prayed these excess could be abated before God in his anger treated England like Sodom and Gomorrah.[85]

In 1559, 1562 and 1566 there were proclamations requiring the enforcement of the statute of apparel passed in the time of Queen Mary. In particular the amount and kind of cloth used by various classes was regulated. Hosiers and tailors were put under bond to guarantee that they would not make 'nether stocks and upper stocks' using more than a yard and three-quarters of broadest kersey cloth. Shirts could not be made with double ruffs. Nor could men wear damascened or gilt swords, rapiers or daggers unless they were knights. Cutlers were forbidden to make daggers longer than twelve inches and swords longer than one and an eighth yards.[86] Henry Machyn, whose trade of drapery was affected by the law, summed it up, calling it a proclamation against 'great ruffs and great breeches'.[87]

Hosiers were singled out because of the popular fashion of wearing 'great hose' – also called trunk hose or breeches – and 'nether stocks' or stockings. The stockings were tied to the hose with laces called points, which were often decorative and expensive. Great hose were swelled out with stuffing of rags, wool, tow or hair to such an enormous size that the wearers had trouble sitting down. In Parliament a scaffold was built around the walls that would allow the Members to rest their feet without actually sitting down. When the fashion changed in the late 1560s the scaffold was removed.[88]

Lord Keeper Bacon explained why the Queen's government was so concerned about enforcing these laws, giving us an insight to their assumptions about how crime was caused by social climbing and greed. Extravagant dress was the thin end of a wedge of criminal deviance, much like the modern belief that marijuana use leads directly to heroin addiction. Addressing an assembly of justices and lawmen during Hilary

Term 1565, he demanded that they enforce the sumptuary laws more thoroughly than hitherto.

Their failure to execute the statute of apparel gave rise to four mischiefs: confusion of social degrees, consumption of patrimonies, the universal impoverishment of the realm and the destruction of persons. As for the first, it was hard these days, he said, to know a serving man from a nobleman by his dress, an evil so evident that he did not gloss it further. For the second, everyone knew that people who should have been spending their money in productive ways were consuming their estates in their mad pursuit of fancy clothes. Even men of years and discretion were seeing their incomes eaten by their dependants' demands for clothes, rather than spending them on 'things of necessity as in marriage of their children, in maintenance of hospitality and so forth'.

Of course buying clothes was a non-productive investment, so it led to the impoverishment of the nation. Clothes produced nothing of value and when they were fancy clothes they tended to be foreign, creating a balance of trade problem.

Costly clothes upset the social and economic balance in such a way that they literally destroyed people by making them criminals. The justices had to inform the people that

> their unreasonable desire to maintain their excess in apparel has moved them to fall to those felonies and robberies for the which so many of them do lose their lives. And who sees not but that it had been much better for them with plain hose and convenient apparel to have lived honestly by labour than with outrageous hose and excess of apparel to suffer execution?

Justices on assize were encouraged by Bacon to single out people in their audiences who were wearing 'excessive' clothes and demand to know what they paid in the last subsidy. If they had not paid taxes appropriate to the clothes they wore they were to be punished.[89]

Tempering people's delight in fine clothes was a constant uphill struggle, but the Crown fought the good fight. In 1564 Exchequer Special Commissions were issued in most shires for investigations to identify men whose wives wore silk or gold jewellry in spite of their husbands' lack of sufficient land to justify their costumes. Any man whose wife wore silk had to keep a horse for the royal service; otherwise she could not wear such fine clothes. The gentlemen detailed to report their neighbours' wives showed little stomach for it, judging by the paucity of the returns.[90]

An easier way to moderate people's fancy dress was by attacking the tailors directly. Hosiers and tailors from London had to post penal bonds guaranteeing they would not make great hose.[91]

Since clothing was one of the few ways Tudor people had of expressing individuality and status in a world remarkably poor in material goods, it is hardly surprising that the Queen's subjects valued it so highly. Their enthusiasm for silks, velvets, felts, satins, Spanish leather and other raw materials of dress that could be taken to their tailors was boundless. And such things were expensive, encouraging people to buy on credit and make corrupt bargains with usurers. In 1563 Parliament passed an Act decreeing that if a merchant sold foreign-made apparel on credit to anyone worth less than £3000 the merchant could not sue for non-payment.[92]

Perhaps such legislation was sparked by cases like that of Sir Nicholas Poines' wife. She bought silks and velvet on credit but then her husband refused to pay for them. The mercer who sold the goods sued her husband, since, as a married woman she could not be sued. The jury decided that her husband was not responsible for her debt, to the horror of Justice Dyer.[93]

The value and desirability of cloth and clothing made it a target of thieves. When a travelling cloth merchant had 'a piece of cloth' stolen while he was staying in an inn in Broadway he sued the innkeeper. The master of the inn responded that he had warned the plaintiff that he would not be responsible for the cloth unless it was locked in a chamber provided for the purpose; since the merchant had left his packs in the courtyard he could take no responsibility for them. The court agreed; the plaintiff ought to have known better.[94]

A class of criminals known as 'hookers' used hooks on long poles to steal clothing from open windows and out of gardens, selling it into a ready market for second-hand clothes, made readier by the custom of masters and mistresses of passing their used clothes on to their servants.

Hookers were a specialists within the great army of criminals known to Elizabethans as 'vagabonds'. The object of hysterical outbursts and penal legislation, the vagabonds were travelling people without visible means of support. Assumed by their more prosperous fellows to be *de facto* criminals because of their masterless state, they were the source of a great deal of petty crime. What modern people call the 'homeless poor', they were symptoms of a bad economy and a population growing faster than the economy could absorb new workers.

Of course Tudor people, like some moderns, assumed that unemployment and homelessness were a matter of personal choice and indicted the lazy, immoral character of the poor. In Calvinist theology this went one step further, so that the poor were associated with the reprobate, their poverty the mark of God's rejection. At any rate, it was held that the 'sturdy beggar' should not be given alms, and could be made to work if enough force and fear were applied. Moreover, people frightened themselves by imagining that the vagrants were organized into a criminal underground, a fear encouraged by books like John Awdley's *The Fraternity of Vagabonds* (1565) and Thomas Harman's *Caveat for Common Cursetors* 1567.

Naturally the sturdy beggars saw things rather differently. Thomas Harman, a Kent justice of the peace and author of a book on vagabonds, interviewed a homeless mother in the summer of 1566 when she came begging to his gate. They talked for awhile and he asked questions for his book (these 'walking mortes' as he called them were unmarried women claiming to be widows whose husbands had died in the army in Newhaven or Ireland). Then he began chastising her for her life-style and threatening hell fire.

> 'God help me,' she responded, 'how should I live? None will take me into service, but I labour in harvest time honestly.'
> 'I think but a while with honesty,' responded Harman, who made it his business to know the evil ways of this criminal class.[95]

In fact she probably did labour honestly in harvest time. The demand for labour in the autumn of the year gave such people a temporary chance to earn a living.

Swelling the numbers of masterless people who travelled the country and were assumed to be criminals were the 'Egyptians', or gypsies. An alien element that had never been tamed, they had an unsavoury reputation as shysters, petty thieves and dissolute people. When news reached the Privy Council that a band of gypsies had been sighted in Oxfordshire in the summer of 1562 they sent the sheriff and justices there an order to round them up and lock them up in Oxford Castle. Another group already in custody was to be moved to Oxford so that all the gypsies could be tried together.[96]

The numbers of vagabonds and gypsies on the roads and the fear they struck into the hearts of settled people encouraged harsh measures to control them. Symptomatic of the hard times and the growing population of poor, they were not appreciated for what they were. Feared, they were not even desirable objects of pious alms. Force was needed to make them into productive, obedient citizens. By statute it was required that any masterless person apprehended by the justices could be whipped from parish to parish until reaching his or her home parish, which was responsible for its own poor.

Lord Keeper Bacon, in the same speech in which he harangued the justices about the laws on apparel, expatiated on the problem of vagabonds.

> As to the statute concerning vagabonds who is so blind that sees not how by the not executing of the law, idleness, the mother of all mischief, is bred, brought forth, nourished and maintained. Of this root springeth all

manner of vice and disorder . . . . But here some perchance will say that
it is a pitiful thing to see whipping . . . meet for dogs by the appointment
of this law imposed upon men. I for my part am very sorry to see a man
whipped, but yet no more sorry to see a man hanged. Were it not much
better, know you, to see a man whipped and thereby unhanged, than
hanged because he was unwhipped?

Half the men hanged annually for robberies and felonies would have
been saved if only the laws on apparel and vagabonds had been properly
enforced, he asserted. Moreover, if the laws against vagabonds were
observed there would be more labourers to employ, and those hired
would be much more tractable.[97]

In the early 1570s, when the nation was troubled by revolts and
rumours of revolts, a concerted drive was made against the vagabonds
by the Privy Council.

If people were more afraid of sturdy beggars and gypsies than reality
warranted they still had a right to fear crimes against their persons and
property. As always with humanity, the sorts of harm people did to
one another are predictable, though the reasons for and responses to
violence are less certain. The murder rate for mid-sixteenth century
England approached an annual average of 1.5 per ten thousand,
making murder and manslaughter comparatively uncommon, but
forty times more frequent than in modern England and Wales. The
typical homicide case heard by the justices involved two or more men,
often neighbours, who got into a quarrel that ended in a death. In one
study domestic murder only accounted for a quarter of all homicides in
Essex, even though the modern ratio is one in two – however, keeping
in mind the case of Lady Dyer we should be careful about believing that
Tudor people were nicer to one another.[98] All murder statistics depend
upon charges being brought and domestic violence is notoriously hard
to document even today.

Property disputes could lead to violent confrontations which often
became more violent in memory as the aggrieved parties prepared
their law suits. To hear Thomas Statham of Southwark tell it in the
Court of Star Chamber he and his relations in Ashford, Derby, were
peaceably harvesting on land he held by copyhold when Thomas
Molder, accompanied by his relatives, entered the field with swords,
pitchforks, staves and other weapons and attacked them, carrying away
the produce.

Molder's version was very different. He claimed that he had leased
the ground from Statham's farmer and had a right to the produce. In
the argument that ensued when the two parties met, Joan Statham had
attacked Edward Molder with a cudgel, prompting him to knock her
down.

A witness who watched from a neighbouring field saw it differently.

He said Edward Molder had hit Joan with a pole, grabbing her hair and throwing her to the ground, where he continued to beat her.[99]

That group violence was still an acceptable way of handling property disputes is demonstrated by another case, too. The servants of Thomas Hare of Water Eaton, Oxfordshire, were attacked and beaten and their master's house was entered by Edward Stafford, gentleman, and his men. The same armed gang beat a woman servant to death during another break in. The justices of the peace ordered an end to the conflict and forced Stafford to post a hundred pound bond, but he ambushed and assaulted Hare anyway. They were fighting over who controlled the manor, Stafford claiming Hare had seized it and that he was only attempting to get back his own property.[100]

More pacific people used the courts to harass their enemies in this litigious age that so disliked lawyers but sent its sons to learn enough law to protect themselves.

Random violence and theft were also a possibility, whether in the town or the country. Travellers and householders faced the possibility that anyone with ready cash or moveable goods had to reckon with theft which was sometimes accompanied by violence. Robert Smith and his wife knew this when they confronted an armed tailor at Hinton Bridge near Cambridge, surrendering a purse containing five marks in cash.[101] When Joan Wright broke into Richard Manning's house in Halton, Lincolnshire, and took twenty marks from his chest, Manning was reminded of the insecurity of a world without banks.[102]

Thefts such as occurred to Manning were hanging matters, though Wright received the Queen's pardon for it, as did the tailor who robbed the Smiths. Petty pilfering was common, if we can believe the concerns people voiced – and the numbers of people noted by Machyn for being punished for thefts too small to deserve the hanging reserved for felons. Another class of criminal played confidence games, pretending to be licensed cripples, shipwrecked seamen, victims of fires, and others down on their luck. And then there were the crooked merchants who overcharged, sold goods at illegal prices or of poor quality, cheated on the weight of bread or the measure of beer, or lent money at interest. All of them were considered to be stealing, directly, indirectly or by means of the market.

The law's answer to crime, whether murder, felonious theft or sharp business practice, was, in theory, severe. The severity, however, was tempered by the realities of enforcement and the cumbersome legal system. Lacking a national police of any kind (there was one royal official for every three thousands subjects) Elizabeth depended upon the voluntary activities of the justices of the peace.[103] These gentlemen had the job of making the royal will felt in the country. Empanelled annually and subject to removal for political reasons, but not receiving any payment for their work, they were backed up by the sheriff of the shire on the one hand and the local constables on the other.

Serving out of a sense of responsibility and, probably, because of the power it gave them over local affairs, the justices frequently had little or no training in the law – a law which, on its higher levels, was conducted in Law French or Latin and was obsessed with proper form. Moreover, they were burdened with an ever greater number of statutes to enforce. As government attempted to respond to crime and economic trouble more and more statutes and royal proclamations were made, each of which was to be enforced by the justices and their equivalents in the towns. Charged with controlling behaviour ranging from how much silk people wore and if they owned a knit cap, to murder, treason and anything else the Crown handed them, they were not very efficient.

Lord Keeper Bacon, in the 1565 speech in which he urged the enforcement of apparel and vagabond laws, admitted as much. Claiming that Elizabeth had done all she could, including doubling the number of justices in order to keep up with the growing pile of laws, he complained that the number of dependable men would be very small 'if out of the whole number of justices that number were taken out which do daily their diligence more to serve the private affection of themselves and friends as in overthrowing an enemy or maintaining a friend, a servant, or a covenant than to maintain the common good of their country respecting more the persons than the matters'.

With these crooked justices removed another group remained: those who served only for reputation's sake, rather than from commitment to justice.[104]

If a malefactor was apprehended and condemned the punishments were quick and painful. Convicted felons were sentenced to hang, while those convicted of lesser crimes were pilloried – exposed to public shame and physical punishment.

Sir Thomas Smith, writing to a French audience, proudly described the English jury trial. He stressed that in England torture was not used as a judicial device, for any true Englishmen, unlike the craven people of other nations, would rather die than suffer torment. Consequently, it was no good torturing them if you wanted the truth to be told. Instead England had the jury of twelve men.

The accused was brought before the justices and the jurors and placed where he or she could hear and see everything that was done. The accuser, the people who had arrested the accused, and other witnesses were sworn to tell the truth and asked what evidence they had against the defendant. After which 'the thief will say no, and so they stand a while in altercation'. After the accusers and the accused had wrangled for a bit the judge would turn to the jury and charge them to do their duty to God and their prince, sequestering them under the watchful eye of a bailiff.

Any jury might hear several cases before it was sequestered, and once they were, they were not allowed any food, drink, or fire – but they could ask to hear evidence again to clarify their deliberations. While the jurors debated the justices went to dinner. When the jury was ready everyone resumed their places and the foreman of the jury was asked 'is he guilty or not guilty?' The foreman answered 'in one word, guilty, or in two, not guilty: the one is deadly, the other acquits the prisoner'.

Only about one prisoner in four received a verdict of guilty, but if the verdict went against him or her it was, in theory, immutable. The convict now had only one barrier between him and the noose: proving 'clergy'. If the offence was one that allowed a plea of clergy, such as theft, the convict could claim to be in the protection of the Church, proving it by reading a sentence from the Psalms. This famous 'neck verse' could, even if poorly read, prompt the bishop's commissary to proclaim that he could *legit ut clericus* – read like a cleric. A decree of *legit* saved his neck from the halter. A ruling of *non legit* allowed the judge to order the sheriff to take the convicted person out and promptly hang him.

Those who saved themselves by their literacy were branded with T for thief, M for manslaughter, or sent to the bishop's prison.[105]

A pregnant woman condemned to die was spared until after the birth of her child. The plea of pregnancy, however, had to be substantiated by a jury of matrons.

The punishments were carried out wholesale and in public in order to maximize their deterrent effect. Machyn's diary frequently records the aftermath of a gaol delivery: 'the eight day of March were hanged at Tyburn ten men.'[106]

The severity and speed of this justice was often softened and slowed by the interference of lawyers, money and powerful people. One might be able to buy a pardon, or use influence to get one, so that the crime was officially forgiven. Or the sheriff could be hobbled by a gift or a threat. For people with access to the powerful, hanging could be escaped with their help.

For instance, in Trinity term in Elizabeth's third year Ellen Lambe brought a charge of rape against Richard Puttenham. He pleaded not guilty, but the jury found against him. Unfortunately, noted Justice Dyer, Puttenham, who was also a bigamist, was 'known to be a clerk' and the justices were forced to grant him his clergy instead of hanging him outright.

Now Puttenham's lawyers and friends became active. A former serv-ant of Queen Elizabeth, she took an interest in his case and appointed a special commission to examine it. The justices were summoned and a long list of objections and questions were laid out concerning the case. Puttenham's lawyers claimed that the indictment was incorrect because it only charged that he had 'feloniously ravished and deflowered her, and carnally knew her', failing to state that the deflowering was felonious, too. Moreover, the indictment did not aver in fact that she had not assented before or after the rape. A series of other legal questions were raised, and the issue was left in legal confusion. Meanwhile, said Dyer, Puttenham 'found favor with the Queen . . . and afterwards being let out of prison he quitted the realm.'[107]

Few criminals had the Queen to intervene on their behalf but the principle was the same, especially since indictments might never be made if the justices of the peace were friends of the accused.

A person sought by officers of the court on a criminal charge had one other way to avoid, at least temporarily, an appearance in court. He or she could take sanctuary in a sanctuary church. In the pre-Reformation era there had been many sanctuary churches in which a person could take shelter for forty days before being forced to trial or to abjure the realm forever. Henry VIII had seen to it that most of the sanctuaries were abolished, for most offences, but in the 1560s there were still places where one could seek shelter from justice. Westminster Abbey, for instance, was a sanctuary. Close enough to the City to be useful to debtors, it was a thorn in the side of the law. The Commons passed a bill in 1563 to abolish sanctuary for debt, but it was never passed in the Lords.[108]

For the lesser offences that the justices of the peace could punish by their own authority, or which town officers had under their jurisdictions, or which fell to the Leet Courts and Courts Baron or other local authorities, the trial was still by jury, but the accused was allowed counsel. There were a number of minor misdemeanours and trespasses in which the justices could make a summary judgement thanks to the extension of a legal fiction.

Punishments meted out for crimes which did not demand the life of the criminal still depended heavily on shame and public punishment. Machyn noted these pilloryings along with the public executions. One person, whose offence was not named, was placed on the pillory first in Westminster and then at the Standard in Cheapside. After his second exposure to public scorn the man's ear was cut off.[109] 'Nailing' of ears – in which the ear was nailed to a post on the pillory and then cut off when the convict had passed enough time on display – was a common punishment, as was whipping, all of which was done as a public spectacle.

The concept of shaming had been borrowed from the Church courts, and it must have been fairly effective. Once a person was publicly identified as a malefactor – and especially if he or she was then marked by the branding iron, the loss of an ear, or slitting of the nose – the community was likely to keep an eye on him or her.

The Church courts had jurisdiction over the souls of England's people, which meant that heresy, blasphemy, matrimony, adultery and divorce, wills and other private spiritual matters were regulated by them. There, too, shame was a primary tool of correction, encouraging repentance. For instances, persons convicted of fornication were forced to stand before the congregation, clothed in a white sheet, and confess their sins on three different Sundays.

The community tended to follow the example of the courts, spontaneously shaming people they considered to be guilty. When the minister of St Mary Abchurch was discovered in Distaff Lane, London, 'using another man's wife as his own . . . and he being so taken at the deed doing (having a wife of his own) was carried to Bridewell [Prison] through all the streets, his breeches hanging about his knees, his gown and his (cover knave) hat born[e] after him with much honour . . .' Perhaps this spontaneous punishment arose from the frustration the public often felt when known malefactors escaped punishment. Stowe notes that the minister was released unpunished from jail and was allowed to keep his church position. The people who had marched him through the streets were 'greatly blamed' by the authorities for what they had done.[110]

Shame, whether applied officially or by popular will, was assumed to be a powerful deterrent. The loss of one's honour could do great damage in a small community – it often literally meant the loss of one's 'credit' or believability.

Given the poor policing and the slipshod manners of the justices of the peace other enforcement mechanisms were used, especially for offences in which the Crown had a financial interest. If one was a smuggler, or broke the usury law, or put horses that were too small on the commons, or failed to observe the apprenticeship rules, one might find oneself reported by an informer. These people made their livings by reporting lawbreakers and collecting half the fine upon conviction, using a *qui tam* action that allowed them to sue on behalf of the monarch, who was the aggrieved party. Frequently, however, the existence of the *qui tam* action turned informers into extortioners, demanding payment upon threat of prosecution.

These informers were hated by the general population. Enforcing laws against things that many thought should be legal, their extortion was deeply resented. Considered to be, as one member of Parliament described them, 'the worst sort of men',[111] they frightened and oppressed their neighbours, even forcing some to become spies in order to work off the debts they owed the informer. When a man was unable to pay the fine owing to the informer Thomas Bunning of Norfolk, Bunning required him to report as many usurers as would give him sixty pounds worth of fines.[112]

In some circumstances the informers also had the right to seize the property of the accused. This became a problem for the fen folk of East Anglia because of a statute made in Henry VIII's time requiring all stallions grazing on commons to be of a certain size.

The Henrician statute was not forgotten in Elizabeth's time; in 1562 a royal proclamation ordered that 'no stoned horse being above the age of two years, and not being of the height of 15 handfuls' could be pastured in any forest, chase or common. Anyone finding such a puny horse had the right to seize it. Worse, the officers of any place containing such grazing ground were instructed to round-up the horses grazing there and kill any small, 'unprofitable' ones they found.[113]

Enforcement of this proclamation grieved the people around the Isle of Ely. The promoters began rounding up and seizing their horses, and nearly all of them were shorter than fifteen hands. Big horses were of little use in the fens because their 'moisture and wateriness, were never able nor yet are to breed, bear, or bring forth such greet breed of stoned horses of such bigness . . . without danger and peril of the miring, drowning, and perishing of the same'. Not daring to pasture their horses, the people around Ely found that the informers were making tillage and carriage unnecessarily difficult.[114]

The peak of the informers' activity came in the 1560s, the year 1566 being an especially active year which saw the all-time high for information against usurers in the Exchequer.[115] In the autumn of 1566 a bill was introduced in the Commons to control them. This bill was rewritten three times before its final version, described as 'touching informers, for execution of penal statutes', was passed and sent to the Lords on 6 November.

That same week informers were being attacked in the streets of Westminster. A Lincolnshire informer was beaten in Whitehall by a gang led by a fellow townsman, and John Chambers, a London bowyer and informer, was involved in a shouting match with a tailor he had reported. On 5 November there was a protest against informers in Westminster, and on 7 November a crowd heckled and jostled one awaiting the trial of his *qui tam* actions in both the Exchequer and the Queen's Bench.[116] These disturbances were serious enough that a royal proclamation was issued on 10 November, condemning the 'light and evil-disposed persons who in great routs and companies have assembled themselves together against such as be informers'. Their rage was disturbing the royal courts, so the informers were placed under royal protection. Anyone attacking them would suffer imprisonment for three months without bail and be whipped on the pillory.[117]

Meanwhile the bill against the informers had entered the Lords, where it became bogged down amidst all the other bills for legal reform proposed that session. It appears that in 1566 everyone was keen on improving enforcement, but the various bills foiled one another and almost all of them were lost when the Queen prorogued Parliament.[118] Another attempt to hobble the informers was made in the Parliament of 1571, but it was 1576 before a statute against their abusive actions was finally enacted.

Informers were enforcing the will of the state as a form of private enterprise which worked fairly well – perhaps better than using police and due process – by frightening wrongdoers, but they added another layer of fear to people's lives. Disease, violence and theft were bad enough, scarcely assuaged by prayers and pleasant distractions.

The informers, and that other caterpillar of the commonwealth, the Queen's purveyor who took food for the Court at prices far under those of the market, compounded the fear of robbery and burglary with the threat of judicial seizure and blackmail. They made it harder than ever to make and keep a decent living in the troubled economy of the 1560s.

10

Making a Living

I

No one in the Shah of Persia's Court had ever heard of England.
His Highness wondered where Arthur Edwards had come from that
spring of 1569, but when Edwards told him 'England' the Shah did not
understand and, turning to his assembled nobles, he asked if they had
heard of such a place. None had.

Running through the names of his native island in different languages
Edwards came to 'Inghliterra' of the Italians and at last there was a spark
of recognition. One of the courtiers had heard of a town called 'Londro',
and it became clear that London 'is better known in far countries out of
Christendom, than is the name of England'. The Shah, surprised that he
had never heard of a country as rich and powerful as the one Edwards
described, asked all sorts of questions about it before demanding details
of the activities of Philip II of Spain, of whose nation he had heard a
great deal.[1]

Edwards was in Persia trying to opening new markets for English
cloth. A servant of the Muscovy Company, he had come overland
through Russia, down the Volga and the Caspian Sea, pioneering a route
the Company hoped would be a 'Northeast Passage' to the riches of the
orient. Pragmatically they speculated that this route would allow them
to tap the silk and spice trade at Hormuz and undercut the Portuguese
who, because it took two years to make a voyage around the Cape of
Good Hope, were vulnerable to anyone who could get spices back to
Europe more quickly.[2]

The underlying causes for Edwards' trip, however, lay in an ailing English economy. Need for new markets and sources of foreign exchange
drove English merchants into the world in a way undreamt by their
fathers. While Edwards and his associates where negotiating with Ivan
the Terrible and fighting off Tartars in their attempts to reach Persia,

John Hawkins and his crews were pioneering English participation in the slave trade. The men who opened up the West African trade had initially hoped to make it an outlet for cloth and other trade goods, getting slaves, gold and other valuables in return, but it became apparent that stealing people was cheaper than buying them.

Sponsored by investors that included the Queen, Leicester and Cecil, Hawkins's first two voyages made enormous profits. Sailing to West Africa, they raided the coastal towns. Carrying their prisoners, people even they referred to as 'prey', they sailed to the West Indies and sold them to the Spanish. Hawkins's sales technique often included threatening to burn the town unless the Spaniards bought his slaves, so it is not surprising that he wore out his welcome. The Spanish ambassador in England began reporting on his movements and his third voyage, in 1567, had to be prepared in secret.

The Spanish, however, were watching for him. When Hawkins was forced to seek shelter at San Juan de Ullua because of a storm, he was attacked by the Spanish fleet. Losing some of his ships and many men (but not the *Judith* or her captain Francis Drake) Hawkins fled out to sea, where he wandered, lost, for fourteen days. Starving, his crew tried to find another Spanish post, but to no avail, eating rats, cats, mice and dogs to survive.

In the end the voyage was a disaster, and Hawkins 'the pirate' as he is called in Spanish sources, lost his investors' money. He wrote afterwards, 'If all the miseries and troublesome affairs of this sorrowful voyage should be perfectly and thoroughly written, there should need a painful man with his pen, and as great a time as he had that wrote the lives and deaths of the Martyrs [John Foxe].'[3]

Anthony Jenkinson and Humphrey Gilbert sought to get west by sailing east to China. In 1565 Jenkinson proved to Elizabeth that such a passage was possible because unicorn horns were found on arctic islands, proving a sea connection with Cathay, where unicorns were raised. Elizabeth invested in his abortive 1566 expedition. That same year Gilbert used the new Act creating a corporation of Merchant Adventurers for the Discovery of New Trades to demand a monopoloy on the proposed route through the arctic seas north of Russia.[4]

The men participating in these ventures were seeing a world unknown to English people. One of Hawkins's men reported eating 'a kind of corn called maize, in bigness of a pea, the ear whereof is much like to a teasel'. He also tasted a potato for the first time, reporting it to be one of the 'most delicate roots that may be eaten, and do far exceed our parsnips or carrots.'[5] Arthur Edwards described another plant upon which English fortunes would be built: cotton. It grows, he said, 'on a little tree or briar' with a slender stalk like a carnation.[6]

Trade into Russia, into Persia, into West Africa, into the Americas, into Morocco, into any place English merchants could go to open new markets, was the entrepreneurial edge in the 1560s. Forced by the decline in domestic and foreign demand for the wool cloth that was the staple of the English economy new markets were sought and the groundwork laid that made England into a sea power.

Making a living required sometimes heroic efforts in the 1560s because a number of things came together in the decade to disturb the economy. The advice written to the Queen at the beginning of the reign touched on a series of economic problems, sometimes called the 'mid-Tudor crisis', that troubled the people and demanded governmental action. Sir Thomas Smith, one of the nation's leading intellectuals, policy adviser, and diplomat had analysed the problems of the nation in his classic *Discourse of the Commonweal* in 1549; the problems he confronted in the 1560s were much the same as they were when he wrote the book, making another edition worth publishing in the 1570s. In this dialogue the Doctor (Smith's voice) defined the griefs of the realm as general dearth, the 'exhausted' treasure of the realm, the loss of arable ground to grazing causing food shortages and unemployment, the decay of towns and villages, and religious division.[7] Armigal Waad in 1559 complained of the poverty of the Queen, the penury of the nobility, the wealth of the meaner sort, the dearth of things, wars, divisions within the realm and want of justice.[8] Both were expressing the national distress at rapid inflation, devaluation, bad harvests and a decline in exports. In human terms these troubles meant that people found it harder to make a living, harder to pay for food and shelter, and harder to plan for the future. In political terms they meant declining tax revenue juxtaposed with rising costs and the pressure to act before the 'hatred conceived between the meaner sort and the gentlemen' flared into yet another local revolt.[9] Unemployment and an increasing population created problems for social order, too, raising concerns for all magistrates.

The responses to economic ills followed the popular academic definitions. Monetarists in their economic theory, most Tudor people thought of the economy as static and of inflation as the result of both greed and money whose face value did not match its bullion content. Quite capable of understanding the need for new markets and willing to use patents and monopolies to encourage new industries, they nevertheless fell back on the assumption that economic behaviour was the product of morality.

Social climbing and greed caused economic dislocation, so strict laws and moral instruction would cure the economy. In her first decade of rule Elizabeth took action to cure the monetary ills, to encourage new markets and trades, to freeze wages and prices, to punish greed, to keep markets open and to protect distressed industries. Her subjects

responded in a variety of ways, depending upon their positions, but
there was a broad acceptance of the monetarist and moral roots of their
troubles.

At the heart of the troubles was inflation. Participating in the great
inflation that overtook all of Europe in the century, England's problems
had been worsened by successive devaluations of its coinage. The coins
produced between 1545 and 1551 had been horribly overvalued,
sometimes deficient in silver content as much as four pence in
the troy pound.[10] Following the 'law' coined by England's greatest
money man of the 1550s and 1560s, Sir Thomas Gresham, this bad
money drove out the good, wreaking havoc in the foreign exchanges
and stimulating an inflationary spiral. A study comparing food prices
and wages demonstrates the impact of the inflation, showing how much
it stressed people's lives. Taking the year 1500 to equal 100, the index
of prices and wages shows the price of food at 217 and wages at 118 in
1550. In 1560 food was at 315 and wages were at 160. By 1570 things
had improved, with food at 298 and wages at 177, but beneath these
statistics is the fact that the buying power of people's incomes had been
drastically reduced in relation to foodstuffs. Manufactured goods had
inflated at about the same rate as wages, so that those selling the goods
found themselves further behind, too.[11]

Although there was general inflation occurring, the English problem
was compounded by the monetary policy of the Crown in the 1540s
and 1550s. As Henry VIII called in coins, melted them, and reissued
them with lower bullion content he made a great profit, adding so much
copper that the new testons (12 penny coins) had a rosy shade. John
Heywood, Thomas Whythorne's old master, wrote an epigram about
the debased coins:

> These testons look red: how like you the same?
> 'Tis a token of grace: they blush with shame.[12]

Henry made a profit, but his subjects found their currency discounted
in the international market. The increasing price of imports was crucial
in a nation that imported most of its raw materials for manufacturing.
Everything from canvas and alum, to steel and copper, came from
abroad.

Although the governments of Edward VI and Mary took some
steps towards improving English money without controlling the price
increases, Elizabeth inherited the belief that if the debased coins could
be replaced with good ones the inflation would stop. As Sir Thomas
Gresham informed her a few days after her accession, if she wished to
restore the realm to its former healthy state she had no choice but to
'bring your base money into fine of 11 ounce fine, and so gold after the
rate'.[13]

As soon as she was on the throne Elizabeth, who herself had written a memorandum on the coinage, began to prepare a recoinage, conceiving it as fiscal chemotherapy, as she said when she ordered it in 1560: 'them, that being sick receive a medicine, and in the taking feel some bitterness, but yet thereby recover health and strength, and save their lives.'[14]

A committee charged with preparing for the change was created in February 1559.[15] Eventually Sir Thomas Gresham found a German firm that would undertake the recoinage for a reasonable rate and a contract was signed in November 1560. As these plans for a new coinage were laid the old coins were revalued, with disturbing results.

In late September 1560 a financial panic swept through England when the Crown proclaimed a 'base' penny was now only worth ¾ of a penny, in accord with its bullion content.[16] The old coins would continue to circulate for four months, during which time they could be exchanged at the Mint for new money.

The proclamation explained that this adulterated money was causing 'all manner of prices of things in this realm necessary for sustentation of the people [to] grow daily excessive . . . to the lamentable and manifest hurt . . . specially of pensioners, soldiers, and all hired servants and other mean people that live by any kind of wages and not by rents of lands or trade of merchandise.'[17]

The people were suspicious, agreeing, perhaps, with the theory but unconvinced that any good would come from it. As the news spread slowly through the realm some refused to accept cash for goods and services, unsure of the value of the money they received. Others simply doubled their prices in order to cover possible losses.[18] On the one hand their quite reasonable reactions created an artificial shortage of goods, and on the other they caused prices to jump even higher.

Behind the panic was the fact that the 'base' coins were not easily told from better ones. Since there had been several mint standards over the past fifteen years one might find that one's good testons, the ones on which the king had a short neck and round face, were trading for the value of the condemned ones, on which the king had a long neck and lean face. Realizing this the government decreed that all the bad coins should be countermarked with a greyhound or a portcullis. The Master of the Mint objected, saying reasonably that this process would make counterfeiting easier, but the order was issued. Then it was noted that making the punches for the countermarks would take time. Even when they were made and distributed to the various sites where mayors and others were ordered to identify and mark the bad coins it was an undependable process. The officials appointed to decide which coins were bad were rejecting many good ones as counterfeit and misidentifying good as bad. It was November before the punches had been distributed and when they were it took time to sort and mark the coins. In London six hammerers of the Armourers' Company spent an entire month marking. In the meantime people were confused about what money to accept at what value, so some simply stopped accepting it.

Unprepared for the furore the proclamation had caused, the Court speeded up the move to a new coinage, but that scarcely reassured the nation. They had seen other recoinages and generally the Crown did not repay in new coins as much as the old coins it took in were worth (and it would not this time, making a profit approaching £50,000). And what if the new coins were going to be debased even further, no matter what the Queen claimed?

Meanwhile, those who believed that the value of the coins would increase rushed to pay their creditors, not wishing to pay contracted debts in money with a higher value.[19] Interest rates plummeted for the same reason.

Those who did not trust the government began hoarding coins. Thinking that the mint would not pay the equivalent in bullion value in new coins, they bought the old ones for export or to be melted into plate in order to maximize their profits.[20] Some of those hoarding the coins were foreign merchants, who were trying to get their profits out of the country before they disappeared.

On 20 September 1561 the mint stopped taking base coins, almost a full year after the devaluation. By October the recoinage had been completed, by which time the panic had subsided and £670,000 of base money had been withdrawn and recoined, its base alloys dumped in the roads to fill holes.[21]

By all rights the members of the Privy Council who had overseen the process had a right to feel relieved that the task was finished. Their economic theory told them that inflation should cease and all would be well with the realm, but they were wrong. Prices did not go down; 'all things were rather more dear, not only victuals but chiefly all kind of merchandise.'

Puzzled by the obstinately high prices of imported goods, the Council summoned the Warden of the Mercers to ask why, if the coins were now worth more, the prices of silk, satin and damasks had not come down as they and others had claimed they would. The mercers were called first, but they insisted that they should not be blamed alone. They would, they said righteously, lower their prices if the rest would. The grocers when called responded that they would peg their prices to those of the mercers.[22]

Representatives of all the haberdashers, merchant tailors, leather sellers, goldsmiths, girdlers, cloth workers, drapers, salters, iron mongers and merchant strangers companies prepared answers as well, their excuses showing that they had a better understanding of international trade than their governors. They could not, they said, sell their wares more cheaply unless they could buy silk more cheaply. Its price had risen in all parts of the world, and especially Spain, where the demand for it had increased.[23] There were too many merchants creating too much demand.

Faced with prices that would not decline and needing to negotiate a large loan in Antwerp, the Queen seems to have flirted with the idea of devaluing the coinage again. It was a time-honoured thing to devalue when borrowing abroad, paying the debt in bad coins as Henry VIII had done. But it was not wise. A rumour that it was about to happen ran through the country in December 1561.

Perhaps it was triggered by the proclamation announcing new denominations of small coins and outlawing foreign coins issued on 15 November. Christopher Bumpstead, ruminating on the shortage of small coins, sketched its logic. The new small coins were worth 6d, 3d, 1 ½d, and ¾d. A devaluation of one-third would give them the value of the old coins of 4d, 2d, 1d, and ½d they were replacing.[24] In early December Robert Jones had caught the rumour, telling Throckmorton: 'Here is great care taken for the perfection of our money: the new silver monies, and the banishment of foreign gold coins . . . make angels and royals to serve abroad, of whom . . . also there is a common opinion, that they shall change their state.' An anonymous courtier said there was 'great talk' in London 'of the fall of money from 5s to 10 grotes the ounce, and the angel to 6s 8d which troubled the merchants very much'.

The courtier and Jones both remarked that it stimulated the real estate and credit markets. Jones informs us that people were willing to pay '36 years' purchase' for land (that is, to pay the equivalent of the annual income from the property times thirty-six). The courtier said that lenders were willing to lend at no interest and for longer than usual terms (two and a half years) if payment was guaranteed in the money then current.[25]

When members of the Privy Council began paying off their creditors ahead of schedule, selling their plate to do it, the panic increased. The Queen made matters worse by offering to pay her creditors the thirty thousand pounds she owed in the City. They could either take their money immediately or she would extend the notes for another nine months. Opinion began to divide on what she was intending to do. London's merchants debated together for two days and split over whether it was better to get the cash now or afterwards, the young men demanding their money immediately while the old men were 'content to tarry for it, fearing [a] fall' of the value. In the end the older men bought out the notes of the younger men and became creditors for the whole debt.

The concern of the great merchants was communicated to the rest of the community. Prices jumped; some refused to sell and others would not take cash, requiring that the bill be paid in six months. The innkeepers would not take cash from carters, trusting them for it. In short the rumour 'made much talk and much unquietness for the time'.[26]

It made so much talk that the Council took action in February, issuing a proclamation bewailing the rumours. The false report of a 'decry' of monies was increasing at every market day, giving covetous people the excuse to raise their prices, it said. People spreading the rumour were to be imprisoned and the officers overseeing the markets were empowered to reduce the price of food to where 'it ought to have been if these vain rumours had not so spread abroad'.[27]

The people in the streets had reason to worry: the courtier historian tells us that a debate was raging at Court about the proposed devaluation. The argument was made sharper, he reflected bitterly, because

> the former fall of the base money was not so much grudged at, as this, for that did touch only the poor sort, for the great and wealthy men had changed all their base money into gold and kept it. This fall toucheth only or most of all the great and rich. Wherefore they do the more grudge at it, and invent all manner of excuses: some that money would be carried over [out of the realm]; some that things would be the better cheap to let it. Whereby we learn that every man is for himself, and none is moved with the hurt or loss of his poor neighbour . . . All things upon bruit of this fall increased a third part at the least in price.

Among those opposed to it was the Lord Treasurer, who said that they did not know what they were doing.[28]

The battle within the Council chamber spilled over when Lord Paget, once Queen Mary's leading adviser, wrote to Elizabeth, warning her that if there was devaluation there would be disturbances and that protest meetings were being held around the country.[29] He seems to have convinced her not to do it for the moment, to the Council's chagrin. When she told them what Paget said they petulantly answered that 'it was but a folly for them to debate things if she followed others' counsel' and demanded that he be brought before them. Elizabeth refused their demand.

The elderly Paget was made to regret his letter. Cecil and Petre interviewed him anyway. He refused to take responsibility for his letter, claiming decay of memory and lack of practice. When they got him to confess that he had raised his rents and had many oxen ready to sell they had what they needed to embarrass him. They told Lord Robert, who told the Queen. She ordered him to summon Paget and Sir Walter Mildmay, a leading Exchequer expert on coinage, to hear what each would say. Once again Paget claimed to know nothing 'for he understood nothing belonging either to money or to the exchange'. When his response was communicated to the Queen she 'said Paget was a busy knave, and willed he should send no more to her. For he was no better than a knave.'[30]

The revaluation had been temporarily stopped but the rumours continued to fly, stimulated by the heavy borrowing being done by Sir Thomas Gresham for the Crown. In early February the ports were closed. The Spanish ambassador was informed by Elizabeth that it was because they feared Henry, Lord Darnley might try to leave the realm, but, he says, many thought it was a trick to give them more time to borrow money in Antwerp on exchange in London. Apparently the Antwerp exchange was reacting to the rumours of a fall in the value of the money.[31] The anonymous courtier confirms this report, adding that only Gresham's posts were allowed to leave the country and that Gresham had borrowed £30,000 in London. He took this as a sign that the money would not fall, but still no one knew.

At the end of February, Gresham went to Flanders to raise more money, again suggesting that the money would not be devalued, but in the meantime people were still refusing to accept cash for wares or for debts, and debtors rushed to pay their creditors.

When Gresham borrowed £40,000 in Flanders the value of the pound dropped. 'The merchants,' wrote the courtier, 'curse Gresham as their cut-throat,' noting that when Gresham arrived in the Low Countries the pound was exchanging at 24s Flemish; afterwards it fell to 22s 6d Flemish for a pound.[32]

Meanwhile the Council prepared to devalue. In early March a proclamation announcing the devaluation was printed, declaring that the angel, currently rated at 10s, was to fall to 6s 8d, as the courtier had foretold. The shilling was to fall from 12d to 8d and the sixpence to 4d.

The logic behind this devaluation shows that it was driven by the Council's frustration over the refusal of prices to decrease. According to all monetarist theory prices should have gone down as the purity of the money increased. Instead prices had jumped sharply because people charged as much or more in the new coins as they had charged when the coinage was debased. It was probably the discussion of this that had set off the rumours about devaluation in December, but the proclamation blamed the people who had been raising prices to offset the effects of the rumoured devaluation. The result was that the 'meaner sorts' and people living by wages could scarcely afford the necessities of life. To correct this and get prices back to where they should be a devaluation of a third was declared.[33]

For reasons that are unclear this proclamation was never issued. Perhaps it dawned on them that the Lord Treasurer was right: they did not know what they were doing. Watching the collapse of the pound in Antwerp must have given them pause for thought. One rumour said that Italian merchants had 'made great friends' with their money to stop the devaluation. Another was that Sir Henry Sidney had written from Wales warning that the people were offended by the thought of devaluation.

They blamed Lord Robert for the threatened devaluation because his father had debased the currency twice. Yet another report had it that some forty persons had attended the sermon at Court the Wednesday before and begged the Queen to do something about the price of food, 'otherwise by reason of the dearth they should starve'. Whatever their logic, instead of devaluing the currency the Queen issued a proclamation piously asserting that anyone who believed that a devaluation was in the wind was wrong.[34]

This proclamation was much gentler than the abandoned one. Noting the troubles and the increased prices caused when 'simple people, of doubtfulness and without evil meaning' believed them, it lamented the greed of the 'cursed sort' who used the excuse to raise prices, feeding their 'unsatiable and unmerciful greediness'. The Queen insisted she had no intention to change the value of the money, and she hoped that the 'honest sort of her subjects' would believe her. The dishonest sort who did not believe and who spread the seditious rumours were to be imprisoned and pilloried.[35] The danger engendered by these rumours was taken so seriously that when, in 1566, a man was sued for defaming another by saying he 'is a traitor and worthy to be hanged, for he said money was fallen a noble in the pound', Justice Brown opined that these rumours were the cause of inflation.[36]

Some of the 'dishonest sort', who learned before the 13 March proclamation was issued that there would be no devaluation, took advantage of the situation to borrow as much money as they could. Since most people still expected a devaluation they were willing to lend free for twelve months, or, more commonly, lent at the astonishingly low rate of eight per cent.[37]

The frustration of people who believed that a restored coinage would lower prices must have been intense, as was their disappointment. 'It was supposed,' wrote the courtier of that March, 'that by the alteration of coin both the exchange would have increased and all kinds of wares would have been better cheap'. But the exchange did not improve, and costs were as high with the teston at 2s silver as they were when it was at 12d.[38]

II

When the revaluation of the coinage failed to stop the inflation (it slowed, but probably not enough to be visible to contemporaries) the other popular economic theory was applied. The government moved to punish greedy people by legislating against the importation of foreign goods, fixing wages and prices, enforcing the statutes regulating apparel, and applying a regulatory solution when the markets failed to respond to the currency cure. Unfortunately, the moves to support home industry and slow the importation of foreign goods caused a trade war with the Spanish governors of the Low Countries.

On another front Elizabethan governors moved to improve the food supply, reasoning that if the price of food was increasing, a larger supply would make it cheaper. Of course an increasing population was driving the demand for food, but in the famines and mortality crises of the late 1550s and early 1560s no one identified population as the problem. Rather, greedy people and sinful people were the problem. God punished sin with bad harvests, while obdurate sinners maximized their income in times of bad harvests.

No one in the 1560s could think about the food supply without contemplating the national famine of 1555–7, followed by the bad harvests of 1559–60, 1561–62, and 1564–5. In the famine people in London had died of starvation, and, as William Cecil recalled, many were driven to live on acorns. The dearth, combined with disease, made 1556–61 the only five-year period in the century when the nation's population actually declined.[39]

Weather (and therefore God) was the chief cause of the bad harvests. In the winter and spring of 1562, for instance, it rained and rained, so that all across northern Europe the grain crops suffered. In March 1562 the anonymous courtier talked about the weather:

All the winter past was very great rain, not only in England, but also in France, Flanders and in the East parts. Such scarcity of corn imagined at Danzig that those merchants that be resident there write how there is no hope of any corn there or to be gotten there this year. Whereupon corn waxeth dear in all places. And now in London meal is sold at 36s the quarter, wheat at 24s.[40]

The government's reaction was to issue a proclamation ordering the covetous persons who had driven up the prices to quit hoarding grain.[41]

The report from Danzig that no grain could be bought there was distressing, since in times of bad harvests it was normal for city governments to import it from the Baltic. These imports, however, were not popular with the farmers. When it was feared that there would be a shortage of wheat in 1561 the merchants of London had imported great quantities. English farmers grumbled that 'they must leave the plough if they might not sell their corn at indifferent [fair] prices', but the surplus in the Baltic was so great that when 160 hulks laden with grain sank in a storm off Norway the prices did not increase.[42]

By Easter of 1562 food was very expensive. Beef had risen to 16d a stone, while pigeons and baby rabbits were selling for 3 or 4s a dozen.[43]

If the rains of 1561–2 had damaged the winter wheat the farmers might hope for a good crop of spring wheat, and by May it was flourishing in the fair weather. The price came down and the fear subsided. But in June it began to rain, raining steadily into mid-July, so that 'the ways were so foul as in winter, the meadows in all places over flown, much hay destroyed, corn grew full of weeds, and that bred a sudden dearth of corn [at] 6d in a bushel'. For thirty days the wind blew steadily from the southwest, bringing in the storms. The anonymous courtier linked this terrible weather with the births of monsters occurring all around. A calf with a child's face, a child with toad's feet, a pig with eight feet, siamese twins, children without arms and legs. Noting the birth of 'many monstrous pigs with men's noses', he said, 'It is thought to be reason of the great moisture of the last winter.'[44]

In 1565–6 all of northern Europe was hungry. Export of English grain was forbidden because, said the Duke of Norfolk, overseas sales increased domestic prices. In London the Aldermen blamed the shortage on the Queen's purveyors – and the Council did sell Antwerp 850 quarters of wheat to ease its bellies.[45]

The official response to famine considered both the present necessity and the future need. Immediate crises were likely to be blamed on engrossers, forestallers, and other greedy people who kept goods off the markets in order to inflate their prices. In the longer term food shortages were blamed on enclosure, as more and more land was turned into sheep pasture to supply the lucrative wool trade and as gentlemen built deer parks.

Regrators, engrossers and forestallers were ancient enemies of the commonweal. In a society that had a labour theory of value the activities of middlemen were looked upon with deep suspicion. Like usurers, their role as facilitators was not recognized, so brokerage was considered criminal. Moreover, it was believed that fair competition was necessary to maintain a just price. Undoubtedly there were people who could and would create local shortages to increase prices, but their impacts were only local, unless there were, as Elizabethans seemed to believe, so many of them and they were so organized that they could act in league. Nonetheless, in markets throughout the land there were pillories where these 'caterpillars' were publicly punished, placarded with declarations of their offences. They were people like John Shef, a leather seller, pilloried in 1561 for selling 'false belts' because he did not have 'the fear and dread of almighty God before his eyes but was seduced by the subtle craft of the Devil and was blinded with the great and horrible vice of covetousness'.[46]

Consequently even when prices rose naturally because of shortages the officers of the market stepped in to force them down again. In inflationary times the regrators and forestallers were imagined to be extraordinarily busy, so there was a tendency to establish legal maximums for prices by statute or by proclamation. Thus when Elizabeth lowered the price of hops in 1564 it was because it had risen from a mark or a pound to six pounds a hundredweight. Rather than reflecting on the market realities affecting such a major import, however, she blamed merchants seeking 'singular gain' who had created a monopoly of hops which, if they were allowed to continue, would encourage others to create monopolies of other things.[47]

During the lean winter of 1564–5 Nicholas Bacon forcefully reminded the justices of their duty to control regrators, forestallers and engrossers. The hurt they did, he said, was clearly demonstrated by the dearth of grain, 'for doubtless, albeit the plenty of some kind of grain in some countries is not so great this year', yet surely it was not so scarce that the shortage should be so large. The 'ill disposition of the people by engrossing and regrating and false bruits raising for greedy gain's sake hath been the chief and principal cause of this dearth and not scarcity alone'. These greedy engrossers were abetted, he said, by the justices who gave licenses for moving grain to anyone who asked, driving up the prices and hurting the very people who granted the licenses.[48]

If the price of food was partially a function of the greed of the seller and the need of the buyer, its supply was affected by the amount of land under cultivation. In the mid-sixteenth century it was widely suspected that high food prices were the result of high wool prices. So much money could be made from wool that arable land was being turned into pasture, decreasing the amount of human food available in the market.

For the theorists enclosure meant a reduced supply of food. For the folk losing access to land it meant loss of livelihood. Sometimes they took justice into their own hands. In Lichfield in the early summer of 1562 nearly three hundred 'lewd fellows' pulled down the fences being built to enclose their commons. A canny lot, when many of them were arrested and questioned about who their leaders were they claimed to have done it with 'common consent, and that every of them is at fault as much as any other'.[49] In 1569 a similar incident occurred in Derbyshire. When an encloser began to hedge and ditch Mayston Field near Chinley the villagers filled in the ditch and tore down the hedge rather than give up their grazing. The developer, Geoffrey Bradshaw, swore out a warrant against their leaders and got an order to desist from the Chancellor of the Duchy of Lancaster, but the villagers took up arms,

Propter iniquitatem auaritiæ eius iratus sum, et percussi eum:
abscondi et indignatus sum: Et abijt vagus in via cordis sui. Esay. 57.
v. 17.

Vt nos eremo, vitam traduximus olim:
    Glandibus igniferis, simplicibusque cibis:
Vt sanctis precibus, siluæ sonuere silentes:
    Sacri scriptores, historiaque docent.
Quem postquam viderant proceres, pietatis amore
    Præbuerant terras, exiguasque domos.
Hæc vt prestigijs, augentur ad prædia nostris:
    Horribili cœpit, viuere quisque modo.
Mollia securi, quæsuimus ocia vita.
    Præcipue viguit, vilis auaritia.

Figure 15 'The Greedy Monk' surveying his lands, an anti-Catholic cartoon from 1567.
The monk's greed for land was matched by the land hunger of the enclosers.

threatened to burn his house, and attacked the village constable trying to serve the warrant.[50]

Villagers losing their commons were disturbed, but they were not alone. Great landlords often found that their farmers were converting their lands to pasture without permission, substantially changing the nature of their revenues. In the early 1570s Sir Francis Hastings undertook an inspection of the lands of the Earl of Huntington in Devon and Cornwall. He enjoyed inspecting the 'gallant hill where there hath been a castle in times past called Camelot wherein Sir Lancelot in K[ing] Arthur's time is fained to have dwelled' now grazed by 280 sheep belonging to four widows, but he also found things that disturbed him. The village of Hardington was gone,

> wholly enclosed and made pasture and no house left but his [the farmer's] own, and he pulls down the church, and it is scant known where the parsonage house stood, to which there is known to be a glebe belonging but where it lyeth will hardly be found. Therefore some speedy care would be had to look to it. This Mr Bamfield denieth my lord's officers from coming upon his ground to seize any stray or other profit for my lord, and denieth also to come to my lord's court and to present any commodity to my lord saving his common fine only which he payeth.[51]

The men and women who were losing their commons saw enclosure as a threat to their livelihoods; landlords saw it as a perversion of their leases; farmers saw it as economic progress. Parliament saw it as the cause of food shortages, high prices and social instability. In 1563 an omnibus Act reformed the laws regulating the conversion of land from arable to pasture. According to this new law any land that had been farmed for four years since the twentieth year of Henry VIII had to be kept in cultivation, under threat of a fine of 10s per acre. If the land had been converted to pasture the farmer had one year to bring it back into production. There were provisos in this statute that made it clear that its authors were aiming to stop the production of wool. If your pasture was for meat animals it was exempted; if your pasture supported your own work and milk animals it was exempted; and if you used the ground to feed deer or rabbits it was exempted. Rabbit warrens came in for special treatment, however, probably at the prompting of people whose gardens had fallen victim to the voracious beasts. No warren could be larger than five acres and none could be established within a mile of a house. Nor could it be close enough to one's neighbours' fields to eat their crops.[52]

Parliament's attempt to stop the enclosures did not work very well, since the leading gentlemen of the counties were also the ones most likely to enclose. Lord Keeper Bacon lamented to the justices in 1565 that if the statute on tillage was properly enforced 'it would not be that so many villages should be decayed neither so many parts of the country so weakly peopled as they now be'.[53]

Other steps encouraged food production too. Technically the export of grain had been illegal since 1361, but statutes were passed in 1555, 1559, 1563 and 1571 that permitted export of any surpluses. If, for instance, the price of wheat did not exceed 10s it could be sold overseas.[54] As a result, said Camden, the country people began farming more enthusiastically, ploughing out land that had been pasture.[55]

Ironically, given the concern over enclosure, the 1560s were a time of agricultural innovation and more land was being brought into cultivation. As the population pressure mounted the demand for food and the need of more land to farm led people to farm where no farming had been. In 1571, for instance, a commission of inquiry found that 545 acres of Westward Forest in Cumbria had been converted into 32 new farms. In Caernarvonshire salt marshes were being converted into pasture.[56] It was the beginning of what has been labelled an agricultural revolution in England.

Protecting the food supply took other forms beyond encouraging tillage and preventing monopolies. Eradicating pests and protecting wild food supplies were part of the effort, too. In 1559 the Commons passed a bill for killing rooks, crows and choughes that ate the crops, as well as one for preserving the fry of salmon, pikes, eels, trout and other fish.[57] People were, 'lamentable and horrible to be reported', catching baby fish in nets and using them to feed pigs and dogs. Tight nets were abolished and people were ordered not to fish out of season. Trout eight inches and salmon sixteen inches in length could be kept, but anything smaller had to be thrown back. Thoughtfully the authors provided an exception for people using nets to catch smelt and other tiny fish.[58]

Fish were a special problem for Elizabeth's government and subjects. The fishing industry was important to the economy and to the navy but it had been dealt a serious blow by the Reformation. Although Anglicans officially observed Lent (an observance backed by an annual proclamation from the Queen), and although they were supposed to eat fish on 'fasting evens' of ascension day, midsummer's day, and St Simon's and St Jude's day and all through Christmas and Easter, they did not eat as much fish they had under Catholicism. Friday had been a universal fish day then, and some people had observed Wednesday as one, too, 'for superstition'. The monasteries, colleges, commanderies and other religious establishments had eaten little flesh at any time. In short, the consumption of fish had declined sharply since the 1530s, and the supply of ships and sailors had declined along with it.[59]

In 1559 someone had introduced a bill late in the parliamentary session 'against eating of flesh on Wednesday by artificers and husbandmen', which suggests an attempt to subsidise fishing, but it died at the prorogation.[60] In 1563 it seems to have slipped into the Commons' agenda through a stratagem. Admiral Winter asked the Commons to consider some way to improve the navy. Obligingly a committee produced the bill 'touching certain politic considerations made for the maintenance of the navy'. Hidden under this vague title was a series of measures to stimulate sea fishing. It ended all tolls on importing or exporting fish caught by subjects of the Crown. It forbade foreign ships from carrying fish, food, or wares from point to point in England, and stopped the importation of French wine in foreign ships. It encouraged ship owners, fishermen, gunners and shipwrights to increase the number of their apprentices. And it required everyone to eat fish every Wednesday.

It was the Wednesday 'political Lent' that made the bill a lightning rod. No one seems to have objected to most of the bill, but to men just escaping from Catholicism eating fish any day of the week looked like papist superstition. Although Cecil himself made a speech favouring it, pointing out that the Anglican Church required fish to be eaten two-fifths of each year anyway, it was forced into committee and heavily amended.

Most notable were the two provisos mitigating the religious offence offered by a fish day. To make it plain that this was not a religious fast, and probably to mollify butchers and flesh lovers, people were allowed one dish of flesh if 'he or she or they have also served to the same table . . . at the same meal, three full competent usual dishes of sea fish'. Even people licensed by the Church to eat flesh in Lent were expected to buy the fish.

The second provision bluntly confronted the confusion between fasting for spiritual reasons and a subsidy. It enacted that anyone who said that it was necessary to eat fish on Wednesday in order to save one's soul would be punished for spreading false news.[61]

When the amended bill came back to the Commons the argument raged for three days before the final vote. Forced to divide the House, the Speaker found 179 in favour and 97 opposed. Sent to the Lords, a ping-pong game of amendments for special interests such as Yarmouth, Chepstow and the Cinque Ports was played before it finally passed.[62]

This law, referred to as 'Cecil's Fast', was intensely disliked by the Godly and it was frequently attacked in later Parliaments, forcing the establishment to defend it. In Lent of 1566 Nicholas Carvell, preaching at Paul's Cross, believed it necessary to explain that their Wednesday civil fast, a sparing of meat for the preservation of the commonwealth, was different from that of the papists, who 'guess that Judas that day conceived in his mind to betray Christ'.[63]

This Act to improve the navy was part of a general effort to control prices and stimulate the economy by stifling foreign imports and giving English manufacturers and ship owners as much of the domestic market as possible. This effort, however, was not one sided. Although Parliament used policy to do this, there were many private interests at work, too. Business people have always known that the cheapest form of competition is legislation.

III

Just how complicated the government's attempts to control prices could become, and just how important it was to business to have law on one's side, is illustrated by the long, sad history of the Vintners' Company. Wine was a valuable and much disputed commodity, carefully regulated by the authorities. Until 1552 the supervision of prices and taverns had belonged to the Vintners' but in Edward VI's last Parliament a group of burghers in the Commons succeeded in passing 7 Edw. VI, c. 5, 'Avoiding the Great Price and Excess of Wine'. It stripped the Vintners' of their authority over the wine trade, giving local mayors the right to license taverns.

The Vintners spent Mary's reign trying for a repeal and when Elizabeth succeeded they sent a bill to her first Parliament. Designed to take away the right of mayors to license the sale of wines, it made it to a third reading in the Commons but died in the prorogation. It did not die for want of trying on the part of the Vintners, however, who spent a great deal promoting it, including giving the London MP John Marshe a hogshead of wine for his pains and sending the officers of the Exchequer wine at Christmas.

Their failure was made more bitter when they found themselves included in the Act for Maintenance of the Navy in 1563. For reasons that are not apparent a section of the statute declared that wines could be retailed at prices fixed by proclamation.[64] Worse, the Queen took this seriously and began setting the prices annually.[65] Naturally these prices were lower than the Vintners thought they ought to be.

Therefore in 1564–6 they made a concerted effort to repeal the statutes that offended them. In a petition to the Queen they asserted that because wine sellers were not governed by a single company the price of wine was artificially high. Moreover, 'the navy of this realm . . . and especially in the west parts thereof is greatly decayed and the number of mariners which should serve therein much diminished' because the trade was poorly managed. (Here they were linking themselves with the fortunes of Bristol, through which most of the Spanish sweet wine passed.) At a time when wood was in short supply (the subject of a bill against the iron smelters) the import of more wine would bring in lots of useful casks, too. Lastly, the four or five hundred men, women and children who earned their livelihoods from the Company would be supported if only they were allowed to control who could sell wine.

With the Vintners managing the taverns, they told Cecil, things would be less merry but much better ordered in England, for they promised to end whoredom, dicing, dancing and banqueting of apprentices and servants, and fast-breaking. Furthermore, usury and 'overhighing' of prices in the trade would end.[66]

To work these miracles Parliament in 1566 was asked for a statute. Leaving no stone unturned and no official unbribed the Vintners sought to smooth the way. They enrolled their petition in Chancery under the Lord Keeper's Great Seal, secured the support of the London aldermen, and consulted the Lord Keeper personally. All of this cost the large sum of £22 3s, but when the bill actually entered the Commons their expenses skyrocketed. Their accounts show payments to the Lord Chief Justice, the Clerk of the Crown and the Master of Requests. Leicester was sent two tuns of wine and Cecil's wife received nearly £40 worth of canvas and napkins.

The Vintners gave a bibulous lunch for the members in a tavern just before the vote. Influenced by the free wine the happy Members passed the bill on a division of 95 to 65, only to change their minds in the clear, sober light of the next Monday morning.[67]

After their bill failed they turned again to the Queen and in 1567 she issued letters patent effectively exempting the Vintners from the offending statute. However, they continued in the 1570s to attempt a full repeal.[68]

The Vintners were unusually persistent and unlucky but the use and abuse of regulation to which they were subjected, and would have liked to use on others, is typical. It is not clear that anyone at the time appreciated the irony of the ways in which government was being used in the economy. On the one hand the guilds insisted that they exercise limited monopolies in their own spheres, while on the other they and their governors complained about the dangers of monopolies that distorted the markets. Richard Porder, attacking usurers from Paul's Cross, outlined the danger of monopolies. Usurers, he said, lend to the rich man, who, having the money

> doth engross the markets, bringeth heaps of commodities into his own hands, and so maketh a Monopoly, and dearth without need. The meaner sort are thereby prevented of their markets, and must glean after the engrosser, and take small leavings or sit still, and so remain mean, or rather become poor: the common sort weep through the dearth, for the rich will be sure to make his common weal to bear out his loss, and pay for that usury, and when many are beggared forever, one is helped with a halfpenny, which is the usurer's charity.[69]

Usurers and rich men engrossing markets were a fear, but the reality was that control of the markets was the goal of the guilds. By extension the policy-makers saw the realm as a single market and tried to give English people a monopoly of their own markets by limiting access to foreign merchants.

The impetus for this came from a number of sources. Of course, the merchant community argued that the best way for them to flourish was to limit competition, and the government agreed. Groups like the Merchant Adventurers, the Muscovy Company, the Merchant Adventurers of Bristol and the other limited trading companies that sprang up in the middle of the century are proof of the common view that everyone benefited if imports and exports were controlled by a few. Economic troubles spurred monopoly, too. Since most luxury goods were imported they were seen as a undermining domestic production, just as the use of foreign ships to carry English goods or the sale of fish caught by foreigners undermined the English navy. Then, too, imports hurt the balance of trade and sucked money out of the nation.

The encouragement of English self-sufficiency required laws that protected native manufactures, built up the merchant fleet and stimulated exports. It created a climate in which all sorts of interests cloaked themselves in the flag and demanded discriminatory rules.

The woolen cap trade, for instance, was hurting because high-crowned hats were becoming fashionable. Made from felt, they were displacing the soft woolen caps that had previously been fashionable. Worse, they were often made by foreign craftsmen of foreign felt. The impact, according to the Company of Cappers, was that the Queen's subjects 'using the art of making woolen caps, are impoverished and decayed by the excessive use of hats and felts, and thereby divers good cities and towns brought to desolation, great plenty of strange [foreign] commodities without necessity consumed, and great number of people enforced to depend upon the having of foreign wools', thus endangering the realm.

This thirst for felt hats encouraged lawbreaking, too, and an Exchequer Special Commission investigated the smuggling of Spanish hats and felts into Devon and Cornwall. The commissioners were trying to find out who was bringing them in and how they were being distributed.[70] Perhaps it was their inability to stop the smuggling that encouraged parliamentary regulation of the market.

The threats to royal revenue and cappers were met by a 1566 law that forbade caps to be made of felt, ordered that no one under the rank of a knight could wear a cap or hat of velvet, and, most importantly, constricted the supply of felt hats by severely limiting the number of hatters in the realm. Significantly, the Haberdashers of London were given the right to enforce the rules about felts. The Haberdashers and

Cappers returned to Parliament in 1571 and secured a statute that ordered everyone except peers of the realm to wear a wool cap on Sundays and holidays. The preamble to this statute was more specific (if hyperbolic) about the plight of the industry, pointing out that it was not just cappers who were suffering. They employed men, women and children, 'and also the halt and the lame', to card, spin, knit, part, force, thick, dress, walk, dye, battle, shear, press, edge, line and band caps. Thrown out of work by felt hats they are forced to beg to live, 'ranging and gadding' through the realm, practicing 'sundry kinds of lewdness'. In short, unemployment in the capping trade vested the nation with a hoard of vagabonds. With eight thousand making caps in London alone the depression in caps was no small problem, if we believe the Act.[71]

Preventing the importation of foreign goods was one way of solving the problem of imports. Another was to encourage the development of domestic sources of supply. In the 1560s patents and monopolies were widely used for this. These monopolies sometimes had the benign purpose of modern patents and copyrights, protecting inventions and encouraging investment. For instance, in 1564 a naturalized citizen who came from Germany received a patent to make white salt in the realm 'without other salt', importing a process. In 1561 a patent was issued for making cakes of white, hard soap of the same quality as soap made in Seville. Inventions were protected, too. Jacob Acontius, the Italian engineer and philosopher of toleration living in exile in London, was licensed in 1565 to be the sole maker of machines for grinding, crushing and wood-cutting consisting of wheels driven by wind power. He also patented a new, efficient wood furnace for making ale and dyes.[72]

Some other patents are clearly tied to national defence. Lacking domestic sources of gunpowder, alum, brass and many other essential goods there was a conscious effort to find or develop them. Patents were issued in the 1560s for a new invention for making saltpetre for gunpowder, for alum and copperas mines, and for mineral mines. In the cases of the mines this meant protecting the investments of men who had 'brought into England workmasters of great knowledge and experience in mineral works and waterworks for draining mines'.[73]

Fighting imports and encouraging the development of native manufactures was one use of law. Another was to impede competition and guarantee profits. Lacking any faith in free enterprise, early Elizabethans assumed that well-ordered markets were the best markets, creating the opportunity for competitors to attack one another through proclamations and parliaments.

That was the source of the battle waged by the Clothworkers Company against the Merchant Adventurers. The Clothworkers, a major livery company with a seat in the Court of Aldermen of London from the 1550s, were troubled by people from other companies working in their trade, beyond their control. Compounding their concerns was the export of undressed cloth to be finished by foreign workers, taking bread from the mouths of the Company's workers.

A statute of Henry VIII had reserved the finishing of expensive kinds of cloth to English workers, but inflation and royal licenses suspending the statute had robbed it of any effect. The Merchant Adventures were exporting huge numbers of unfinished clothes by the 1560s. After the plague of 1563 interrupted the export trade the Clothworkers were in great distress and, when the trade reopened in January 1565, they resented the fact that the Merchant Adventurers were again exporting unfinished cloth.

In the summer of 1565 they petitioned the Privy Council for help in their misery. The Council was sympathetic – perhaps because the harvest was bad and the price of bread was high – so it asked the Merchant Adventurers why it was necessary to export the cloth unfinished. They answered that English finished cloth was of too poor a quality to sell in continental markets. Incensed, the Clothworkers demanded an impartial test of the quality of their goods against continental cloth and were declared the winners.

With this victory under their belts they set out to get control of cloth finishing in London, reasoning that the problem of quality was really one of lack of control. With the officers of the Company regulating apprenticeship and production the quality could be guaranteed. To secure this control they needed an act of Parliament, so the Company began a lobbying effort, spending lavishly with gifts to the Lord Keeper, dinners at the King's Head in Fleet Street for the Members, burnt sack and muscatel for the councillors, and a swan for the Speaker.

In the Commons they met serious opposition, especially from the Merchant Adventurers whose Master, John Marshe, was on the committee that examined their bill. After an attempt to split the Clothworkers in two by moving the artisans of the Company into the Merchant Tailors failed a compromise was reached that ordered the Merchant Adventurers to export one finished cloth for every four unfinished. This was amended to one in ten before the battle was over, but the Merchant Adventurers were severely annoyed nonetheless.

The necessity of shipping finished cloth to a market which did not want it was bad enough, but it was compounded by the fact that it complicated their lading methods. Moreover, the Merchant Adventurers only shipped twice a year, in early summer and in winter. Dressing and dying of cloth could only be done in the warm summer months, so that there was little finished cloth to ship in the winter. When they tried to concentrate all the finished cloth in the summer shipment, however, the Clothworkers would not agree to it, and neither would the Privy Council.[74]

This kind of interference in the cloth trade with Antwerp worsened an already bad situation for English exports. For years Antwerp had been the centre of English exporting activities, giving their cloth access to continental customers via the Rhine and the Baltic. In the 1560s, however, that trade was disrupted by plague, wars and politics.

IV

Early in 1558 two events had set the stage for what happened to the Flanders trade in the 1560s: Calais was lost and the customs duties were raised. Until the fall of Calais raw English wool was sold to continental manufacturers by the Company of Merchant Staplers operating from that city. Afterwards they reopened the wool staple in Bruges, further concentrating English exports in the Spanish Netherlands. At the same time Mary reformed her customs book, significantly increasing the export duty on English cloth.

At the end of 1558 Mary died, dissolving the marriage bond that had tied England and the Netherlands together as possessions of Philip II of Spain, while the Protestantism of Elizabeth did little to endear her or her merchants to the conservative Margaret of Parma, governor of the Spanish Low Countries.

The alliance between England and the Burgundian lands of Flanders was an old one, and the regions were economically interdependent, but in the early 1560s relations with Spain were strained and Margaret – resenting English encouragement of heretics in her territories, the unwillingness of Elizabeth to stop piracy aimed at Flemish ships, the statutes that discriminated against her merchants and their goods, and the high English tariffs – sought to bring the English to heel. With the approval of Philip II she complained to the English in 1563 about their policies and, when she was not satisfied with their answers, she began a trade embargo to teach them a lesson.

Embargoes were not new in the relationship; there had been two others, both of which taught Margaret that the English needed the Antwerp trade more than the Flemings needed the English. Conveniently the plague struck England in the summer of 1563, giving her an excuse to ban the entry of English goods into the Low Countries in November. Elizabeth retaliated by halting imports from the Low Countries in March 1564.[75]

Thomas Cooper remembered that this embargo caused 'all manner of wares to grow unto great and excessive prices', while the incomes of people in the cloth industry shrank. Although it was claimed that the plague was the reason for the ban, many, Cooper reported, said the Lords of Antwerp, 'whose pride is great', and the Catholic clergy there who bore malice towards the English because of their religion, had stopped the trade to cause a 'mutiny' in England. For months the Merchant Adventurers waited for an opportunity to ship their cloth until finally, driven by desperation, they begged the Queen to allow them to take their trade to some other country. Emden was settled on, and they set out. 'Thither they are gone,' said Cooper, 'with 40 sail of good ships laden with English clothes. God send them a good market with a prosperous and profitable return.'[76]

To the surprise of Margaret and her advisers the move to Emden worked well enough that the English were unwilling to give in to their demands and they found that the embargo was hurting Antwerp more than London. Moreover, to teach Margaret that England did not need Flanders Elizabeth stopped the Merchant Staplers from shipping the wool to Bruges that supplied the Flemish weaving industry. Although it damaged English trade, it was thought that the Staplers should share in the misery of the Merchant Adventurers in order to get better terms for all. Otherwise, 'it is like that we should set their people on work and suffer our own to go a begging to the great hurt and decay of the common weal of England'.[77]

After thirteen months of the embargo, with workers and merchants on both sides suffering, the two governments finally agreed to resume trading on 1 January 1565. The issues between them would be settled by negotiating teams to meet at Bruges. In the meantime the laws and taxes that had so offended the Netherlanders would be suspended pending the outcome of the talks. Having returned to the *status quo ante* of 1 January 1559 they prepared to negotiate.[78]

The talks at Bruges dragged on into 1566 and ended with nothing resolved. The problem, seen from the Scheldt, was that the English had been erecting trade barriers between the countries while exploiting the Antwerp market. Besides the increase in the customs the English had prohibited the export of salted hides, backs and tallow, sheepskins, pelts, white ashes (for soap making), wood, beer (described as a 'very necessary kind of victual'), herring and several other things. They would not let herring out of the realm and they would not let salt cod and ling in. And then there were the navigation acts of 1559 and 1563. In 1559 it was ruled that any English person shipping goods in a 'stranger's bottom' was to pay the customs charged to foreigners; in 1563 foreigners were cut out of the coasting trade altogether.[79] Most of the laws to which they were objecting had been passed in the previous two Parliaments, demonstrating how the attempts to keep English goods for the English while exporting to the foreigners had boomeranged.

While they negotiated trade rebounded and 1565 was an especially good year for English cloth exports. All seemed well, but politics and religion in the Netherlands dictated otherwise. Antwerp was boiling with tensions that spilled over in the summer of 1566. Calvinist preachers stirred the people there and dissident Protestant nobles, known as *Gueux* or Beggars, allied with them, provoking iconoclastic rioting. The interruption of the trade with England in 1563–4 had been followed by two bad harvests, unemployment and high food prices fueling the revolt, making it a difficult place in which to do business.

In the spring of 1566 Philip II crossed 'a rubicon of Spanish imperialism' ordering the Duke of Alva and a Spanish army to the Netherlands to restore order.[80] In March 1567 a full-scale revolt against Spanish rule was attempted, but it was too late. The *Gueux* were defeated and Antwerp was occupied by the Spaniards. The vicious repression that followed, and the mere presence of a Spanish army in the Netherlands, frightened Elizabeth and her Council. Both they and the French Huguenots, established in their Atlantic base at La Rochelle, feared that when the Netherlands were tamed Alva and his battle-hardened *tercios* would be ordered to repress the other heretics in north-west Europe. Of course, it was assumed that the Spanish Inquisition would follow in their bloody footsteps. Adding to the confusion was the rumour that a Huguenot army was marching to aid their co-religionists in the Netherlands.

Late in 1567 Margaret of Parma was removed from the government of the Netherlands and Alva, declaring 'There is a new world to be created here', began ruling the country with Spaniards and Italians. Some fighting continued into 1568 before an uneasy quiet settled over Flanders while the anti-Spanish forces licked their wounds and prepared for the next round of the civil war.[81]

All these troubles meant financial turmoil in England, too. The Flemish pound fluctuated wildly on the exchanges and, since Elizabeth owed over £40,000 in Antwerp, there was a chance to pay off the debt at a discount when the pound Flemish went below twenty-three shillings.[82] On the downside, customs revenues declined as the disturbances bit into the volume of cloth going abroad. The proscriptions, exiles and executions of leading Antwerp merchants caused trouble too, since they left many debts to English people unpaid and Alva showed little willingness to help them collect.

For the Merchant Adventurers there were other threatening signs. Most importantly the 'double toll' reappeared. Each province of the Netherlands had the right to levy its own tolls, but by custom the English merchants only paid that of Brabant in which Antwerp was situated. To their surprise, in 1566 Zealand arrested an Englishman for not paying the toll, resulting in a long legal wrangle and a declaration that the English could be charged tolls by more than one province. If acted upon this decree would make trading in Antwerp too expensive.

One other outcome of the troubles in 1566–8 was the collapse of the

Antwerp alum staple. Alum, an essential mordant in cloth dying, had been exported to Antwerp from Italy, where it was produced under a papal monopoly. When the English staple moved to Emden they managed to get alum sent there, and in 1568 the Genoese who managed the alum monopoly began shipping directly to England. This was a wonderful stimulus for English trade to the Mediterranean.[83]

Alva's activities in the Spanish Netherlands remained a source of concern to Elizabeth and her Council, combining neatly with a financial opportunity in 1568. In late November a Spanish fleet carrying money for Alva's government from Spain was driven into port in Devon and Cornwall by the swarms of privateers and pirates operating out of New Rochelle and the Low Countries. When the Spanish treasure ships entered English waters Elizabeth decided to keep the money on board for her own use.

Naturally this set off an intense diplomatic battle that almost led to war. The official English explanation for the seizure was that the money did not yet belong to Spain. It had been borrowed from Genoese financiers and Elizabeth was simply taking over the contract; the owners of the money would lose nothing. Beneath this peculiar excuse were other concerns. John Hawkins's brother William had just heard of his brother's disaster at San Juan de Ulloa and was urging that Spanish property be seized to pay for the damage done to English ships. Cecil, and others yearning for active intervention on the side of Protestant rebels in the Low Countries, saw the seizure as a blow to Spanish power and a move in support of Protestantism. And of course there was the opportunity for Elizabeth's financially strained government to get £85,000 at a time when its primary tax, customs revenue, had been sharply reduced and access to credit on the Antwerp bourse was disrupted.

Predictably the Spanish reacted by seizing English property in Flanders and Spain. The English retaliated by seizing all Flemish and Spanish property in England, any Spanish ships in the Channel, and the Spanish ambassador, who was placed under house arrest. Perhaps if the Spanish had not been so weak there would have been bloodshed, but by the summer of 1569 the political crisis had passed, although the economic problems it perpetuated had not.

In the process English foreign policy accidentally changed tracks. Having lived uncomfortably with the Spanish alliance for a decade Elizabeth had defied the greatest power in her world. Philip of Spain was now her enemy.[84] Although the disturbances in the trade with Antwerp did not end England's use of the Netherlands as its major outlet for cloth, its confidence had been shaken. As the Merchant Adventurers and the Privy Council worked their way through the crises they began thinking of other markets.

For some of the families who had spent their lives in the Antwerp trade, however, the disruptions were a personal tragedy. John Isham, for instance, found that it was impossible for him to continue the business he had been building there since he apprenticed as a Mercer in 1542. He had always traded in Antwerp and he had no interest in learning a new market. Instead he took his profits and retired to his country house at Lamport in 1572. His brother Henry went into another business, buying the post of customs collector.[85]

Other merchants were more resolute, responding to the trade crisis by diverting some of their traffic to the Baltic, where it boomed. The trade with the Barbary Coast was picking up, too. As we have seen, the Muscovy Company was attempting to cut out the Portuguese spice merchants selling their goods in Antwerp by importing spices from Persia. Attempts were being made to establish a triangular trade between England, West Africa and the West Indies, too – though John Hawkins's subtle salesmanship did not help its prospects.

Thomas Whythorne, who by 1562 had become the tutor of Richard Bromfield's son and entered the world of great London merchants, was struck by the conversations he heard among them. 'My friend,' he recalled, 'had doings for merchandise and ventures . . . about this time, not only to Muscovy, in Russia, but also in Tartaria, and Persia. Then had he also, ventures to Guinea, in Ethiopia, and also, to Magrobumba, and Nova Spania and also to Terra Florida in America.' Among these men, he said, the subject of conversation was

> of gain and loss, and such merchandise as was best for them to transport into this country and into that country for gain, and likewise of the commodities of other countries to be brought hither wherein gain was to be gotten. And then for the exchange of money how that went from time to time as well beyond the seas as here in England. There was no other talk among all these . . . but of gain and riches.[86]

All of these venturers borrowed and lent capital in London where, as people like Thomas Gresham knew, there was a great deal of money looking for opportunities. This, plus the disturbances in Antwerp, was an impetus to the creation of an English analogue to the New Bourse in Antwerp, a central place for the negotiation of capital contracts.

Gresham took the lead in creating the Royal Exchange. Begun in 1566 and completed in 1570, it copied the New Bourse both spiritually and physically. He imported the architecture, the labour, and even the marble for the piazza from Antwerp. The new exchange would give London its own place for money dealing, but its construction was a major redevelopment project in itself. About sixty houses near the Conduit in Cornhill were sold to anyone who would tear them down and remove the rubble. The destruction began in early February and by Whit Sunday it was done. Gresham laid the corner stone on 17 June 1566.[87]

The creation of a London bourse was followed in 1571 by the passage of the Act Against Usury. *De facto*, permitting loans under ten per cent, it gave people enough security to create a credit market. Taken together with the trouble in the Netherlands these developments meant that Elizabeth began fully financing her government at home for the first time.

V

Razing the buildings and constructing the Exchange provided work for some of the people suffering from the economic ills of the 1560s, but for many existence was hand-to-mouth. Working as day labour, they were treated with suspicion. A Lincoln ordinance of 1562 hints at the aldermens' attitudes toward the jobless and casual labourers. They were ordered to gather every morning, with their tools, at the Stonebow and wait there at least an hour for someone to hire them. If they did not look for work in this way they could be imprisoned.[88]

Lord Keeper Bacon demonstrated a similar attitude in his discussion of farm labour in an address to justices of the leet courts in 1559. These local courts were charged with overseeing wage rates and other things concerning rural labour, and, he told them, with supplying obedient, docile and well-ordered labour. Their neglect had created a stubborn, disobedient work force, people who were not content labouring in husbandry, taking up other occupations or taking to the highway. They should see to it that no one who should be a farm worker was permitted to work at anything else.[89]

Of course speeches like Bacon's prove the fears of the ruling groups more than a disorderly work force. At most they indicate more mobility and ambidexterity than the masters liked to see among people who, as Bacon noted, outnumbered them two to one.

When Norwich surveyed its poor in 1570 it found about twenty per cent of its population living in poverty, but most of them were working. In the parish of St Giles, William Barker was a 28-year-old butcher, married to Joan, aged forty-two, who was a spinner of white warp. Their 10-year-old was also a spinner, but their 8-year-old was attending school. They received no alms from the parish, and were described as 'very poor'. Their neighbour Thomas Caly was employeed as a sawyer, while his wife and all nine of their children were spinners of white warp. Caly was poor, but another member of the parish was much worse off; 60-year-old Maude House was described as 'a widow that is a desolate thing and beggeth'.[90]

Many of the poor in the Norwich survey had trades, but they had no work. In All Saints Parish there lived unemployed men whose occupations included labourers, slaughtermen, weavers, tailors, carpenters, butchers, hatters and sawyers. None of the women, most of whom were weavers, were out of work, but since they did piece work they would not be counted as 'out of labour.' The three harlots living in the parish were not classified as 'out of labour,' but their presence in a census of the poor indicates their economic status.[91]

Many of the poor of Norwich were living in houses they owned and they were established residents of the community. Conditions for the floating world of servants were different, for they were living and travelling with their masters and mistresses.

Thomas Brown was a horse-keeper in the house of John Stanhope. Earning forty shillings a year in cash plus a per diem for room and board, he was on the lower end of the pay scale established by the royal proclamation regulating London wages, a financial equal of porters and watermen. For much of the decade he had worked for Lord Willoughby, before joining Stanhope (perhaps he left Willoughby because of the infighting among the servants caused by the quarrels between Willoughby and his wife Elizabeth). When we meet him in 1572 he is living at The Boar's Head in Westminster, sharing a chamber with the horse-keeper of Sir John Salisbury and eating most of his meals at his host's table.

His job was caring for horses and waiting on his master in the most literal sense. He would rise about six to curry the horses, clean the stalls and work on the harness until his master needed him. On a typical day he might accompany Stanhope to pay a call in the City and wait with the horses in the street until his master returned. Sometimes he waited for hours, and one day he admitted he had spent his time lying in the hay in the barn for three hours. Early or late, he was expected to be there with the horses, and whenever he returned to The Boar's Head he had to give his charges 'bread, hay and litter' before he could retire.

Brown's irregular hours meant that he ate at odd times and sometimes not at all, either because he had no chance, or because his per diem had already been spent. He did keep convivial company, however. Sometimes the servants of Stanhope's house dined together, but Brown had his own circle. One evening he encountered his friend Cragge in the street and they went together to another friend's home, where they were joined by Cragge's wife and a servant of the Earl of Oxford 'who looked as though he was sick because he had a kerchief on his head'. They shared a cold shoulder of mutton, bread and drink and 'there was much talk'.[92]

Gilbert Clark, 'a poor young man,' was a personal servant to William Stanton, Underkeeper of the Exchequer. Living and working in the palace of Westminster with his master, he was an intimate, trusted employee. He helped his master dress in the mornings and accompanied him when he went out on business, unless one of the other servants went instead. In that case he did whatever his mistress instructed him to do. When his master and mistress received guests Clark was present, and when they attended church at St Margaret's, Westminster, he accompanied them. Clark spent part of his time in the kitchen sewing money bags for the Exchequer.

Some of his time was spent running messages. On one particular day he was called by his master early in the morning and sent to find out if the Lord Treasurer was in town. He went to Cecil's house and enquired, returning to find his master still in bed. When he reported, Stanton called for his clothes, Clark helped him dress, and then went into London. Clark stayed with Stanton until another servant arrived with Stanton's 'clock bag' at 8 a.m. Clark was then sent home to Westminster. Arriving, his mistress sent him with their daughter Ann to church.

Clark spent that afternoon with Ann and all the maids playing 'stall ball' until his master came home about 5 p.m. Supper followed, and the young people returned to their ball game in Westminster Hall. When the game finally ended they gathered in the kitchen with the master and mistress.

> Mistress Stanton said, 'good folks you may all get you to bed in God's name'.
> Clark asked his master, 'Shall not we help you to bed first?'
> Stanton answered, 'No, those [servants] that lay below should help your master to bed', so Clark and his chamber mate Edmund went up the stairs to their room in the roof.[93]

The wages for work were set, at least in theory, by local authorities under the authority of the Statute of Artificers. Besides setting the conditions for apprenticeship nationwide the Statute had empowered the justices of the peace to set wages for their cities and counties. Each year they were to consult with the mayors and aldermen of their towns and, considering the 'plenty or scarcity of the time', determine what a fair wage would be, distinguishing between wages with and without food and drink.[94] This new system of fixing wages prevented competition while allowing flexibility in the face of inflation and fluctuating food prices.

Accordingly there was a burst of wage regulations in the summer of 1563. Tiny Rutlandshire's wages were the first to be confirmed by a royal proclamation that June. Other counties and towns followed with their orders, regulating all the occupations they could think of, and showing a lively appreciation of the seasons of agricultural labour. A result was that wages varied from area to area, but within jurisdictions competition for labour was, theoretically, stifled.

In Rutland a mower was paid 5d a day if he was fed, 10d if he was not; in Kent a mower received 6d or 11d. A reaper in Rutland received 4d 'with meat,' and 8d without; a woman reaper there was paid 3d 'with meat', and 6d without. In Kent, male reapers received 6d or 11d; female 4d or 7d. If paying by the acre the farmer took into account the crop harvested: in Kent the wage was 5d an acre for oats, 11d for grass, 6d for barley, and 10d for marsh ground.

A similar principle was applied to all other trades, with distinctions made according to the unit of production, the time of the year, and the expertise of the worker. Thus for every thousand bricks a brick-maker produced he was paid 2s for 'digging the earth, making, striking, and burning, having all other necessaries brought to him without meat and drink'. Even marital status could affect the wages. In New Windsor the bailiff of husbandry, the chief carter and chief shepherd were paid 46s 8d if they were married, plus 10s for livery. If they were unmarried the wage was reduced to 40s a year and 6s 8d for clothes.[95]

In Lincoln the mayor and justices carefully constructed their table of wages to take into account the high price of food. With wheat at 40s a quarter, beans at 26s 8d a quarter, eggs five for a penny, and butter and cheese equally costly they had to pay enough to allow labourers to eat. Like most locales, they had the wage schedule published for easy distribution. Of course the Lincoln aldermen also did what they could to keep prices under control. They were especially worried about the cost and volume of ale and beer consumed in the city. Those selling them were ordered to keep inexpensive small ale and single beer on sale for the poor, and to shut their shops during sermon time. Two years later this was followed with an order forbidding any labourer or artificer to spend more than 4d a day on drink.[96] The moral in Lincoln: a decently paid, well-disciplined work force with clear heads should have plenty of cheap, weak drink.

The aldermen of Lincoln wanted a tractable, regulated work force, but they also wanted their city to be financed without taxation, so they invested £7 10s in the new lottery.[97]

In 1567 the Privy Council proclaimed a 'very rich lottery' for the reparation of harbours and 'other public works'. Offering nearly thirty thousand prizes in money, plate and goods, an entry cost a shilling. A list of prizes was published and sales began. Unfortunately the lottery did not produce the expected revenue. The logistics were very difficult to manage, and sales were not brisk. Perhaps the potential betters did not trust an official lottery – they had seen too many 'loans' extorted by the government that had never been repaid. The sceptics were right. The date for the drawing was changed by the Queen in a proclamation that touchily said that anyone who doubted her honesty should go see the treasurer of his or her shire for reassurance. In the end the lottery

was a failure. The prizes had to be drastically reduced: the Grand Prize
of five thousand pounds was worth only £416 13s 4d when it was drawn
in early 1569.[98]

In the hard economic times of the late 1560s the lottery was a chance
to escape one's financial problems without effort. Those with more
energy could take another sort of gamble and go west to Ireland.
People like John Denton, a London Merchant-Tailor, turned to Ireland
in search of new markets. In 1563 Denton, finding conditions poor
in England, took a load of goods to sell to the Irish 'captains'.[99] By
the 1550s the English were once again considering Ireland as ripe for
colonization, inspired by the example of Spanish colonization of the
New World. Making an analogy between the 'savages' of the New World
and the 'Wild Irish', some English people contemplated the 'conquest'
of Ireland by settlement.[100]

Before plantations could be established, however, the political situation in Ireland had to stabilize. Faction fights between Dudley and the
Earl of Sussex, Lord Lieutenant of Ireland, had helped incapacitate Irish
government in the early 1560s, giving more power to Shane O'Neill
in Ulster, and the Earls of Desmond and Ormond in Munster. Their
battles with one another and with the English and Scots settlers kept
Ireland disturbed. Finally, when Desmond and Ormond met in open
battle at Affane in 1565, the last private battle in Tudor history, they
were ordered to London for disciplining. O'Neill, who wanted to be
recognized as Earl of Ulster but was refused, had been to London earlier
to plead his case.

After he returned to Ulster, O'Neill began presenting himself as
defender of the Catholic faith against English Protestantism, plotting
with the Scots and French against Elizabeth, and arming the peasants of
Tyrone. In retaliation an English army was sent to attack O'Neill in the
winter of 1566–7. The attack was a success, but O'Neill himself escaped,
only to be defeated by the O'Donnells in May.

Fleeing the field, O'Neill tried to raise more forces by negotiating
with Alexander MacDonald, who had just landed with a force of
Scots in the employee of the English. O'Neill hoped to get them to
change allegiances. MacDonald invited him to a feast, during which a
quarrel began over whether O'Neill was good enough to marry Mary of
Scotland, and O'Neill was stabbed to death. His head was packed in salt
and sent to Dublin, where it was posted on the castle gate. The reward
of 1000 marks was duly sent to the killers.[101]

His death temporarily pacified Ireland and by 1568 the government
was bent on planting English settlers on the lands of both the Old
English inhabitants and the Gaels. Ulster, shorn of O'Neill, was chosen
as the region most promising for these settlements and Cecil plotted the
establishment of fourteen garrisons to protect them from the wrath of

the Gaels and Scots they would displace. In the end this plan did not materialize, but others did. For instance Sir Richard Grenville and 106 followers created an English settlement at Kerrycurrihy near Cork.[102]

This was so resented by the Gaels that in June 1569 James Fitzmaurice led 2000 men against the settlement, chasing the settlers into Cork and besieging them. Fitzmaurice, in an attempt to talk the citizens of Cork into joining him, declared that he had revolted because the Queen was intending to impose a 'newly invented kind of religion' and urged that they expel the 'Huguenots'. In spite of this pious appeal Cork resisted, perhaps sensing that this was, in the end, a feudal revolt, not a religious one. It took the English until 1573 to suppress the rebels.[103]

The tentative moves toward colonization in Ireland reflect the same yearning for new markets and new ways of making a living that sent Arthur Edwards to Persia and prompted the development of new industries in the 1560s. Pestered by inflation and recoinage, disruption of the traditional trade networks, the expenses and confusions of war and disease, unemployment, and ham-fisted policy that sought to prevent social change rather than to ease economic troubles, structural and institutional problems made the 1560s a hard time to make a living.

There were also human reasons recognized by contemporaries. Thomas Whythorne, failing to marry the widow's twenty pounds, had taken a job with a gentleman in his country home, tutoring his children. He quit when his employer refused to pay him what had been agreed. Nursing his pride and his purse he mused on his treatment. Recalling that work was the curse God laid on Adam, he realized that 'the world is so corrupt, that whosoever knoweth not how to dissemble cannot live'. A world so troubled by 'wicked rich men' who despised the learned and virtuous, so filled with vanity, was subject to God's wrath. But he took consolation in the words of the Preacher: 'What profit hath man of all his labours, in the which he doth trouble himself under the sun?' 'I have . . . beheld all things that be done under the sun, and behold they are all but vanity, and affliction of the mind.'[104] Forgetting God and pursuing mammon made the commonwealth miserable.

11

Epilogue

On Corpus Christi day, 25 May 1570, the servants of Bishop Grindal found a papal bull stuck on his door. *Regnans in Excelsis* was Pius V's response to the pleas for help from the Northern Earls, issued secretly on 25 February. Coming too late to help the rebels, it declared that Elizabeth was an excommunicated heretic and supporter of heretics bound in the bonds of anathema. Freeing all people from their obedience to her, it cursed all who supported her, resolving the moral conflict felt by the rebels who had qualms because she was an anointed queen.[1] The bull was never officially served on Elizabeth but in 1570 her government began a counter-offensive against the papacy and Roman Catholics in general that drew a firm line in both domestic and international politics. The confusion and indecision that had marked politics and religion in the 1560s had resolved into a firmly anti-Catholic policy at home and abroad.

At the same time the continental battles over religion and the struggle for a positive balance of trade had been disrupting the economy long enough that new patterns were beginning to emerge. English merchants were reaching out to new markets while at home new processes were being encouraged to replace imports. The Crown was withdrawing from the continental money markets and borrowing its money domestically.

But for people who had lived through the decade these developments were only partially visible. Certainly some of the events had marked the nation and touched most lives. No one could have been unaware of the rebellion in the North and the government's anti-Catholic reaction. The revolt had the effect of galvanizing people's opinions, helping to create a new loyalty to the Elizabethan regime for many, and forcing devout Catholics to directly confront their places within it.

In the Parliament that met in April 1571 the new hostility towards Catholics was codified in a series of statutes. A new treason law, a law against anyone bringing in bulls from the See of Rome, and an Act against Catholic fugitives who had fled the realm generalized the anger expressed in the attainder of Westmoreland, Northumberland, and their supporters, ordering their executions and seizing their property.[2]

The arrival of the new decade marked very little, but processes begun in the 1560s were bearing fruit. By the time Parliament assembled in 1571 it was ready to enact a series of important laws born of experience. The collapse of the markets had caused a rash of bankruptcies in the 1560s, setting in train the discussions that led to the bankruptcy statute whose mechanism we still use. The Act Against Usury, permitting, after a fashion, the borrowing and lending of money at 10 per cent interest changed the way in which English people did business. Both the bankruptcy Act and the usury Act had been proposed in 1566.[3]

Continuing the general interest in improving the economy and protecting domestic producers and workers, Parliament tightened the laws protecting the makers of woolen caps, extended the navigation law of 1563 (remarking that it had been very effective), and loosened the export laws so that grain could be sold abroad without special licenses in order to 'increase tillage'. The law-makers, still worried about archery and illegal games, made another shot at guaranteeing a supply of cheap bows by ordering the Hanse merchants to import bow staves with every load of goods they brought to London.[4]

The year 1571 saw the completion, or perhaps the deliberate incompletion, of the settlement of religion. Convocation in 1563 had outlined the legislation needed to complete the newly re-established Protestant church. Bills to enact it had been introduced in 1566, but stopped by the Queen. In 1571 the Queen in Parliament approved the Thirty-nine Articles, giving official authority to the statement of belief that would now define the Anglican faith. Incorporated into a bill to reform 'disorders touching ministers', the Articles became a test of ideological loyalty for the present and future clergy of the Church of England. Men too Catholic or deviantly Protestant could be excluded, keeping the realm safe from counter-revolutionary preaching.[5]

An attempt to make the laity take the same ideological test by requiring that everyone attend church and take communion – an action impossible for a devout Catholic – failed to become law after long and bitter debate. Many members believed that anyone who would not take communion should be discovered and cast out – dangerous tares in the garden of Godly England – but the lawyers among them were worried about the proposed persecution's legal effectiveness.

In the same Parliament motions were made to reform the Book of Common Prayer, excising all the 'popish superstition' remaining in it. Further reforms of the canon law were discussed and demands were made for restructuring the form of episcopal jurisdiction. They came to naught, but they were expressed with great conviction.

Elizabeth's refusal to permit changes in the Book of Common Prayer frustrated those who believed them necessary. By 1572 Puritanism and Presbyterianism had come out of the shadows, given form by Thomas Cartwright's lectures on the Primitive Church at Cambridge in 1570 and the brilliant invective known as the *Admonition to Parliament* aimed at the assembly of 1572.

The great events of the 1560s touched everyone's lives, and the memories of those who survived into the 1570s were ringed like a tree with experiences personal, local and national. None knew what would happen in the new decade, but they all struggled on in the roles in which they had been cast by accidents of birth, gender, predilection and history.

Sir Anthony Mildmay and Thomas Cecil both served in the Queen's forces during the Revolt of the Northern Earls. Mildmay's subsequent career was ignominious, leading John Chamberlain, the diarist of the 1590s, to disparage him as 'not much of a man'. Thomas, despite his father's scorn, proved to be a good soldier, commanding a troop of three hundred horsemen. In that same year Thomas had become a Justice of the Peace for Kesteven, Lincolnshire, and he was beginning to perform the leadership roles expected of a gentleman of his connections and wealth. He became the Sheriff of Northamptonshire in 1579, but high office eluded him as long as his father was alive. Once his half-brother Robert became Principal Secretary, Thomas was made Lord President of the North, a member of the Privy Council and Earl of Exeter.

His wife Dorothy found herself in 1569 tending their infant son William and wondering if Thomas would come back from the rebellion. When he did return she quickly became pregnant again. She would eventually bear three sons and eight daughters. Grace Mildmay, who seems to have been very much in love with Sir Anthony in spite of his fecklessness, waited for his return from the North alone. They only had one daughter, born in the 1570s. James I was much taken with her confectionery, and she became a devout Puritan.

The persecution of Catholics that followed the Northern Rebellion sent Edmund Campion into exile. He had already resigned all his posts in Oxford and sought safety in Ireland, but he was present for the execution of Doctor Story in London. A member of Parliament in 1559, Story had been identified as a traitor. Kidnapped and brought back from exile to England, Story was hanged, drawn and quartered. According to Catholic tradition Story's blood splashed down from the scaffold onto Campion, solidifying his determination to become a Jesuit. After joining Thomas Stapleton at Louvain he returned to England as a missionary priest. He was hanged, drawn and quartered just as Story had been.

Robert Jones, whose chatty correspondence with his diplomatic friends ended when he went up to Cambridge in 1564, stayed there at least through 1566, taking an MA and become a fellow-commoner and sizar of Trinity Hall. In 1562 he became a prebendary of Gloucester Cathedral, providing him with an income to support his education.[6]

Henry Machyn, the lively, gossiping draper whose diary is such an enlightening source of knowledge of London in the 1550s and early 1560s died of the plague in 1563, just at the moment when all the dogs of London were being killed to prevent the spread of the disease.

Machyn's near neighbor, Thomas Earl, Vicar of St Mildred's, Bread Street, survived the plague and everything else, ministering to his charges until 1604. He had been suspended during the vestiarian controversy because of his refusal to wear the 'popish rags' of the vestments, but returned to his parish shortly after; the experience changed his life. He became a Puritan and he stuck to his principles. In 1595 his churchwardens reported he was still refusing to wear his surplice.[7]

Katherine Grey, whose improper marriage to the Earl of Hertford had prompted Elizabeth to imprison her, was kept under house arrest until, sick and afraid, she died on 27 October 1568, a prisoner in the home of Owen Hopton.[8]

The Earl of Hertford, her husband, for so he thought of himself, did not remarry until 1595 and never ceased trying to get his two sons declared legitimate. Unfortunately Elizabeth had a very long memory. In October 1595 he put a record into the Court of Arches to prove his first marriage to Katherine Grey legal and his children legitimate. In November the Queen committed him to the Tower for his audacity and stripped young Edward of his title of Lord Beauchamp. It was rumoured that the new Lady Hertford had gone stark mad because of the Queen's actions, and Elizabeth refused to see her – though she sent a message assuring her that Hertford's lands would not be taken from him.[9] Only when Elizabeth was safely dead and the succession established did James I declare Edward legitimate, allowing him to inherit his father's title when he died in 1621.

Thomas Whythorne, whose religious meditations might have led him to Puritanism, discovered that the church was still willing to support musicians. In 1571 he was chosen over Thomas Tallis and William Byrd to become the Master of Music in Archbishop Parker's palace at Lambeth. It appears that he got the job because in 1569 he had decided to publish a collection of his songs, appearing in 1571 as *Songes for three, foure and five Voices*. He finally succeeded in marrying in 1577 when he was 49. He died in 1596, leaving his estate to his wife Elizabeth 'for I have none other to give it unto', suggesting that he had no surviving children. His wife remarried less than three months after his death.[10]

Writing his farewell to his audience as he ended his memoirs in the early 1570s, Whythorne meditated on the meaning of life, reflecting that people are but the prey of Time. Playing their tragic and comic roles upon the stage, they hand them on to their children at their exits, to be acted again. As usual he wrote a poem about it, giving him my last words:

> Ponder the proof so far as you
> in worldly works be tried shall,
> how vain they are in deed and show
> how dangerous to deal withall,
> and nothing else thou shalt then find,
> the world thus working in his kind,
> but [a] wide scaffold for us each one
> to play our tragedies upon.[11]

Notes

CHAPTER 2   IN THE BEGINNING: 1559

1. Machyn, p. 178.
2. PRO SP 12/1/fos. 147–54.
3. HMC Salisbury, 9, i, p. 151.
4. 5 Eliz. I, c. 20.1.
5. Hatfield House, Herts, Cecil Papers, 152, fos. 96–96v.
6. Ibid., fo. 97.
7. 1 Eliz. I, c. 9.1.
8. Hatfield House, Herts., Cecil Papers, 152, fo. 96v.
9. Bodl., Laud 683, fo. 145v.
10. J. M. Cowper (ed.), *The Selected Works of Robert Crowley* (London, 1872), pp. 49–51.
11. Hatfield House, Herts., Cecil Papers, 152, fo. 98v.
12. 1 Eliz. I, c. 8.1.
13. 1 Eliz. I, c. 10.1.
14. I Eliz. I, c. 12.1.
15. Joan Thirsk, *Economic Policy and Projects* (Oxford, 1988), appendix 1, pp. 181–5.
16. Hatfield House, Herts., Cecil Papers, 152, fo. 97v.
17. Bodl., Laud 683, fos. 139–42.
18. C. E. Challis, *The Tudor Coinage* (Manchester, 1978), p. 118.
19. Tawney and Power, II, p. 194.
20. Ibid., p. 386.
21. 1&2 Philip & Mary, c.5.1.
22. Quoted in D. M. Palliser, *The Age of Elizabeth* (London, 1983), pp. 48–9.
23. Bullein, fo. 26.
24. Ibid., fo. 16.
25. PRO SP 12/1/fo. 150v.
26. PRO SP 12/1/fo. 158.
27. BL, Cotton, Vespasian D.18, fo. 97.
28. Ibid., fo. 105; 103v.
29. [John Wigand], *De Neutralibus et Mediis. Grossly Englished, Jacke of both Sides* Tr. anon. (1562), Sig. Bi. [STC 25612].

30. Bullein, fos. 8–8v.
31. *Zurich Letters*, I, p. 23.
32. H&L, II, p. 102.
33. CSP Ven., VII, p. 2.
34. Hartley, *Proceedings*, I, p. 51.
35. CSP For., I, p. 218.
36. Bodl., Laud 683, fo. 148v.
37. HLRO, Commons Ms. Journals, I, fo. 165v. 4 and 6 Feb.
38. BL, Add. 35,830, fo. 159v.
39. Arcandam, *The most Excellent Booke to fynd the Fatal Desteny of Every Man* [1562?], sig. B 1. [STC 724].
40. Bullein, fos. 56–56v.
41. BL, Add. 48,023, fo. 363v.
42. 5 Eliz. I, c. 15.
43. Whythorne, *Autobiography*, p. 120.

CHAPTER 3   THE UNSETTLED SETTLEMENT OF RELIGION

1. Bodl., MS Top. Yorks. C. 14, fos. 83–84.
2. BL Lansd. 101, fos. 163–4.
3. Samuel Tymms (ed.), *Wills and Inventories from the Registers of the Commissary of Bury St. Edmund's and the Archdeacon of Sudbury. Camden Society* (1850), pp. 153–4.
4. Hugh Aveling, *Northern Catholics. The Catholic Recusants of the North Riding of Yorkshire 1558–1790* (London, 1966), p. 51.
5. Johann Wigand, *De Neutralibus et Mediis. Grossly Englished, Jacke of both Sides. A Godly and necessary Catholike Admonition, touching those that be neuters, holding by no certain religion or doctrine, and such as hold with both partes, or rather of no parte, very necessarye to stay and stablysh Gods elect in the true Catholic faith against this present wicked world.* Anon. tr. (London, 1562), Sig. B.i. [STC 25612].
6. Hartley, p. 51.
7. Parker, p. 105.
8. Bullein, fos. 8–8v. This description also occurs in the 1564 edition. [STC 4036.5].
9. Quoted in Marvin R. O'Connell, *Thomas Stapleton and the Counter Reformation* (New Haven, 1964), pp. 10–11.
10. Strype, *Annals*, I, ii, pp. 406–7.
11. N. L. Jones, *Faith by Statute. Parliament and the Settlement of Religion, 1559* (London, 1982), pp. 130–1. ZL, I, p. 1.
12. CSP Ven., VII, p. 64.
13. 1 Eliz. I, c. I.11.
14. Thomas Brice, *A Compendious Register in metre, containing the names and patient sufferings of the members of Jesus Christ, and the tormented, and cruelly burned within England . . .1559.* In A. F. Pollard (ed.), *Tudor Tracts 1532–88* (Westminster, 1903), pp. 270, 285, 288.
15. Strype, *Annals*, I, ii, p. 408.
16. HLRO Commons Ms. Journal I, fo. 202v. CSP Ven., VII, p. 52. Jones,

Faith by Statute, pp. 99–103.

17. Jones, *Faith by Statute*, pp. 123–9.
18. Ibid., pp. 140–51.
19. ZL, I, p. 10.
20. Adrian Morey, *The Catholic Subjects of Queen Elizabeth* (Totowa, NJ, 1978), p. 41.
21. Corp. of London, Guildhall Library, Ms. 11,588, Vol. I, fos. 23v, 33v.
22. Machyn, p. 200.
23. CUL Mm.1.29, fo. 45.
24. BCP, p. 264.
25. Parker, p. 65.
26. W. H. Frere (ed.), *Visitation Articles and Injunctions of the Period of the Reformation, III, 1559–1575* (London, 1910), pp. 10–11.
27. Ibid., p. 11. Margaret Aston, *England's Iconoclasts. Vol. I Laws against Images* (Oxford, 1988), p. 300.
28. John Jewel, *Apology*, in *The Works of John Jewel*, John Ayre (ed.) (Cambridge, 1845), Vol. III, p. 94.
29. David M. Loades, 'The Piety of the Catholic Restoration in England, 1553–1558', in James Kird (ed.), *Humanism and Reform: The Church in Europe, England, and Scotland, 1400–1643. Studies in Church History, Subsidia* 8 (1991), pp. 297–8, 303. Eamon Duffy, *The Stripping of the Altars* (New Haven, 1992), pp. 543–64.
30. Christopher Kitching (ed.), *The Royal Visitation of 1559. Act Book of the Northern Province. Surtees Society* 187 (1975), p. xxi.
31. Ibid., p. 85.
32. Thomas Wright (ed.), *Churchwardens Accounts of the Town of Ludlow, in Shropshire, from 1540 to the End of the Reign of Queen Elizabeth. Camden Society* 102 (1869), pp. 93–4.
33. Duffy, *Stripping*, pp. 569–78.
34. Machyn, pp. 207, 208.
35. ZL, I, pp. 44–5.
36. Aston, *Iconoclasts*, p. 13.
37. Bullein, fo. 8.
38. Felicity Heal, 'The Bishops and the Act of Exchange of 1559', *Historical Journal* (1974), pp. 227–46.
39. Justin McCann and Hugh Connolly (eds), 'Memorials of Father Augustine Baker, O.S.B.' *Catholic Record Society*, 33 (1933), p. 16.
40. Nicholas Sanders, *Rise and Growth of the Anglican Schism*, David Lewis, trans. and ed. (London, 1877), pp. 264–5.
41. Ibid., p. 267, n. 1.
42. Strype, *Annals*, I, i, p. 257.
43. Parker, pp. 132–4.
44. Aston, *Iconoclasts*, pp. 367–8.
45. Norman Jones, 'Elizabeth, Edification and the Latin Prayer Book of 1560', *Church History*, 53, 2 (1984), pp. 174–86.
46. ZL, I, p. 74.
47. ZL, I, p. 63.
48. ZL, I, p. 23.

49. HEH El 2529, fo. 15.

50. Mary Bateson, 'A Collection of Original Letters from the Bishops to the Privy Council, 1564', *Camden Society Miscellanea*, 9 (1895), pp. 1–84.

51. Mary A. E. Green (ed.), 'The Life of Mr William Whittingham, Dean of Durham', *Camden Society Miscellanea*, 6 (1870), p. 16.

52. BL Add. 35830, fo. 107v.

53. 2 Dyer, 203a–203b, 231b: ER 73, 448–9, 511–12.

54. CSPF, 1561–2, pp. 103–4.

55. Conyers Read, *Mr Secretary Cecil and Queen Elizabeth* (London, 1965), pp. 208–9. MacCaffrey, pp. 108–9.

56. BL Add 48,023 fo. 354v. PRO SP 12/16/fos. 119–20, 115, 136. Pole's trial is recorded in PRO KB 8/40, Trinity, 5 Eliz. Sentenced to death, he was reprieved.

57. PRO SP 12/16/fo. 20. J. H. Pollen, 'Official Lists of Prisoners for Religion from 1562 to 1580', *Cath. Rec. Soc. Miscellanea*, I (1905), pp. 53; 55; 56.

58. Machyn, p. 261.

59. Strype, *Annals*, I, i, p. 11.

60. PRO SP 12/16/fo. 136.

61. Strype, *Annals*, I, i, p. 521.

62. 5 Eliz. I, c. 16.

63. 5 Eliz. I, c. 15.

64. PRO SP 12/17/fos. 35, 38, 39–39v, 41–2. M. A. R. Green (ed.), *CPSD, 1601–1603, with Addenda, 1547–1565* (London, 1870), pp. 509–10, 512.

65. Cyprian Leowitz, *De Coniunctionibus Magnis Insignioribus Superiorum planetarum . . . cum eorundem effectuum historia expostione* (London, 1573). [STC 479.8]. The book had appeared in Germany in 1563. Camden bought it in May 1573 and carefully noted the prophecies that had been fulfilled.

66. Lewis Vaughan, *A Prognostication for the yere of our Lorde God MDCLIX. Wherin ye may se to fore hande the mutacions of the ayre, that shall happen throughoute the whoole yeare. Declaringe also what dyseases, warres, pestilence, and derth of vitaliles, shall happen . . .* (London, 1558), unpaginated. [STC 520].

67. Quoted in Sanford V. Larkey, 'Astrology and Politics in the First Years of Elizabeth's Reign', *Bulletin of the Institute of the History of Medicine*, III (1935), pp. 180–81.

68. Parker, pp. 59–60.

69. William Fulke, *Antiprognosticon; that is to saye an invective against the astrologians* (London, 1560), Sig. A.vij–viij verso. [STC 11420].

70. Francis Coxe, *A short treatise declaring the detestable wickednesse of magicall sciences* (London, 1561), Sig. A.iiij.–A.v. [STC 5950] *The Unfained retraction of Fraunces Cox, which he uttered at the pillorye in Chepesyde and els where according to the counsels commaundment, Ao 1561, the 25 of June. Beyng accused for the use of certayne sinistral and divelysh Artes.* London, Society of Antiquaries, Lemon 55. My thanks to the Society for allowing me to see their unique copy. [STC 5951].

71. John Hall, *A poesie in Forme of a vision, briefly inveying aginst the*

moste hatefull, and prodigious Artes of Necromancie, Witchcraft, Sorcerie, incantations, and divers other detestable and devilishe practises, dayly used under colour of Judiciall Astrologie (London, 1563), Sig. B.iiij. verso; B.v. [STC 12633].

72.   His story is known from his examination before Grindal, PRO SP 12/23/fos. 91–92 and his examination before the commissioners, Bodl., Tanner 50, fos. 16–16v.

73.   5 Eliz. I, c. 15.

74.   BL Add. 48,023, fo. 363v.

75.   PRO PROB 11/45/fo. 58. They included the calf with a child's face, siamese twin pigs, a pig with human hands, a limbless child, and the monster from Chichester. John D., *A description of a monstrous chylde borne at Chychester . . . , MCCCCCLXII*, in Henry Huth (ed.), *Ancient Ballads and Broadsides* (London, 1867), p. 301. [STC 61].

76.   *The true discription of two monstrous chyldren borne at herne in Kent. The .xxvii. daie of Auguste in the yere our of [sic] Lorde. MCCCCCLXV. They were booth women Chyldren and were Chrystened, and lyved halfe a daye. The one departed afore the other almoste an howre. 1565.* [STC 6774].

77.   Bullein, fos. 56–56v.

78.   *The True Report of the Burning of the Steeple and Church of Paul's in London . . . 1561* in A. F. Pollard (ed.), *Tudor Tracts 1532–1588* (Westminster, 1903), p. 406. Stowe, p. 116.

79.   *The Burning of St. Paul's Church* in James Scholefield (ed.), *The Works of James Pilkington* (Cambridge, 1842), pp. 479–645.

80.   My emphasis. Henry Bull, *Christian Prayers and Holy Meditations as well for Private as for Public Exercise* (Cambridge, 1842), p. 84.

81.   Bullein, fos. 53v–54.

82.   BL, Lansd. 101, fos. 21–33.

83.   Grindal, p. 306.

84.   HEH, HM 1340, fo. 28.

CHAPTER 4   PROTESTANT DISCONTENTS

1.   Bullein, fo. 41.

2.   Whythorne, p. 158.

3.   Ibid., pp. 164–5.

4.   William Birch, *The Complaint of a Sinner Vexed with Pain, Desyring the ioye, that ever shall remain* (1563). [STC 3076].

5.   Parker, pp. 183–5.

6.   Grindal, pp. 81–120, 87.

7.   William Fuller, 'A copie of Mr Fullers booke to the Queene', in Albert Peel (ed.), *The Seconde Parte of a Register* (Cambridge, 1915), p. 60.

8.   Parker, pp. 132–4.

9.   Ibid., p. 66.

10.   Ibid., p. 146. M. A. R. Green (ed.), *CSPD. 1601–1603, with Addenda, 1547–1565* (London, 1870), p. 515.

11.   James Pilkington, 'The Burning of St. Paul's Church: Confutation of

an Addition', in *The Works of James Pilkington*, ed. James Scholefield, (Cambridge, 1842), pp. 544, 553, 564–5.

12. Strype, *Annals*, I, i, 473–84. William Haugaard, *Elizabeth and the English Reformation* (Cambridge, 1970), pp. 346–8.

13. E. J. Bicknell, *A Theological Introduction to the Thirty-Nine Articles of the Church of England*, 3rd edn, H. J. Carpenter (ed.), (London, 1955), p. 249.

14. ZL, I, pp. 1–2.

15. ZL, II, pp. 25, 32.

16. Bodl., Tanner 79, fo. 16.

17. Collinson, *Grindal*, p. 172.

18. Haugaard, *English Reformation*, pp. 209–11.

19. Parker, pp. 223–7.

20. Haugaard, *English Reformation*, pp. 212–15.

21. Parker, p. 235. C. M. Dent, *Protestant Reformers in Elizabethan Oxford* (Oxford, 1983), pp. 35–9.

22. H. C. Porter, *Reformation and Reaction in Tudor Cambridge* (Hamden, Conn., 1972), pp. 114–127. Strype, *Annals*, I, ii, pp. 153–62.

23. Patrick Collinson, 'The "Nott Conformytye" of the Young John Whitgift', in his *Godly People* (London, 1983), pp. 326–7.

24. Parker, p. 268.

25. Parker, pp. 269–70.

26. CUL, Mm.1.29, fo. 3.

27. Ibid., fo. 3v.

28. Ibid., fo. 1v.

29. Ibid., fo. 3v.

30. Stowe, p. 138.

31. Ibid., pp. 135–6.

32. *A briefe discourse against the outwarde apparrell and Ministring garmentes of the popishe church.* (1566). [STC 6078].

33. Stowe, p. 139.

34. Ibid. Grindal, p. 289.

35. Ibid. p. 140.

36. Ibid.

37. Patrick Collinson, 'The Role of Women in the English Reformation Illustrated by the Life and Friendships of Anne Locke', *Godly People. Essays on English Protestantism and Puritanism* (London, 1983), pp. 274–6.

38. Ibid., pp. 279–83.

39. Grindal, pp. 288–9.

40. Collinson, *Grindal*, p. 177.

41. Parker, p. 284.

42. Ibid.

43. G. R. Elton, *The Parliament of England, 1559–1581* (Cambridge, 1986), pp. 199–214.

44. Parker, pp. 291–2.

45. Grindal, p. 214.

46. Ibid., p. 209.

47. Collinson, *Grindal*, p. 180.

CHAPTER 5   CATHOLIC CONFUSION

1. Quoted in Peter Holmes, *Resistance and Compromise. The Political Thought of Elizabethan Catholics* (Cambridge, 1982), p. 16.
2. Ibid., p. 15.
3. Nicholas Sander, 'Dr Nicholas Sander's Report to Cardinal Moroni', A. J. Pollen (ed.), *Catholic Record Society Miscellanea* I (1905), pp. 36–7.
4. Ibid., p. 39.
5. Nicholas Sander, *The Rise and Growth of the Anglican Schism*, David Lewis, trans. and ed. (London, 1877), p. 265.
6. Eamon Duffy, *The Stripping of the Altars. Traditional Religion in England 1400–1580* (New Haven, 1992), pp. 565–93.
7. McCann and Connolly (eds), 'Baker', pp. 18–19.
8. John Jewel, *The Works of John Jewel*, ed. John Ayre (Cambridge, 1845), I, pp. 20–1.
9. Ibid., pp. 26–31.
10. Ibid., p. 36.
11. Ibid., pp. 40–89.
12. Haugaard, *English Reformation*, pp. 242–7.
13. Jewel, *Works*, III, p. 77.
14. Ibid., p. 106.
15. Adrian Morey, *The Catholic Subjects of Queen Elizabeth* (Totowa, NJ, 1978), pp. 45–6.
16. 5 Eliz. I, c. 1.
17. Quoted in J. E. Neale, *Elizabeth I and her Parliaments* (London, 1953), I, p. 117.
18. Hartley, I, pp. 96–101.
19. Strype, *Annals*, I, i, 442–6. For analyses of the passage of this bill see Jones, *Faith by Statute*, pp. 171–6 and Elton, *Parliament*, pp. 178–81.
20. Parker, pp. 174–5.
21. Leslie Ward, 'The Treason Act of 1563: A Study of the Enforcement of anti-Catholic Legislation', *Parliamentary History* 8, 2 (1989), pp. 290–4. 2 Dyer, 234a: ER 73, p. 517.
22. 8 Eliz. I, c. 1.
23. Mary Bateson, 'A Collection of Original Letters from the Bishops to the Privy Council, 1564', *Camden Society, Miscellany 9* (1895), pp. 16, 38, 66.
24. Morey, *Catholic Subjects*, p. 48.
25. MacCaffrey, pp. 186–7.
26. PRO C 115/M16. Bateman, 'Letters from the Bishops', p. 12.
27. Marvin R. O'Connell, *Thomas Stapleton and the Counter Reformation* (New Haven, 1964), pp. 26–61.
28. Jennifer Loach, 'Reformation Controversies' in J. McConica (ed.), *The History of the University of Oxford, III, the Collegiate University* (Oxford, 1986), pp. 378–87.
29. DNB; Evelyn Waugh, *Edmund Campion* (New York, 1935), pp. 6–50.
30. Christopher Haigh, *Reformation and Reaction in Tudor Lancashire* (Cambridge, 1975), pp. 209–23.

31. Hugh Aveling, *Northern Catholics. The Catholic Recusants of the North Riding of Yorkshire 1558–1790* (London, 1966), pp. 21, 51–2.

32. Haigh, *Tudor Lancashire*, p. 216.

33. J. C. H. Aveling, *Catholic Recusancy in the City of York 1558–1790. Catholic Record Society Monograph Series*, 2 (1970), pp. 31–2.

34. PRO SP 12/60/fo. 214v.

35. Roger Manning, *Religion and Society in Elizabethan Sussex* (Leicester, 1969), pp. 41–2.

36. Parker, p. 149.

37. Diarmaid MacCulloch, *Suffolk and the Tudors. Politics and Religion in an English County 1500–1600* (Oxford, 1986), pp. 181–91.

38. Steven G. Ellis, *Tudor Ireland. Crown, Community and the Conflict of Cultures 1470–1603* (London, 1985), pp. 259–61.

39. Neville Williams, *A Tudor Tragedy. Thomas Howard Fourth Duke of Norfolk* (London, 1964), pp. 126–72.

40. R. R. Reid, 'The Rebellion of the Earls, 1569', *Transactions of the Royal Historical Society*, 2nd ser., 20 (1906), p. 197. MacCaffrey, pp. 340–1.

41. Morey, *Catholic Subjects*, pp. 53–4.

42. Cuthbert Sharp, *Memorials of the Rebellion of 1569* (London, 1840), pp. 97–8.

43. ZL, I, pp. 214, 218.

44. J. B. Black, *The Reign of Elizabeth 1558–1603* 2nd edn (Oxford, 1965), pp. 140–42.

45. Sharp, *Rebellion*, pp. 130–1.

46. Ibid., pp. 133, 140–1, 143–4.

47. Letmeke Avale, compiler, *A Commemoration or Dirige of Bastarde Edmonde Bonner* (1569), Sig. C.iii. [STC 977].

48. PRO SP 12/60/fo. 136, 137.

49. PRO SP 12/60/fos. 130–130v, 135.

50. Bateman, 'Letters from the Bishops', p. 12. PRO SP 12/60/fo. 67.

51. Sander, *Schism*, p. 264.

52. PRO SP 12/60/fo. 202–202v.

CHAPTER 6 MARRIAGE

1. Frederick J. Furnivall (ed.), *Child-Marriages, Divorces and Ratifications . . . the Diocese of Chester, A.D. 1561–66*, Early English Text Society, orig. ser., 108 (1897), p. 22.

2. Hartley, pp. 44–5.

3. BL, Lansd. 120, fo. 81. The biblical quotations are from *The Geneva Bible. A Facsimile of the 1560 ed.* (Madison, Wisc., 1969).

4. Edmund Tilney, *A briefe and pleasant discourse of duties in mariage, called the flower of friendshippe* (London, 1568), Sig. B vii verso–D i verso. [STC 24076.3].

5. BL, Lansd. 120, fo. 82.

6. Gloss on 1 Peter 3:1–6.

7. Tilney, *Duties*, Sig. D iiii verso–D vii verso.

8. Ibid. E iiii–verso.

9. William Painter, *The Palace of Pleasure* (London, 1567), II, fos. 218v–246. [STC 19124].

10. 'Love me Little, Love me Long', in Norman Ault (ed.), *Elizabethan Lyrics* (London, 1986), pp. 61–2.

11. CPR, 1560–63, pp. 526–7.

12. Patrick Collinson, *The Birthpangs of Protestant England. Religious and Cultural Change in the Sixteenth and Seventeenth Centuries* (New York, 1988), pp. 67–8. Mary Prior, 'Reviled and Crucified Marriages: The Position of Tudor Bishops' Wives', in Mary Prior (ed.), *Women in English Society 1500–1800* (London, 1985), pp. 134–8.

13. Nicholas Sander, *The Rise and Growth of the Anglican Schism*, ed. David Lewis (London, 1877), pp. 279–80.

14. PRO SP 12/28/fos. 125v–127v.

15. Parker, 146, 148.

16. Sander, *Schism*, p. 280.

17. Ibid., p. 151.

18. 'Lady Mildmay's Meditations', Northampton, Central Library, Phillipps Ms. 2569, pp. 37–8. My thanks to Retha Warnicke for supplying a copy of this manuscript.

19. PRO SP 12/21/fos. 54–54v.

20. BL, Lansd. 7, fos. 79–83.

21. Barbara J. Todd, 'The Remarrying Widow: A Stereotype Reconsidered', in Mary Prior (ed.), *Women in English Society 1500–1800* (London, 1985), p. 63.

22. Whythorne, pp. 43, 185–200.

23. J. F. Pound (ed.), *The Norwich Census of the Poor, 1570. Norfolk Record Society*, 40 (1971), pp. 16–17, 99.

24. Tawney and Power, I, 356. 5 Eliz. I, c. 4.19.

25. Steve Rappaport, *Worlds Within Worlds: Structures of Life in Sixteenth-Century London* (Cambridge, 1989), pp. 236–7, 313.

26. PRO E 163/13/18 fo. 3.

27. Caroline Barron, Christopher Coleman, and Claire Gobbi (eds), 'The London Journal of Alessandro Magno 1562', *The London Journal* 9, 2 (1983), p. 144.

28. Whythorne, pp. 30–2.

29. BL, Lansd. 101, fo. 21.

30. 4&5 Philip & Mary, c. 8.

31. 39 Eliz. I, c. 9.

32. CSP Sp., 1558–67, p. 45.

33. Bodl., Tanner 193, fo. 224.

34. HMC, Bath, IV, p. 178.

35. This is a reconstruction of events based on the transcript of their trial in Bodl., Tanner 84, fos. 105–97. See especially fos. 148v–149, 166–67.

36. BL, Add. 35830, fo. 104.

37. PRO SP 12/18/fo. 141; SP 12/19/fo. 29.

38. BL Add. 35830, fos. 183, 185, 189v, 191–191v.

39. Machyn, pp. 267–8. BL, Add. 48023, fo. 357.

40. CSP Rome, p. 51.

41. BL Add. 35830, fo. 185.
42. Mortimer Levine, *The Early Elizabethan Succession Question, 1558–1568* (Stanford, 1966), 14. PRO SP 12/21/fos. 76–77.
43. Bodl., Tanner 84, fo. 191; 196v. CSPD, Add., 535.
44. Bodl., Tanner 193, fo. 226.
45. Machyn, p. 300.
46. HMC Salisbury, XIII, pp. 66–7.
47. Quoted in Ralph A. Houlbrooke, *The English Family 1450–1700* (London, 1988), p. 81.
48. William Haugaard, *Elizabeth and the English Reformation* (Cambridge, 1970), pp. 172–3.
49. BCP, pp. 290–9.
50. Bodl., Tanner 50, fos. 29–29v.
51. Houlbrooke, *English Family*, pp. 86–7.
52. Machyn, p. 300.
53. Ibid., p. 240.
54. Ibid., p. 219.
55. Edward Cardwell, *Documentary Annals of the Reformed Church of England* (Oxford, 1844), I, pp. 316–20. Parker, p. 354. R. H. Helmholz, *Roman Canon Law in Reformation England* (Cambridge, 1990), pp. 69–79.
56. James C. Spalding (ed.), *The Reformation of the Ecclesiastical Laws of England. Sixteenth Century Essays and Studies* XIX (1992), p. 106.
57. 2 Leonard, 169: ER 74, 449–53.
58. Furnivall, *Child divorce*, pp. 137–8.
59. 2 Dyer, 178b–179a: ER 73, 394.
60. Houlbrooke, *English Family*, pp. 114–18.
61. Smith, p. 58.
62. HEH, Ms. 1340, fos. 72v–73.
63. Nottingham, University of Nottingham Library, MSS Division, Middleton Collection, Mi 26, fos. 67–68.
64. BL, Cotton, Titus, B.II, fo. 352.
65. HMC, Exeter, p. 24.
66. Stowe, p. 132.
67. A. L. Rowse, *The Elizabethan Renaissance: The Life of the Society* (London, 1974), pp. 180–2. Parker, pp. 406, 407–8.
68. BL, Lansd. 7, fo. 177.
69. 3 Dyer, 256b: ER 73, pp. 568–9.
70. Houlbrooke, *English Family*, p. 118.
71. 'Forman's Autobiography', in A. L. Rowse, *Simon Forman. Sex and Society in Shakespeare's Age* (London, 1974), pp. 275–6.
72. Thomas Harman, *A Caveat or Warning of Common Cursetors* (London, 1573), Sig. F.ij–F.iiij. [STC 12788]. The first edition was published in 1567.

CHAPTER 7   ROYAL MARRIAGE

1. Stowe, p. 137.
2. Victor von Klarwill (ed.), *Queen Elizabeth and Some Foreigners* (London,

1928), p. 94.
3. Hartley, pp. 44–5.
4. Klarwill, *Foreigners*, pp. 86–7.
5. Ibid.
6. John Bruce (ed.), *Annals of the First Four Years of the Reign of Queen Elizabeth, by Sir John Hayward. Camden Society*, 7 (1840), p. 37.
7. Ibid., p. 145.
8. BL, Add. 48023, fo. 354.
9. HMC Salisbury, I, 261.
10. Machyn, pp. 265, 267, 268. BL Add. 48023, fos. 356v, 357v. BL Add. 35830, fo. 107v.
11. BL, Add. 48023, fo. 258. BL, Add. 35830, fo. 107v.
12. BL, Add. 48023, fo. 366. CSPF, 1562, pp. 173, 190, 216–27, 228. APC, n.s., VII, p. 123. CSP Sp, 1558–1567, p. 257.
13. James Bell, *Queen Elizabeth and a Swedish Princess. Being an Account of the Visit of Princess Cecilia of Sweden to England in 1565*, ed. Ethel Seaton (London, 1926), pp. 15–28.
14. Klarwill, *Foreigners*, p. 171.
15. J. E. Neale, *Queen Elizabeth I* (London, 1957), pp. 78–9.
16. Klarwill, *Foreigners*, pp. 113–15.
17. BL, Add. 48023, fo. 352.
18. HMC Salisbury, I, p. 257.
19. PRO, SP 12/13/fo. 21.
20. MacCaffrey, pp. 95–7.
21. CSP Sp, 1558–67, pp. 174–5.
22. Ibid., p. 176.
23. BL, Add. 48023, fo. 353.
24. Machyn, pp. 242–3.
25. CSPF, 1560–61, pp. 348–9.
26. Samuel Rhea Gammon, *Statesman and Schemer. William, First Lord Paget Tudor Minister* (Hamden, Conn., 1973), pp. 247–8. PRO SP 70/20/fos. 14–15; 21/fos. 63–4.
27. 'Sir Thomas Smith's orations for and against the Queen's marriage', in John Strype, *The Life of the Learned Sir Thomas Smith* (Oxford, 1820), appendix 3, pp. 184–259.
28. MacCaffrey, pp. 104–15.
29. BL, Add. 35830, fo. 159v.
30. Quoted in Jasper Ridley, *John Knox* (Oxford, 1968), pp. 270–1.
31. M. A. R. Green (ed.), *CPSD, 1601–1603, with Addenda, 1547–1565* (London, 1870), p. 534.
32. BL, Add. 48023, fo. 364.
33. F. A. Inderwick (ed.), *A Calendar of the Inner Temple Records* (London, 1896), I, 215–9. BL, Add. 48023, fo. 358v.
34. Ibid., I, 219, 219–20, 220.
35. BL, Add. 48023, fo. 359v.
36. Thomas Sackville and Thomas Norton, *Gorboduc or Porrex and Ferrex*, ed. Irby B. Cauthen, jr (Lincoln, Nebraska, 1970), pp. 63–4.
37. Ibid., p. 73.

38. Machyn, p. 275.
39. Hartley, pp. 58–62, 87–90, 90–5.
40. Ibid., p. 115.
41. C. J. Gutherie (ed.), *The History of the Reformation of Religion Within the Realm of Scotland written by John Knox* (Edinburgh, 1982), p. 238.
42. Jones, *Faith by Statute*, pp. 54–6.
43. Quoted in Antonia Fraser, *Mary Queen of Scots* (New York, 1969), p. 114.
44. BL, Add. 48023, fo. 353v.
45. Ibid., fo. 357v.
46. Ibid., fo. 362v.
47. Ibid., fo. 361. CSP Sp, 1558–1567, p. 315.
48. H&L, II, 229. MacCaffrey, pp. 121–30.
49. CSP Sp, 1558–1567, p. 338.
50. Ibid., p. 313.
51. Quoted in J. B. Black, *The Reign of Elizabeth*, 2nd edn (Oxford, 1959), p. 80.
52. Klarwill, *Foreigners*, p. 173.
53. Ibid., pp. 182–9.
54. Ibid., pp. 197–9.
55. Ibid., p. 267.
56. BL, Add. 48023, fo. 362.
57. Strype, *Annals*, I, ii, p. 122.
58. HEH, EL 7976, no. 4, 'The Kinges Castell'. Another copy is in Bodl., Rawlinson D, 718, fo. 32 ff. The Huntington's late sixteenth-century copy is attributed to Roger Andrews and dated c. 1566, but the catalog description implies that Andrews was the copyist, not the author, assigning him a death date of 1635. It is possible that it is earlier – though not later – than this, because of his exhortation to Elizabeth to reform religion. However, his remarks about the behaviour of Parliament suggest 1566.
59. Hartley, pp. 145–9.
60. Ibid., p. 138.
61. Ibid., pp. 129–39. See G. R. Elton's consideration of this episode in *The Parliaments of England 1558–1581* (Cambridge, 1986), pp. 370–2. Hartley did not identify the man who gave this speech, but Elton has.
62. Hartley, *Proceedings*, p. 140.
63. Ibid., I, pp. 155–7.
64. Ibid., I, pp. 158–9.
65. CUL, Ff.v.14, fo. 83v.
66. Hartley, pp. 160–2.
67. PRO SP 12/41/fo. 75.
68. Klarwill, *Foreigners*, pp. 297, 299.
69. Susan Doran, 'Religion and Politics at the Court of Elizabeth I: The Habsburg Marriage Negotiations of 1559–1567', *English Historical Review* 104 (1989), pp. 908–26.
70. Gordon Donaldson, *The First Trial of Mary, Queen of Scots* (New York, 1969), pp. 29–59.

71. Gordon Donaldson (ed.), *The Memoirs of Sir James Melville of Halhill* (London, 1969), pp. 67–9.

72. G. B. Harrison (ed.), *The Letters of Queen Elizabeth I* (London, 1968), p. 50.

73. Donaldson, *Melville*, pp. 76–8.

74. Donaldson, *Trial*, pp. 191–209. MacCaffrey, pp. 247–67.

CHAPTER 8 FAMILY VALUES

1. BL, Lansd. 101, fos. 27–28v.

2. Thomas Raynalde, *The Byrth of Mankynde, otherwyse named the Womans Booke* (London, 1560), fos. CXXv–CXXI. [STC 21156]. Thomas Vicary, *A Profitable Treatise of the Anatomie of mans Bodye . . . 1577*, ed. Fredrick J. Furnivall and Percy Furnivall, *Early English Text Society* 53 (London, 1888), pp. 78–9.

3. Raynalde, *Byrth*, fo. XXI.

4. Thomas Hill, *The Gardener's Labyrinth*, ed. Richard Mabey (Oxford, 1988), pp. 142, 201, 206.

5. Raynalde, *Byrth*, fo. CXXIII–CXXIIIv.

6. Audrey Eccles, *Obstetrics and Gynaecology in Tudor and Stuart England* (Kent, Ohio, 1982), pp. 68–71.

7. Thomas R. Forbes, 'By What Disease or Casualty: The Changing Face of Death in London,' in Charles Webster (ed.), *Health, Medicine and Mortality in the Sixteenth Century* (Cambridge, 1979), pp. 127–8.

8. 'Sir Thomas Smith's Oration for and against the Queen's Marriage', in John Strype, *The Life of the Learned Sir Thomas Smith* (Oxford, 1820), appendix III, p. 186.

9. Keith Wrightson and David Levine, *Poverty and Piety in an English Village. Terling, 1525–1700* (New York, 1979), pp. 57–8.

10. Eccles, *Obstetrics*, pp. 101–8.

11. BCP, pp. 314–15.

12. Machyn, p. 301.

13. Edgar Powell (ed.), 'The Travels and Life of Sir Thomas Hoby . . . written by Himself', in *Camden Society Miscellanea X*, 3rd ser., 4 (1902), p. 128.

14. BCP, pp. 269–81.

15. William P. Haugaard, *Elizabeth and the English Reformation* (Cambridge, 1970), pp. 121–2.

16. Machyn, p. 249.

17. Machyn, pp. 288–9.

18. J. S. Cockburn (ed.), *Calendar of Assize Records. Sussex Indictments, Elizabeth I* (London, 1975), p. 15.

19. 2 Dyer, 186a: ER 73, 410–11.

20. Machyn, p. 298.

21. Raynalde, *Byrth*, fos. XCIX–XCIXv.

22. Forbes, 'Death in London', 133, 136. Lawrence Stone, *The Family Sex and Marriage in England 1500–1800* (New York, 1977), pp. 473–4.

23. D. M. Palliser, *The Age of Elizabeth. England under the Later Tudors 1547–1603* (London, 1983), p. 44.

24. Roger Schofield and E. A. Wrigley, 'Infant and Child Mortality in England in the Late Tudor and Stuart Period', in Webster (ed.), *Mortality*, p. 61.

25. Schofield and Wrigley, 'Mortality', pp. 62–3. Houlbrooke, *English Family*, pp. 136–8.

26. Ephesians 6:1–3.

27. Ecclesiasticus 3:8;6; 13.

28. BL, Lansd. 120, fo. 81.

29. Roger Ascham, *The Scholemaster* (1570), fos. 15–16. [STC 832].

30. Whythorne, p. 8.

31. David Siegenthaler, 'Religious Education For Citizenship: Primer and Catechism,' in John E. Booty (ed.), *The Godly Kingdom of Tudor England: Great Books of the English Reformation* (Wilton, Conn., 1981), p. 240.

32. BCP, p. 289.

33. Ibid., p. 286.

34. Strype, *Annals*, I, ii, pp. 567–8. Haugaard, *English Reformation*, pp. 170–1.

35. Haugaard, *English Reformation*, pp. 277–8.

36. G. E. Corrie (ed.), *A Catechism written in Latin by Alexander Nowell, . . . together with the same Catechism translated into English by Thomas Norton* (Cambridge, 1853), pp. 130–1.

37. Proverbs 22:6.

38. David Cressy, *Literacy and the Social Order. Reading and Writing in Tudor and Stuart England* (Cambridge, 1980), pp. 166–9.

39. Ibid., pp. 127–34.

40. John Hart, *A Methode, or Comfortable Beginning for all Unlearned to Read English* (1570), Sig. Aiiii verso. [STC 12889].

41. Cressy, *Literacy*, pp. 20–2.

42. Rowse, *Forman*, pp. 269–70.

43. Roger Ascham, *The Scholemaster* (1570), fo. 1. [STC 832].

44. Proverbs 23:13–14; 13:24; 22:15. Ecclesiasticus 30:12. Ascham, *Scholemaster*, fo. 12.

45. Machyn, p. 311. Stowe, p. 125.

46. Rowse, *Forman*, pp. 174, 276–8.

47. Margaret Gay Davies, *The Enforcement of English Apprenticeship 1563–1642* (Cambridge, Mass., 1956), p. 11.

48. Whythorne, pp. 19–21.

49. 5 Eliz. I, c. 4.

50. Steve Rappaport, *Worlds within Worlds: Structures of Life in Sixteenth Century London* (Cambridge, 1989), pp. 295–6. Tawney and Power, *Tudor Economic Documents*, I, p. 356.

51. Tawney and Power, I, p. 357.

52. Ibid. pp. 350–1.

53. Rowse, *Forman*, pp. 271–6.

54. Charles Carlton, *The Court of Orphans* (Leicester, 1974), pp. 29–31.

55. HLRO, Original Acts, 5 Eliz. no. 34, 'Confirming Liberties Granted to the City of Exeter.'

56. Joel Hurstfield, *The Queen's Wards. Wardship and Marriage under Elizabeth I* (Cambridge, Mass., 1958), p. 115.
57. Smith, p. 129.
58. PRO SP 12/26/ fo.113.
59. HMC Bath, IV, pp. 134–5.
60. Thomas Blage, *A Schole of Wise Conceits* (1569), p. 173. [STC 3114].
61. Smith, p. 134.
62. 'Don't do what is doubtful' and 'What is not from faith is sin.' Hartley, I, p. 237.
63. Louis B. Wright, *Middle Class Culture in Elizabethan England* (Ithaca, 1958), pp. 359–60.
64. M. St. Clare Byrne (ed.), *The Elizabethan Home Discovered in Two Dialogues by Claudius Hollyband and Peter Erondell* (London, 1930), pp. vii–ix, 9, 13–17. Quoting Hollyband's *The Frenche Littleton* (1566). [STC 6738].
65. BL, Harelian 3638, fos. 106–106v.
66. PRO SP 12/18/fo. 33.
67. PRO SP 12/18/fos. 92–3.
68. PRO SP 12/18/fo. 141.
69. BL, Add. 35831, fo. 36.
70. CSPF, 1561–1562, p. 635.
71. CSPF, 1562, p. 81.
72. PRO SP 12/22/fo. 40.
73. PRO SP 12/22/fo. 79.
74. PRO SP 12/24/ fo. 17.
75. PRO SP 12/26/ fo. 17.
76. PRO SP 12/26/ fo. 22.
77. S. L. Greenslade, 'The Faculty of Theology', in J. McConica (ed.), *The History of the University of Oxford, III, The Collegiate University* (Oxford, 1986), pp. 297, 305.
78. PRO SP 46/13/fos. 279–279v.
79. Whythorne, pp. 22–34.
80. Mildmay said she read it in Bartholomew Vigoe, but she must have meant Johannes de Vigo whose *The Most Excellent Workes of Chirurgerye* were first translated in 1543 and went through several editions in mid-century [STC 24720].
81. 'Lady Mildmay's Meditations,' Northampton, Northamptonshire Libraries, Phillipps Ms. 2569, pp. 9–15.

CHAPTER 9 *CARPE DIEM*

1. BL Add. 35831, fo. 188.
2. Paul Slack, *The Impact of Plague in Tudor and Stuart England* (Oxford, 1990), pp. 71–2.
3. Black, *Reign of Elizabeth*, p. 61.
4. CSPD Add., p. 540.
5. CSPF, 1563, p. 439.
6. Ibid., pp. 443, 453. BL Add. 35831, fos. 145v–146.
7. Ibid., p. 448.

8. Ibid., p. 473.
9. Ibid., p. 483.
10. LRO, Repertories 15, fos. 257v; 260.
11. Bullein, fos. 26–27v.
12. Stowe, pp. 122–3. Machyn, p. 310. LRO, Repertories 15, p. 260.
13. LRO, Repertories, 15, fo. 260v.
14. LRO, Journal 18, fo. 143v; 152v; 156v.
15. Machyn, p. 312. LRO, Repertories 15, p. 276.
16. H&L, II, p. 229.
17. Grindal, p. 258. 'Cito fuge, procul fuge, sero revertere.'
18. Grindal, p. 269.
19. LRO Journal 18, fo. 184.
20. Stowe, pp. 124–5.
21. Slack, *Impact of Plague*, p. 148.
22. Thomas Cooper, *Coopers Chronicle conteyning the whole discourse of the histories . . . augmented unto the .vii. year of the raigne of . . . Elizabeth* (1565), Sig. D.iii. [STC 15220]. Cooper estimated the death toll to be 23,000.
23. Machyn, p. 312.
24. Bullein, fo. 28.
25. Ibid., fos. 29–29v.
26. Bullein, fos. 30v–31v. Slack, *Impact of Plague*, 30–31. Whitney R. D. Jones, *William Turner Tudor Naturalist Physician and Divine* (London, 1988), pp. 122–3.
27. Thomas Gale, *An Antidotarie conteyning hidde and secrete medicines simple and compound*, in his *Certaine Workes of Chirrugerie, newly compiled* (1563), fo. 76. [STC 11529].
28. Bullein, fos. 31v–32. Slack, *Impact of Plague*, p. 30.
29. Bodl. Rawlinson C. 816, fo. 85v.
30. Grindal, pp. 96–110.
31. Stowe, pp. 128, 126.
32. H&L, II, 236–40.
33. Stowe, p. 127.
34. Grindal, p. 272.
35. H&L, II, 318–20.
36. LRO, Repertories, 15, fo. 281.
37. Corp. of London, Guildhall Library, Ms. 11,588, Vol. I, fo. 97.
38. Slack, *Impact of Plague*, pp. 205, 272. A. A. Van Schelven (ed.), *Kerkeraads-Protocollen der Nederduitsche Vluchtelingen-Kerk te Londen, 1560–1563* (Amsterdam, 1921), pp. 428–35.
39. Rappaport, *Worlds Within Worlds*, p. 73.
40. Stowe, pp. 128–9.
41. BL, Lands. 114, fos. 171–2.
42. BL, Lansd. 102, fo. 87. Stowe, pp. 130–1.
43. BL, Add. 48023, fo. 369v.
44. Grindal, pp. 280–1.
45. F. G. Emmison, *Tudor Secretary. Sir William Petre at Court and Home* (Cambridge, Mass., 1961), pp. 251–3.
46. Margaret Pelling and Charles Webster, 'Medical Practitioners', in Charles

Webster (ed.), *Health, Medicine and Mortality in the Sixteenth Century* (Cambridge, 1979), p. 219.

47. H&L, II, 233; 235.
48. Thomas Gale, *Certaine workes of Galens called Methodus Medendi* (1586), fo. 32. [STC 11531]. This is a reprint of the 1567 edn, STC 11529a.
49. Ibid., 32–32v.
50. Cockburn, *Surrey Indictments*, pp. 64–5.
51. Cockburn, *Kent Indictments*, pp. 58, 72.
52. Thomas Gale, *Enchiridion* in *Works* (1563), Sig. Aiii.
53. Pelling and Gilbert, 'Practitioners', p. 176. Machyn, pp. 251–2.
54. Stowe, p. 130.
55. Marjorie McIntosh, *A Community Transformed. The Manor and Liberty of Havering, 1500–1620* (Cambridge, 1991), p. 83.
56. Gale, *Enchiridion*, fos. 50v–54.
57. Ibid., fos. 51v–57.
58. John Jones, *The Benefit of the Auncient Bathes of Buckstones, which cureth most greevous Sicknesses, never before published* (1572), fos. 2v–3; 20v; 11–12v. bound with John Jones, *The Bathes of Bathes Ayde: Wonderful and most excellent against very many sickness, approved by authority, confirmed by reason, and daily tried by experience: with the antiquity, commoditie, propertie, knowledge, use, aphorismes, diet, medicine, and other things to be considered and observed.* (1574) [STC 14725]. VCH Yorkshire, III, p. 470. William Turner, *A booke of the natures and properties of the bathes in England* (1562) [STC 24351; 24352]. Jones, *Turner*, pp. 123–9.
59. Bullein, fo. 33.
60. CSPD, Addendum, p. 80.
61. 8 Eliz. I, c. 10.
62. HMC, Exeter, p. 9.
63. 33 Henry VIII, c. 9; 5&6 Edw. VI, c. 25. H&L, II, p. 361.
64. Thomas Isham, 'The Life of John Isham', in G. D. Ramsay (ed.), *John Isham Mercer and Merchant Adventurer. Two Account Books of a London Merchant in the Reign of Elizabeth I. Northamptonshire Record Society*, 21 (1962), p. 171.
65. A. Hassell Smith, G. M. Baker and R. W. Kenny, (eds), *The Papers of Nathaniel Bacon of Stiffkey, Vol. I, 1556–1577* (Norwich, 1979), p. 7.
66. Caroline Barron, Christopher Coleman and Claire Gobbi (eds), 'The London Journal of Alessandro Magno 1562', *The London Journal*, 9 (1983), pp. 143–4.
67. McIntosh, *Havering*, p. 65.
68. Emmison, *Tudor Secretary*, p. 217.
69. H&L, II, pp. 115–16. CSP Rome, I, p. 9. LRO, Repertories 14, 13 April 1559. CSP Sp, 1559, p. 62.
70. APC, ns, VII, p. 331. Charles Plummer (ed.), *Elizabethan Oxford. Reprints of Rare Tracts. Oxford Historical Society* 8 (1886), pp. 123–5, 127–9, 138–9.
71. Bodl., Tanner 207, fo. 44.
72. STC 25584.
73. Whythorne, p. 245.

74. ZL, I, p. 178. ZL, II, p. 150.
75. *The Whole Psalter translated into English metre* (1567?) [STC 2729].
76. Patrick Collinson, *The Religion of Protestants* (Oxford, 1982), p. 237.
77. J. Utenhove, trans., *Hondert psalmen Davids* (1561) [STC 2739]. *De psalmen Davidis in Nederlandischer sangs-ryme* (1566) [STC 2740].
78. Norman Ault (ed.), *Elizabethan Lyrics* (London, 1949), pp. 56–7.
79. William Harrison, *The Description of England*, ed. Georges Edelen (Ithaca, 1969), 141.
80. Ibid., pp. 139, 247.
81. 'Magno Journal', p. 146.
82. Ibid., pp. 148–9.
83. For the concentration of highway robberies in Kent see Caroline Patrick-Jones, 'Subsistence Methods in Elizabethan Kent: A Field Guide to Sixteenth Century Survival' (unpublished MA thesis, Utah State University, 1993), pp. 63, 55, 53. J. S. Cockburn (ed.), *Calendar of Assize Records: Kent Indictments, Elizabeth I* (London, 1979), ind. 304, 247.
84. Bullein, fos. 72v–73.
85. Harrison, *Description*, p. 148.
86. H&L, II, pp. 136–8, 187–94, 278–83.
87. Machyn, p. 281.
88. Frances Elizabeth Baldwin, *Sumptuary Legislation and Personal Regulation in England* (Baltimore, 1926), p. 206.
89. HEH, HM 1340, fos. 26v–27v; 30–30v.
90. PRO E 178/3058; 469; 512; 570; 733; 1052; 2004; 2396; 2473; 2952; 3299. PRO SP 12/23, fo. 8.
91. PRO SP 12/23/fo. 25.
92. 5 Eliz. I, c. 6.
93. 2 Dyer, 234b: ER 73, 518–19.
94. 3 Dyer, 266b: ER 73, 591–2.
95. Thomas Harman, *A Caveat or Warning of Common Cursetors* (1573), Sig. F. i. verso–F.iiii. verso [STC 12788]. The first edition appeared in 1567 but Harman added a number of illustrated tales for the 1573 edition.
96. APC, ns, VII, 125.
97. HEH, HM 1340, fos. 27v–28.
98. D. M. Palliser, *The Age of Elizabeth. England under the Later Tudors 1547–1603* (London, 1983), p. 312.
99. PRO STAC 5/54/36. 3 Eliz.
100. PRO STAC 5/H39/3. 11 Eliz.
101. CPR, 1560–63, p. 406.
102. Ibid., pp. 405–6.
103. Palliser, *Age of Elizabeth*, p. 303.
104. HEH, HM 1340, fos. 29–30.
105. Smith, pp. 111–16.
106. Machyn, p. 301.
107. 2 Dyer, 202a: ER 73, 445–6. CSPD, 16, no. 61.
108. HLRO, Commons Ms. Journals, I, fos. 234, 251.
109. Machyn, p. 286.
110. Stowe, p. 127.

111. Hartley, p. 201.
112. PRO E 133/2/284.
113. H&L, II, pp. 196–7.
114. 8 Eliz. 1, C. 8.
115. Jones, *God and the Moneylenders*, p. 95.
116. D. R. Lidington, 'Parliament and the Enforcement of the Penal Statutes: The History of the Act "In Restraint of Common Promoters" (18 Eliz. I, c. 5)', in Norman Jones and David Dean (eds), *Interest Groups and Legislation in Elizabethan Parliaments: Essays Presented to Sir Geoffrey Elton. Parliamentary History*, 8 (1989), p. 311.
117. H&L, II, pp. 288–9.
118. Lidington, 'Penal Statutes', pp. 311–12.

CHAPTER 10 MAKING A LIVING

1. Richard Hakluyt, *Voyages* (London, 1962), II, pp. 113–14.
2. Ibid., II, p. 117. BL Add. 48020, fo. 331.
3. Ibid., VII, pp. 53–62.
4. Noel W. Sainsbury (ed.), *Calendar of State Papers, Colonial Series, East Indies, China and Japan, 1513–1616* (London, 1862), pp. 4–7. HLRO, Orig. Acts, 8 Eliz. no. 17.
5. Ibid., VII, p. 22.
6. Ibid., II, p. 118.
7. Mary Dewar (ed.), *A Discourse of the Commonweal of this Realm of England attributed to Sir Thomas Smith* (Charlottesville: 1969), pp. 95–6.
8. PRO SP 12/1/fo. 147.
9. PRO SP 12/1/fo. 150.
10. C. E. Challis, *The Tudor Coinage* (Manchester, 1978), p. 260.
11. Palliser, *Age of Elizabeth*, p. 141.
12. John Heywood, *Iohn Heywoodes Workes* (1566), Sig. Aa. iii. [STC 13286].
13. Quoted in Stanford E. Lehmberg, *Sir Walter Mildmay and Tudor Government* (Austin, Texas, 1964), p. 60.
14. Quoted in Challis, *Tudor Coinage* p. 122.
15. CPR, I, pp. 66–7.
16. H&L, II, pp. 150–4. Challis, *Tudor Coinage*, pp. 122–3.
17. H&L, II, pp. 150–4.
18. BL Add. 48023, fos. 358v; 360.
19. Ibid., fo. 354.
20. H&L, II, pp. 155–8.
21. Challis, *Tudor Coinage*, p. 126.
22. Corp. of London Guildhall Library, Ms. 11,588, vol. I, fo. 56.
23. BL Add. 48023, fos. 58; 58v. PRO SP 12/20/fos. 135–6. Ramsay, *Isham*, pp. xxxi–xxxii.
24. Challis, *Tudor Coinage*, pp. 127–8. Tract by Christopher Bumpstead, BL Add. 48020, fo. 231–2.
25. BL Add. 35830, fo. 210v. BL Add. 48023, fo. 360.
26. BL Add. 48023, fo. 360.
27. H&L, II, p. 181.

28.   BL Add. 48023, fo. 360v.
29.   CSP Span., 1558–67, p. 228.
30.   BL Add. 48023, fo. 361.
31.   CSP Span., 1558–67, p. 228.
32.   BL Add. 48023, fo. 361v.
33.   H&L, II, pp. 183–5. There has been a debate over this proclama-
        tion, with some scholars refusing to believe that Elizabeth intended
        to devalue. The evidence in BL Add. 48023 makes it clear that a
        devaluation was being planned. For the debate see Challis, *Coinage*,
        p. 128, n. 348.
34.   BL Add. 48023, fo. 362v.
35.   H&L, II, pp. 185–6.
36.   R. H. Helmholtz (ed.), *Select Cases on Defamation to 1600* (London, 1985),
        pp. 76–8.
37.   BL Add. 48023, fo. 362v.
38.   BL Add. 48023, fo. 362v.
39.   Palliser, *Age of Elizabeth*, pp. 189–92.
40.   BL Add. 48023, fo. 362. H&L, II, p. 182.
41.   H&L, II, p. 182.
42.   BL Add. 48023, fo. 355v.
43.   BL Add. 48023, fo. 362v.
44.   BL Add. 48023, fos. 363v, 364, 364v, 365.
45.   Carlos Wyffels, 'Documenten over de Engeland reis in november-
        december 1565 van Jakob Van Wesenbeke, Pensionaris van de stad
        Antwerpen', *Bulletin de la Commission Royale d'Histoire*, 150 (1984),
        pp. 357–63.
46.   LRO, Journals, 17, fo. 336v.
47.   H&L, II, pp. 242–3.
48.   HEH HM 1340, fos. 28v–29.
49.   BL Add. 35830, fo. 141.
50.   R. H. Tawney, *The Agrarian Problem of the Sixteenth Century* (London,
        1912), pp. 327–8.
51.   HEH, HAP Box 12, (9).
52.   5 Eliz. I, c. 2.
53.   HEH HM 1340, fo. 29.
54.   5 Eliz. I, c. 5.15.
55.   Palliser, *Age of Elizabeth*, p. 193.
56.   Ibid., p. 194.
57.   HLRO, Commons Ms. Journals, I, fos. 200, 210.
58.   1 Eliz. I, c. 17.
59.   Hartley, pp. 106–7.
60.   HLRO, Commons Ms. Journals, I, fo. 212.
61.   5 Eliz. I, c. 5. HLRO, Original Acts, 5 Eliz. c. 5 shows that the two
        provisoes were written by the committee and submitted together.
62.   Mea culpa! In my book *Faith by Statute*, pp. 184–5 I give the division
        as 147–77, a misreading of the manuscript as wrong as J. E. Neale,
        Elizabeth I and Her Parliaments (London, 1953), I, p. 116, who gives it
        as 149–77. Both are incorrect, as an examination of HLRO, Commons

Ms. Journals, I, fo. 238v shows. Mea maxima culpa! A look at HLRO, Original Acts, 5 Eliz. c. 5 shows that the proviso I took to be the one on false rumors in *Faith by Statute* is actually one that declares that the Act will not infringe on existing franchises.

63. Eric R. Olsen, 'The Paul's Cross Sermons of March 1566' (unpublished MA thesis, Utah State University, 1992), pp. 15–16, 40. The quote is from Oxford, Bodl., Tanner 50, fo. 44.
64. 5 Eliz. I, c. 5.16.
65. H&L, II, pp. 257, 273–5.
66. HMC Pepys, pp. 93–5.
67. J. E. Neale, *The Elizabethan House of Commons* (Harmondsworth, 1969), pp. 361–2.
68. Edwin Green, 'The Vintners' Lobby, 1552–1568', *Guildhall Studies in History* 1 (1974), pp. 47–58.
69. Richard Porder, *A Sermon of Gods Fearefull Threatenings for Idolatrye, Mixing of Religion, Retayning Idolatrous Remnants, and other Wickednesse: With a Treatise Against Usurie Preached in Paules Churche the XI Daye of Maye 1570* (London, 1570), fos. 59–59v. [STC 20117].
70. PRO E 178/636. 4 Eliz.
71. 8 Eliz. I, C. 11. 13 Eliz. I, c. 19. G. R. Elton, *The Parliament of England 1559–1581* (Cambridge, 1986), p. 253.
72. CPR, 1563–64, pp. 119, 331. Ibid., 1561–1563, p. 213. Ibid., 1564–1565, p. 331. J. A. van Dorsten *The Radical Arts. The First Decade of an Elizabethan Renaissance* (London, 1970), p. 17.
73. CPR, 1560–1563, p. 98. Ibid., 1563–1564, p. 119. Ibid., 1564–1565, pp. 330–1.
74. G. D. Ramsay, 'Industrial Discontent in Early Elizabethan London: Clothworkers and Merchant Adventurers in Conflict', *The London Journal* 1 (1975), pp. 227–39.
75. H&L, II, pp. 247–8.
76. Thomas Cooper, *Coopers Chronicle conteyning the whole discourse of the histories . . . augmented unto the .vii. year of the reigne of . . . Elizabeth* (London, 1565), Sig. D.iii verso–D.iiii. [STC 15220].
77. G. D. Ramsay, *The Queen's Merchants and the Revolt of the Netherlands. The End of the Antwerp Mart* (Manchester, 1986), II, pp. 10–15. Cooper, *Chronicle*, Sig. D.iiii.
78. H&L, II, pp. 259–60.
79. 'Royal instructions to the commissioners sent to Bruges, 1565', in Ramsay, *Queen's Merchants*, appendix, pp. 206–20.
80. Geoffrey Parker, *The Dutch Revolt* (Harmondsworth, 1985), p. 90.
81. Ibid., p. 106.
82. Ramsay, *Queen's Merchants*, pp. 34–61.
83. Ibid., II, pp. 73–8.
84. MacCaffrey, pp. 189–95.
85. Ramsay, *Isham*, lxxx–xci, pp. 170–2.
86. Whythorne, pp. 138–9.
87. Stowe, pp. 134–5.
88. HMC, 14th Report, Appx. 8, p. 54.

89. HEH, El 2579, fos. 14–14v.
90. J. F. Pound (ed.), *The Norwich Census of the Poor 1570. Norfolk Record Society* (1971), pp. 50–1.
91. Ibid., pp. 39–42.
92. PRO E 163/13/18 fos. 17–18v.
93. PRO E 163/13/18 fos. 2–4v.
94. 5 Eliz. I, c. 4.11.
95. H&L, II, pp. 210–19.
96. HMC, 14th Report, Appx. 8, p. 56.
97. Ibid., p. 63.
98. H&L, II, pp. 291–2, 294–5, 298, 306–7. C. L'Estrange Ewen, *Lotteries and Sweepstakes* (London, 1932), pp. 34–63. HMC, *Appendix to the Seventh Report*, pp. 620–1.
99. Nicholas P. Canny, *The Elizabethan Conquest of Ireland: A Pattern Established 1565–76* (Hassocks, Sussex, 1976), p. 5.
100. Steven G. Ellis, *Tudor Ireland. Crown, Community and the Conflict of Cultures 1470–1603* (London, 1985), pp. 248–9.
101. Myles V. Ronan, *The Reformation in Ireland under Elizabeth 1560–1580 (from Original Sources)* (London, 1930), pp. 216–18.
102. Ellis, *Ireland*, pp. 255–7.
103. Ibid., pp. 259–61.
104. Whythorne, pp. 207–10.

CHAPTER 11 EPILOGUE

1. Philip E. Hughes, *The Reformation in England*, rev. edn (London, 1963), pp. 272, 418–20.
2. 13 Eliz. I, c. 1, 2, 3, 16.
3. 13 Eliz. 1, c. 7, 8.
4. 13 Eliz. I, c. 11, 13, 14, 19.
5. 13 Eliz. I, c. 12.
6. CPR, 1560–63, p. 223. Venn, *Alumni Cantabrigiensis*.
7. CUL Mm.1.29, fo. 49–49v.
8. PRO SP 12/46/fos. 1, 28.
9. HMC, De L'Isle, II, pp. 177, 183, 184, 197. PRO SP 12/46/fo. 1 (no. 12).
10. Whythorne, pp. xlvi–lii.
11. Whythorne, pp. 210–11.

Suggestions for Further Reading

PRIMARY SOURCES

Any student researching Elizabethan history will find the great series of calendars essential. Lists of documents arranged chronologically, they are guides to the archives from which they are taken. The better ones, such as the *Calendar of State Papers, Spain, Venice* and *Rome* provide long translations or summaries of the documents. These are detailed enough that there is little need to consult the originals – although in interpretations that turn around the wording of the document it is still necessary to check the passage in the original language.

The *Calendar of State Papers, Foreign Series*, summarizing the documents generated by the English in dealing with foreign governments, is less detailed than the calendars for foreign archives, but still provides the broad details. There are separate calendars for Scottish and Irish affairs.

The most important papers for writing the history of England in the 1560s are listed in the *Calendar of State Papers, Domestic*. Describing what passes for the central archive of Elizabeth's government, the manuscripts it covers are in the Public Record Office. Unfortunately, this calendar is nothing more than a list of documents and their topics. Useful as a finding guide, it cannot be used for primary research of a very detailed kind. The fact that the calendar is poor may account for the relative paucity of studies on early Elizabethan government in comparison with those of Henry VIII's reign, for which a superb calendar exists.

Because William Cecil was Elizabeth's principal secretary his personal archive, held at Hatfield House in Hertfordshire, is another important source. Like so many collections, it has been calendared by the Historical Manuscripts Commission as the Salisbury Manuscripts. This calendar is rather detailed and can generally be depended upon without reference to the manuscripts. The other volumes of the Historical Manuscript Commission vary enormously in their quality and detail, but they are an indispensable access tool for Elizabethan historical sources outside the Public Record Office.

There is one other calendar that students of the 1560s ought to consult, the *Acts of the Privy Council*. Although the register is missing for both the early and late 1560s, it is an indispensable guide to the concerns of the central administration. Often one can move from the Privy Council to the proclamations it ordered in the Queen's name by consulting Hughes and Larkins's *Tudor Royal Proclamations.*

Besides archival series there are the many individual documents published in local and specialized record society publications. Groups like the Surtees Society and the Camden Society have been publishing documents since the nineteenth century. As early as 1848 the Camden Society printed *The Diary of Henry Machyn,* one of the richest sources for London life in the middle of the sixteenth century.

Another record society whose books are essential to the study of the 1560s is the Parker Society. In the middle of the nineteenth century it produced editions of the correspondence, theology, polemics and liturgies of the first generation of Elizabethan divines. The *Zurich Letters,* which contains letters written by English Protestants to their friends in Switzerland, the *Correspondence of Matthew Parker,* the *Remains of Edmund Grindal* and the *Works* of John Jewel all appear in this collection. The collective index to the Parker Society volumes is an indispensable tool for anyone interested in religion and social thought in early Elizabethan England.

Although he was not an Elizabethan, the works of John Strype, written in the late-seventeenth and eighteenth centuries, also provide an important source. Because he had access to the great Cotton Library before it burned, Strype saw, and often published, documents that no longer exist. His narrative of the 1560s is contained in his *Annals of the Reformation,* but he also did biographies, with documentary appendices, on Parker, Smith, Grindal and other leading Elizabethans. What remain of the Cotton manuscripts, along with other collections such as the Landsdowne and Yelverton manuscripts, which are full of sixteenth-century material, are in the British Library.

WORKS BY MODERN HISTORIANS

There are very few books which concentrate directly on the 1560s since they fall in the crack between the turbulent 1550s and the glories and drama of the later Elizabethan years. The exceptions to that rule cluster around seminal events: the Elizabethan Settlement of Religion and the succession crisis. The one book which unites all of these themes by dealing with the high politics from the accession until 1572 is Wallace MacCaffrey's *The Shaping of the Elizabethan Regime.* A useful introduction to the politics of the 1560s is my 'Elizabeth's First Year: The Conception and Birth of the Elizabethan Political World,' in Christopher Haigh (ed.), *The Reign of Elizabeth I* (1984).

The Elizabethan Settlement and its aftermath was subjected to careful scrutiny in the early twentieth century and again in the 1970s and 1980s. The standard treatment of the Parliamentary history of the Settlement is my *Faith by Statute. Parliament and the Settlement of Religion, 1559* (1982), which should be read in conjunction with Winthrop Hudson's *The Cambridge Connection and the Elizabethan Settlement of 1559* (1980). Hudson's book traces the personal ties between Cecil, Bacon and the other leaders of the new regime to demonstrate why the Settlement had the shape it did. William Haugaard's *Elizabeth I and the English Reformation* (1968) is, despite its title, about the attempts of the early Elizabethan clergy and episcopate to shape their new church. It is flawed by its dependence of J. E. Neale's now discredited belief in a 'Puritan conspiracy', but still extremely useful for the study of the early Elizabethan church.

Products of the turn-of-the-century debate over the Settlement that are still useful include Henry Gee's, *The Elizabethan Clergy and the Settlement of Religion 1558–1564* (1898), and his, *The Elizabethan Prayer-book and Ornaments* (1902). C. G. Bayne's, *Anglo-Roman Relations 1558–1564* (1913), provides a look at the ecclesiastical diplomacy of the change in religion. The debate in which these books took a part was highly sectarian, with Catholic, Anglo-Catholic, High Anglican and Low Church exponents using history as a club with which to beat one another, so one must be aware of the biases of authors on this subject. One Catholic historian whose detailed work on the 1560s reflects the special concern Catholics have about their first generation of martyrs is Philip E. Hughes. His *The Reformation in England*, rev. edn (1963) is a valuable reference tool even though it must sometimes be taken with a grain of salt. Christopher Haigh's work is an excellent introduction to current thought on Catholicism in Elizabethan England, especially his *Reformation and Resistance in Tudor Lancashire* (1975) and his edited work *The Reformation Revised* (1987).

For the beginnings of Puritanism in the 1560s the works of Patrick Collinson are the obvious starting point. His *The Elizabethan Puritan Movement* (1967) is a classic; his *Archbishop Grindal, 1519–1583: The Struggle for a Reformed Church* (1980) is especially useful for its study of the conflicts within the emerging establishment in the 1560s.

The succession crisis of the 1560s has been treated by Mortimer Levine in his *The Early Elizabethan Succession Question 1558–1568* (1966). The only work to treat it as a whole, it should be used with some care, since it is makes some insupportable assumptions about some aspects of the issue, especially the Hertford-Grey marriage. For the negotiations with the Habsburgs see Susan Doran, 'Religion and Politics at the Court of Elizabeth I: the Habsburg Marriage Negotiations of 1559–1567', *English Historical Review*, 104 (1989), pp. 908–26.

Mary, Queen of Scots has been the subject of many works, most badly flawed by nationalist and romantic assumptions. One lively and respectable biography is Antonia Fraser, *Mary Queen of Scots* (1969). For a more scholarly treatment of the people and issues around Mary and her relations with England see Gordon Donaldson, *All the Queen's Men: Power and Politics in Mary Stewart's Scotland* (1983), and his *The First Trial of Mary, Queen of Scots* (1969).

Social history does not focus on decades, but students interested in topics such as birth, death, marriage and crime might consult some of the excellent surveys. J. A. Sharpe, *Crime in Early Modern England 1550–1750* (1984) provides a useful introduction to criminal acts and the courts that tried them. R. A. Houlbrooke, *The English Family 1450–1700* (1988) surveys family structure, marriage, child-bearing and education. A. L. Beier, *Masterless Men: The Vagrancy Problem in England 1560–1640* (1985) considers the social, legal and economic sides of this popular problem. D. M. Palliser's *The Age of Elizabeth: England under the Later Tudors, 1547–1603* (1983) surveys the social and economic history of the period. Paul Slack is most useful on disease, both in his *The Impact of Plague on Tudor and Stuart Britain* (1985) and 'Mortality Crises and Epidemic Disease in England, 1485–1610', in C. Webster (ed.), *Health, Medicine and Mortality in the Sixteenth Century* (1979), pp. 9–59. In addition Slack's *Poverty and Policy in Tudor and Stuart England* (1988) reviews the economic and social issues of the period.

Index